W9-CPE-780

Microsoft® SQL Server® 2008 T-SQL Fundamentals

Itzik Ben-Gan

PUBLISHED BY
Microsoft Press
A Division of Microsoft Corporation
One Microsoft Way
Redmond, Washington 98052-6399

Library of Congress Control Number: 2008938209

Printed and bound in the United States of America.

1 2 3 4 5 6 7 8 9 QWT 3 2 1 0 9 8

Distributed in Canada by H.B. Fenn and Company Ltd.

A CIP catalogue record for this book is available from the British Library.

Microsoft Press books are available through booksellers and distributors worldwide. For further information about international editions, contact your local Microsoft Corporation office or contact Microsoft Press International directly at fax (425) 936-7329. Visit our Web site at www.microsoft.com/mspress. Send comments to mspinput@microsoft.com.

Microsoft, Microsoft Press, MSDN, SQL Server, and Windows are either registered trademarks or trademarks of the Microsoft group of companies. Other product and company names mentioned herein may be the trademarks of their respective owners.

The example companies, organizations, products, domain names, e-mail addresses, logos, people, places, and events depicted herein are fictitious. No association with any real company, organization, product, domain name, e-mail address, logo, person, place, or event is intended or should be inferred.

This book expresses the author's views and opinions. The information contained in this book is provided without any express, statutory, or implied warranties. Neither the authors, Microsoft Corporation, nor its resellers, or distributors will be held liable for any damages caused or alleged to be caused either directly or indirectly by this book.

Acquisitions Editor: Ken Jones
Developmental Editor: Sally Stickney
Project Editor: Maria Gargiulo
Editorial Production: S4Carlisle Publishing Services
Technical Reviewer: Ron Talmage ; Technical Review services provided by Content Master, a member of CM Group, Ltd.
Cover: Tom Draper Design

Body Part No. X15-12280

To Dato

To live in hearts we leave behind,
    Is not to die.

        —*Thomas Campbell*

Contents at a Glance

Table of Contents

What do you think of this book? We want to hear from you!

Microsoft is interested in hearing your feedback so we can continually improve our books and learning resources for you. To participate in a brief online survey, please visit:

www.microsoft.com/learning/booksurvey/

What do you think of this book? We want to hear from you!

Microsoft is interested in hearing your feedback so we can continually improve our books and learning resources for you. To participate in a brief online survey, please visit:

www.microsoft.com/learning/booksurvey/

Acknowledgments

Many people have contributed to the book, directly and indirectly, and I'd like to acknowledge their contributions.

To Ron Talmage, the book's technical editor: I've asked Microsoft Press to work with you for a reason. You seek a true understanding of things; you look for subtleties; you appreciate SQL and logic; and on top of all this you have superb English. You've done an outstanding job!

To Dejan Sarka: I'd like to thank you for your help with the first chapter of the book, and for your insights regarding set theory, predicate logic, and the relational model. I like the fact that you always question things, even those that most people take for granted. You're one of the people whose thoughts and ideas I heed most. Your understanding of the relational model and your capacity for drinking beer are truly admirable, albeit that the examples you choose for demonstrating your ideas are not always politically correct. ;-)

Several people from Microsoft Press and S4Carlisle Publishing Services are due thanks. To Ken Jones, the project planner: it's a real pleasure working with you. I appreciate your attentiveness and the way you manage to handle us authors and our tempers. I also appreciate your friendship. Thanks to Sally Stickney, the development editor, for lifting the project off the ground, and to Maria Gargiulo, the project editor, for managing the project on a day-to-day basis. It was great to work with you! Thanks is also due to Christian Holdener and Tracy Ball, the vendor project managers, and to Becka McKay, the copy editor.

I'd like to thank my company, Solid Quality Mentors, for the best job I could ever hope for, which mainly involves teaching, and for making me feel like I'm part of family and friends. Fernando G. Guerrero, Brian Moran, and Douglas McDowell, who manage the company: you have a lot to be proud of. The company has grown and matured, and has accomplished great things. To my friends and colleagues from the company, Ron Talmage, Andrew J. Kelly, Eladio Rincón, Dejan Sarka, Herbert Albert, Fritz Lechnitz, Gianluca Hotz, Erik Veerman, Daniel A. Seara, Davide Mauri, Andrea Benedetti, Miguel Egea, Adolfo Wiernik, Javier Loria, Rushabh B. Mehta, and many others: it's an honor and pleasure to be part of the gang; I always look forward to spending more time with you over beer talking about SQL and other things! I'd like to thank Jeanne Reeves for making many of my classes possible, and all the back office team for their support. I'd also like to thank Kathy Blomstrom for managing our writing projects and for your excellent edits.

To Lubor Kollar, who's with the Microsoft SQL Server Customer Advisory Team (SQL CAT): I'd like to thank you for being such a great example, and for your friendship. You're always there to help or to find the right address for help when I have a question about SQL Server, and this contributed a lot to my T-SQL understanding. I always look forward to spending time together!

I'd like to thank several people from the product team. To Michael Wang, Michael Rys, and all others involved in the development of T-SQL: thanks for making T-SQL such a great language, notwithstanding the fact that the OVER clause is not yet fully implemented ;-). To Umachandar Jayachandran (UC); I know very few people who understand the true depths of T-SQL the way you do, and I can't tell you how glad I was when you joined the programmability team. I knew that T-SQL was in good hands!

To Sensei Yehuda Pantanowitz: you were my greatest teacher, and a friend; your passing away is unbearable.

To the team at *SQL Server Magazine:* Megan Bearly, Sheila Molnar, Mary Waterloo, Karen Forster, Michele Crockett, Mike Otey, Lavon Peters, and Anne Grubb: we've been working together for almost 10 years now, and I feel like it's my home. Thanks for giving me the freedom to write every month about a subject that is burning in my veins, and for all the work you do to enable the articles to be published.

I'd like to thank my fellow MVPs for your contribution to the SQL community and to my knowledge. A few deserve special thanks: Steve Kass, when I grow up, I want to be just like you! To Erland Sommarskog, Alejandro Mesa, Aaron Bertrand, and Tibor Karaszi: your participation in the newsgroups is truly astounding! Erland, your papers are a great source of information. To Marcello Poletti (Marc): I believe that we share similar feelings towards SQL and puzzles; your puzzles are wicked and they have deprived me of sleep more than once.

My true passion is for teaching; I'd like to thank my students for enabling me to fulfill my passion. Student questions and inquiries make me do a lot of research, and a lot of my knowledge today is due to those questions.

I'd like to thank my family for their support. To my parents, Gabriel and Emilia Ben-Gan, for supporting me in pursuing my passion, even if it means that we see each other less. And to my brother, Michael Ben-Gan and my sister, Ina Aviram, for being there for me.

Finally, Lilach, you give meaning to everything I do; contrary to the common cliché, I probably could finish the book without you. But then, why would I want to?

Introduction

This book walks you through your first steps in T-SQL (also known as Transact-SQL), which is the Microsoft SQL Server dialect of the standard ANSI-SQL language. You'll learn the theory behind T-SQL querying and programming, how to develop T-SQL code to query and modify data, and get an overview of programmable objects.

Although this book is intended for beginners, it is not merely a step-by-step book. It goes beyond the syntactical elements of T-SQL and explains the logic behind the language and its elements.

Occasionally the book covers subjects that may be considered advanced for readers who are new to T-SQL; therefore, those sections are optional reading. If you already feel comfortable with the material discussed in the book up to that point, you may want to tackle the more advanced subjects; otherwise, feel free to skip those sections and return to them after you've gained more experience. The text will indicate when a section may be considered more advanced and is provided as optional reading.

Many aspects of SQL are unique to the language, and are very different from other programming languages. This book helps you adopt the right state of mind and gain a true understanding of the language elements. You learn how to think in terms of sets and follow good SQL programming practices.

The book is not version-specific; it does, however, cover language elements that were introduced in recent versions of SQL Server, including SQL Server 2008. When I discuss language elements that were introduced recently, I specify the version in which they were added.

To complement the learning experience, the book provides exercises that enable you to practice what you've learned. The book occasionally provides optional exercises that are more advanced. Those exercises are intended for readers who feel very comfortable with the material and want to challenge themselves with more difficult problems. The optional exercises for advanced readers are labeled as such.

Who This Book Is For

This book is intended for T-SQL programmers, DBAs, architects, analysts, and SQL Server power users who just started working with SQL Server and need to write queries and develop code using Transact-SQL.

What This Book Is About

The book starts with both a theoretical background to T-SQL querying and programming in Chapter 1, laying the foundations for the rest of the book, and also coverage of creating tables and defining data integrity. The book moves on to various aspects of querying and modifying data, in Chapters 2 through 8, then to a discussion of concurrency and transactions in Chapter 9, and finally provides an overview of programmable objects in Chapter 10. The following section lists the chapter titles along with a short description:

Chapter 1, "Background to T-SQL Querying and Programming," provides a theoretical background about SQL, set theory, and predicate logic; examines the relational model and more; describes SQL Server's architecture; and explains how to create tables and define data integrity.

Chapter 2, "Single-Table Queries," covers various aspects of querying a single table using the *SELECT* statement.

Chapter 3, "Joins," covers querying multiple tables using joins, including cross joins, inner joins, and outer joins.

Chapter 4, "Subqueries," covers queries within queries, otherwise known as subqueries.

Chapter 5, "Table Expressions," covers derived tables, CTEs, views, inline table-valued functions, and the APPLY operator.

Chapter 6, "Set Operations," covers the set operations UNION, INTERSECT, and EXCEPT.

Chapter 7, "Pivot, Unpivot, and Grouping Sets," covers data-rotation techniques and working with grouping sets.

Chapter 8, "Data Modification," covers inserting, updating, deleting, and merging data.

Chapter 9, "Transactions and Concurrency," covers concurrency of user connections that work with the same data simultaneously; it covers concepts including transactions, locks, blocking, isolation levels, and deadlocks.

Chapter 10, "Programmable Objects," provides an overview to the T-SQL programming capabilities in SQL Server.

The book also provides an appendix, "Getting Started," to help you set up your environment, download the book's source code, install the sample database TSQLFundamentals2008, start writing code against SQL Server, and learn how to get help by working with SQL Server Books Online.

Companion Content

This book features a companion Web site that makes available to you all the code used in the book, the errata, additional resources, and more. The companion Web site is *http://www.insidetsql.com*. Please refer to Appendix A, "Getting Started," for details about the source code.

Hardware and Software Requirements

In Appendix A, "Getting Started," I explain which editions of SQL Server 2008 you can use to work with the code samples included with this book. Each edition of SQL Server may have different hardware and software requirements, and those requirements are well-documented in SQL Server Books Online under "Hardware and Software Requirements for Installing SQL Server 2008." Appendix A also explains how to work with SQL Server Books Online.

Find Additional Content Online

For more great information from Microsoft Press, visit the new Microsoft Press Online sites— your one-stop online resource for access to updates, sample chapters, articles, scripts, and e-books related to our industry-leading Microsoft Press titles. Check out the following sites: *http://www.microsoft.com/learning/books/online/developer* and *http://www.microsoft.com/ learning/books/online/serverclient*.

Support for This Book

Every effort has been made to ensure the accuracy of this book and the contents of the companion Web site. As corrections or changes are collected, they will be added to a Microsoft Knowledge Base article.

Microsoft Press provides support for books at the following Web site:

http://www.microsoft.com/learning/support/books/

Questions and Comments

If you have comments, questions, or ideas regarding the book, or questions that are not answered by visiting the sites above, please send them to me via e-mail at:

itzik@SolidQ.com

Or via postal mail at:

Microsoft Press
Attn: *Microsoft SQL Server 2008 T-SQL Fundamentals* Editor
One Microsoft Way
Redmond, WA 98052-6399

Please note that Microsoft software product support is not offered through the above addresses.

Chapter 1
Background to T-SQL Querying and Programming

You're about to embark on a journey in a land that is like no other—a land that has its own set of laws. Assuming that reading this book is your first step in learning Transact-SQL (T-SQL), you should feel like Alice just before she started her adventures in Wonderland. For me, the journey has not ended; instead it's an ongoing path filled with new discoveries. I envy you—some of the most exciting discoveries are still ahead of you!

I've been involved with T-SQL for many years, teaching, speaking, writing, and consulting about it. For me, T-SQL is more than just a language—it's a way of thinking. I've taught and written extensively on advanced topics, and kept postponing writing about fundamentals. This is not because T-SQL fundamentals are too simple or easy, but the opposite: The apparent simplicity of the language is misleading. I could explain the language syntax elements in a superficial manner and you could be writing queries within minutes. But this approach will only hold you back in the long run and make it harder for you to understand the essence of the language.

Acting as your guide while you take the first steps in this realm is a big responsibility. I wanted to make sure that I spent enough time and effort exploring and understanding the language before writing about fundamentals. T-SQL is deep; learning the fundamentals the right way involves much more than just understanding the syntax elements and coding a query that returns the right output. You pretty much need to forget what you know about other programming languages and start thinking in terms of T-SQL.

Theoretical Background

SQL stands for *Structured Query Language*. SQL is a standard language that was designed to query and manage data in relational database management systems (RDBMSs). An RDBMS is a database management system based on the relational model (a semantic model for representing data), which in turn is based on two mathematical branches: set theory and predicate logic. Many other programming languages and various aspects of computing evolved pretty much as a result of intuition. To the degree that SQL is based on the relational model, it is based on a firm foundation—applied mathematics. T-SQL sits on these very wide and solid shoulders. Microsoft provides T-SQL as a dialect of, or extension to, SQL in Microsoft SQL Server, its RDBMS.

This section provides a brief theoretical background about SQL, set theory and predicate logic, the relational model, and the data life cycle. Because this book is neither a mathematics book nor a design/data modeling book, the theoretical information provided here is informal and by no means complete. The goals are to give you a context for the T-SQL language and deliver the key points that are integral to correctly understanding T-SQL later in the book.

Language Independence

The relational model is language-independent. That is, you can implement the relational model with languages other than SQL, for example, with C# in a class model. Today it is common to see RDBMSs that support languages other than a dialect of SQL, such as CLR integration in SQL Server.

Also, you should realize from the start that SQL deviates from the relational model in a number of ways, and some "relational model purists" say that a new language that more closely follows the relational model should replace SQL. But to date, SQL is the de facto industrial language used by all leading RDBMSs.

SQL

SQL is both an ANSI and ISO standard language based on the relational model, designed for querying and managing data in an RDBMS.

In the early 1970s, IBM developed a language called SEQUEL (short for Structured English QUEry Language) for their RDBMS product called System R. The name of the language was later changed from SEQUEL to SQL because of a trademark dispute. SQL first became an ANSI standard in 1986, and an ISO standard in 1987. Since 1986, ANSI and ISO have been releasing revisions for the SQL standard every few years. So far, the following standards have been released: SQL-86 (1986), SQL-89 (1989), SQL-92 (1992), SQL:1999 (1999), SQL:2003 (2003), SQL:2006 (2006), and SQL:2008 (2008).

Interestingly, SQL resembles English and is also very logical. Unlike many other programming languages, SQL requires you to specify *what* you want to get and not *how* to get it. The task of the RDBMS is to figure out the physical mechanics of processing your request.

SQL has several categories of statements, including Data Definition Language (DDL), Data Manipulation Language (DML), and Data Control Language (DCL). DDL deals with object definitions and includes statements such as *CREATE, ALTER,* and *DROP*. DML allows you to query and modify data and includes statements such as *SELECT, INSERT, UPDATE, DELETE,* and *MERGE*. It's a common misunderstanding that DML includes only data modification statements, but as I mentioned, it also includes *SELECT*. DCL deals with permissions and includes statements such as *GRANT* and *REVOKE*. This book's focus is DML.

T-SQL is based on standard SQL and also provides some nonstandard/proprietary extensions. When describing a language element for the first time, I'll typically mention whether it is standard.

Set Theory

Set theory, which originated with the mathematician Georg Cantor, is one of the mathematical branches on which the relational model is based. Cantor's definition of a set follows:

> By a "set" we mean any collection M *into a whole of definite, distinct objects* m
> *(which are called the "elements" of* M) *of our perception or of our thought.*
>
> —*Joseph W. Dauben,* Georg Cantor *(Princeton University Press, 1990)*

Every word in the definition has deep and crucial meaning. But to avoid getting lost in symbols and mathematical lingo, let's look at a more informal definition:

A set is any collection of definite, distinct objects of our perception or our thought considered as a whole. The objects are considered the elements or members of the set.

The definitions of a set and set membership are axioms that are not supported by proofs. Each element belongs to a universe, and either is or is not a member of the set.

Let's start with the word *whole* in Cantor's definition. A set should be considered a single entity. Your focus should be the collection of objects as opposed to the individual objects that make up the collection. Later on, when you write T-SQL queries against tables in a database (such as a table of Employees), you should think of the set of employees as a whole rather than the individual employees. This might sound trivial and simple enough, but apparently many programmers have difficulty adopting this way of thinking.

The word *distinct* means that every element of a set must be unique. Jumping ahead to tables in a database, you can enforce the uniqueness of rows in a table by defining key constraints. Without a key, you won't be able to uniquely identify rows, and therefore the table won't qualify as a set. Rather, the table would be a *multiset,* or *bag*.

The phrase *of our perception or our thought* implies that the definition of a set is subjective. Consider a classroom: One person might perceive a set of people, whereas another might perceive a set of students and a set of teachers. Therefore, you have substantial freedom in defining sets. When you design a data model for your database, the design process should carefully consider the subjective needs of the application to determine adequate definitions for the entities involved.

As for the word *object*, the definition of a set is not restricted to physical objects such as cars or employees, but rather is relevant to abstract objects as well, such as prime numbers or lines.

What Cantor's definition of a set leaves out is probably as important as what it includes. Notice that the definition doesn't mention any order among the set elements. The order in which set elements are listed is not important. The formal notation used to list set elements is with curly brackets: {a, b, c}. Because order has no relevance, the same set can be expressed as {b, a, c} or {b, c, a}. The elements of a set are described by their attributes—not by the order of elements. Having unique attribute names enforces this requirement (irrelevance of order). Many programmers have a hard time adapting to the idea that when querying tables, there is no order among the set elements. In other words, a query against a table can return the table rows in any order unless you explicitly ask the data to be sorted for presentation purposes.

Predicate Logic

Predicate logic, whose roots reach back to ancient Greece, is another branch of mathematics that the relational model is based on. Dr. Edgar F. Codd, in creating the relational model, had the insight to connect predicate logic to both management and querying of data. Loosely speaking, a *predicate* is a property or an expression that either holds or doesn't hold—in other words, is either true or false. In the relational model, predicates are used to maintain the logical integrity of the data and define its structure. One example of a predicate used to enforce integrity is a constraint defined in a table of Employees that allows only employees with a salary greater than zero in the table. The predicate is "salary greater than zero" (T-SQL expression: salary > 0).

You can also use predicates when filtering data to define subsets, and so on. For example, if you need to query the Employees table and return only rows for employees from the sales department, you would use the predicate "department equals sales" in your query filter (T-SQL expression: department = 'sales').

In set theory, you can use predicates to define sets. This is helpful because you can't always define a set by listing all its elements (for example, infinite sets), and sometimes for brevity it's more convenient to define a set based on a property. As an example of an infinite set defined with a predicate, the set of all prime numbers can be defined with the following predicate: "*x* is a positive integer greater than 1 that is divisible only by 1 and itself." For any given value, the predicate either holds true or does not hold true. The set of all prime numbers is the set of all elements for which the predicate holds true. As an example of a finite set defined with a predicate, the set {0, 1, 2, 3, 4, 5, 6, 7, 8, 9} can be defined as the set of all elements for which the following predicate holds true: "*x* is an integer greater than or equal to 0 and smaller than or equal to 9."

The Relational Model

The relational model is a semantic model for representing data and is based on set theory and predicate logic. As mentioned, it was created by Dr. Edgar F. Codd, and later explained and developed by Chris Date, Hugh Darwen, and others. The first version of the relational model was proposed by Codd in 1969 in an IBM research report called "Derivability, Redundancy, and Consistency of Relations Stored in Large Data Banks." A revised version was proposed by Codd in 1970 in a paper called "A Relational Model of Data for Large Shared Data Banks" published in the journal *Communications of the ACM*.

The goal of the relational model is to enable consistent representation of data with minimal or no redundancy and without sacrificing completeness, and to define data integrity (enforcement of data consistency) as part of the model. An RDBMS is supposed to implement the relational model and provide the means to store, manage, enforce the integrity of, and query data. The fact that the relational model is based on a strong mathematical foundation means that given a certain data model instance (from which a physical database will later be generated), you can tell with certainty when a design is flawed, rather than relying solely on intuition.

The relational model involves concepts such as propositions, domains, n-ary relations, n-tuples, ordered pairs, and so on. For non-mathematicians these concepts can be quite intimidating. The sections that follow cover some of the key aspects of the model in an informal, nonmathematical manner and explain how they relate to databases.

Propositions, Predicates, and Relations

The common belief that the term *relational* stems from relationships between tables is incorrect. "Relational" actually pertains to the mathematical term *relation*. A relation is a representation of a set in set theory. In the relational model, a relation is a set of related information, with the implementation in the database being a table. A key point in the relational model is that a single relation should represent a single set (for example, Customers). It is interesting to note that operations on relations (based on relational algebra) result in a relation (for example, a join between two relations).

When you design a data model for a database, you represent all data with relations (tables). You start by identifying propositions that you will need to represent in your database. A proposition is an assertion or a statement that must be true or false. For example, the statement "employee Itzik Ben-Gan was born on February 12, 1971 and belongs to department IT" is a proposition. If this proposition is true, it will manifest itself as a row in a table of Employees. A false proposition simply won't manifest itself.

The next step is to formalize propositions. You do this by taking out the actual data (the body of the relation) and defining the structure (the heading of the relation)—for example, by creating predicates out of propositions. The heading of a relation comprises a set of attributes. Note the use of the term "set"; in the relational model, attributes are unordered. An attribute is identified by an attribute name and a domain (type) name. For example, the heading of an Employees relation might consist of the following attributes (expressed as pairs of attribute name and type name): employeeid integer, firstname character string, lastname character string, birthdate date, departmentid integer. A domain or type is one of the most fundamental relational building blocks. A domain is the set of possible/valid values for an attribute. For example, the domain INT is the set of all integers in the range –2,147,483,648 to 2,147,483,647. A domain is one of the simplest forms of a predicate in our database be-cause it restricts the attribute values that are allowed. For example, the database would not accept a proposition where an employee birth date is February 31, 1971 (not to speak of birth date "abc"!). Note that domains are not restricted to base types such as integers or character strings. For example, a domain can be an enumeration of possible values, such as an enumeration of possible job positions. A domain can be complex. Probably the best way to think of a domain is as a class—encapsulated data and the behavior supporting it. An example of a complex domain would be a geometry domain that supports polygons.

Missing Values

One aspect of the relational model is the source of many passionate debates—whether propositions should be restricted to use two-valued predicate logic. That is, using two-valued predicate logic, a proposition is either true or false. If a proposition is not true, it must be false. However, some say that there's room for three-valued predicate logic (or even four-valued), taking into account cases where something is unknown. Take, for example, a cellphone attribute of an Employees relation. Suppose that a certain employee's cell phone number is missing. How do you represent this fact in the database? In a three-valued logic implementa-tion, the cellphone attribute should allow a special mark for a missing value.

Some people believe that three-valued predicate logic is nonrelational, while others believe that it is relational. Codd actually advocated four-valued predicate logic, saying that there were two different cases of missing values: missing but applicable, and missing but not applicable. An example of missing but applicable is when an employee has a cell phone, but we don't know what the cell phone number is. An example of missing but not applicable is when an employee doesn't have a cell phone at all. Per Codd, two special markers should be used to support these two cases of missing values. SQL implements three-valued predicate logic by supporting the NULL mark to signify the generic concept of a missing value. Support for NULLs and three-valued predicate logic in SQL is the source of a great deal of confusion and complexity, though one can argue that missing values are part of reality and the alternative—using two-valued predicate logic—is no less problematic.

Constraints

One of the greatest benefits of the relational model is having data integrity defined as part of the model. Integrity is achieved through rules, or *constraints*, that are defined in the data model and enforced by the RDBMS. The simplest methods of enforcing integrity are the attribute type and its NULLability (whether it supports or doesn't support NULLs), which enforce domain integrity. Constraints are also enforced through the model itself; for example, the relation Orders(orderid, orderdate, duedate, shipdate) allows three distinct dates per order, while the relations Employees(empid) and EmployeeChildren(empid, childname) allow zero to countable infinity of children per employee.

Other examples of constraints include candidate keys that provide entity integrity and foreign keys that provide referential integrity. A candidate key is a key defined on one or more attributes preventing more than one occurrence of the same tuple (row) in a relation. A predicate based on a candidate key can uniquely identify a row (such as an employee). You can define multiple candidate keys in a relation. For example, in an Employees relation you can define candidate keys on employeeid, on ssn (social security number), and others. One of the candidate keys is arbitrarily chosen as the primary key (say, employeeid in the Employees relation), and is used as the preferred way to identify a row. All other candidate keys are also known as alternate keys.

Foreign keys are used to enforce referential integrity. A foreign key is defined on one or more attributes of a relation (known as the referencing relation) and references a candidate key in another (or possibly the same) relation. This constraint restricts the values in the referencing relation's foreign key attributes to the values that appear in the referenced relation's candidate key attributes. For example, say that the Employees relation has a foreign key defined on the attribute departmentid, referencing the primary key attribute departmentid in the Departments relation. This means that the values in Employees.departmentid are restricted to the values that appear in Departments.departmentid.

Normalization

The relational model also defines normalization rules (also known as normal forms). Normalization is a formal mathematical process to guarantee that each entity will be represented by a single relation. In a normalized database you avoid anomalies upon data modification and keep redundancy to a minimum without sacrificing completeness. If you follow Entity Relationship Modeling (ERM), and represent each entity and its attributes, you probably won't need normalization; rather you will apply normalization only to reinforce and assure that the model is correct. The following sections briefly cover the first three normal forms (1NF, 2NF, and 3NF) introduced by Codd.

1NF   The first normal form says that rows in the table must be unique, and attributes should be atomic. This is a redundant definition of a relation; in other words, if a table truly represents a relation, it is in first normal form.

Uniqueness of rows is achieved by defining a unique key in the table.

You can only operate on attributes with operations defined as part of the attribute's data-type. Atomicity of attributes is subjective in the same way that the definition of a set is subjective. For example, take an employee name in an Employees relation. Should it be expressed with one attribute (fullname), two (firstname and lastname), or three (firstname, middlename, and lastname)? That depends on the application. If the application will need to manipulate the employee name parts separately (such as for search purposes), it makes sense to break them apart; otherwise, it doesn't.

In the same way that an attribute might not be atomic enough based on the needs of the application, an attribute might be subatomic. For example, if an address attribute is considered atomic for a given application, not including the city as part of the address would violate the first normal form.

This normal form is often misunderstood. Some people think that an attempt to mimic arrays violates the first normal form. An example would be defining a YearlySales relation with the following attributes: salesperson, qty2006, qty2007, and qty2008. However, in this example you don't really violate the first normal form; you simply impose a constraint—restricting the data to three specific years: 2006, 2007, and 2008.

2NF The second normal form involves two rules. One rule is that the data must meet the first normal form. The other rule addresses the relationship between nonkey and candidate key attributes. For every candidate key, every nonkey attribute has to be fully functionally dependent on the entire candidate key. In other words, a nonkey attribute cannot be fully functionally dependent on part of a candidate key. Informally, if you need to obtain any nonkey attribute value, you need to provide the values of all attributes of a candidate key from the same row. You can find any value of any attribute of any row if you know all attribute values of a candidate key.

As an example of violating the second normal form, suppose that you define a relation called Orders that represents information about orders and order details (see Figure 1-1). The Orders relation contains the following attributes: orderid, productid, orderdate, qty, customerid, and companyname. The primary key is defined on orderid and productid.

Orders	
PK	**orderid**
PK	**productid**
	orderdate
	qty
	customerid
	companyname

FIGURE 1-1 Data model before applying 2NF

The second normal form is violated in Figure 1-1 because there are nonkey attributes that depend only on part of a candidate key (the primary key in this example). For example, you can find the orderdate of an order, as well as customerid and companyname, based on the orderid alone. To conform to the second normal form, you would need to split your original relation into two relations: Orders and OrderDetails (as shown in Figure 1-2). The Orders relation would include the attributes: orderid, orderdate, customerid, and companyname. The primary key is defined on orderid. The OrderDetails relation would include the following attributes: orderid, productid, and qty, with the primary key defined on orderid, productid.

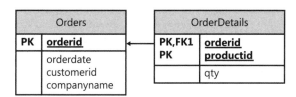

FIGURE 1-2 Data model after applying 2NF and before 3NF

3NF   The third normal form also has two rules. The data must meet the second normal form. Also, all nonkey attributes must be dependent on candidate keys nontransitively. Informally this rule means that all nonkey attributes must be mutually independent. In other words, one nonkey attribute cannot be dependent on another nonkey attribute.

Our Orders and OrderDetails relations now conform to the second normal form. Remember that the Orders relation at this point contains the attributes orderid, orderdate, customerid, and companyname with the primary key defined on orderid. Both customerid and companyname depend on the whole primary key—orderid. For example, you need the whole primary key to find the customerid who placed the order. Similarly, you need the whole primary key to find the company name of the customer who placed the order. However, customerid and companyname are also dependent on each other. To meet the third normal form, you need to add a Customers relation (shown in Figure 1-3) with attributes customerid (primary key) and companyname and remove the companyname attribute from the Orders relation.

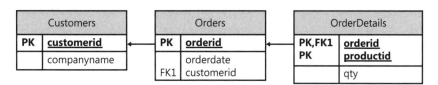

FIGURE 1-3 Data model after applying 3NF

Informally, 2NF and 3NF are commonly summarized with the sentence: "Every nonkey attribute is dependent on the key, the whole key, and nothing but the key—so help me Codd."

There are higher normal forms beyond Codd's original first three normal forms that involve compound primary keys and temporal databases, but they are outside the scope of this book.

The Data Life Cycle

Data is usually perceived as something static that is entered into a database and later queried. But in many environments, data is actually more similar to a product in an assembly line moving from one environment to another and undergoing transformations along the way. This section describes the different environments that data can reside in and the characteristics of both the data and the environment in each stage in the data life cycle. Figure 1-4 illustrates the data life cycle.

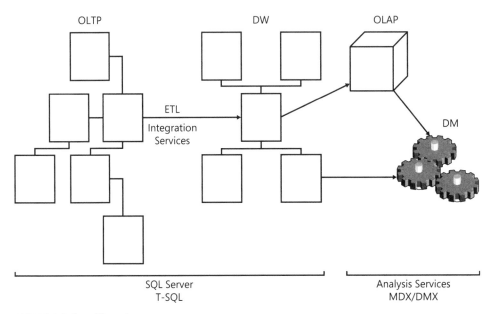

FIGURE 1-4 Data life cycle

OnLine Transactional Processing

Data is entered initially into an OnLine Transactional Processing (OLTP) system. The focus of an OLTP system is data entry and not reporting—transactions mainly insert, update, and delete data. The relational model is targeted mainly at OLTP systems, where a normalized model provides both good performance for data entry and data consistency. In a normalized environment each table represents a single entity and redundancy is at a minimum. When you need to modify a fact you need to modify it in only one place, resulting in optimized performance for modifications and little chance for error.

An OLTP environment is not suitable for reporting purposes because a normalized model usually involves many tables (one for each entity) with complex relationships. Even simple reports require joining many tables, resulting in complex and poorly performing queries.

You can implement an OLTP database in SQL Server and both manage it and query it with T-SQL.

Data Warehouse

A data warehouse (DW) is an environment designed for data retrieval/reporting purposes. When serving an entire organization such an environment is called a data warehouse; when serving part of the organization (such as a specific department) it is called a data mart. The data model of a data warehouse is designed and optimized mainly to support data retrieval needs. The model has intentional redundancy, which allows fewer tables and simpler relationships, ultimately resulting in simpler and more efficient queries compared to an OLTP environment.

The simplest design of a data warehouse is called a star schema, which includes several dimension tables and a fact table. Each dimension table represents a subject by which data is analyzed. For example, in a system that deals with orders and sales, you will probably want to analyze data by customers, products, employees, time, and so on. In a star schema each dimension is implemented as a single table with redundant data. For example, a product dimension could be implemented as a single ProductDim table instead of three normalized tables: Products, ProductSubCategories, and ProductCategories. If you normalize a dimension table, resulting in multiple tables representing the dimension, you get what's known as a *snowflake dimension*. A schema that contains snowflake dimensions is known as a *snowflake schema* (as opposed to a star schema).

The fact table holds the facts and measures such as quantity and value for each relevant combination of dimension keys. For example, for each relevant combination of customer, product, employee, and day there will be a row with the quantity and value in the fact table. Note that data in a data warehouse is typically pre-aggregated to a certain level of granularity (such as a day), unlike data in an OLTP environment, which is usually recorded at the transaction level.

Historically, early versions of SQL Server mainly targeted OLTP environments, but eventually SQL Server also started targeting data warehouse systems and data analysis needs. You can implement a data warehouse as a SQL Server database and manage and query it with T-SQL.

The process that pulls data from source systems (OLTP and others), manipulates it, and loads it into the data warehouse is called Extract Transform and Load, or ETL. SQL Server provides a tool called Microsoft SQL Server Integration Services (SSIS) to handle ETL needs.

OnLine Analytical Processing

OnLine Analytical Processing (OLAP) systems support dynamic, online analysis of aggregated data.

Consider a data warehouse that you implemented as a relational database in SQL Server. Whenever a user makes a request for aggregated data, the application submits a query to the database, typically scanning and aggregating large amounts of base data. Even though it is more efficient to handle such requests against a relational data warehouse compared to an

OLTP environment, that approach might not be efficient enough. Online dynamic analysis of aggregated data usually involves frequent requests for different levels of aggregations, which require slicing and dicing the data. Each such request might end up being very expensive if it needs to scan and aggregate large amounts of data, and chances are the response time will not be satisfactory.

To handle such needs you can pre-calculate different levels of aggregations. For example, you can pre-calculate yearly, monthly, and daily with the time dimension; category, subcategory, and product with the product dimension, and so on. When you pre-calculate aggregates, requests for aggregated data can be satisfied more quickly.

One option to implement this idea is to calculate and store the different levels of aggregations in the relational data warehouse. This involves writing a sophisticated process to handle the initial processing of the aggregates and the incremental updates. Another option is to use a special product designed for OLAP needs—Microsoft SQL Server Analysis Services (SSAS or AS). Note that SSAS is a separate service/engine from the SQL Server service. SSAS supports calculating different levels of aggregations and storing them in optimized multidimensional structures known as cubes. The source data for SSAS cubes can—and usually is—a relational data warehouse. Besides supporting large volumes of aggregated data, SSAS also provides many rich and sophisticated data analysis capabilities. The language used to manage and query SSAS cubes is called Multidimensional Expressions (MDX).

Data Mining

OLAP systems provide the user with answers to all possible questions, but the user's task is to ask the right questions—to sift anomalies, trends, and other useful information from the sea of data. In the dynamic analysis process the user navigates from one view of aggregates to another—again, slicing and dicing the data—to find useful information.

Data mining (DM) is the next step; instead of letting the user look for useful information in the sea of data, data mining models can do this for the user. That is, data mining algorithms comb the data and sift the useful information from it. Data mining has enormous business value for organizations, helping to identify trends, figure out which products are purchased together, predict customer choices based on given parameters, and so on.

SSAS supports data mining algorithms—including clustering, decision trees, and others—to address such needs. The language used to manage and query data mining models is Data Mining Extensions (DMX).

SQL Server Architecture

This section will introduce you to the SQL Server architecture, the entities involved—SQL Server instances, databases, schemas, and database objects—and the purpose of each entity.

SQL Server Instances

A SQL Server instance, illustrated in Figure 1-5, is an installation of a SQL Server database engine/service. You can install multiple instances of SQL Server on the same computer. Each instance is completely independent of the others in terms of security, the data that it manages, and in all other respects. At the logical level, two different instances residing on the same computer have no more in common than two instances residing on two separate computers. Of course, they do share the server's physical resources such as CPU, memory, and disk.

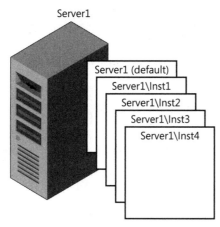

FIGURE 1-5 Instances

One of the instances on the computer can be set up as the *default instance*, while all others must be *named instances*. You determine whether an instance is the default or a named one upon installation; you cannot change this later. For a client application to connect to a default instance, it needs to specify the computer's name or IP address. To connect to a named instance, the client needs to specify the computer's name or IP address, followed by a backslash (\), followed by the instance name (as provided upon installation). For example, say you have two instances of SQL Server installed on a computer called Server1. One of the instances was installed as the default instance, and the other was installed as a named instance called Inst1. To connect to the default instance you need to specify Server1 as the server name; to connect to the named instance you need to specify Server1\Inst1.

There are various reasons why you might want to install multiple instances of SQL Server on the same computer. I'll mention only a couple here. One reason is to save costs for the support department of the organization. To be able to test functionality of features in response to support calls, reproduce errors that users face in production environment, and so on, the support department needs local installations of SQL Server that represent the user environment in terms of version, edition, and service pack of SQL Server. If an organization has multiple user environments, the support department needs multiple installations of SQL

Server. Rather than having multiple computers, each hosting a different installation of SQL Server that needs to be supported, the support department can have one computer with multiple instances.

As another example, take people like me who teach and lecture about SQL Server. For us it is very convenient to be able to install multiple instances of SQL Server on the same laptop. This way we can perform demonstrations against different versions of the product, showing differences in behavior between versions, and so on.

As a final example, providers of database services sometimes need to guarantee their customers complete security separation of their data from other customers' data. The database provider can have a very powerful data center hosting multiple instances of SQL Server, instead of needing to maintain multiple less-powerful computers, each hosting a different instance.

Databases

You can think of a database as a container of objects such as tables, views, stored procedures, and so on. Each instance of SQL Server can contain multiple databases, as illustrated in Figure 1-6. When you install SQL Server, the setup program creates several system databases that hold system data and serve internal purposes. After installation you can create your own user databases that will hold application data.

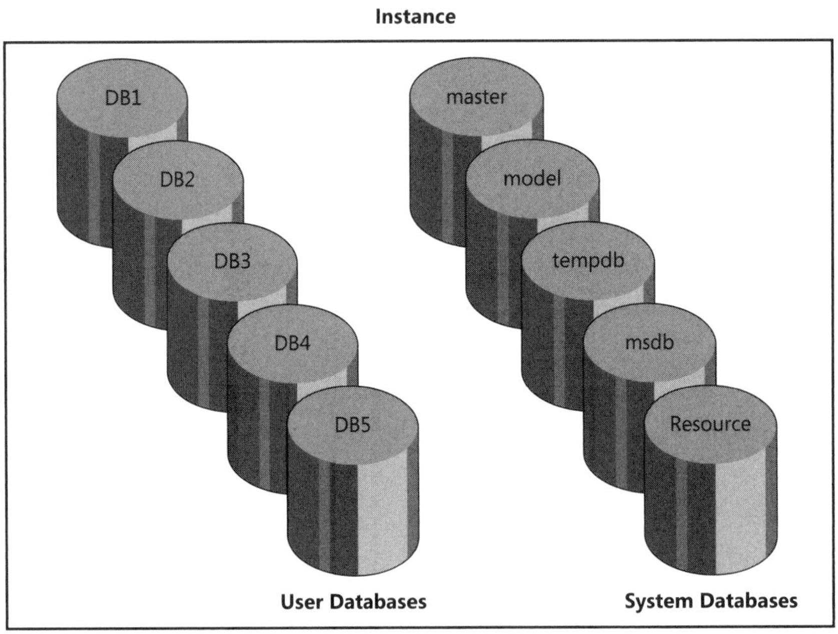

FIGURE 1-6 Databases

The system databases that the setup program creates include master, Resource, model, tempdb, and msdb. A description of each follows.

- **master**   The master database holds instance-wide metadata information, server configuration, information about all databases in the instance, and initialization information.

- **Resource**   The Resource database was added as of SQL Server 2005 and it holds all system objects. When you query metadata information in a database, this information appears to be local to the database but in practice it resides in the Resource database.

- **model**   The model database is used as a template for new databases. Every new database that you create is initially created as a copy of model. So if you want certain objects (such as data types) to appear in all new databases that you create, or certain database properties to be configured in a certain way in all new databases, you need to create those objects and configure those properties in the model database. Note that changes you apply to the model database will not impact existing databases—only new databases that you create in the future.

- **tempdb**   The tempdb database is where SQL Server stores temporary data such as work tables, sort space, row versioning information, and so on. SQL Server allows you to create temporary tables for your own use, and the physical location of those temporary tables is tempdb. Note that this database is destroyed and recreated as a copy of the model every time you restart the instance of SQL Server. For this reason, when I need to create objects for test purposes and I don't want the objects to remain in the database, I usually create them in tempdb. I know that even if I forget to clear those objects, they will be automatically cleared after restart.

- **msdb**   The msdb database is where a service called SQL Server Agent stores its data. SQL Server Agent is in charge of automation, which includes entities such as jobs, schedules, and alerts. The SQL Server Agent is also the service in charge of replication. The msdb database also holds information related to other SQL Server features such as Database Mail and Service Broker.

You can create as many user databases as you might need within an instance. A user database will hold objects and data for an application.

You can define a property called *collation* at the database level that will determine language support, case sensitivity, and sort order for character data in that database. If you do not specify a collation for the database when you create it, the default collation of the instance (chosen upon installation) will be assumed.

To run T-SQL code against a database, a client application needs to connect to a SQL Server instance and be in the context of, or use, the relevant database.

In terms of security, to be able to connect to a SQL Server instance, the DBA must create a *login* for you. The login can be tied to your Windows credentials, in which case it is called a Windows authenticated login. With a Windows authenticated login, you won't need to provide login and password information when connecting to SQL Server because you already provided those when you logged on to Windows. The login can also be independent of your Windows credentials, in which case it is called a SQL Server authenticated login. When connecting to SQL Server using a SQL Server authenticated login, you will need to provide both a login name and a password.

The DBA needs to map your login to a *database user* in each database that you are supposed to have access to. The database user is the entity that will be granted permissions to objects in the database.

So far, I've mainly mentioned the logical aspects of databases. Figure 1-7 shows a diagram of the physical database layout.

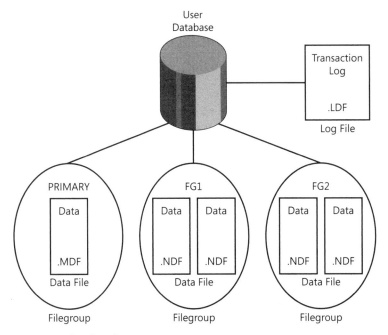

FIGURE 1-7 Database layout

The database is made of data and transaction log files. When you create a database, you can define various properties for each file, including the file name, location, initial size, maximum size, and an autogrowth increment. Each database must have at least one data file and at least one log file (the default in SQL Server). The data files hold object data, and the log files hold information that SQL Server needs to maintain transactions.

Although SQL Server can write to multiple data files in parallel, it can only write to one log file at a time, in a sequential manner. Therefore, unlike with data files, having multiple log files does not result in performance benefit. You might need to add log files if the disk drive where the log resides runs out of space.

Data files are organized in logical groups called filegroups. A filegroup is the target for creating an object, such as a table or an index. The object data will be spread across the files that belong to the target filegroup. Filegroups are your way to control what will be the physical locations of your objects. A database must have at least one filegroup called PRIMARY, and optionally other user filegroups as well. The PRIMARY filegroup contains the primary data file (extension .mdf), and the database's system catalog. You can optionally add secondary data files (extension .ndf) to PRIMARY. User filegroups contain only secondary data files. You can determine which of the filegroups is marked as the default filegroup. An object is created on the default filegroup when the object creation statement does not explicitly specify the target filegroup.

File Extensions .mdf, .ldf and .ndf

The database file extensions .mdf and .ldf are quite straightforward. The extension .mdf stands for Master Data File (not to be confused with the master database) and .ldf stands for Log Data File. One anecdote states that when discussing the extension for the secondary data files, one of the developers suggested, tongue in cheek, using .ndf for Not Master Data File, and the idea was accepted.

Schemas and Objects

When I said earlier that a database is a container of objects, I simplified things a bit. As illustrated in Figure 1-8, a database contains schemas, and schemas contain objects. You can think of a schema as a container of objects such as tables, views, stored procedures, and others.

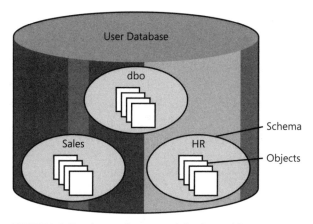

FIGURE 1-8 Database, schemas, and database objects

You can control permissions at the schema level. For example, you can grant a user SELECT permissions on a schema, allowing the user to query data from all objects in the schema. So security is one of the considerations for determining how to arrange objects in schemas.

The schema is also a namespace—it is used as a prefix to the object name. For example, say you have a table called Orders in a schema called Sales. The schema-qualified object name (also known as the two-part object name) is Sales.Orders. If you omit the schema name when referring to an object, SQL Server will apply a process to resolve the schema name such as checking whether the object exists in the user's default schema, and if it doesn't, checking whether it exists in the dbo schema. It is recommended that when you refer to objects in your code you always use the two-part object names. Some insignificant extra costs are involved in resolving the object name when it's not explicitly specified. As insignificant as this extra cost might be, why pay it? Also, if multiple objects with the same name exist in different schemas, you might end up getting a different object than the one you wanted.

Creating Tables and Defining Data Integrity

In this section I'll describe the fundamentals of creating tables and defining data integrity using T-SQL. Feel free to run the included code samples in your environment. If you don't know yet how to run code against SQL Server, Appendix A will help you get started.

As I mentioned earlier, DML rather than DDL is the focus of this book. Still, it is important that you understand how to create tables and define data integrity. I will not go into the gory details here, but I will provide a brief description of the essentials.

Before you look at the code for creating a table, remember that tables reside within schemas, and schemas reside within databases. My examples use a database called testdb and a schema called dbo. You can create a database called testdb in your environment by running the following code:

```
IF DB_ID('testdb') IS NULL
  CREATE DATABASE testdb;
```

If a database called testdb does not exist, this code creates a new one. The *DB_ID* function accepts a database name as input, and returns its internal database ID. If a database with the input name does not exist, the function returns a NULL. This is a simple way to check whether a database exists. Note that in this simple *CREATE DATABASE* statement I relied on defaults in terms of file settings such as location and initial size. In production environments you will usually explicitly specify all desired database and file settings, but for our purposes, the default settings are perfectly fine.

I will use a schema called dbo that is created automatically in every database, and is also used as the default schema for users that were not associated explicitly with another schema.

Creating Tables

The following code creates a table called Employees in the testdb database:

```
USE testdb;

IF OBJECT_ID('dbo.Employees', 'U') IS NOT NULL
  DROP TABLE dbo.Employees;

CREATE TABLE dbo.Employees
(
  empid     INT          NOT NULL,
  firstname VARCHAR(30)  NOT NULL,
  lastname  VARCHAR(30)  NOT NULL,
  hiredate  DATE         NOT NULL,
  mgrid     INT          NULL,
  ssn       VARCHAR(20)  NOT NULL,
  salary    MONEY        NOT NULL
);
```

The *USE* statement changes the current database context to that of testdb. It is important to incorporate the *USE* statement in scripts that create objects to ensure that the objects will be created in the desired database.

The *IF* statement invokes the *OBJECT_ID* function to check whether the Employees table already exists in the current database. The *OBJECT_ID* function accepts an object name and type as inputs. The type 'U' represents a user table. This function returns the internal object ID if an object with the given input name and type exists, and NULL otherwise. If the function returns a NULL, you know that the object doesn't exist. In our case, the code drops the table if it already exists, and then creates a new one. Of course you could have chosen a different treatment, such as simply not creating the object if it already exists.

The *CREATE TABLE* statement is in charge of defining what I referred to earlier as the body of the relation. Here you specify the name of the table and, in parentheses, the definition of its attributes (columns).

Notice the use of the two-part name dbo.Employees for the table name, as recommended earlier. If you omit the schema name, SQL Server will assume the default schema associated with the database user running the code.

For each attribute you specify the attribute name, datatype, and NULLability.

In our Employees table the attributes empid (employee ID) and mgrid (manager ID) are defined as *INT* (four byte integer); firstname, lastname, and ssn (social security number) are defined as *VARCHAR* (variable length character string with the specified max supported number of characters); hiredate is defined as *DATE* and salary is defined as *MONEY*. Note that the datatype *DATE* was added in SQL Server 2008. If you are working with an earlier version of the product, use the *DATETIME* or *SMALLDATETIME* data type instead.

If you don't explicitly specify whether a column allows or disallows NULLs, SQL Server will have to rely on defaults. ANSI dictates that when a column NULLability is not specified, the assumption should be NULL (allowing NULLs), but SQL Server has settings that can change this behavior. I strongly recommend being explicit in this sense and not relying on defaults. Also, I strongly recommend defining a column as NOT NULL unless you have a compelling reason to support NULLs. If a column is not supposed to allow NULLs and you don't enforce this with a NOT NULL constraint, you can rest assured that NULLs will get there. In our Employees table all columns are defined as NOT NULL except for the mgrid column. A NULL in the mgrid attribute would represent the fact that the employee has no manager, as in the case of the CEO of the organization.

Coding Style

You should be aware of a few general notes regarding coding style, the use of white spaces (space, tab, new line, and so on), and semicolons. I'm not aware of any formal coding styles. My advice is that you use a style that you and your fellow developers feel comfortable with. What ultimately matters most is consistency and the readability and maintainability of your code. I have tried to reflect these aspects in my code through-out the book.

T-SQL allows you to use white spaces quite freely in your code. You can take advantage of this fact to facilitate readability. For example, I could have written the code in the previous section in one line. However, it wouldn't have been as readable as when I break it into multiple lines and use indentation.

The practice of using a semicolon to terminate statements is standard and is also a re-quirement in several other database platforms. In SQL Server you are required to use a semicolon only in particular cases, but in cases where a semicolon is not required, it doesn't interfere. I strongly recommend that you adopt the practice of terminating all statements with a semicolon. This will improve the readability of your code and in some cases will even save you some grief. (When a semicolon is required and is not specified, the error message SQL Server produces is not always very clear.)

Defining Data Integrity

As mentioned earlier, one of the great benefits in the relational model is that data integrity is an integral part of it. Data integrity that is enforced as part of the model—namely, as part of the table definitions—is considered *declarative data integrity*. Data integrity that is enforced with code—such as with stored procedures or triggers—is considered *procedural data integrity*.

Data type and NULLability choices for attributes and even the data model itself are examples of declarative data integrity constraints. In this section I will describe other examples for declarative constraints, including primary key, unique, foreign key, check, and default constraints. You can define such constraints when creating a table as part of the *CREATE TABLE* statement, or after the table was already created using an *ALTER TABLE* statement. All types of constraints except for default can be defined as composite ones—that is, based on more than one attribute.

Primary Key Constraints

A primary key constraint enforces uniqueness of rows and also disallows NULLs in the constraint attributes. Each unique set of values in the constraint attributes can appear only once in the table—in other words, only in one row. An attempt to define a primary key constraint on a column that allows NULLs will be rejected by the RDBMS. Each table can have only one primary key.

Here's an example of defining a primary key constraint on the empid column in the Employees table that you created earlier:

```
ALTER TABLE dbo.Employees
  ADD CONSTRAINT PK_Employees
  PRIMARY KEY(empid);
```

With this primary key in place, you can be assured that all empid values will be unique and known. An attempt to insert or update a row such that the constraint would be violated will be rejected by the RDBMS and result in an error.

To enforce the uniqueness of the logical primary key constraint, SQL Server will create a unique index behind the scenes. A unique index is a physical mechanism used by SQL Server to enforce uniqueness. Indexes (not necessarily unique ones) are also used to speed up queries by avoiding unnecessary full table scans (similar to indexes in books).

Unique Constraints

A unique constraint enforces uniqueness of rows, allowing you to implement the concept of alternate keys from the relational model in your database. Unlike primary keys, multiple unique constraints can be defined in the same table. Also, a unique constraint is not restricted to columns defined as NOT NULL. ANSI SQL supports two types of unique constraints—one that allows a single NULL in a column with a unique constraint and another that allows multiple NULLs. SQL Server implemented only the former.

The following code defines a unique constraint on the ssn column in the Employees table:

```
ALTER TABLE dbo.Employees
  ADD CONSTRAINT UNQ_Employees_ssn
  UNIQUE(ssn);
```

As with a primary key constraint, SQL Server will create a unique index behind the scenes as the physical mechanism to enforce the logical unique constraint.

Foreign Key Constraints

A foreign key enforces referential integrity. This constraint is defined on a set of attributes in what's called the *referencing* table, and points to a set of candidate key (primary key or unique constraint) attributes in what's called the *referenced* table. Note that the referencing and referenced tables can be one and the same. The foreign key's purpose is to restrict the domain of values allowed in the foreign key columns to those that exist in the referenced columns.

The following code creates a table called Orders with a primary key defined on the orderid column:

```
IF OBJECT_ID('dbo.Orders', 'U') IS NOT NULL
  DROP TABLE dbo.Orders;

CREATE TABLE dbo.Orders
(
  orderid   INT         NOT NULL,
  empid     INT         NOT NULL,
  custid    VARCHAR(10) NOT NULL,
  orderts   DATETIME    NOT NULL,
  qty       INT         NOT NULL,
  CONSTRAINT PK_Orders
    PRIMARY KEY(OrderID)
);
```

Say you want to enforce an integrity rule that restricts the domain of values supported by the empid column in the Orders table to the values that exist in the empid column in the Employees table. You can achieve this by defining a foreign key constraint on the empid column in the Orders table pointing to the empid column in the Employees table like so:

```
ALTER TABLE dbo.Orders
  ADD CONSTRAINT FK_Orders_Employees
  FOREIGN KEY(empid)
  REFERENCES dbo.Employees(empid);
```

Similarly, if you want to restrict the domain of values supported by the mgrid column in the Employees table to the values that exist in the empid column of the same table, you can do so by adding the following foreign key:

```
ALTER TABLE dbo.Employees
  ADD CONSTRAINT FK_Employees_Employees
  FOREIGN KEY(mgrid)
  REFERENCES Employees(empid);
```

Note that NULLs are allowed in the foreign key columns (mgrid in the last example) even if there are no NULLs in the referenced candidate key columns.

The preceding two examples are basic definitions of foreign keys that enforce a referential action called *no action*. No action means that attempts to delete rows from the referenced table or update the referenced candidate key attributes will be rejected if related rows exist in the referencing table. For example, if you try to delete an employee row from the Employees table when there are related orders in the Orders table, the RDBMS will reject such an attempt and produce an error.

You can define the foreign key with actions that will compensate for such attempts (to delete rows from the referenced table or update the referenced candidate key attributes when related rows exist in the referencing table). You can define the options *ON DELETE* and *ON UPDATE* with actions like *CASCADE*, *SET DEFAULT*, and *SET NULL* as part of the foreign key definition. *CASCADE* means that the operation (delete or update) will be cascaded to related rows. For example, *ON DELETE CASCADE* means that when you delete a row from the referenced table, the RDBMS will delete the related rows from the referencing table. *SET DEFAULT* and *SET NULL* mean that the compensating action will set the foreign key attributes of the related rows to the column's default value or NULL respectively. Note that regardless of which action you chose, the referencing table will only have orphaned rows in the case of the exception with NULLs that I mentioned earlier.

Check Constraints

A check constraint allows you to define a predicate that a row must meet to enter the table or to be modified. For example, the following check constraint ensures that the salary column in the Employees table will support only positive values:

```
ALTER TABLE dbo.Employees
  ADD CONSTRAINT CHK_Employees_salary
  CHECK(salary > 0);
```

An attempt to insert or update a row with a nonpositive salary value will be rejected by the RDBMS. Note that a check constraint rejects an attempt to insert or update a row when the predicate evaluates to FALSE. The modification will be accepted when the predicate evaluates to either TRUE or UNKNOWN. For example, salary -1000 will be rejected, while salaries 50000 and NULL will both be accepted.

When adding CHECK and FOREIGN KEY constraints, you can specify an option called WITH NOCHECK telling the RDBMS that you want it to bypass constraint checking for existing data. This is considered a bad practice because you cannot be sure that your data is consistent. You can also disable or enable existing CHECK and FOREIGN KEY constraints.

Default Constraints

A default constraint is associated with a particular attribute. It is an expression that is used as the default value when an explicit value is not specified for the attribute when you insert a row. For example, the following code defines a default constraint for the orderts attribute (representing the order's timestamp):

```
ALTER TABLE dbo.Orders
  ADD CONSTRAINT DFT_Orders_orderts
  DEFAULT(CURRENT_TIMESTAMP) FOR orderts;
```

The default expression invokes the *CURRENT_TIMESTAMP* function, which returns the current date and time value. Once this default expression is defined, whenever you insert a row in the Orders table and do not explicitly specify a value in the orderts attribute, SQL Server will set the attribute value to *CURRENT_TIMESTAMP*.

Conclusion

This chapter provided a brief background to T-SQL querying and programming. It presented a theoretical background, explaining the strong foundations that T-SQL is based on. It gave an overview of the SQL Server architecture, and concluded with sections that demonstrated how to use T-SQL to create tables and define data integrity. I hope that by now you see that there's something special about SQL, and that it's not just a language that can be learned as an afterthought. This chapter equipped you with fundamental concepts—the actual journey is just about to begin.

Chapter 2
Single-Table Queries

This chapter introduces you to the fundamentals of the *SELECT* statement, focusing for now on queries against a single table. The chapter starts by describing logical query processing—namely, the series of logical phases involved in producing the correct result set of a given SELECT query. The chapter then covers other aspects of single-table queries, including operators, NULLs, manipulation of character and temporal data, ranking, CASE expressions, and querying metadata. Many of the code samples and exercises in this book use a sample database called TSQLFundamentals2008. You can find the instructions for downloading and installing this sample database in Appendix A, "Getting Started."

Elements of the SELECT Statement

The purpose of a *SELECT* statement is to query tables, apply some logical manipulation, and return a result. In this section, I talk about the phases involved in logical query processing. I describe the logical order in which the different query clauses are processed, and what happens in each phase.

Note that by "logical query processing," I'm referring to the conceptual way ANSI SQL defines that a query should be processed and the final result achieved. Don't be alarmed if some logical processing phases that I'll describe here seem inefficient. The Microsoft SQL

Server engine doesn't have to follow logical query processing to the letter; rather, it is free to physically process a query differently by rearranging processing phases, as long as the final result would be the same as dictated by logical query processing. SQL Server can—and in fact often does—make many shortcuts in the physical processing of a query.

To describe logical query processing and the various SELECT query clauses, I use the query in Listing 2-1 as an example. For now, don't worry about understanding what this query does; I'll explain the query clauses one at a time, and gradually build this query.

LISTING 2-1 Sample Query

```
USE TSQLFundamentals2008;

SELECT empid, YEAR(orderdate) AS orderyear, COUNT(*) AS numorders
FROM Sales.Orders
WHERE custid = 71
GROUP BY empid, YEAR(orderdate)
HAVING COUNT(*) > 1
ORDER BY empid, orderyear;
```

The code starts with a *USE* statement that sets the database context of your session to the TSQLFundamentals2008 sample database. If your session is already in the context of the database you need to query, the *USE* statement is not required.

Before getting into the details of each phase of the *SELECT* statement, notice the order in which the query clauses are logically processed. In most programming languages the lines of code are processed in the order that they are written. In SQL things are different. Even though the SELECT clause appears first in the query, it is logically processed almost last. The clauses are logically processed in the following order:

1. FROM

2. WHERE

3. GROUP BY

4. HAVING

5. SELECT

6. ORDER BY

So even though syntactically our sample query in Listing 2-1 starts with a SELECT clause, logically its clauses are processed in the following order:

```
FROM Sales.Orders
WHERE custid = 71
GROUP BY empid, YEAR(orderdate)
HAVING COUNT(*) > 1
SELECT empid, YEAR(orderdate) AS orderyear, COUNT(*) AS numorders
ORDER BY empid, orderyear
```

Or to present it in a more readable manner, here's what our statement does:

1. Queries the rows *from* the Sales.Orders table

2. Filters only orders *where* the customer ID is equal to 71

3. *Groups* the orders by employee ID and order year

4. Filters only groups (employee ID and order year) *having* more than one order

5. *Selects* (returns) for each group the employee ID, order year, and number of orders

6. *Orders* (sorts) the rows in the output *by* employee ID and order year

Unfortunately, we cannot write the query in correct logical order. We have to start with the SELECT clause as shown in Listing 2-1.

Now that you understand the order in which the query clauses are logically processed, the next sections explain the details of each phase.

When discussing logical query processing, I refer to query *clauses* and query *phases*, (the WHERE clause and the WHERE phase, for example). A query clause is a syntactical component of a query, so when discussing the syntax of a query element I usually use the term clause (for example, "In the WHERE clause you specify a predicate."). When discussing the logical manipulation taking place as part of logical query processing, I usually use the term phase (for example, "The WHERE phase returns rows for which the predicate evaluates to TRUE").

Recall my recommendation from the previous chapter regarding the use of a semicolon to terminate statements. SQL Server doesn't require you to terminate all statements with a semicolon. This is a requirement only in particular cases where the meaning of the code might otherwise be ambiguous. However, I recommend that you terminate all statements with a semicolon because it is standard, it improves the code readability, and it is likely that SQL Server will require this in more cases in the future. Currently, when a semicolon is not required, adding one doesn't interfere. Therefore I recommend that you make it a practice to terminate all statements with a semicolon.

The FROM Clause

The FROM clause is the very first query clause that is logically processed. In this clause you specify the names of the tables that you want to query and table operators that operate on those tables. This chapter doesn't get into table operators; I describe those in Chapter 5, "Table Expressions". For now, the FROM clause is simply where you specify the name of the table you want to query. The sample query in Listing 2-1 queries the Orders table in the Sales schema, finding 830 rows shown in the output below:

```
FROM Sales.Orders
```

Recall the recommendation I gave in the previous chapter to always schema-qualify object names in your code. When you don't specify the schema name explicitly, SQL Server must resolve it implicitly. This creates some minor cost, and also leaves it to SQL Server to decide which object to use in case of ambiguity. By being explicit, you ensure that you get the object that you intended to get, and that you don't pay any unnecessary penalties.

To return all rows from a table with no special manipulation, all you need is a query with a FROM clause where you specify the table you want to query, and a SELECT clause where you specify the attributes you want to return. For example, the following statement queries all rows from the Orders table in the Sales schema, selecting the attributes orderid, custid, empid, orderdate, and freight:

```
SELECT orderid, custid, empid, orderdate, freight
FROM Sales.Orders;
```

The output of this statement is shown here in abbreviated form:

```
orderid     custid      empid       orderdate                      freight
----------- ----------- ----------- ------------------------------ --------------
10248       85          5           2006-07-04 00:00:00.000        32.38
10249       79          6           2006-07-05 00:00:00.000        11.61
10250       34          4           2006-07-08 00:00:00.000        65.83
10251       84          3           2006-07-08 00:00:00.000        41.34
10252       76          4           2006-07-09 00:00:00.000        51.30
10253       34          3           2006-07-10 00:00:00.000        58.17
10254       14          5           2006-07-11 00:00:00.000        22.98
10255       68          9           2006-07-12 00:00:00.000        148.33
10256       88          3           2006-07-15 00:00:00.000        13.97
10257       35          4           2006-07-16 00:00:00.000        81.91
...

(830 row(s) affected)
```

Although it might seem that the output of the query is returned in a particular order, this is not guaranteed. I'll elaborate on this point later in the chapter in the sections "The SELECT Clause" and "The ORDER BY Clause."

Delimiting Identifier Names

As long as identifiers in your query comply with rules for the format of regular identifiers, you don't need to delimit the identifier names used for schemas, tables, and columns. The rules for the format of regular identifiers can be found in SQL Server Books Online under "Identifiers." If an identifier is irregular—for example, has embedded spaces or special characters, starts with a digit, or is a reserved keyword—you have to delimit it. You can delimit identifiers in SQL Server in a couple of ways. The ANSI SQL form is to use double quotes—for example, "Order Details". The SQL Server specific form is to use square brackets—for example, [Order Details], but it also supports the standard form.

With identifiers that do comply with the rules for the format of regular identifiers, delimiting is optional. For example, a table called Order Details residing in the Sales schema can be referred to as Sales."Order Details" or "Sales"."Order Details". My personal preference is not to use delimiters when they are not required because they tend to clutter the code. Also, when you're in charge of assigning identifiers, I recommend always using regular ones, for example, OrderDetails instead of Order Details.

The WHERE Clause

In the WHERE clause, you specify a predicate or logical expression to filter the rows returned by the FROM phase. Only rows for which the logical expression evaluates to TRUE are returned by the WHERE phase to the subsequent logical query processing phase. In the sample query in Listing 2-1, the WHERE phase filters only orders placed by customer 71:

```
FROM Sales.Orders
WHERE custid = 71
```

Out of the 830 rows returned by the FROM phase, the WHERE phase filters only the 31 rows where the customer ID is equal to 71. To see which rows you get back after applying the filter custid = 71, run the following query:

```
SELECT orderid, empid, orderdate, freight
FROM Sales.Orders
WHERE custid = 71;
```

This query generates the following output:

```
orderid     empid        orderdate                      freight
----------- ------------ ------------------------------ -------------
10324       9            2006-10-08 00:00:00.000        214.27
10393       1            2006-12-25 00:00:00.000        126.56
10398       2            2006-12-30 00:00:00.000        89.16
10440       4            2007-02-10 00:00:00.000        86.53
10452       8            2007-02-20 00:00:00.000        140.26
10510       6            2007-04-18 00:00:00.000        367.63
10555       6            2007-06-02 00:00:00.000        252.49
10603       8            2007-07-18 00:00:00.000        48.77
10607       5            2007-07-22 00:00:00.000        200.24
10612       1            2007-07-28 00:00:00.000        544.08
10627       8            2007-08-11 00:00:00.000        107.46
10657       2            2007-09-04 00:00:00.000        352.69
10678       7            2007-09-23 00:00:00.000        388.98
10700       3            2007-10-10 00:00:00.000        65.10
10711       5            2007-10-21 00:00:00.000        52.41
10713       1            2007-10-22 00:00:00.000        167.05
10714       5            2007-10-22 00:00:00.000        24.49
```

10722	8	2007-10-29 00:00:00.000	74.58
10748	3	2007-11-20 00:00:00.000	232.55
10757	6	2007-11-27 00:00:00.000	8.19
10815	2	2008-01-05 00:00:00.000	14.62
10847	4	2008-01-22 00:00:00.000	487.57
10882	4	2008-02-11 00:00:00.000	23.10
10894	1	2008-02-18 00:00:00.000	116.13
10941	7	2008-03-11 00:00:00.000	400.81
10983	2	2008-03-27 00:00:00.000	657.54
10984	1	2008-03-30 00:00:00.000	211.22
11002	4	2008-04-06 00:00:00.000	141.16
11030	7	2008-04-17 00:00:00.000	830.75
11031	6	2008-04-17 00:00:00.000	227.22
11064	1	2008-05-01 00:00:00.000	30.09

```
(31 row(s) affected)
```

The WHERE clause has significance when it comes to query performance. Based on what you have in the filter expression, SQL Server evaluates the use of indexes to access the required data. By using indexes, SQL Server can sometimes get the required data with much less work compared to applying full table scans. Query filters also reduce the network traffic created by returning all possible rows to the caller and filtering on the client side.

Earlier I mentioned that only rows for which the logical expression evaluates to TRUE are returned by the WHERE phase. Always keep in mind that T-SQL uses three-valued predicate logic, where logical expressions can evaluate to TRUE, FALSE, or UNKNOWN. With three-valued logic, saying "returns TRUE" is not the same as saying "does not return FALSE." The WHERE phase returns rows for which the logical expression evaluates to TRUE, and doesn't return rows for which the logical expression evaluates to FALSE or UNKNOWN. I elaborate on this point later in this chapter in the section "NULLs."

The GROUP BY Clause

The GROUP BY phase allows you to arrange the rows returned by the previous logical query processing phase in groups. The groups are determined by the elements you specify in the GROUP BY clause. For example, the GROUP BY clause in the query in Listing 2-1 has the elements *empid* and *YEAR(orderdate)*:

```
FROM Sales.Orders
WHERE custid = 71
GROUP BY empid, YEAR(orderdate)
```

This means that the GROUP BY phase produces a group for each unique combination of employee ID and order year values that appears in the data returned by the WHERE phase. The expression YEAR(orderdate) invokes the *YEAR* function to return only the year part from the orderdate column.

The WHERE phase returned 31 rows, within which there are 16 unique combinations of employee ID and order year values, as shown here:

```
empid       YEAR(orderdate)
----------- ---------------
1           2006
1           2007
1           2008
2           2006
2           2007
2           2008
3           2007
4           2007
4           2008
5           2007
6           2007
6           2008
7           2007
7           2008
8           2007
9           2006
```

Thus the GROUP BY phase creates 16 groups, and associates each of the 31 rows returned from the WHERE phase with the relevant group.

If the query involves grouping, all phases subsequent to the GROUP BY phase—including HAVING, SELECT, and ORDER BY—must operate on groups as opposed to operating on individual rows. Each group is ultimately represented by a single row in the final result of the query. This implies that all expressions that you specify in clauses that are processed in subsequent phases to the GROUP BY phase are required to guarantee returning a scalar (single value) per group.

Expressions based on elements that participate in the GROUP BY list meet the require-ment because by definition each group has only one unique occurrence of each GROUP BY element. For example, in the group for employee ID 8 and order year 2007, there's only one unique employee ID value and only one unique order year value. Therefore, you're allowed to refer to the expressions empid and YEAR(orderdate) in clauses that are processed in phases subsequent to the GROUP BY phase, such as the SELECT clause. The following query, for example, returns 16 rows for the 16 groups of employee ID and order year values:

```
SELECT empid, YEAR(orderdate) AS orderyear
FROM Sales.Orders
WHERE custid = 71
GROUP BY empid, YEAR(orderdate);
```

This query returns the following output:

```
empid       orderyear
----------- -----------
1           2006
1           2007
```

```
1          2008
2          2006
2          2007
2          2008
3          2007
4          2007
4          2008
5          2007
6          2007
6          2008
7          2007
7          2008
8          2007
9          2006
```

(16 row(s) affected)

Because an aggregate function returns a single value per group, elements that do not participate in the GROUP BY list are only allowed as inputs to an aggregate function such as *COUNT, SUM, AVG, MIN*, or *MAX*. For example, the following query returns the total freight and number of orders per each employee and order year:

```
SELECT
  empid,
  YEAR(orderdate) AS orderyear,
  SUM(freight) AS totalfreight,
  COUNT(*) AS numorders
FROM Sales.Orders
WHERE custid = 71
GROUP BY empid, YEAR(orderdate);
```

This query generates the following output:

```
empid        orderyear    totalfreight           numorders
-----------  -----------  ---------------------  -----------
1            2006         126.56                 1
2            2006         89.16                  1
9            2006         214.27                 1
1            2007         711.13                 2
2            2007         352.69                 1
3            2007         297.65                 2
4            2007         86.53                  1
5            2007         277.14                 3
6            2007         628.31                 3
7            2007         388.98                 1
8            2007         371.07                 4
1            2008         357.44                 3
2            2008         672.16                 2
4            2008         651.83                 3
6            2008         227.22                 1
7            2008         1231.56                2
```

(16 row(s) affected)

The expression SUM(freight) returns the sum of all freight values in each group, and the function *COUNT(*)* returns the count of rows in each group—which in our case means number of orders. If you try to refer to an attribute that does not participate in the GROUP BY list (such as freight) and not as an input to an aggregate function in any clause that is processed after the GROUP BY clause, you get an error—in such a case there's no guarantee that the expression will return a single value per group. For example, the following query will fail:

```
SELECT empid, YEAR(orderdate) AS orderyear, freight
FROM Sales.Orders
WHERE custid = 71
GROUP BY empid, YEAR(orderdate);
```

SQL Server produces the following error:

```
Msg 8120, Level 16, State 1, Line 1
Column 'Sales.Orders.freight' is invalid in the select list because it is not contained in
either an aggregate function or the GROUP BY clause.
```

Note that all aggregate functions ignore NULLs with one exception—*COUNT(*)*. For example, consider a group of five rows with the values 30, 10, NULL, 10, 10 in a column called qty. The expression COUNT(*) would return 5 because there are five rows in the group, while COUNT(qty) would return 4 because there are four known values. If you want to handle only distinct occurrences of known values, specify the *DISTINCT* keyword in the parentheses of the aggregate function. For example, the expression COUNT(DISTINCT qty) would return 2 since there are two distinct known values. The *DISTINCT* keyword can be used with other functions as well. For example, while the expression SUM(qty) would return 60, the expression SUM(DISTINCT qty) would return 40. The expression AVG(qty) would return 15 while the expression AVG(DISTINCT qty) would return 20. As an example of using the DISTINCT option with an aggregate function in a complete query, the following code returns the number of distinct (different) customers handled by each employee in each order year:

```
SELECT
  empid,
  YEAR(orderdate) AS orderyear,
  COUNT(DISTINCT custid) AS numcusts
FROM Sales.Orders
GROUP BY empid, YEAR(orderdate);
```

This query generates the following output:

```
empid       orderyear   numcusts
----------- ----------- -----------
1           2006        22
2           2006        15
3           2006        16
4           2006        26
5           2006        10
6           2006        15
7           2006        11
```

8	2006	19
9	2006	5
1	2007	40
2	2007	35
3	2007	46
4	2007	57
5	2007	13
6	2007	24
7	2007	30
8	2007	36
9	2007	16
1	2008	32
2	2008	34
3	2008	30
4	2008	33
5	2008	11
6	2008	17
7	2008	21
8	2008	23
9	2008	16

```
(27 row(s) affected)
```

The HAVING Clause

With the HAVING clause you can specify a predicate/logical expression to filter groups as opposed to filtering individual rows, which happens in the WHERE phase. Only groups for which the logical expression in the HAVING clause evaluates to TRUE are returned by the HAVING phase to the next logical query processing phase. Groups for which the logical expression evaluates to FALSE or UNKNOWN are filtered out.

Because the HAVING clause is processed after the rows have been grouped, you can refer to aggregate functions in the logical expression. For example, in the query from Listing 2-1 the HAVING clause has the logical expression COUNT(*) > 1, meaning that the HAVING phase filters only groups (employee and order year) with more than one row. The following fragment of the Listing 2-1 query shows what steps have been processed so far:

```
FROM Sales.Orders
WHERE custid = 71
GROUP BY empid, YEAR(orderdate)
HAVING COUNT(*) > 1
```

Recall that the GROUP BY phase created 16 groups of employee ID and order year. Seven of those groups have only one row, so after the HAVING clause is processed, nine groups remain. Run the following query to return those nine groups:

```
SELECT empid, YEAR(orderdate) AS orderyear
FROM Sales.Orders
WHERE custid = 71
GROUP BY empid, YEAR(orderdate)
HAVING COUNT(*) > 1;
```

This query returns the following output:

```
empid       orderyear
----------- -----------
1           2007
3           2007
5           2007
6           2007
8           2007
1           2008
2           2008
4           2008
7           2008

(9 row(s) affected)
```

The SELECT Clause

The SELECT clause is where you specify the attributes (columns) that you want to return in the result table of the query. You can base the expressions in the SELECT list on attributes from the queried tables, with or without further manipulation. For example, the SELECT list in Listing 2-1 has the following expressions: empid, YEAR(orderdate), and COUNT(*). If an expression refers to an attribute with no manipulation, such as empid, the name of the target attribute is the same as the name of the source attribute. You can optionally assign your own name to the target attribute by using the AS clause—for example, empid AS employee_id. Expressions that do apply manipulation, such as YEAR(orderdate), or are not based on a source attribute, such as a call for the function *CURRENT_TIMESTAMP*, don't have a name in the result of the query if you don't alias them. T-SQL allows a query to return result columns with no names in certain cases, but the relational model doesn't. It's strongly recommended that you alias such expressions as YEAR(orderdate) AS orderyear so that all result attributes have names. In this respect, the result table returned from the query would be considered relational.

T-SQL supports, in addition to the AS clause, a couple of other forms with which you can alias expressions, but to me, the AS clause seems the most readable and intuitive form and therefore I recommend using it. I will cover the other forms for the sake of completeness and also in order to describe an elusive bug related to one of them. Besides the form <expression> AS <alias>, T-SQL also supports the forms <alias> = <expression> (alias equals expression), and <expression> <alias> (expression space alias). An example of the former is orderyear = YEAR(orderdate), and an example of the latter is YEAR(orderdate) orderyear. I find the latter form in which you specify the expression followed by a space and the alias, particularly unclear, and I strongly recommend that you avoid using it.

It is interesting to note that if by mistake you don't specify a comma between two column names in the SELECT list, your code won't fail. Rather SQL Server will assume that the second name is an alias for the first column name. As an example, suppose that you wanted to write a query that selects the orderid and orderdate columns from the Sales.Orders table, and by mistake didn't specify the comma between the column names, as follows:

```
SELECT orderid orderdate
FROM Sales.Orders;
```

This query is considered syntactically valid, as if you intended to alias the orderid column as orderdate. In the output you will get only one column holding the order IDs, with the alias orderdate:

```
orderdate
-----------
10248
10249
10250
10251
10252
...

(830 row(s) affected)
```

It can be hard to detect such a bug, so the best you can do is to be alert when writing code.

With the addition of the SELECT phase, the following query clauses from the query in Listing 2-1 have been processed so far:

```
SELECT empid, YEAR(orderdate) AS orderyear, COUNT(*) AS numorders
FROM Sales.Orders
WHERE custid = 71
GROUP BY empid, YEAR(orderdate)
HAVING COUNT(*) > 1
```

The SELECT clause produces the result table of the query. In the case of the query in Listing 2-1, the heading of the result table has the attributes empid, orderyear, and numorders, and the body has nine rows (one for each group). Run the following query to return those nine rows:

```
SELECT empid, YEAR(orderdate) AS orderyear, COUNT(*) AS numorders
FROM Sales.Orders
WHERE custid = 71
GROUP BY empid, YEAR(orderdate)
HAVING COUNT(*) > 1;
```

This query generates the following output:

```
empid       orderyear   numorders
----------- ----------- -----------
1           2007        2
3           2007        2
5           2007        3
6           2007        3
8           2007        4
1           2008        3
2           2008        2
```

4	2008	3
7	2008	2

(9 row(s) affected)

Remember that the SELECT clause is processed after the FROM, WHERE, GROUP BY, and HAVING clauses. This means that aliases assigned to expressions in the SELECT clause do not exist as far as clauses that are processed before the SELECT clause are concerned. A very typical mistake made by programmers who are not familiar with the correct logical processing order of query clauses is to refer to expression aliases in clauses that are processed prior to the SELECT clause. Here's an example of such an invalid attempt in the WHERE clause:

```
SELECT orderid, YEAR(orderdate) AS orderyear
FROM Sales.Orders
WHERE orderyear > 2006;
```

On the surface this query might seem valid, but if you consider the fact that the column aliases are created in the SELECT phase—which is processed after the WHERE phase—you can see that the reference to the orderyear alias in the WHERE clause is invalid. And in fact, SQL Server produces the following error:

```
Msg 207, Level 16, State 1, Line 3
Invalid column name 'orderyear'.
```

One way around this problem is to repeat the expression YEAR(orderdate) in both the WHERE and the SELECT clauses:

```
SELECT orderid, YEAR(orderdate) AS orderyear
FROM Sales.Orders
WHERE YEAR(orderdate) > 2006;
```

It's interesting to note that SQL Server is capable of identifying the repeated use of the same expression—YEAR(orderdate)—in the query. It only needs to be evaluated or calculated once.

The following query is another example of an invalid reference to a column alias. The query attempts to refer to a column alias in the HAVING clause, which is also processed before the SELECT clause:

```
SELECT empid, YEAR(orderdate) AS orderyear, COUNT(*) AS numorders
FROM Sales.Orders
WHERE custid = 71
GROUP BY empid, YEAR(orderdate)
HAVING numorders > 1;
```

This query fails with an error saying that the column name numorders is invalid. You would also need to repeat the expression COUNT(*) in both clauses:

```
SELECT empid, YEAR(orderdate) AS orderyear, COUNT(*) AS numorders
FROM Sales.Orders
WHERE custid = 71
GROUP BY empid, YEAR(orderdate)
HAVING COUNT(*) > 1;
```

In the relational model, operations on relations are based on relational algebra and result in a relation (a set). In SQL, things are a bit different in the sense that a SELECT query is not guaranteed to return a true set—namely, unique rows with no guaranteed order. To begin with, SQL doesn't require a table to qualify as a set. Without a key, uniqueness of rows is not guaranteed, in which case the table isn't a set; it's a multiset or a bag. But even if the tables you query have keys and qualify as sets, a SELECT query against the tables can still return a result with duplicate rows. The term result set is often used to describe the output of a SELECT query, but a result set doesn't necessarily qualify as a set in the mathematical sense. For example, even though the Orders table is a set because uniqueness is enforced with a key, a query against the Orders table returns duplicate rows, as shown in Listing 2-2:

LISTING 2-2 Query Returning Duplicate Rows

```
SELECT empid, YEAR(orderdate) AS orderyear
FROM Sales.Orders
WHERE custid = 71;
```

This query generates the following output:

```
empid       orderyear
----------- -----------
9           2006
1           2006
2           2006
4           2007
8           2007
6           2007
6           2007
8           2007
5           2007
1           2007
8           2007
2           2007
7           2007
3           2007
5           2007
1           2007
5           2007
8           2007
3           2007
6           2007
2           2008
4           2008
4           2008
1           2008
7           2008
2           2008
1           2008
4           2008
7           2008
6           2008
1           2008

(31 row(s) affected)
```

SQL provides the means to guarantee uniqueness in the result of a *SELECT* statement in the form of a DISTINCT clause that removes duplicate rows, as shown in Listing 2-3:

LISTING 2-3 Query with a DISTINCT Clause

```
SELECT DISTINCT empid, YEAR(orderdate) AS orderyear
FROM Sales.Orders
WHERE custid = 71;
```

This query generates the following output:

```
empid       orderyear
----------- -----------
1           2006
1           2007
1           2008
2           2006
2           2007
2           2008
3           2007
4           2007
4           2008
5           2007
6           2007
6           2008
7           2007
7           2008
8           2007
9           2006

(16 row(s) affected)
```

Of the 31 rows in the multiset returned by the query in Listing 2-2, 16 rows are in the set returned by the query in Listing 2-3 after removal of duplicates.

SQL supports the use of an asterisk (*) in the SELECT list to request all attributes from the queried tables instead of listing them explicitly, as in the following example:

```
SELECT *
FROM Sales.Shippers;
```

Such use of an asterisk is a bad programming practice in most cases, with very few exceptions. It is recommended that you explicitly specify the list of attributes that you need even if you need all of the attributes from the queried table. There are many reasons for this recommendation. Unlike the relational model, SQL keeps ordinal positions for columns based on the order in which the columns were specified in the *CREATE TABLE* statement. By specifying SELECT *, you're guaranteed to get the columns back in order based on their ordinal positions. Client applications can refer to columns in the result by their ordinal positions (a bad practice in its own right) instead of by name. Any schema changes applied to the table—such as adding or removing columns, rearranging their order, and so on—might result in failures in the client application, or even worse, logical bugs that will go unnoticed. By specifying the attributes that you need explicitly, you always get the right ones, as long as the columns exist in the table. If a column referenced by the query was dropped from the table, you get an error and can fix your code accordingly.

Some people wonder whether there's any performance difference between specifying an asterisk and explicitly listing column names. Some extra work may be required in resolving column names when using the asterisk, but it is usually so negligible compared to other costs involved in the query that it is unlikely to be noticed. If there is any performance difference, as minor as it may be, it is most probably in the favor of explicitly listing column names. Because that's the recommended practice anyway, it's a win-win situation.

Within the SELECT clause you are still not allowed to refer to a column alias that was created in the same SELECT clause, regardless of whether the expression that assigns the alias appears to the left or right of the expression that attempts to refer to it. For example, the following attempt is invalid:

```
SELECT orderid,
  YEAR(orderdate) AS orderyear,
  orderyear + 1 AS nextyear
FROM Sales.Orders;
```

As explained earlier in this section, one of the ways around this problem is to repeat the expression:

```
SELECT orderid,
  YEAR(orderdate) AS orderyear,
  YEAR(orderdate) + 1 AS nextyear
FROM Sales.Orders;
```

The ORDER BY Clause

The ORDER BY clause allows you to sort the rows in the output for presentation purposes. In terms of logical query processing, ORDER BY is the very last clause to be processed. The sample query shown in Listing 2-4 sorts the rows in the output by employee ID and order year:

LISTING 2-4 Query Demonstrating the ORDER BY Clause

```
SELECT empid, YEAR(orderdate) AS orderyear, COUNT(*) AS numorders
FROM Sales.Orders
WHERE custid = 71
GROUP BY empid, YEAR(orderdate)
HAVING COUNT(*) > 1
ORDER BY empid, orderyear;
```

This query generates the following output:

```
empid       orderyear   numorders
----------- ----------- -----------
1           2007        2
1           2008        3
2           2008        2
3           2007        2
4           2008        3
5           2007        3
6           2007        3
7           2008        2
8           2007        4

(9 row(s) affected)
```

One of the most important points to understand about SQL is that a table has no guaranteed order, because a table is supposed to represent a set (or multiset if it has duplicates), and a set has no order. This means that when you query a table without specifying an ORDER BY clause, the query returns a table result, and SQL Server is free to return the rows in the output in any order. The only way for you to guarantee that the rows in the result are sorted is to explicitly specify an ORDER BY clause. However, if you do specify an ORDER BY clause, the result cannot qualify as a table because the order of the rows in the result is guaranteed. A query with an ORDER BY clause results in what ANSI calls a cursor—a nonrelational result with order guaranteed among rows. You're probably wondering why it matters whether a query returns a table result or a cursor. Some language elements and operations in SQL expect to work with table results of queries and not with cursors; examples include table expressions and set operations, which I cover in detail later in the book.

Notice that the ORDER BY clause refers to the column alias orderyear, which was created in the SELECT phase. The ORDER BY phase is in fact the only phase in which you can refer to column aliases created in the SELECT phase, because it is the only phase that is processed after the SELECT phase.

When you want to sort by an expression in ascending order, you either specify ASC right after the expression, such as orderyear ASC, or don't specify anything after the expression because ASC is the default. If you want to sort in descending order, you need to specify DESC after the expression, such as orderyear DESC.

SQL and T-SQL both allow you to specify in the ORDER BY clause ordinal positions of columns based on the order in which the columns appear in the SELECT list. For example, in the query in Listing 2-4, instead of using:

```
ORDER BY empid, orderyear
```

You could use:

```
ORDER BY 1, 2
```

However, this is considered bad programming practice for a couple of reasons. First, in the relational model attributes don't have ordinal positions and need to be referred to by name. Second, when you make revisions to the SELECT clause, you might forget to make the corresponding revisions in the ORDER BY clause. When you use column names, your code is safe from this type of mistake.

T-SQL allows you to specify elements in the ORDER BY clause that do not appear in the SELECT clause, meaning that you can sort by something that you don't necessarily want to return in the output. For example, the following query sorts the employee rows by hire date without returning the hiredate attribute:

```
SELECT empid, firstname, lastname, country
FROM HR.Employees
ORDER BY hiredate;
```

However, when DISTINCT is specified, you are restricted in the ORDER BY list only to elements that appear in the SELECT list. The reasoning behind this restriction is that when DISTINCT is specified, a single result row might represent multiple source rows; therefore, it might not be clear which of the multiple possible values in the ORDER BY expression should be used. Consider the following invalid query:

```
SELECT DISTINCT country
FROM HR.Employees
ORDER BY empid;
```

There are nine employees in the Employees table—five from the USA and four from the UK. If you omit the invalid ORDER BY clause from this query, you get two rows back—one for each distinct country. Because each country appears in multiple rows in the source table, and each such row has a different employee ID, the meaning of ORDER BY empid is not really defined.

The TOP Option

The TOP option is a proprietary T-SQL feature that allows you to limit the number or percentage of rows that your query returns. When an ORDER BY clause is specified in the query, the TOP option relies on it to define the logical precedence among rows. For example, to return from the Orders table the five most recent orders, you would specify TOP (5) in the SELECT clause and orderdate DESC in the ORDER BY clause, as shown in Listing 2-5:

LISTING 2-5 Query Demonstrating the TOP Option

```
SELECT TOP (5) orderid, orderdate, custid, empid
FROM Sales.Orders
ORDER BY orderdate DESC;
```

This query returns the following output:

```
orderid     orderdate                    custid      empid
----------- ---------------------------  ----------- -----------
11077       2008-05-06 00:00:00.000      65          1
11076       2008-05-06 00:00:00.000      9           4
11075       2008-05-06 00:00:00.000      68          8
11074       2008-05-06 00:00:00.000      73          7
11073       2008-05-05 00:00:00.000      58          2

(5 row(s) affected)
```

In terms of logical query processing, the TOP option is processed as part of the SELECT phase, right after the DISTINCT clause is processed (if one exists). Note that when TOP is specified in a query the ORDER BY clause serves a dual purpose. That is, as part of the SELECT phase the TOP option relies on the ORDER BY clause to determine logical precedence among rows, and based on this precedence filters as many as were requested. Later, as part of the ORDER BY phase that follows the SELECT phase, the very same ORDER BY clause is used to sort the rows in the output for presentation purposes. For example, the query in Listing 2-5 returns the five rows with the highest orderdate values, and sorts the rows in the output by orderdate DESC for presentation purposes.

If you're confused about whether a TOP query returns a table result or a cursor, you have every reason to be. When TOP is used, the same ORDER BY clause serves both the purpose of determining logical precedence for TOP, and the normal meaning—presentation—that changes the nature of the result from a table to a cursor with guaranteed order. For example, you can't specify in the same query that you want the logical precedence among rows to be determined by one ORDER BY list for the TOP option, while you want to sort the rows in the output for presentation purposes by another, or not at all. To achieve this, you have to use a table expression, but I'll save the discussion of table expressions for Chapter 5. All I want to say for now is that if the design of the TOP option seems confusing, there's a good reason. In other words, it's not you—it's the feature's design.

You can use the TOP option with the *PERCENT* keyword, in which case SQL Server calculates the number of rows to return based on a percentage of the number of qualifying rows, rounded up. For example, the following query requests the top one percent of the most recent orders:

```
SELECT TOP (1) PERCENT orderid, orderdate, custid, empid
FROM Sales.Orders
ORDER BY orderdate DESC;
```

This query generates the following output:

```
orderid     orderdate                    custid      empid
----------- ---------------------------  ----------- -----------
11074       2008-05-06 00:00:00.000      73          7
11075       2008-05-06 00:00:00.000      68          8
11076       2008-05-06 00:00:00.000      9           4
```

11077	2008-05-06 00:00:00.000	65	1
11070	2008-05-05 00:00:00.000	44	2
11071	2008-05-05 00:00:00.000	46	1
11072	2008-05-05 00:00:00.000	20	4
11073	2008-05-05 00:00:00.000	58	2
11067	2008-05-04 00:00:00.000	17	1

```
(9 row(s) affected)
```

The query returns 9 rows because the Orders table has 830 rows, and 1 percent of 830, rounded up, is 9.

In the query in Listing 2-5, you might have noticed that the ORDER BY list is not unique because no primary key or unique constraint is defined on the orderdate column. Multiple rows can have the same order date. In a case where no tiebreaker is specified, precedence among rows in case of ties (rows with the same order date) is undefined. This fact makes the query nondeterministic—more than one result can be considered correct. In case of ties, SQL Server chooses rows based on whichever row it physically happens to access first.

Notice in the output for the query in Listing 2-5 that the minimum order date out of the rows returned is May 5, 2008, and one row in the output has that date. Other rows in the table may have the same order date, and with the existing non-unique ORDER BY list, there is no guarantee which of those will be returned.

If you want the query to be deterministic, you need to make the ORDER BY list unique; in other words, add a tiebreaker. For example, you can add orderid DESC to the ORDER BY list as shown in Listing 2-6 so that in case of ties, precedence is determined by order ID descending:

LISTING 2-6 Query Demonstrating TOP with Unique ORDER BY List

```
SELECT TOP (5) orderid, orderdate, custid, empid
FROM Sales.Orders
ORDER BY orderdate DESC, orderid DESC;
```

This query returns the following output:

orderid	orderdate	custid	empid
11077	2008-05-06 00:00:00.000	65	1
11076	2008-05-06 00:00:00.000	9	4
11075	2008-05-06 00:00:00.000	68	8
11074	2008-05-06 00:00:00.000	73	7
11073	2008-05-05 00:00:00.000	58	2

```
(5 row(s) affected)
```

If you examine the results of the queries from Listing 2-5 and Listing 2-6, you'll notice that they seem to be the same. The important difference is that the result shown in the query output for Listing 2-5 is one of several possible valid results for this query, while the result shown in the query output for Listing 2-6 is the only possible valid result.

Instead of adding a tiebreaker to the ORDER BY list, you can request to return all ties. For example, besides the five rows that you get back from the query in Listing 2-5, you can ask to return all other rows from the table that have the same sort value (order date in our case) as the last one found (May 5, 2008 in our case). You achieve this by adding the *WITH TIES* option as shown in the following query:

```
SELECT TOP (5) WITH TIES orderid, orderdate, custid, empid
FROM Sales.Orders
ORDER BY orderdate DESC;
```

This query returns the following output:

```
orderid     orderdate                   custid      empid
----------- --------------------------- ----------- -----------
11077       2008-05-06 00:00:00.000     65          1
11076       2008-05-06 00:00:00.000     9           4
11075       2008-05-06 00:00:00.000     68          8
11074       2008-05-06 00:00:00.000     73          7
11073       2008-05-05 00:00:00.000     58          2
11072       2008-05-05 00:00:00.000     20          4
11071       2008-05-05 00:00:00.000     46          1
11070       2008-05-05 00:00:00.000     44          2

(8 row(s) affected)
```

Notice that the output has eight rows even though you specified TOP (5). SQL Server first returned the TOP (5) rows based on orderdate DESC precedence, and also all other rows from the table that had the same *orderdate* value as in the last of the five rows that was accessed.

The OVER Clause

The OVER clause exposes a window of rows to certain kinds of calculations. Think of a window of rows simply as a certain set of rows that the calculation operates on. Aggregate and ranking functions, for example, are the types of calculations that support the OVER clause. Because the OVER clause exposes a window of rows to those functions, they are known as window functions.

Because the whole point of an aggregate function is to aggregate a set of values, aggregate functions traditionally operate in the context of GROUP BY queries. Recall from earlier discussions in the section "The GROUP BY Clause" that once you group data, the query returns only one row for each group; therefore, all your expressions are restricted to returning a single value per group.

An aggregate window function operates against a set of values in a window of rows that you expose to it using the OVER clause, and not in the context of a GROUP BY query. Therefore, you don't have to group the data, and you can return base row attributes and aggregates in the same row.

To understand the OVER clause, think of the Sales.OrderValues view. I will discuss views in Chapter 10, "Programmable Objects," but for now, simply think of a view as if it were a table. The Sales.OrderValues view has a row for each order, with the order ID (orderid), customer ID (custid), employee ID (empid), shipper ID (shipperid), order date (orderdate) and order value (val).

An OVER clause with empty parentheses exposes all rows to the calculation. The phrase "all rows" doesn't necessarily mean all rows from the table that appears in the FROM clause; rather the rows exposed are those available after the FROM, WHERE, GROUP BY and HAVING phases are completed. Note that the OVER clause is allowed only in the SELECT and ORDER BY phases. In order not to overwhelm you with too much information at this early stage, I'll focus on using the OVER clause in the SELECT phase. So, for example, if you specify the expression SUM(val) OVER() in the SELECT clause of a query against the OrderValues view, the function calculates the total value out of all rows that the SELECT phase operates on. If the query doesn't filter data or apply any other logical phases before the SELECT phase, the expression returns the total value out of all OrderValues rows.

If you want to restrict or partition the rows, you can use the PARTITION BY clause. For example, if instead of returning the total value of all OrderValues rows, you want to return the total value of the current customer (out of all rows with the same custid as in the current row), specify SUM(val) OVER(PARTITION BY custid).

To demonstrate both nonpartitioned and partitioned expressions, the following query returns all OrderValues rows. Additionally, in each row except for the base attributes, the query returns the grand total value and the customer total value:

```
SELECT orderid, custid, val,
  SUM(val) OVER() AS totalvalue,
  SUM(val) OVER(PARTITION BY custid) AS custtotalvalue
FROM Sales.OrderValues;
```

This query returns the following output:

```
orderid      custid       val           totalvalue        custtotalvalue
-----------  -----------  ------------  ----------------  ---------------
10643        1            814.50        1265793.22        4273.00
10692        1            878.00        1265793.22        4273.00
10702        1            330.00        1265793.22        4273.00
10835        1            845.80        1265793.22        4273.00
10952        1            471.20        1265793.22        4273.00
11011        1            933.50        1265793.22        4273.00
10926        2            514.40        1265793.22        1402.95
10759        2            320.00        1265793.22        1402.95
10625        2            479.75        1265793.22        1402.95
10308        2            88.80         1265793.22        1402.95
10365        3            403.20        1265793.22        7023.98
...

(830 row(s) affected)
```

The totalvalue column has, in all result rows, the total value out of all rows. The custtotalvalue column has the total value out of all rows that have the same custid value as in the current row.

One benefit of the OVER clause is that by enabling you to return base row attributes and aggregate them in the same row, it also enables you to write expressions that mix the two. For example, the following query calculates for each OrderValues row the percentage of the current value out of the grand total, and also the percentage of the current value out of the customer total:

```
SELECT orderid, custid, val,
  100. * val / SUM(val) OVER() AS pctall,
  100. * val / SUM(val) OVER(PARTITION BY custid) AS pctcust
FROM Sales.OrderValues;
```

Note that the reason that I specified the decimal value 100. (one hundred dot) in the expressions instead of the integer 100 is in order to cause implicit conversion of the integer values val and SUM(val) to decimal values. Otherwise, the division would have been an integer division and the fractional part would have been truncated.

This query returns the following output:

```
orderid      custid val         pctall                          pctcust
------------ ------ ----------- ------------------------------- ----------------------------
10643        1      814.50      0.0643470029014691672941        19.0615492628130119354083
10692        1      878.00      0.0693636200705830925528        20.5476246197051252047741
10702        1      330.00      0.0260706089103558320528        7.7229113035338169904048
10835        1      845.80      0.0668197606556938265161        19.7940556985724315469225
10952        1      471.20      0.0372256694501808123130        11.0273812309852562602387
11011        1      933.50      0.0737482224782338461253        21.8464778843903580622513
10926        2      514.40      0.0406385491620819394181        36.6655974910011048148544
10759        2      320.00      0.0252805904585268674452        22.8090808653195053280587
10625        2      479.75      0.0379011352264945770526        34.1958017035532271285505
10308        2      88.80       0.0070153638522412057160        6.3295199401261627285362
10365        3      403.20      0.0318535439777438529809        5.7403352515240647040566
...

(830 row(s) affected)
```

The OVER clause is also supported with four ranking functions: *ROW_NUMBER, RANK, DENSE_RANK,* and *NTILE*. The following query demonstrates the use of these functions:

```
SELECT orderid, custid, val,
  ROW_NUMBER() OVER(ORDER BY val) AS rownum,
  RANK()       OVER(ORDER BY val) AS rank,
  DENSE_RANK() OVER(ORDER BY val) AS dense_rank,
  NTILE(100)   OVER(ORDER BY val) AS ntile
FROM Sales.OrderValues
ORDER BY val;
```

This query generates the following output:

```
orderid      custid       val        rownum   rank    dense_rank ntile
-----------  -----------  ---------  -------  -------  ---------- -----
10782        12           12.50      1        1        1          1
10807        27           18.40      2        2        2          1
10586        66           23.80      3        3        3          1
10767        76           28.00      4        4        4          1
10898        54           30.00      5        5        5          1
10900        88           33.75      6        6        6          1
10883        48           36.00      7        7        7          1
11051        41           36.00      8        7        7          1
10815        71           40.00      9        9        8          1
10674        38           45.00      10       10       9          1
...
10691        63           10164.80   821      821      786        10
10540        63           10191.70   822      822      787        10
10479        65           10495.60   823      823      788        10
10897        37           10835.24   824      824      789        10
10817        39           10952.85   825      825      790        10
10417        73           11188.40   826      826      791        10
10889        65           11380.00   827      827      792        10
11030        71           12615.05   828      828      793        10
10981        34           15810.00   829      829      794        10
10865        63           16387.50   830      830      795        10

(830 row(s) affected)
```

The *ROW_NUMBER* function assigns incrementing sequential integers to the rows in the result set of a query, based on logical order that is specified in the ORDER BY subclause of the OVER clause. In our sample query, the logical order is based on the val column; therefore, you can see in the output that when the value increases the row number increases as well. However, even when the ordering value doesn't increase, the row number still must increase. Therefore, if the *ROW_NUMBER* function's ORDER BY list is non-unique, as in the preceding example, the query is nondeterministic. That is, more than one correct result is possible. For example, observe that two rows with the value 36.00 got the row numbers 7 and 8. Any arrangement of these row numbers would have been considered correct. If you want to make a row number calculation deterministic, you need to add elements to the ORDER BY list to make it unique; meaning that the list of elements in the ORDER BY clause would uniquely identify rows. For example, you can add the orderid column as a tiebreaker to the ORDER BY list to make the row number calculation deterministic.

As I mentioned earlier, the *ROW_NUMBER* function must produce unique values even when there are ties in the ordering values. If you want to treat ties in the ordering values the same way, you will probably want to use the *RANK* or *DENSE_RANK* function instead. Both are similar to the *ROW_NUMBER* function, but they produce the same ranking value in all rows that have the same logical ordering value. The difference between *RANK* and *DENSE_RANK* is that *RANK* indicates how many rows have a lower ordering value, while *DENSE_RANK* indicates how many distinct ordering values are lower. For example, in our sample query, a rank 9 indicates 8 rows with lower values. A dense rank 9 indicates 8 distinct lower values.

The *NTILE* function allows you to associate the rows in the result with tiles (equally sized groups of rows) by assigning a tile number to each row. You specify as input to the function how many tiles you are after, and in the OVER clause you specify the logical ordering. Our sample query has 830 rows and the request was for 10 tiles; therefore, the tile size is 83 (830 divided by 10). Logical ordering is based on the val column. This means that the 83 rows with the lowest values are assigned with tile number 1, the next 83 with tile number 2, the next 83 with tile number 3, and so on. The *NTILE* function is logically related to the *ROW_NUMBER* function. It's as if you assigned row numbers to the rows based on val ordering, and based on the calculated tile size 83 assigned tile number 1 to rows 1 through 83, tile number 2 to rows 84 through 166, and so on. If the number of rows doesn't divide evenly by the number of tiles, from the remainder an extra row is added to each of the first tiles. For example, if there had been 102 rows and 5 tiles were requested, the first two tiles would have had 21 rows instead of 20.

Like aggregate window functions, ranking functions also support a PARTITION BY clause in the OVER clause. It's probably easy to understand the meaning of the PARTITION BY clause in the context of ranking calculations; think of it as making the calculation independent for each partition, or window. For example, the expression ROW_NUMBER() OVER(PARTITION BY custid ORDER BY val) assigns row numbers for each subset of rows with the same custid independently, as opposed to assigning those across the whole set. Here's the expression in a query:

```
SELECT orderid, custid, val,
  ROW_NUMBER() OVER(PARTITION BY custid
                    ORDER BY val) AS rownum
FROM Sales.OrderValues
ORDER BY custid, val;
```

This query generates the following output:

```
orderid      custid       val          rownum
-----------  -----------  -----------  -------
10702        1            330.00       1
10952        1            471.20       2
10643        1            814.50       3
10835        1            845.80       4
10692        1            878.00       5
11011        1            933.50       6
10308        2            88.80        1
10759        2            320.00       2
10625        2            479.75       3
10926        2            514.40       4
10682        3            375.50       1
...

(830 row(s) affected)
```

As you can see in the output, the row numbers are calculated independently for each customer, as though the calculation were reset for each customer.

Note that the logical ORDER BY specified in the OVER clause has nothing to do with presentation, and does not change the nature of the result from being a table. If you do not specify a presentation ORDER BY in the query, as explained earlier, you don't have any guarantees in terms of the order of the rows in the output. If you need to guarantee presentation order, you have to add a presentation ORDER BY clause, as I did in the last two queries demonstrating the use of ranking functions.

If specified in the SELECT phase, window calculations are processed before the DISTINCT clause (if one exists).

To put it all together, the following list presents the logical order in which all clauses discussed so far are processed:

- FROM
- WHERE
- GROUP BY
- HAVING
- SELECT
  - OVER
  - DISTINCT
  - TOP
- ORDER BY

Are you wondering why it matters that the DISTINCT clause is processed after window calculations that appear in the SELECT clause are processed, and not before? I'll explain with an example. Currently the OrderValues view has 830 rows with 795 distinct values. Consider the following query and its output:

```
SELECT DISTINCT val, ROW_NUMBER() OVER(ORDER BY val) AS rownum
FROM Sales.OrderValues;
```

```
val         rownum
----------  -------
12.50       1
18.40       2
23.80       3
28.00       4
30.00       5
33.75       6
36.00       7
36.00       8
40.00       9
```

```
45.00      10
...
12615.05   828
15810.00   829
16387.50   830
```

```
(830 row(s) affected)
```

The *ROW_NUMBER* function is processed before the DISTINCT clause. First, unique row numbers are assigned to the 830 rows from the OrderValues view. Then the DISTINCT clause is processed—therefore, no duplicate rows to remove. You can consider it a best practice not to specify both DISTINCT and ROW_NUMBER in the same SELECT clause as the DISTINCT clause has no effect in such a case. If you want to assign row numbers to the 795 unique values, you need to come up with a different solution. For example, because the GROUP BY phase is processed before the SELECT phase, you could use the following query:

```
SELECT val, ROW_NUMBER() OVER(ORDER BY val) AS rownum
FROM Sales.OrderValues
GROUP BY val;
```

This query generates the following output:

```
val       rownum
--------- -------
12.50     1
18.40     2
23.80     3
28.00     4
30.00     5
33.75     6
36.00     7
40.00     8
45.00     9
48.00     10
...
12615.05  793
15810.00  794
16387.50  795
```

```
(795 row(s) affected)
```

Here, the GROUP BY phase produces 795 groups for the 795 distinct values, and then the SELECT phase produces a row for each group with the value and a row number based on val order.

Predicates and Operators

T-SQL has different language elements where logical expressions can be specified—for example, query filters such as WHERE and HAVING, CHECK constraints, and others. Logical expressions can make use of various predicates (expressions that evaluate to TRUE, FALSE or UNKNOWN) and operators.

Examples for predicates supported by T-SQL include IN, BETWEEN, and LIKE. The IN predicate allows you to check whether a value, or scalar expression, is equal to at least one of the elements in a set. For example, the following query returns orders where the order ID is equal to 10248 or 10249 or 10250:

```
SELECT orderid, empid, orderdate
FROM Sales.Orders
WHERE orderid IN(10248, 10249, 10250);
```

The BETWEEN predicate allows you to check whether a value is in a specified range, inclusive of the two specified boundary values. For example, the following query returns all orders in the range 10300 through 10310:

```
SELECT orderid, empid, orderdate
FROM Sales.Orders
WHERE orderid BETWEEN 10300 AND 10310;
```

The LIKE predicate allows you to check whether a character string value meets a specified pattern. For example, the following query returns employees whose last name starts with D:

```
SELECT empid, firstname, lastname
FROM HR.Employees
WHERE lastname LIKE N'D%';
```

Later in the chapter I'll elaborate on pattern matching and the LIKE predicate.

If you're curious about the use of the letter N to prefix the string 'D%', it stands for *National* and is used to denote that a character string is of a Unicode data type (NCHAR or NVARCHAR), as opposed to a regular character data type (CHAR or VARCHAR). Because the data type of the lastname attribute is NVARCHAR(40), the letter N is used to prefix the string. Later in the chapter, in the section "Working with Character Data," I elaborate on the treatment of character strings.

T-SQL supports the following comparison operators: =, >, <, >=, <=, <>, !=, !>, !<, out of which the last three are not standard. Because the nonstandard operators have standard alternatives (such as <> instead of !=), I recommend that you avoid the use of the nonstandard operators. For example, the following query returns all orders placed on or after January 1, 2008:

```
SELECT orderid, empid, orderdate
FROM Sales.Orders
WHERE orderdate >= '20080101';
```

If you need to combine logical expressions, you can use the logical operators OR and AND. If you want to negate an expression, you can use the NOT operator. For example, the following query returns orders placed on or after January 1, 2008, and were handled by one of the employees 1, 3, 5:

```
SELECT orderid, empid, orderdate
FROM Sales.Orders
WHERE orderdate >= '20080101'
  AND empid IN(1, 3, 5);
```

T-SQL supports the four obvious arithmetic operators: +, –, *, /, and also the % operator (modulo) that returns the remainder of integer division. For example, the following query calculates the net value as a result of arithmetic manipulation of the quantity, unitprice, and discount attributes:

```
SELECT orderid, productid, qty, unitprice, discount,
  qty * unitprice * (1 - discount) AS val
FROM Sales.OrderDetails;
```

Note that the data type of a scalar expression involving two operands is determined in T-SQL by the higher of the two in terms of data type precedence. If both operands are of the same data type, the result of the expression is of the same data type as well. For example, a division between two integers (INT) yields an integer. The expression 5/2 returns the integer 2 and not the numeric 2.5. This is not a problem when dealing with constants because you can always specify the values as numeric ones with a decimal point. But when dealing with, say, two integer columns, such as col1/col2, you need to cast the operands to the appropriate type if you want the calculation to be a numeric one: CAST(col1 AS NUMERIC(12, 2))/ CAST(col2 AS NUMERIC(12, 2)). The data type NUMERIC(12, 2) has precision 12 and scale 2, meaning twelve digits in total, two of which are after the decimal point.

If the two operands are of different types, the one with the lower precedence is promoted to the one that is higher. For example, in the expression 5/2.0 the first operand is INT and the second is NUMERIC. Because NUMERIC is considered higher than INT, the INT operand 5 is implicitly converted to the NUMERIC 5.0 before the arithmetic operation, and you get the result 2.5.

You can find the precedence order among types in SQL Server Books Online under "Data Type Precedence."

When multiple operators appear in the same expression, SQL Server evaluates them based on operator precedence rules. The following list has the precedence among operators, from highest to lowest:

1. ( ) (Parentheses)
2. * (Multiply), / (Division), % (Modulo)
3. + (Positive), – (Negative), + (Add), (+ Concatenate), – (Subtract)
4. =, >, <, >=, <=, <>, !=, !>, !< (Comparison operators)
5. NOT
6. AND
7. BETWEEN, IN, LIKE, OR
8. = (Assignment)

For example, in the following query, AND has precedence over OR:

```
SELECT orderid, custid, empid, orderdate
FROM Sales.Orders
WHERE
        custid = 1
    AND empid IN(1, 3, 5)
    OR  custid = 85
    AND empid IN(2, 4, 6);
```

The query returns orders that were either placed by customer 1 and handled by employees 1, 3, or 5 or placed by customer 85 and handled by employees 2, 4, or 6.

Parentheses have the highest precedence, so they give you full control. For the sake of other people who need to review or maintain your code and for readability purposes, it's a good practice to use parentheses even when not required, as well as indentation. For example, the following query is the logical equivalent of the previous query, only its logic is much clearer:

```
SELECT orderid, custid, empid, orderdate
FROM Sales.Orders
WHERE
      (custid = 1
        AND empid IN(1, 3, 5))
    OR
      (custid = 85
        AND empid IN(2, 4, 6));
```

Using parentheses to force precedence with logical operators is similar to using parentheses with arithmetic operators. For example, without parentheses in the following expression multiplication precedes addition:

```
SELECT 10 + 2 * 3;
```

Therefore, this expression returns 16. You can use parentheses to force the addition to be calculated first:

```
SELECT (10 + 2) * 3;
```

This time the expression returns 36.

CASE Expressions

A CASE expression is a scalar expression that returns a value based on conditional logic. Note that CASE is an expression and not a statement; that is, it doesn't let you control flow of activity or do something based on conditional logic. Instead, the value it returns is based on conditional logic. Because CASE is a scalar expression, it is allowed wherever scalar expressions are allowed, such as the SELECT, WHERE, HAVING, and ORDER BY clauses; CHECK constraints; and so on.

The two forms of CASE expression are *simple* and *searched*. The simple form allows you to compare one value, or scalar expression, with a list of possible values, and return a value back for the first match. If no value in the list is equal to the tested value, the CASE expression returns the value that appears in the ELSE clause (if one exists). If a CASE expression doesn't have an ELSE clause, it defaults to ELSE NULL.

For example, the following query against the Production.Products table uses a CASE expression in the SELECT clause to produce the description of the categoryid column value:

```
SELECT productid, productname, categoryid,
  CASE categoryid
    WHEN 1 THEN 'Beverages'
    WHEN 2 THEN 'Condiments'
    WHEN 3 THEN 'Confections'
    WHEN 4 THEN 'Dairy Products'
    WHEN 5 THEN 'Grains/Cereals'
    WHEN 6 THEN 'Meat/Poultry'
    WHEN 7 THEN 'Produce'
    WHEN 8 THEN 'Seafood'
    ELSE 'Unknown Category'
  END AS categoryname
FROM Production.Products;
```

This query produces the following output, shown in abbreviated form:

```
productid   productname          categoryid  categoryname
----------- -------------------- ----------- ----------------
1           Product HHYDP        1           Beverages
2           Product RECZE        1           Beverages
3           Product IMEHJ        2           Condiments
4           Product KSBRM        2           Condiments
5           Product EPEIM        2           Condiments
6           Product VAIIV        2           Condiments
7           Product HMLNI        7           Produce
8           Product WVJFP        2           Condiments
9           Product AOZBW        6           Meat/Poultry
10          Product YHXGE        8           Seafood
...

(77 row(s) affected)
```

The preceding query is a simple example of using the CASE expression. Unless the set of categories is very small and static, your best design choice is probably to maintain the product categories in a table, and join that table with the Products table when you need to get the category descriptions. In fact, the TSQLFundamentals2008 database has just such a Categories table.

Again demonstrating the simple form of the CASE expression, the following query against the Sales.OrderValues view produces three tiles based on val logical order, and translates the tile numbers to tile descriptions (Low, Medium, and High):

```
SELECT orderid, custid, val,
  CASE NTILE(3) OVER(ORDER BY val)
    WHEN 1 THEN 'Low'
    WHEN 2 THEN 'Medium'
    WHEN 3 THEN 'High'
    ELSE 'Unknown'
  END AS titledesc
FROM Sales.OrderValues
ORDER BY val;
```

This query generates the following output:

```
orderid      custid       val       titledesc
-----------  -----------  --------  ---------
10782        12           12.50     Low
10807        27           18.40     Low
10586        66           23.80     Low
10767        76           28.00     Low
10898        54           30.00     Low
...
10632        86           589.00    Low
11044        91           591.60    Low
10584        7            593.75    Low
10704        62           595.50    Low
10654        5            601.83    Low
10813        67           602.40    Medium
10656        32           604.22    Medium
10888        30           605.00    Medium
10300        49           608.00    Medium
10493        41           608.40    Medium
...
10645        34           1535.00   Medium
10667        20           1536.80   Medium
10461        46           1538.70   Medium
10878        63           1539.00   Medium
10553        87           1546.30   Medium
10362        9            1549.60   High
10250        34           1552.60   High
10799        39           1553.50   High
10722        71           1570.00   High
11018        48           1575.00   High
...
10417        73           11188.40  High
10889        65           11380.00  High
11030        71           12615.05  High
10981        34           15810.00  High
10865        63           16387.50  High

(830 row(s) affected)
```

The simple CASE form has a single test value, or expression, right after the *CASE* keyword that is compared with a list of possible values in the WHEN clauses. The searched CASE form is more flexible because it allows you to specify predicates, or logical expressions, in the WHEN clauses rather than restricting you to equality comparisons. The searched CASE expression returns the value in the THEN clause that is associated with the first WHEN logical expression that evaluates to TRUE. If none of the WHEN expressions evaluates to TRUE, the CASE expression returns the value that appears in the ELSE clause (or NULL if an ELSE clause is not specified). For example, the following query produces a value category description based on whether the value is less than 1,000.00, between 1,000.00 and 3,000.00, or greater than 3,000.00:

```
SELECT orderid, custid, val,
  CASE
    WHEN val < 1000.00                          THEN 'Less then 1000'
    WHEN val BETWEEN 1000.00 AND 3000.00 THEN 'Between 1000 and 3000'
    WHEN val > 3000.00                          THEN 'More than 3000'
    ELSE 'Unknown'
  END AS valuecategory
FROM Sales.OrderValues;
```

This query generates the following output:

```
orderid      custid       val      valuecategory
-----------  -----------  -------- ----------------------
10248        85           440.00   Less then 1000
10249        79           1863.40  Between 1000 and 3000
10250        34           1552.60  Between 1000 and 3000
10251        84           654.06   Less then 1000
10252        76           3597.90  More than 3000
10253        34           1444.80  Between 1000 and 3000
10254        14           556.62   Less then 1000
10255        68           2490.50  Between 1000 and 3000
10256        88           517.80   Less then 1000
10257        35           1119.90  Between 1000 and 3000
...

(830 row(s) affected)
```

You can see that every simple CASE expression can be converted to the searched CASE form, but not necessarily the other way around.

So far I've just used a few examples to familiarize you with the CASE expression. Even though it might not be apparent at this point from these examples, the CASE expression is an extremely powerful and useful language element.

NULLs

As explained in Chapter 1, "Background to T-SQL Querying and Programming," SQL supports the NULL mark to represent missing values, and uses three-valued logic, meaning that predicates can evaluate to TRUE, FALSE, or UNKNOWN. T-SQL follows the standard in this respect. Treatment of NULLs and UNKNOWN in SQL can be very confusing because intuitively people are more accustomed to thinking in terms of two-valued logic (TRUE, FALSE). To add to the confusion, different language elements in SQL treat NULLs and UNKNOWN differently.

Let's start with three-valued predicate logic. A logical expression involving only existing or present, values evaluates to either TRUE or FALSE, but when the logical expression involves a missing value, it evaluates to UNKNOWN. For example, consider the predicate salary > 0. When salary is equal to 1000, the expression evaluates to TRUE. When salary is equal to –1000, the expression evaluates to FALSE. When salary is NULL, the expression evaluates to UNKNOWN.

SQL treats TRUE and FALSE in an intuitive and probably expected manner. For example, if the predicate salary > 0 appears in a query filter (the WHERE and HAVING clauses), rows or groups for which the expression evaluates to TRUE are returned, while those for which the expression evaluates to FALSE are filtered out. Similarly, if the predicate salary > 0 appears in a CHECK constraint in a table, *INSERT* or *UPDATE* statements for which the expression evaluates to TRUE are accepted, while those for which the expression evaluates to FALSE are rejected.

SQL has different treatments for UNKNOWN in different language elements (and for some people, not necessarily the expected treatments). The correct definition of the treatment SQL has for query filters is "accept TRUE," meaning that both FALSE and UNKNOWN are filtered out. Conversely, the definition of the treatment SQL has for CHECK constraints is "reject FALSE," meaning that both TRUE and UNKNOWN are accepted. If SQL used two-valued predicate logic, there wouldn't be a difference between the definitions "accept TRUE" and "reject FALSE." But with three-valued predicate logic, "accept TRUE" rejects UNKNOWN (accepts TRUE, hence rejects both FALSE and UNKNOWN) while "reject FALSE" accepts it (rejects FALSE, hence accepts both TRUE and UNKNOWN). Using the predicate salary > 0 from the previous example, a NULL salary would cause the expression to evaluate to UNKNOWN. If this predicate appears in a query's WHERE clause, a row with a NULL salary would be filtered out. If this predicate appears in a CHECK constraint in a table, a row with a NULL salary would be accepted.

One of the tricky aspects of UNKNOWN is that when you negate it, you still get UNKNOWN. For example, given the predicate NOT (salary > 0), when salary is NULL, salary > 0 evaluates to UNKNOWN, and NOT UNKNOWN remains UNKNOWN.

What some people find surprising is that an expression comparing two NULLs (NULL = NULL) evaluates to UNKNOWN. The reasoning for this is that a NULL represents a missing or unknown value, and you can't really tell whether one unknown value is equal to another. Therefore, SQL provides you with the predicates IS NULL and IS NOT NULL, which you should use instead of = NULL and <> NULL.

To make things a bit more tangible, I'll demonstrate the aforementioned aspects of the three-valued predicate logic. The Sales.Customers table has three attributes called country, region, and city, where the customer's location information is stored. All locations have existing countries and cities. Some have existing regions (such as country: USA, region: WA, city: Seattle), yet for some the region element is missing or inapplicable (such as country: UK, region: NULL, city: London). Consider the following query that attempts to return all customers where the region is equal to WA:

```
SELECT custid, country, region, city
FROM Sales.Customers
WHERE region = N'WA';
```

This query generates the following output:

```
custid       country           region            city
-----------  ----------------  ----------------  --------------
43           USA               WA                Walla Walla
82           USA               WA                Kirkland
89           USA               WA                Seattle
```

Out of the 91 rows in the Customers table, the query returns the three rows where the region attribute is equal to WA. The query neither returns rows where the value in the region attribute is present and different than WA (predicate evaluates to FALSE) nor those where the region attribute is NULL (predicate evaluates to UNKNOWN).

The following query attempts to return all customers where the region is different than WA:

```
SELECT custid, country, region, city
FROM Sales.Customers
WHERE region <> N'WA';
```

This query generates the following output:

```
custid       country           region            city
-----------  ----------------  ----------------  --------------
10           Canada            BC                Tsawassen
15           Brazil            SP                Sao Paulo
21           Brazil            SP                Sao Paulo
31           Brazil            SP                Campinas
32           USA               OR                Eugene
33           Venezuela         DF                Caracas
34           Brazil            RJ                Rio de Janeiro
35           Venezuela         Táchira           San Cristóbal
36           USA               OR                Elgin
37           Ireland           Co. Cork          Cork
38           UK                Isle of Wight     Cowes
42           Canada            BC                Vancouver
45           USA               CA                San Francisco
46           Venezuela         Lara              Barquisimeto
47           Venezuela         Nueva Esparta     I. de Margarita
48           USA               OR                Portland
51           Canada            Québec            Montréal
```

```
55        USA          AK           Anchorage
61        Brazil       RJ           Rio de Janeiro
62        Brazil       SP           Sao Paulo
65        USA          NM           Albuquerque
67        Brazil       RJ           Rio de Janeiro
71        USA          ID           Boise
75        USA          WY           Lander
77        USA          OR           Portland
78        USA          MT           Butte
81        Brazil       SP           Sao Paulo
88        Brazil       SP           Resende
```

(28 row(s) affected)

If you expected to get 88 rows back (91 rows in the table minus 3 returned by the previous query), you might find the fact that this query returned only 28 rows surprising. But remember, a query filter "accepts TRUE," meaning that it rejects both rows for which the logical expression evaluates to FALSE and those for which it evaluates to UNKNOWN. So this query returned rows in which a value was present in the region attribute and that value was different than WA. It returned neither rows where the region attribute was equal to WA nor rows where region was NULL. You will get the exact same output if you use the predicate NOT (region = N'WA') because in the rows where region is NULL and the expression region = N'WA' evaluates to UNKNOWN, NOT (region = N'WA') evaluates to UNKNOWN also.

If you want all rows where region is NULL, do not use the predicate region = NULL, because the expression evaluates to UNKNOWN in all rows—both those where the value is present and those where the value is missing (is NULL). The following query returns an empty set:

```
SELECT custid, country, region, city
FROM Sales.Customers
WHERE region = NULL;
```

```
custid       country          region           city
-----------  ---------------  ---------------  ---------------
```

(0 row(s) affected)

Instead, you should use the IS NULL predicate:

```
SELECT custid, country, region, city
FROM Sales.Customers
WHERE region IS NULL;
```

This query generates the following output, shown in abbreviated form:

```
custid       country          region           city
-----------  ---------------  ---------------  ---------------
1            Germany          NULL             Berlin
2            Mexico           NULL             México D.F.
3            Mexico           NULL             México D.F.
4            UK               NULL             London
```

5	Sweden	NULL	Luleå
6	Germany	NULL	Mannheim
7	France	NULL	Strasbourg
8	Spain	NULL	Madrid
9	France	NULL	Marseille
11	UK	NULL	London

...

```
(60 row(s) affected)
```

If you want to return all rows where the region attribute is not WA, including those in which the value is present and different than WA along with those in which the value is missing, you need to include an explicit test for NULLs, like so:

```
SELECT custid, country, region, city
FROM Sales.Customers
WHERE region <> N'WA'
   OR region IS NULL;
```

This query generates the following output, shown in abbreviated form:

```
custid       country          region           city
-----------  ---------------  ---------------  ---------------
1            Germany          NULL             Berlin
2            Mexico           NULL             México D.F.
3            Mexico           NULL             México D.F.
4            UK               NULL             London
5            Sweden           NULL             Luleå
6            Germany          NULL             Mannheim
7            France           NULL             Strasbourg
8            Spain            NULL             Madrid
9            France           NULL             Marseille
10           Canada           BC               Tsawassen
...

(88 row(s) affected)
```

SQL also treats NULLs inconsistently in different language elements for comparison and sorting purposes. Some elements treat two NULLs as equal to each other and others as different.

For example, for grouping and sorting purposes, two NULLs are considered equal. That is, the GROUP BY clause arranges all NULLs in one group just like present values, and the ORDER BY clause sorts all NULLs together. ANSI SQL leaves it to the product implementation as to whether NULLs sorts before present values or after. T-SQL sorts NULLs before present values.

As mentioned earlier, query filters "accept TRUE." An expression comparing two NULLs yields UNKNOWN; therefore, such a row is filtered out.

ANSI SQL has two kinds of UNIQUE constraint: one that treats NULLs as equal (allowing only one NULL) and one that treats NULLs as different (allowing multiple NULLs). T-SQL implemented only the former.

Keeping in mind the inconsistent treatment SQL has for UNKNOWN and NULLs and the potential for logical errors, you should explicitly think of three-valued logic in every query that you write. If the default treatment is not the one you desire, you have to intervene explicitly; otherwise, just ensure that the default behavior is in fact the one you are after.

All-At-Once Operations

SQL supports a concept called all-at-once operations, which means that all expressions that appear in the same logical query processing phase are evaluated as if at the same point in time.

This concept explains why, for example, you cannot refer to column aliases assigned in the SELECT clause within the same SELECT clause, even if it seems intuitively that you should be able to. Consider the following query:

```
SELECT
  orderid,
  YEAR(orderdate) AS orderyear,
  orderyear + 1 AS nextyear
FROM Sales.Orders;
```

The reference to the column alias orderyear is invalid in the third expression in the SELECT list, even though the referencing expression appears "after" the one where the alias is assigned. The reason is that logically there is no order of evaluation of the expressions in the SELECT list—it's a set of expressions. At the logical level all expressions in the SELECT list are evaluated at the same point in time. Therefore this query generates the following error:

```
Msg 207, Level 16, State 1, Line 4
Invalid column name 'orderyear'.
```

Here's another example of the relevance of all-at-once operations: Suppose you had a table called T1 with two integer columns called col1 and col2, and you wanted to return all rows where col2/col1 is greater than 2. Because there may be rows in the table where col1 is equal to 0, you need to ensure that the division doesn't take place in those cases—otherwise, the query fails because of a divide-by-zero error. So if you write a query using the following format:

```
SELECT col1, col2
FROM dbo.T1
WHERE col1 <> 0 AND col2/col1 > 2;
```

You assume that SQL Server evaluates the expressions from left to right, and that if the expression col1 <> 0 evaluates to FALSE, SQL Server will short-circuit; that is, it doesn't bother to evaluate the expression 10/col1 > 2 because at this point it is known that the whole expression is FALSE. So you might think that this query never produces a divide-by-zero error.

SQL Server does support short circuits, but because of the all-at-once operations concept in ANSI SQL, SQL Server is free to process the expressions in the WHERE clause in any order that it likes. SQL Server usually makes decisions like this based on cost estimations, meaning that typically the expression that is cheaper to evaluate is evaluated first. You can see that if SQL Server decides to process the expression 10/col1 > 2 first, this query might fail because of a divide-by-zero error.

You have several ways to try and avoid a failure here. For example, the order in which the WHEN clauses of a CASE expression are evaluated is guaranteed. So you could revise the query as follows:

```
SELECT col1, col2
FROM dbo.T1
WHERE
  CASE
    WHEN col1 = 0 THEN 'no' — or 'yes' if row should be returned
    WHEN col2/col1 > 2 THEN 'yes'
    ELSE 'no'
  END = 'yes';
```

In rows where col1 is equal to zero, the first WHEN clause evaluates to TRUE and the CASE expression returns the string 'no' (replace with 'yes' if you want to return the row when col1 is equal to zero). Only if the first CASE expression does not evaluate to TRUE—meaning that col1 is not 0—does the second WHEN clause check whether the expression 10/col1 > 2 evaluates to TRUE. If it does, the CASE expression returns the string 'yes.' In all other cases, the CASE expression returns the string 'no.' The predicate in the WHERE clause returns TRUE only when the result of the CASE expression is equal to the string 'yes.' This means that there will never be an attempt here to divide by zero.

This workaround turned out to be quite convoluted, and in this particular case we can use a simpler mathematical workaround that avoids division altogether:

```
SELECT col1, col2
FROM dbo.T1
WHERE col1 <> 0 and col2 > 2*col1;
```

I included this example to explain the unique and important all-at-once operations concept, and the fact that SQL Server guarantees the processing order of the WHEN clauses in a CASE expression.

Working with Character Data

In this section, I cover query manipulation of character data, including data types, collation, operators and functions, and pattern matching.

Data Types

SQL Server supports two kinds of character data types—regular and Unicode. Regular data types include CHAR and VARCHAR, and Unicode data types include NCHAR and NVARCHAR. The difference is that regular characters use one byte of storage for each character, while Unicode characters require two bytes per character. With one byte of storage per character, a choice of a regular character type for a column restricts you to only one language in addition to English because only 256 (2^8) different characters can be represented by a single byte. The language support for the column is determined by the column's effective collation, which I'll describe shortly. With Unicode data types, 65,536 (2^{16}) distinct characters can be represented because two bytes of storage are used for each character. All languages can be represented in the same Unicode table, so when using a Unicode data type for a column, you can mix multiple languages rather than being restricted to only one in addition to English.

The two kinds of character data types also differ in the way literals are expressed. When expressing a regular character literal, you simply use single quotes: 'This is a regular character string literal'. When expressing a Unicode character literal, you need to specify the character N (for National) as a prefix: N'This is a Unicode character string literal'.

Any data type without the VAR element (CHAR, NCHAR) in its name is fixed length, which means that SQL Server preserves space in the row based on the column's defined size and not on the actual number of characters in the character string. For example, defining a column as CHAR(25) means that SQL Server preserves space for 25 characters in the row regardless of the length of the stored character string. Because no expansion of the row is required when the strings are expanded, fixed-length data types are more suited for write-focused systems. But because storage consumption is not optimal, you pay more when reading data.

A data type with the VAR element (VARCHAR, NVARCHAR) in its name is variable length, which means that SQL Server uses as much storage space in the row as required to store the characters that appear in the character string, plus two extra bytes for offset data. For example, defining a column as VARCHAR(25) means that the maximum number of characters supported will be 25, but in practice, the actual number of characters in the string determines storage. Because storage consumption is reduced when compared to that of fixed-length types, read operations are faster. However, updates might result in row expansion, which may result in data movement outside the current page. Therefore, updates of data having variable-length data types are less efficient than updates of data having fixed-length data types.

You can also define the variable-length data types with the MAX specifier instead of a maximum number of characters. When the column is defined with the MAX specifier, a value with a size up to a certain threshold (8,000 bytes by default) is stored inline in the row. A value with a size above the threshold is stored external to the row as a large object (LOB).

Later in this chapter, in the section "Querying Metadata," I will explain how you can obtain metadata information about objects in the database, including the data types of columns.

Collation

Collation is a property of character data that encapsulates several aspects, including language support (relevant to regular types because Unicode supports all languages), sort order, case sensitivity, accent sensitivity, and more. To get the set of supported collations and their descriptions, you can query the table function *fn_helpcollations* as follows:

```
SELECT name, description
FROM sys.fn_helpcollations();
```

For example, the collation Latin1_General_CI_AS means that:

- **Latin1_General**   The supported language is English.

- **Dictionary sorting**   Sorting and comparison of character data is based on dictionary order ('A' and 'a' < 'B' and 'b').

  You determine that it is dictionary order because that's the default when no other ordering is defined explicitly. More specifically, the element **BIN** doesn't explicitly appear in the collation name. If the element BIN appeared, it would mean that sorting and comparison of character data was based on the binary representation of characters ('A' < 'B' < 'a' < 'b').

- **CI**   The data is case insensitive ('a' = 'A').

- **AS**   The data is accent sensitive ('à' <> 'ä').

Collation can be defined at four different levels: instance, database, column, and expression. The lowest level is the effective one.

The collation of the instance is chosen as part of the setup program. It determines the collations of all system databases, and is used as the default for user databases.

When you create a user database, you can specify a collation for the database using the COLLATE clause. If you don't, the instance's collation is assumed by default.

The database collation determines the collation of metadata of objects in the database, and is used as the default for user table columns. It is important to emphasize that the database collation determines the collation of metadata, including object and column names. For example, if the database collation is case insensitive, you can't create two tables called T1 and t1 within the same schema, but if the database collation is case sensitive you can.

You can explicitly specify a collation for a column as part of its definition using the COLLATE clause. If you don't, the database collation is assumed by default.

You can convert the collation of an expression using the COLLATE clause. For example, in a case-insensitive environment the following query uses a case-insensitive comparison:

```
SELECT empid, firstname, lastname
FROM HR.Employees
WHERE lastname = N'davis';
```

The following query returns the row for Sara Davis even though the casing doesn't match because the effective casing is insensitive:

```
empid        firstname  lastname
-----------  ---------- --------------------
1            Sara       Davis
```

If you want to make the filter case sensitive even though the column's collation is case insensitive, you can convert the collation of the expression like so:

```
SELECT empid, firstname, lastname
FROM HR.Employees
WHERE lastname COLLATE Latin1_General_CS_AS = N'davis';
```

This time the query returns an empty set because no match is found when using a case-sensitive comparison.

Quoted Identifiers

In standard SQL, single quotes are used to delimit literal character strings (for example, 'literal') and double quotes are used to delimit irregular identifiers like table or column names that include a space or start with a digit (for example, "Irregular Identifier"). In SQL Server, there's a setting called QUOTED_IDENTIFIER that controls the meaning of double quotes. This setting can be applied either at the database level using the *ALTER DATABASE* command or at the session level using the *SET* command. When the setting is turned on, the behavior is according to standard SQL, meaning that double quotes are used to delimit identifiers. When the setting is turned off, the behavior is nonstandard, and double quotes are used to delimit literal character strings. It is strongly recommended to follow best practices and stick to standard behavior (setting is on). Most database interfaces including OLEDB and ODBC turn this setting on by default.

> **Tip** As an alternative to using double quotes to delimit identifiers, SQL Server also supports square brackets (for example, [Irregular Identifier]).

Regarding single quotes that are used to delimit literal character strings, if you want to incorporate a single quote character as part of the string, you need to specify two single quotes. For example, to express the literal abc'de, specify 'abc''de'.

Operators and Functions

This section covers string concatenation and functions that operate on character strings.

String Concatenation (Plus Sign [+] Operator)

T-SQL provides the plus sign (+) operator to concatenate strings. For example, the following query against the Employees table produces the fullname result column by concatenating firstname, a space, and lastname:

```
SELECT empid, firstname + N' ' + lastname AS fullname
FROM HR.Employees;
```

This query produces the following output:

```
empid       fullname
----------- ------------------------------
1           Sara Davis
2           Don Funk
3           Judy Lew
4           Yael Peled
5           Sven Buck
6           Paul Suurs
7           Russell King
8           Maria Cameron
9           Zoya Dolgopyatova
```

ANSI SQL dictates that a concatenation with a NULL should yield a NULL. This is the default behavior of SQL Server. For example, consider the query against the Customers table shown in Listing 2-7:

LISTING 2-7 Query Demonstrating String Concatenation

```
SELECT custid, country, region, city,
  country + N',' + region + N',' + city AS location
FROM Sales.Customers;
```

Some of the rows in the Customers table have a NULL in the region column. For those, SQL Server returns by default a NULL in the location result column:

```
custid      country         region city            location
----------- --------------- ------ --------------- -------------------
1           Germany         NULL   Berlin          NULL
2           Mexico          NULL   México D.F.     NULL
3           Mexico          NULL   México D.F.     NULL
4           UK              NULL   London          NULL
5           Sweden          NULL   Luleå           NULL
6           Germany         NULL   Mannheim        NULL
7           France          NULL   Strasbourg      NULL
8           Spain           NULL   Madrid          NULL
9           France          NULL   Marseille       NULL
10          Canada          BC     Tsawassen       Canada,BC,Tsawassen
11          UK              NULL   London          NULL
```

```
12          Argentina       NULL   Buenos Aires   NULL
13          Mexico          NULL   México D.F.    NULL
14          Switzerland     NULL   Bern           NULL
15          Brazil          SP     Sao Paulo      Brazil,SP,Sao Paulo
16          UK              NULL   London         NULL
17          Germany         NULL   Aachen         NULL
18          France          NULL   Nantes         NULL
19          UK              NULL   London         NULL
20          Austria         NULL   Graz           NULL
...

(91 row(s) affected)
```

You can change the way SQL Server treats concatenation by setting a session option called CONCAT_NULL_YIELDS_NULL to OFF. SQL Server treats a NULL set to OFF as an empty string for concatenation purposes. To demonstrate this behavior, run the following code to set the option to OFF, and then rerun the query in Listing 2-7:

```
SET CONCAT_NULL_YIELDS_NULL OFF;
```

The query now treats NULLs as empty strings for concatenation purposes, and you get the following output, shown here in abbreviated form:

```
custid      country         region city            location
----------- --------------- ------ --------------- -------------------
1           Germany         NULL   Berlin          Germany,,Berlin
2           Mexico          NULL   México D.F.     Mexico,,México D.F.
3           Mexico          NULL   México D.F.     Mexico,,México D.F.
4           UK              NULL   London          UK,,London
5           Sweden          NULL   Luleå           Sweden,,Luleå
6           Germany         NULL   Mannheim        Germany,,Mannheim
7           France          NULL   Strasbourg      France,,Strasbourg
8           Spain           NULL   Madrid          Spain,,Madrid
9           France          NULL   Marseille       France,,Marseille
10          Canada          BC     Tsawassen       Canada,BC,Tsawassen
11          UK              NULL   London          UK,,London
12          Argentina       NULL   Buenos Aires    Argentina,,Buenos Aires
13          Mexico          NULL   México D.F.     Mexico,,México D.F.
14          Switzerland     NULL   Bern            Switzerland,,Bern
15          Brazil          SP     Sao Paulo       Brazil,SP,Sao Paulo
16          UK              NULL   London          UK,,London
17          Germany         NULL   Aachen          Germany,,Aachen
18          France          NULL   Nantes          France,,Nantes
19          UK              NULL   London          UK,,London
20          Austria         NULL   Graz            Austria,,Graz
...

(91 row(s) affected)
```

It is strongly recommended that you avoid changing the standard behavior; most programmers expect the code to behave in a standard manner. If you want to treat a NULL as an empty string, you can do so programmatically. But before I demonstrate how, first make sure you set the CONCAT_NULL_YIELDS_NULL option back to ON in your session:

```
SET CONCAT_NULL_YIELDS_NULL ON;
```

To treat a NULL as an empty string—or more accurately, to substitute a NULL with an empty string—you can use the *COALESCE* function. This function accepts a list of input values and returns the first that is not NULL. Here's how you can revise the query from Listing 2-7 to substitute NULLs with empty strings programmatically:

```
SELECT custid, country, region, city,
  country + N',' + COALESCE(region, N'') + N',' + city AS location
FROM Sales.Customers;
```

T-SQL provides a set of functions that manipulate character strings, including *SUBSTRING, LEFT, RIGHT, LEN, CHARINDEX, PATINDEX, REPLACE, REPLICATE, STUFF, UPPER, LOWER, RTRIM, LTRIM,* and others. In the following sections, I'll describe the commonly used ones.

The SUBSTRING Function

The *SUBSTRING* function extracts a substring from a string.

Syntax
SUBSTRING(*string, start, length*)

The function operates on the input *string*, and extracts a substring starting at position *start*, *length* characters long. For example, the following code returns the output 'abc':

```
SELECT SUBSTRING('abcde', 1, 3);
```

If the value of the third argument exceeds the end of the input string, the function returns everything until the end without raising an error. This can be convenient when you want to return everything from a certain point until the end of the string—you can simply specify a very large value or a value representing the full length of the input string.

The LEFT and RIGHT Functions

The *LEFT* and *RIGHT* functions are abbreviations of the *SUBSTRING* function, returning a requested number of characters from the left or right of the input string.

Syntax
LEFT(*string, n*), RIGHT(*string, n*)

The first argument, *string*, is the string the function operates on. The second argument, *n*, is the number of characters to extract from the left or right of the string. For example, the following code returns the output 'cde':

```
SELECT RIGHT('abcde', 3);
```

The LEN and DATALENGTH Functions

The *LEN* function returns the number of characters in the input string.

Syntax
LEN(*string*);

Note that this function returns the number of characters in the input string and not necessarily the number of bytes. With regular characters, both numbers are the same because each character requires one byte of storage. With Unicode characters each character requires two bytes of storage; therefore, the number of characters is half the number of bytes. To get the number of bytes, use the *DATALENGTH* function instead of *LEN*. For example, the following code returns 5:

```
SELECT LEN(N'abcde');
```

The following code returns 10:

```
SELECT DATALENGTH(N'abcde');
```

Another difference between *LEN* and *DATALENGTH* is that the former excludes trailing blanks while the latter doesn't.

The CHARINDEX Function

The *CHARINDEX* function returns the position of the first occurrence of a substring within a string.

Syntax
CHARINDEX(*substring*, *string* [, *start_pos*])

The function returns the position of the first argument, *substring*, within the second argument, *string*. You can optionally specify a third argument, *start_pos*, to tell the function the position from which to start looking. If you don't specify the third argument, the function starts looking from the first character. If the substring is not found, the function returns 0. For example, the following code returns the first position of a space in 'Itzik Ben-Gan,' and returns the output 6:

```
SELECT CHARINDEX(' ','Itzik Ben-Gan');
```

The PATINDEX Function

The *PATINDEX* function returns the position of the first occurrence of a pattern within a string.

Syntax
PATINDEX(*pattern*, *string*)

The argument *pattern* uses similar patterns to those used by the LIKE predicate in T-SQL. I'll explain patterns and the LIKE predicate shortly, in the section "The LIKE Predicate." Even though I haven't explained yet how patterns are expressed in T-SQL, the following example shows how to find the position of the first occurrence of a digit within a string:

```
SELECT PATINDEX('%[0-9]%', 'abcd123efgh');
```

This code returns the output 5.

The REPLACE Function

The *REPLACE* function replaces all occurrences of a substring with another.

Syntax
REPLACE(string, substring1, substring2)

The function replaces all occurrences of *substring1* in *string* with *substring2*. For example, the following code substitutes all occurrences of a dash in the input string with colons:

```
SELECT REPLACE('1-a 2-b', '-', ':');
```

This code returns the output: '1:a 2:b'.

You can use the *REPLACE* function to count the number of occurrences of a character within a string. To achieve this you replace all occurrences of the character with an empty string (zero characters), and calculate the original length of the string minus the new length. For example, the following query returns, for each employee, the number of times the character 'e' appears in the lastname attribute:

```
SELECT empid, lastname,
  LEN(lastname) - LEN(REPLACE(lastname, 'e', '')) AS numoccur
FROM HR.Employees;
```

This query generates the following output:

```
empid       lastname             numoccur
----------- -------------------- -----------
5           Buck                 0
8           Cameron              1
1           Davis                0
9           Dolgopyatova         0
2           Funk                 0
7           King                 0
3           Lew                  1
4           Peled                2
6           Suurs                0
```

The REPLICATE Function

The *REPLICATE* function replicates a string a requested number of times.

Syntax
REPLICATE(*string, n*)

For example, the following code replicates the string 'abc' three times returning the string 'abcabcabc':

```
SELECT REPLICATE('abc', 3);
```

The next example demonstrates using the *REPLICATE* function, along with the *RIGHT* function and string concatenation. The following query against the Production.Suppliers table generates a 10-digit string representation of the integer supplier ID with leading zeros:

```
SELECT supplierid,
  RIGHT(REPLICATE('0', 9) + CAST(supplierid AS VARCHAR(10)), 10) AS strsupplierid
FROM Production.Suppliers;
```

The expression producing the result column strsupplierid replicates the character '0' nine times (producing the string '000000000') and concatenates the string representation of the supplier ID to form the result. The string representation of the integer supplier ID is produced by the *CAST* function, which is used to convert the data type of the input value. Finally, the expression extracts the 10 rightmost characters of the result string, returning the 10-digit string representation of the supplier ID with leading zeros. Here's the output of this query, shown in abbreviated form:

```
supplierid  strsupplierid
----------- -------------
29          0000000029
28          0000000028
4           0000000004
21          0000000021
2           0000000002
22          0000000022
14          0000000014
11          0000000011
25          0000000025
7           0000000007
...

(29 row(s) affected)
```

The STUFF Function

The *STUFF* function allows you to remove a substring from a string and insert a new substring instead.

Syntax

STUFF(string, pos, delete_length, insertstring)

The function operates on the input parameter *string*. It deletes as many characters as the number specified in the *delete_length* parameter starting at the character position specified in the *pos* input parameter. The function inserts the string specified in the *insertstring* parameter in position *pos*. For example, the following code operates on the string 'xyz', removes one character from the second character, and inserts the substring 'abc' instead:

```
SELECT STUFF('xyz', 2, 1, 'abc');
```

The output of this code is 'xabcz'.

The UPPER and LOWER Functions

The *UPPER* and *LOWER* functions return the input string with all uppercase or lowercase characters.

Syntax

UPPER(*string*), LOWER(*string*)

For example, the following code returns 'ITZIK BEN-GAN':

```
SELECT UPPER('Itzik Ben-Gan');
```

The following code returns 'itzik ben-gan':

```
SELECT LOWER('Itzik Ben-Gan');
```

The RTRIM and LTRIM Functions

The *RTRIM* and *LTRIM* functions return the input string with leading or trailing spaces removed.

Syntax

RTRIM(*string*), LTRIM(*string*)

If you want to remove both leading and trailing spaces, use the result of one function as the input to the other. For example, the following code removes both leading and trailing spaces from the input string returning 'abc':

```
SELECT RTRIM(LTRIM('   abc   '));
```

The LIKE Predicate

T-SQL provides a predicate called LIKE that allows you to check whether a character string matches a specified pattern. Similar patterns are used by the *PATINDEX* function described earlier. The following section describes the wildcards supported in the patterns and demonstrates their use.

The % (Percent) Wildcard

The percent sign represents a string of any size, including an empty string. For example, the following query returns employees where the last name starts with 'D':

```
SELECT empid, lastname
FROM HR.Employees
WHERE lastname LIKE N'D%';
```

This query returns the following output:

```
empid       lastname
----------- --------------------
1           Davis
9           Dolgopyatova
```

The _ (Underscore) Wildcard

An underscore represents a single character. For example, the following query returns employees where the second character in the last name is 'e':

```
SELECT empid, lastname
FROM HR.Employees
WHERE lastname LIKE N'_e%';
```

This query returns the following output:

```
empid       lastname
----------- --------------------
3           Lew
4           Peled
```

The [<List of Characters>] Wildcard

Square brackets with a list of characters (such as '[ABC]') represent a single character that must be one of the characters specified in the list. For example, the following query returns employees where the first character in the last name is 'A', 'B' or 'C':

```
SELECT empid, lastname
FROM HR.Employees
WHERE lastname LIKE N'[ABC]%';
```

This query returns the following output:

```
empid       lastname
----------- --------------------
5           Buck
8           Cameron
```

The [<Character>-<Character>] Wildcard

Square brackets with a character range (such as '[A-E]') represent a single character that must be within the specified range. For example, the following query returns employees where the first character in the last name is 'A' through 'E':

```
SELECT empid, lastname
FROM HR.Employees
WHERE lastname LIKE N'[A-E]%';
```

This query returns the following output:

```
empid       lastname
----------- --------------------
5           Buck
8           Cameron
1           Davis
9           Dolgopyatova
```

The [^<Character List or Range>] Wildcard

Square brackets with a caret sign (^) followed by a character list or range (such as '[^A-E]') represent a single character not in the specified character list or range. For example, the following query returns employees where the first character in the last name is not A through E:

```
SELECT empid, lastname
FROM HR.Employees
WHERE lastname LIKE N'[^A-E]%';
```

This query returns the following output:

```
empid        lastname
-----------  --------------------
2            Funk
7            King
3            Lew
4            Peled
6            Suurs
```

The ESCAPE Character

If you want to look for a character that is also used as a wildcard, ('%', '_', '[', ']', for example) you can use an escape character. Specify a character that you know for sure doesn't appear in the data as the escape character in front of the character you are looking for, and specify the keyword *ESCAPE* followed by the escape character right after the pattern. For example, to check whether a column called col1 contains an underscore, use col1 LIKE '%!_%' ESCAPE '!'.

For wildcards '%', '_', and '[' you can use square brackets instead of an escape character. Instead of col1 LIKE '%!_%' ESCAPE '!' you can use col1 LIKE '%[_]%'.

Working with Date and Time Data

Working with date and time data in SQL Server is not trivial. You will face several challenges in this area, such as expressing literals in a language-neutral manner, working separately with date and time, and so on.

In this section, I first introduce the date and time data types supported by SQL Server, then I explain the recommended way to work with those types, and finally I cover date- and time-related functions.

Date and Time Data Types

Prior to SQL Server 2008, SQL Server supported two temporal data types called *DATETIME* and *SMALLDATETIME*. Both types include date and time components that are inseparable. The two data types differ in their storage requirements, their supported date range, and their accuracy. SQL Server 2008 introduces separate DATE and TIME data types: *DATETIME2*, which has a bigger date range and better accuracy than *DATETIME*, and *DATETIMEOFFSET*, which also has a time zone component. Table 2-1 lists details about date and time data types, including storage requirements, supported date range, accuracy, and recommended entry format.

TABLE 2-1 Date and Time Data Types

Data Type	Storage (bytes)	Date Range	Accuracy	Recommended Entry Format and Example
DATETIME	8	January 1, 1753 through December 31, 9999	3 1/3 milliseconds	'YYYYMMDD hh:mm:ss.nnn' '20090212 12:30:15.123'
SMALLDATETIME	4	January 1, 1900 through June 6, 2079	1 minute	'YYYYMMDD hh:mm' '20090212 12:30'
DATE	3	January 1, 0001 through December 31, 9999	1 day	'YYYY-MM-DD'
TIME	3 to 5		100 nanoseconds	'hh:mm:ss.nnnnnnn' '12:30:15.1234567'
DATETIME2	6 to 8	January 1, 0001 through December 31, 9999	100 nanoseconds	'YYYY-MM-DD hh:mm:ss.nnnnnnn' '2009-02-12 12:30:15.1234567'
DATETIMEOFFSET	8 to 10	January 1, 0001 through December 31, 9999	100 nanoseconds	'YYYY-MM-DD hh:mm:ss.nnnnnnn [+|-] hh:mm' '2009-02-12 12:30:15.1234567 +02:00'

The storage requirements for the last three data types in Table 2-1 (*TIME*, *DATETIME2*, and *DATETIMEOFFSET*) depend on the accuracy you choose. You specify the accuracy as an integer in the range 0 to 7 representing the fractional second precision. For example, *TIME(0)* means 0 fractional second precision—in other words, one-second accuracy. *TIME(3)* means one-millisecond accuracy, and *TIME(7)* means 100-nanosecond accuracy. If you don't specify a fractional second precision, SQL Server assumes 7 by default with all three aforementioned types.

Literals

When you need to specify a literal (constant) of a date and time data type, you should consider several things. First, though it might sound a bit strange, SQL Server doesn't provide the means to express a date and time literal; instead, it allows you to specify a literal of a different type that can be converted—explicitly or implicitly—to a date and time data type. It is a best practice to use character strings to express date and time values, as shown in the following example:

```
SELECT orderid, custid, empid, orderdate
FROM Sales.Orders
WHERE orderdate = '20070212';
```

SQL Server recognizes the literal '20070212' as a character string literal and not as a date and time literal, but because the expression involves operands of two different types, one operand needs to be converted to the other's type. When an expression involves two operands of different types, one of the operand will need to be implicitly converted to the other's type. Normally, implicit conversion between types is based on what's called datatype precedence. SQL Server defines precedence among datatypes, and will usually implicitly covert the operand that has lower datatype precedence to the one that has higher precedence. In our example the character string literal is converted to the column's data type (*DATETIME*) because character strings are considered lower in terms of data type precedence with respect to date and time data types. Implicit conversion rules are not always that simple, and in fact there are different rules applied in cases of filters and in other expressions, but for the purposes of our discussion we'll keep things simple. For the complete list of data type precedence please see "Data Type Precedence" in SQL Server Books Online.

The point I'm trying to make is that in the preceding example, implicit conversion takes place behind the scenes. This query is logically equivalent to the following one, which converts the character string to a *DATETIME* data type explicitly:

```
SELECT orderid, custid, empid, orderdate
FROM Sales.Orders
WHERE orderdate = CAST('20070212' AS DATETIME);
```

It is important to note that some character string formats of date and time literals are language-dependent, meaning that when you convert them to a date and time data type, SQL Server may interpret the value differently based on the language setting in effect in the session. Each login defined by the DBA has a default language associated with it, and unless changed explicitly, that language becomes the effective language in the session. You can overwrite the default language in your session by using the *SET LANGUAGE* command, but this is generally not recommended because some aspects of the code might rely on the user's default language.

The effective language in the session sets several language-related settings behind the scenes, among them one called *DATEFORMAT* that determines how SQL Server interprets literals you enter when converted from a character string type to a date and time type. The *DATEFORMAT* setting is expressed as a combination of the characters d, m, and y. For example, the us_english language setting sets the *DATEFORMAT* to mdy, while the British language setting sets the *DATEFORMAT* to dmy. You can overwrite the *DATEFORMAT* setting in your session by using the *SET DATEFORMAT* command, but as mentioned earlier, changing language-related settings is generally not recommended.

Consider, for example, the literal '02/12/2007'. SQL Server can interpret the date as either February 12, 2007 or December 2, 2007 when you convert this literal to one of the following types: *DATETIME*, *DATE*, *DATETIME2*, or *DATETIMEOFFSET*. The effective LANGUAGE/ DATEFORMAT setting is the determining factor. To demonstrate different interpretations of the same character string literal, run the following code:

```
SET LANGUAGE British;
SELECT CAST('02/12/2007' AS DATETIME);

SET LANGUAGE us_english;
SELECT CAST('02/12/2007' AS DATETIME);
```

Notice in the output that the literal was interpreted differently in the two different language environments:

```
Changed language setting to British.

-----------------------
2007-12-02 00:00:00.000

Changed language setting to us_english.

-----------------------
2007-02-12 00:00:00.000
```

Note that the LANGUAGE/DATEFORMAT setting only affects the way the values you enter are interpreted; these settings have no impact on the format used in the output for presentation purposes, which is determined by the database interface used by the client tool (such as OLEDB) and not by the LANGUAGE/DATEFORMAT setting. For example, OLEDB and ODBC present DATETIME values in the format 'YYYY-MM-DD hh:mm:ss.nnn'.

Because the code you write might end up being used by international users with different language setting for their logins, understanding that some formats of literals are language-dependent is crucial. It is strongly recommended that you phrase your literals in a language-neutral manner. Language-neutral formats are always interpreted by SQL Server the same way, and are not affected by language-related settings. Table 2-2 provides literal formats that are considered neutral for each of the date and time types.

TABLE 2-2 Date and Time Data Type Formats

Data Type	Language-Neutral Formats	Examples
DATETIME	'YYYYMMDD hh:mm:ss.nnn'	'20090212 12:30:15.123'
	'YYYY-MM-DDThh:mm:ss.nnn'	'2009-02-12T12:30:15.123'
	'YYYYMMDD'	'20090212'
SMALLDATETIME	'YYYYMMDD hh:mm'	'20090212 12:30'
	'YYYY-MM-DDThh:mm'	'2009-02-12T12:30'
	'YYYYMMDD'	'20090212'

TABLE 2-2 Date and Time Data Type Formats

Data Type	Language-Neutral Formats	Examples
DATE	'YYYYMMDD'	'20090212'
	'YYYY-MM-DD'	'2009-02-12'
DATETIME2	'YYYYMMDD hh:mm:ss.nnnnnnn'	'20090212 12:30:15.1234567'
	'YYYY-MM-DD hh:mm:ss.nnnnnnn'	'2009-02-12 12:30:15.1234567'
	'YYYY-MM-DDThh:mm:ss.nnnnnnn'	'2009-02-12T12:30:15.1234567'
	'YYYYMMDD'	'20090212'
	'YYYY-MM-DD'	'2009-02-12'
DATETIMEOFFSET	'YYYYMMDD hh:mm:ss.nnnnnnn [+|-]hh:mm'	'20090212 12:30:15.1234567 +02:00'
	'YYYY-MM-DD hh:mm:ss.nnnnnnn [+|-]hh:mm'	'2009-02-12 12:30:15.1234567 +02:00'
	'YYYYMMDD'	'20090212'
	'YYYY-MM-DD'	'2009-02-12'
TIME	'hh:mm:ss.nnnnnnn'	'12:30:15.1234567'

Note a couple of things about Table 2-2. With all types that include both date and time components, if you don't specify a time part in your literal, SQL Server assumes midnight. If you don't specify a time zone, SQL Server assumes 00:00. It is also important to note that the formats 'YYYY-MM-DD' and 'YYYY-MM-DD hh:mm...' are language-dependent when converted to *DATETIME* or *SMALLDATETIME*, and language-neutral when converted to *DATE*, *DATETIME2* and *DATETIMEOFFSET*.

For example, notice in the following code that the language setting has no impact on how a literal expressed with the format 'YYYYMMDD' is interpreted when converted to *DATETIME*:

```
SET LANGUAGE British;
SELECT CAST('20070212' AS DATETIME);

SET LANGUAGE us_english;
SELECT CAST('20070212' AS DATETIME);
```

The output shows that the literal was interpreted in both cases as February 12, 2007:

```
Changed language setting to British.

-----------------------
2007-02-12 00:00:00.000

Changed language setting to us_english.

-----------------------
2007-02-12 00:00:00.000
```

I probably can't emphasize enough that using language-neutral formats like 'YYYYMMDD' is a best practice since such formats are interpreted the same way regardless of the LANGUAGE/DATEFORMAT settings.

If you insist on using a language-dependent format to express literals, you can use the *CONVERT* function to explicitly convert the character string literal to the desired data type, and in the third argument specify a number representing the style you used. SQL Server Books Online has a table with all style numbers and the formats they represent under the section "The CAST and CONVERT Functions." For example, if you want to specify the literal '02/12/2007' with the format mm/dd/yyyy, use style number 101, as shown here:

```
SELECT CONVERT(DATETIME, '02/12/2007', 101);
```

The literal is interpreted as February 12, 2007 regardless of the language setting that is in effect.

If you want to use the format dd/mm/yyyy, use style number 103:

```
SELECT CONVERT(DATETIME, '02/12/2007', 103);
```

This time the literal is interpreted as December 2, 2007.

Working with Date and Time Separately

SQL Server 2008 introduced separate *DATE* and *TIME* data types, but in previous versions there is no separation between the two components. If you want to work only with dates or only with times in versions of SQL Server prior to SQL Server 2008, you can use one of the data types *DATETIME* or *SMALLDATETIME* that contain both components. You can also use types like integers or character strings where you implement the date and time logic, but I won't discuss this option here. If you want to use the *DATETIME* or *SMALLDATETIME* types, when you want to work only with dates you store the date with a value of midnight (all zeros in the time parts). When you want to work only with times, you store the time with the base date January 1, 1900.

For example, the orderdate column in the Sales.Orders table is of a *DATETIME* data type, but because only the date component is actually relevant, all values were stored at midnight. When you need to filter only orders from a certain date, you don't have to use a range filter. Instead, you can use the equality operator like so:

```
SELECT orderid, custid, empid, orderdate
FROM Sales.Orders
WHERE orderdate = '20070212';
```

When the character string literal gets converted to *DATETIME*, SQL Server assumes midnight as the time component if time is not specified. Because all values in the orderdate column were stored with midnight in the time component, you get all orders placed on the requested date.

If the time component is stored with non-midnight values, you can use a range filter like so:

```
SELECT orderid, custid, empid, orderdate
FROM Sales.Orders
WHERE orderdate >= '20070212'
  AND orderdate < '20070213';
```

If you want to work only with times in versions prior to SQL Server 2008, you can store all values using the base date January 1, 1900. When SQL Server converts a character string literal that contains only a time component to *DATETIME* or *SMALLDATETIME*, SQL Server assumes you mean the base date. For example, run the following code:

```
SELECT CAST('12:30:15.123' AS DATETIME);
```

You get the following output:

```
-----------------------
1900-01-01 12:30:15.123
```

Suppose you had a table with a column called tm of a *DATETIME* data type and you stored all values using the base date. To return all rows where the time value is 12:30:15.123, you use the filter WHERE tm = '12:30:15.123'. Because you did not specify a date component, SQL Server assumes you mean the base date when it implicitly converts the character string to a *DATETIME* data type.

If you want to work only with dates or only with times, but the input values you get include both date and time components, you need to apply some manipulation on the input values to "zero" the irrelevant part. That is, set the time component to midnight if you want to work only with dates, and set the date component to the base date if you want to work only with times. I'll explain how you can achieve this shortly, in the section "Date and Time Functions."

Filtering Date Ranges

When you need to filter a range of dates, such as a whole year or a whole month, it seems natural to use functions such as *YEAR* and *MONTH*. For example, the following query returns all orders placed in the year 2007:

```
SELECT orderid, custid, empid, orderdate
FROM Sales.Orders
WHERE YEAR(orderdate) = 2007;
```

However, you should be aware that in most cases, when you apply manipulation on the filtered column you cannot use an index in an efficient manner. This is probably hard to understand without some background about indexes and performance, which are outside the scope of this book, but for now, just keep this general point in mind: To have the potential to use an index efficiently, you need to revise the predicate so that there is no manipulation on the filtered column, like so:

```
SELECT orderid, custid, empid, orderdate
FROM Sales.Orders
WHERE orderdate >= '20070101' AND orderdate < '20080101';
```

Similarly, instead of using functions to filter orders placed on a particular month, like so:

```
SELECT orderid, custid, empid, orderdate
FROM Sales.Orders
WHERE YEAR(orderdate) = 2007 AND MONTH(orderdate) = 2;
```

use a range filter, like so:

```
SELECT orderid, custid, empid, orderdate
FROM Sales.Orders
WHERE orderdate >= '20070201' AND orderdate < '20070301';
```

Date and Time Functions

In this section, I describe functions that operate on date and time data types, including *GETDATE*, *CURRENT_TIMESTAMP*, *GETUTCDATE*, *SYSDATETIME*, *SYSUTCDATETIME*, *SYSDATETIMEOFFSET*, *CAST*, *CONVERT*, *SWITCHOFFSET*, *TODATETIMEOFFSET*, *DATEADD*, *DATEDIFF*, *DATEPART*, *YEAR*, *MONTH*, *DAY*, and *DATENAME*. Note that the functions *SYSDATETIME*, *SYSUTCDATETIME*, *SYSDATETIMEOFFSET*, *SWITCHOFFSET*, and *TODATETIMEOFFSET* are new in SQL Server 2008, while the others were available in previous versions as well. The functions available prior to SQL Server 2008 were enhanced to support the new date and time data types and the new date and time parts.

Current Date and Time

The following parameterless functions return the current date and time values in the system where the SQL Server instance resides: *GETDATE*, *CURRENT_TIMESTAMP*, *GETUTCDATE*, *SYSDATETIME*, *SYSUTCDATETIME*, and *SYSDATETIMEOFFSET*. Table 2-3 provides the description of these functions.

TABLE 2-3 Functions Returning Current Date and Time

Function	Return Type	Description	New in SQL Server 2008?
GETDATE	*DATETIME*	Current date and time	No
CURRENT_TIMESTAMP	*DATETIME*	Same as *GETDATE* but ANSI	No
GETUTCDATE	*DATETIME*	Current date and time in UTC	No
SYSDATETIME	*DATETIME2*	Current date and time	Yes
SYSUTCDATETIME	*DATETIME2*	Current date and time in UTC	Yes
SYSDATETIMEOFFSET	*DATETIMEOFFSET*	Current date time including time zone	Yes

Note that you need to specify empty parentheses with all functions that should be specified without parentheses, except the ANSI function *CURRENT_TIMESTAMP*. Also, because *CURRENT_TIMESTAMP* and *GETDATE* return the same thing but only the former is standard, it is recommended that you use the former. This is a practice that I try to follow in general—when I have several options that do the same thing with no functional or performance difference, and one is standard while others aren't, my preference is to use the standard option.

The following code demonstrates using the current date and time functions:

```
SELECT
  GETDATE()           AS [GETDATE],
  CURRENT_TIMESTAMP   AS [CURRENT_TIMESTAMP],
  GETUTCDATE()        AS [GETUTCDATE],
  SYSDATETIME()       AS [SYSDATETIME],
  SYSUTCDATETIME()    AS [SYSUTCDATETIME],
  SYSDATETIMEOFFSET() AS [SYSDATETIMEOFFSET];
```

As you probably noticed, none of the new functions in SQL Server 2008 return only the current system date or only the current system time. However, you can get those easily by converting *CURRENT_TIMESTAMP* or *SYSDATETIME* to *DATE* or *TIME* like so:

```
SELECT
  CAST(SYSDATETIME() AS DATE) AS [current_date],
  CAST(SYSDATETIME() AS TIME) AS [current_time];
```

The CAST and CONVERT Functions

The *CAST* and *CONVERT* functions are used to convert the data type of a value.

Syntax
CAST(*value* AS *datatype*)

CONVERT (*datatype, value* [, *style_number*])

Both functions convert the input *value* to the specified *datatype*. In some cases, *CONVERT* has a third argument with which you can specify the style of the conversion. For example, when converting from a character string to one of the date and time data types (or the other way around), the style number indicates the format of the string. For example, style 101 indicates 'MM/DD/YYYY', while style 103 indicates 'DD/MM/YYYY'. You can find the full list of style numbers and their meanings in SQL Server Books Online under "CAST and CONVERT." As mentioned earlier, when converting from a character string to one of the date and time data types, some of the string formats are language-dependent. I recommend either using one of the language-neutral formats, or using the *CONVERT* function and explicitly specifying the style number you used. This way your code is interpreted the same way regardless of the language of the login running it.

Note that *CAST* is ANSI and *CONVERT* isn't, so unless you need to use the style number, it is recommended that you use the *CAST* function; this way your code is as standard as possible.

Following are a few examples of using the *CAST* and *CONVERT* functions with date and time data types. The following code converts the character string literal '20090212' to a *DATE* data type:

```
SELECT CAST('20090212' AS DATE);
```

The following code converts the current system date and time value to a *DATE* data type, practically extracting only the current system date:

```
SELECT CAST(SYSDATETIME() AS DATE);
```

The following code converts the current system date and time value to a *TIME* data type, practically extracting only the current system time:

```
SELECT CAST(SYSDATETIME() AS TIME);
```

Remember that the *DATE* and *TIME* data types were introduced in SQL Server 2008. As suggested earlier, if you want to work only with dates or only with times in a version prior to SQL Server 2008, you can "zero" the irrelevant part in the *DATETIME* or *SMALLDATETIME* value. In other words, to work only with dates, you set the time to midnight. To work only with time, you set the date to the base date January 1, 1900. I will describe techniques to zero the irrelevant part in a given date and time value, such as *CURRENT_TIMESTAMP*.

The following code converts the current date and time value to CHAR(8) using style 112 ('YYYYMMDD'):

```
SELECT CONVERT(CHAR(8), CURRENT_TIMESTAMP, 112);
```

For example, if the current date is February 12, 2009, this code returns '20090212'. Remember that this style is language-neutral, so when the code is converted back to *DATETIME*, you get the current date at midnight:

```
SELECT CAST(CONVERT(CHAR(8), CURRENT_TIMESTAMP, 112) AS DATETIME);
```

Similarly, to zero the date portion to the base date, you can first convert the current date and time value to *CHAR(12)* using style 114 ('hh:mm:ss.nnn'):

```
SELECT CONVERT(CHAR(12), CURRENT_TIMESTAMP, 114);
```

When the code is converted back to *DATETIME*, you get the current time in the base date:

```
SELECT CAST(CONVERT(CHAR(12), CURRENT_TIMESTAMP, 114) AS DATETIME);
```

The SWITCHOFFSET Function

The *SWITCHOFFSET* function adjusts an input *DATETIMEOFFSET* value to a specified time zone.

Syntax
SWITCHOFFSET(datetimeoffset_value, time_zone)

For example, the following code adjusts the current system *datetimeoffset* value to time zone -05:00:

```
SELECT SWITCHOFFSET(SYSDATETIMEOFFSET(), '-05:00');
```

So if the current system *datetimeoffset* value is February 12, 2009 10:00:00.0000000 -08:00, this code returns the value: February 12, 2009 13:00:00.0000000 -05:00.

The following code adjusts the current *datetimeoffset* value to UTC:

```
SELECT SWITCHOFFSET(SYSDATETIMEOFFSET(), '+00:00');
```

Assuming the aforementioned current *datetimeoffset* value, this code returns the value: February 12, 2009 18:00:00.0000000 +00:00.

The TODATETIMEOFFSET Function

The *TODATETIMEOFFSET* function sets the time zone offset of an input date and time value.

Syntax

TODATETIMEOFFSET(*date_and_time_value, time_zone*)

This function is different from *SWITCHOFFSET* in a couple of ways. First, it's not restricted to a *datetimeoffset* value as input, rather any date and time data type. Second, it doesn't try to adjust the time based on the time zone difference between the source value and the specified time zone, rather simply returns the input date and time value with the specified time zone as a *datetimeoffset* value. For example, if the current system *datetimeoffset* value is February 12, 2009 10:00:00.0000000 -08:00, and you run the following code:

```
SELECT TODATETIMEOFFSET(SYSDATETIMEOFFSET(), '-05:00');
```

You get back the value: February 12, 2009 10:00:00.0000000 -05:00. Remember that the *SWITCHOFFSET* function returned February 12, 2009 13:00:00.0000000 -05:00 because it adjusted the time based on the time zone differences between the input (-08:00) and the specified time zone (-05:00).

As I mentioned, you can use the *TODATETIMEOFFSET* function with any date and time data type as input. For example, the following code takes the current system date and time value and returns it as a *datetimeoffset* value with a time zone -05:00:

```
SELECT TODATETIMEOFFSET(SYSDATETIME(), '-05:00');
```

The DATEADD Function

The *DATEADD* function allows you to add a specified number of units of a specified date part to an input date and time value.

Syntax

DATEADD(*part, n, dt_val*)

Valid values for the *part* input include *year, quarter, month, dayofyear, day, week, weekday, hour, minute, second, millisecond, microsecond,* and *nanosecond.* The last two are new in SQL Server 2008. You can also specify the part in abbreviated form, such as *yy* instead of *year.* Please refer to SQL Server Books Online for details.

The return type for a date and time input is the same type as the input's type. If given a string literal as input, the output is *DATETIME.*

For example, the following code adds 1 year to February 12, 2009:

```
SELECT DATEADD(year, 1, '20090212');
```

This code returns the following output:

```
-----------------------
2010-02-12 00:00:00.000
```

The DATEDIFF Function

The *DATEDIFF* function returns the difference between two date and time values in terms of a specified date part.

Syntax
DATEDIFF(*part, dt_val1, dt_val2*)

For example, the following code returns the difference in terms of days between two values:

```
SELECT DATEDIFF(day, '20080212', '20090212');
```

This code returns the output 366.

Ready for a bit more sophisticated use of the *DATEADD* and *DATEDIFF* functions? You can use the following code in versions prior to SQL Server 2008 to set the time component of the current system date and time value to midnight:

```
SELECT
  DATEADD(
    day,
    DATEDIFF(day, '20010101', CURRENT_TIMESTAMP), '20010101');
```

This is achieved by first using the *DATEDIFF* function to calculate the difference in terms of whole days between an anchor date at midnight ('20010101' in this case) and the current date and time (call that difference *diff*). Then, the *DATEADD* function is used to add *diff* days to the anchor. You get the current system date at midnight.

Interestingly, if you use this expression with a month part instead of day, and make sure to use an anchor that is the first day of a month (as in our example), you get the first day of the current month:

```
SELECT
  DATEADD(
    month,
    DATEDIFF(month, '20010101', CURRENT_TIMESTAMP), '20010101');
```

Similarly, by using a year part and an anchor that is the first day of a year, you get back the first day of the current year.

If you want the last day of the month or year, simply use an anchor that is the last day of a month or year. For example, the following expression returns the last day of the current month:

```
SELECT
  DATEADD(
    month,
    DATEDIFF(month, '19991231', CURRENT_TIMESTAMP), '19991231');
```

The DATEPART Function

The *DATEPART* function returns an integer representing a requested part of a given date and time value.

Syntax
DATEPART(dt_val, part)

Valid values for the part argument include *year, quarter, month, dayofyear, day, week, weekday, hour, minute, second, millisecond, microsecond, nanosecond, TZoffset,* and *ISO_WEEK.* The last four parts are new in SQL Server 2008. As I mentioned earlier, you can use abbreviations for the date and time parts, such as *yy* instead of *year, mm* instead of *month, dd* instead of *day,* and so on.

For example, the following code returns the month part of the input value:

```
SELECT DATEPART(month, '20090212');
```

This code returns the integer 2.

The YEAR, MONTH and DAY Functions

The *YEAR, MONTH,* and *DAY* functions are abbreviations for the *DATEPART* function returning the integer representation of the year, month, and day parts of an input date and time value.

Syntax
YEAR(dt_val)

MONTH(dt_val)

DAY(dt_val)

For example, the following code extracts the day, month, and year parts of an input value:

```
SELECT
  DAY('20090212') AS theday,
  MONTH('20090212') AS themonth,
  YEAR('20090212') AS theyear;
```

This code returns the following output:

```
theday      themonth    theyear
----------- ----------- -----------
12          2           2009
```

The DATENAME Function

The *DATENAME* function returns a character string representing the part of a given date and time value.

Syntax
DATENAME(dt_val, part)

This function is similar to *DATEPART*, and in fact has the same options for the part input. However, when relevant it returns the name of the requested part rather than the number. For example, the following code returns the month name of the given input value:

```
SELECT DATENAME(month, '20090212');
```

Recall that *DATEPART* returned the integer 2 for this input. *DATENAME* returns the name of the month, which is language-dependent. If your session's language is one of the English languages (us_english, British, and so on), you get back the value 'February'. If your session's language is Italian you get back the value 'febbraio'. If a part is requested that has no name, but only a numeric value (such as *year*), the *DATENAME* function returns its numeric value as a character string. For example, the following code returns '2009':

```
SELECT DATENAME(year, '20090212');
```

The ISDATE Function

The *ISDATE* function accepts a character string as input and returns 1 if it is convertible to a date and time data type and 0 if it isn't.

Syntax
ISDATE(string)

For example, the following code returns 1:

```
SELECT ISDATE('20090212');
```

And the following code returns 0:

```
SELECT ISDATE('20090230');
```

Querying Metadata

SQL Server provides tools for getting information about metadata of objects, such as information about tables in a database, columns in a table, and so on. Those tools include catalog views, information schema views, system stored procedures, and functions. This area is documented well in SQL Server Books Online in the section "Querying the SQL Server System Catalog," so I won't cover it in great detail here. I'll just give a couple of examples of each metadata tool to give you a sense of what's available and get you started.

Catalog Views

Catalog views provide very detailed information about objects in the database, including information that is SQL Server–specific. For example, if you want to list the tables in the database along with their schema names, you can query the sys.tables view as follows:

```
USE TSQLFundamentals2008;

SELECT SCHEMA_NAME(schema_id) AS table_schema_name, name AS table_name
FROM sys.tables;
```

The function *SCHEMA_NAME* is used to convert the integer schema ID to its name. This query returns the following output:

```
table_schema_name  table_name
------------------ -------------
HR                 Employees
Production         Suppliers
Production         Categories
Production         Products
Sales              Customers
Sales              Shippers
Sales              Orders
Sales              OrderDetails
```

To get information about columns in a table, you can query the sys.columns table. For example, the following code returns information about columns in the Sales.Orders table including column names, data types (system type ID translated to name using the *TYPE_NAME* function), maximum length, collation name, and NULLability:

```
SELECT
  name AS column_name,
  TYPE_NAME(system_type_id) AS column_type,
  max_length,
  collation_name,
  is_nullable
FROM sys.columns
WHERE object_id = OBJECT_ID(N'Sales.Orders');
```

This query returns the following output:

```
column_name        column_type      max_length collation_name            is_nullable
---------------    ---------------   ---------- ------------------------  -----------
orderid            int              4          NULL                      0
custid             int              4          NULL                      0
empid              int              4          NULL                      0
orderdate          datetime         8          NULL                      0
requireddate       datetime         8          NULL                      0
shippeddate        datetime         8          NULL                      1
shipperid          int              4          NULL                      0
freight            money            8          NULL                      0
shipname           nvarchar         80         Latin1_General_CI_AI      0
shipaddress        nvarchar         120        Latin1_General_CI_AI      0
shipcity           nvarchar         30         Latin1_General_CI_AI      0
shipregion         nvarchar         30         Latin1_General_CI_AI      1
shippostalcode     nvarchar         20         Latin1_General_CI_AI      1
shipcountry        nvarchar         30         Latin1_General_CI_AI      0
```

Information Schema Views

Information schema views are a set of views that reside in a schema called INFORMATION_
SCHEMA and provide metadata information in a standard manner. That is, the views are
defined in the ANSI SQL standard, so naturally they don't cover SQL Server specific aspects.

For example, the following query against the INFORMATION_SCHEMA.TABLES view lists the
user tables in the current database along with their schema names:

```
SELECT TABLE_SCHEMA, TABLE_NAME
FROM INFORMATION_SCHEMA.TABLES
WHERE TABLE_TYPE = N'BASE TABLE';
```

The following query against the INFORMATION_SCHEMA.COLUMNS view provides most of
the available information about columns in the Sales.Orders table:

```
SELECT
  COLUMN_NAME, DATA_TYPE, CHARACTER_MAXIMUM_LENGTH,
  COLLATION_NAME, IS_NULLABLE
FROM INFORMATION_SCHEMA.COLUMNS
WHERE TABLE_SCHEMA = N'Sales'
  AND TABLE_NAME = N'Orders';
```

System Stored Procedures and Functions

System stored procedures and functions internally query the system catalog and give you
back more "digested" metadata information. Again, you can find the full list of objects
and their detailed descriptions in SQL Server Books Online, but here are a few examples.
The sp_tables stored procedure returns a list of objects (such as tables and views) that can be
queried in the current database:

```
EXEC sys.sp_tables;
```

Note that the sys schema was introduced in SQL Server 2005. In previous versions, the system stored procedures resided in the dbo schema.

The sp_help procedure accepts an object name as input and returns multiple result sets with general information about the object, and also information about columns, indexes, constraints, and more. For example, the following code returns detailed information about the Orders table:

```
EXEC sys.sp_help
  @objname = N'Sales.Orders';
```

The sp_columns procedure returns information about columns in an object. For example, the following code returns information about columns in the Orders table:

```
EXEC sys.sp_columns
  @table_name = N'Orders',
  @table_owner = N'Sales';
```

The sp_helpconstraint procedure returns information about constraints in an object. For example, the following code returns information about constraints in the Orders table:

```
EXEC sys.sp_helpconstraint
  @objname = N'Sales.Orders';
```

One set of functions returns information about properties of entities such as the SQL Server instance, database, object, column, and so on. The *SERVERPROPERTY* function returns the requested property of the current instance. For example, the following code returns the product level (such as RTM, SP1, SP2, and so on) of the current instance:

```
SELECT
  SERVERPROPERTY('ProductLevel');
```

The *DATABASEPROPERTYEX* function returns the requested property of the given database name. For example, the following code returns the collation of the TSQLFundamentals2008 database:

```
SELECT
  DATABASEPROPERTYEX(N'TSQLFundamentals2008', 'Collation')
```

The *OBJECTPROPERTY* function returns the requested property of the given object name. For example, the output of the following code indicates whether the Orders table has a primary key:

```
SELECT
  OBJECTPROPERTY(OBJECT_ID(N'Sales.Orders'), 'TableHasPrimaryKey');
```

Notice the nesting of the function *OBJECT_ID* within *OBJECTPROPERTY*. The *OBJECTPROPERTY* function expects an object ID and not a name, so the *OBJECT_ID* function is used to return the ID of the Orders table.

The *COLUMNPROPERTY* function returns the requested property of a given column. For example, the output of the following code indicates whether the shipcountry column in the Orders table is NULLable:

```
SELECT
  COLUMNPROPERTY(OBJECT_ID(N'Sales.Orders'), N'shipcountry', 'AllowsNull');
```

Conclusion

This chapter introduced you to the *SELECT* statement, logical query processing, and various other aspects of single-table queries. I covered quite a few subjects here, including many new and unique concepts. If you're new to T-SQL, you might feel overwhelmed at this point. But remember, this chapter introduces some of the most important points about SQL that might be hard to digest at the beginning. If some of the concepts weren't completely clear, you might want to revisit sections from this chapter later on, after you've had a chance to sleep on it.

For an opportunity to practice what you've learned and absorb the material better, I recommend going over the chapter exercises.

Exercises

This section contains exercises to practice the subjects discussed in this chapter. Solutions to the exercises appear in the section that follows.

This section occasionally provides optional exercises that are more advanced. Those exercises are intended for readers who feel very comfortable with the material and want to challenge themselves with more difficult problems. The optional exercises for advanced readers are labeled as such.

You can find instructions for downloading and installing the TSQLFundamentals2008 sample database in Appendix A, "Getting Started."

1

Return orders placed in June 2007.

Tables involved: TSQLFundamentals2008 database, Sales.Orders table.

Desired output (abbreviated):

```
orderid      orderdate               custid      empid
-----------  ----------------------- ----------- -----------
10555        2007-06-02 00:00:00.000 71          6
10556        2007-06-03 00:00:00.000 73          2
10557        2007-06-03 00:00:00.000 44          9
```

```
10558          2007-06-04 00:00:00.000 4              1
10559          2007-06-05 00:00:00.000 7              6
10560          2007-06-06 00:00:00.000 25             8
10561          2007-06-06 00:00:00.000 24             2
10562          2007-06-09 00:00:00.000 66             1
10563          2007-06-10 00:00:00.000 67             2
10564          2007-06-10 00:00:00.000 65             4
...

(30 row(s) affected)
```

2 (Optional, Advanced)

Return orders placed on the last day of the month.

Tables involved: Sales.Orders table.

Desired output (abbreviated):

```
orderid        orderdate                  custid       empid
-----------    ----------------------     -----------  -----------
10269          2006-07-31 00:00:00.000 89             5
10317          2006-09-30 00:00:00.000 48             6
10343          2006-10-31 00:00:00.000 44             4
10399          2006-12-31 00:00:00.000 83             8
10432          2007-01-31 00:00:00.000 75             3
10460          2007-02-28 00:00:00.000 24             8
10461          2007-02-28 00:00:00.000 46             1
10490          2007-03-31 00:00:00.000 35             7
10491          2007-03-31 00:00:00.000 28             8
10522          2007-04-30 00:00:00.000 44             4
...

(26 row(s) affected)
```

3

Return employees with last name containing the letter 'a' twice or more.

Tables involved: HR.Employees table.

Desired output:

```
empid          firstname  lastname
-----------    ---------- --------------------
9              Zoya       Dolgopyatova

(1 row(s) affected)
```

4

Return orders with total value (quantity * unitprice) greater than 10,000, sorted by total value.

Tables involved: Sales.OrderDetails table.

Desired output:

```
orderid      totalvalue
-----------  --------------------
10865        17250.00
11030        16321.90
10981        15810.00
10372        12281.20
10424        11493.20
10817        11490.70
10889        11380.00
10417        11283.20
10897        10835.24
10353        10741.60
10515        10588.50
10479        10495.60
10540        10191.70
10691        10164.80

(14 row(s) affected)
```

5

Return the three ship countries with the highest average freight in 2007.

Tables involved: Sales.Orders table.

Desired output:

```
shipcountry     avgfreight
--------------  ---------------------
Austria         178.3642
Switzerland     117.1775
Sweden          105.16

(3 row(s) affected)
```

6

Calculate row numbers for orders based on order date ordering (using order ID as tiebreaker) for each customer separately.

Tables involved: Sales.Orders table.

Desired output (abbreviated):

```
custid       orderdate                  orderid     rownum
-----------  -------------------------  ----------  --------------------
1            2007-08-25 00:00:00.000    10643       1
1            2007-10-03 00:00:00.000    10692       2
1            2007-10-13 00:00:00.000    10702       3
1            2008-01-15 00:00:00.000    10835       4
1            2008-03-16 00:00:00.000    10952       5
1            2008-04-09 00:00:00.000    11011       6
2            2006-09-18 00:00:00.000    10308       1
2            2007-08-08 00:00:00.000    10625       2
2            2007-11-28 00:00:00.000    10759       3
2            2008-03-04 00:00:00.000    10926       4
...

(830 row(s) affected)
```

7

Figure out the *SELECT* statement that returns for each employee the gender based on the title of courtesy. For 'Ms.' and 'Mrs.' return 'Female'; for 'Mr.' return 'Male'; and in all other cases (for example, 'Dr.') return 'Unknown'.

Tables involved: HR.Employees table.

Desired output:

```
empid        firstname  lastname              titleofcourtesy            gender
-----------  ---------  --------------------  -------------------------  -------
1            Sara       Davis                 Ms.                        Female
2            Don        Funk                  Dr.                        Unknown
3            Judy       Lew                   Ms.                        Female
4            Yael       Peled                 Mrs.                       Female
5            Sven       Buck                  Mr.                        Male
6            Paul       Suurs                 Mr.                        Male
7            Russell    King                  Mr.                        Male
8            Maria      Cameron               Ms.                        Female
9            Zoya       Dolgopyatova          Ms.                        Female

(9 row(s) affected)
```

8

Return for each customer the customer ID and region. Sort the rows in the output by region, having NULLs sort last (after non-NULL values). Note that the default sort behavior of NULLs in T-SQL is to sort first (before non-NULL values).

Tables involved: Sales.Customers table.

Desired output (abbreviated):

```
custid       region
-----------  ---------------
55           AK
10           BC
42           BC
45           CA
37           Co. Cork
33           DF
71           ID
38           Isle of Wight
46           Lara
78           MT
...
1            NULL
2            NULL
3            NULL
4            NULL
5            NULL
6            NULL
7            NULL
8            NULL
9            NULL
11           NULL
...

(91 row(s) affected)
```

Solutions

This section provides the solutions to the exercises for this chapter, accompanied by explanations where needed.

1

You may have considered using the *YEAR* and *MONTH* functions in the WHERE clause of your solution query, like so:

```
USE TSQLFundamentals2008;

SELECT orderid, orderdate, custid, empid
FROM Sales.Orders
WHERE YEAR(orderdate) = 2007 AND MONTH(orderdate) = 6;
```

This solution is valid and returns the correct result. However, I explained that if you apply manipulation on the filtered column, in most cases SQL Server can't use an index efficiently if such manipulation exists on that column. Therefore, I advised using a range filter instead:

```
SELECT orderid, orderdate, custid, empid
FROM Sales.Orders
WHERE orderdate >= '20070601'
  AND orderdate < '20070701';
```

2

As part of the discussion about date and time functions, I provided the following expression format to calculate the last day of the month corresponding to a given date:

```
DATEADD(month, DATEDIFF(month, '19991231', date_val), '19991231')
```

This expression first calculates the difference in terms of whole months between an anchor last day of some month (December 31, 1999 in our case) and the given date. Call this difference *diff*. By adding *diff* months to the anchor date, you get the last day of the given date's month. Here's the full solution query returning only orders where the order date is equal to the last day of the month:

```
SELECT orderid, orderdate, custid, empid
FROM Sales.Orders
WHERE orderdate = DATEADD(month, DATEDIFF(month, '19991231', orderdate), '19991231');
```

3

This exercise involves using pattern matching with the LIKE predicate. Remember that the percent sign (%) represents a character string of any size, including an empty string. Therefore, you can use the pattern '%a%a%' to express at least two occurrences of the character 'a' anywhere in the string. Here's the full solution query:

```
SELECT empid, firstname, lastname
FROM HR.Employees
WHERE lastname LIKE '%a%a%';
```

4

This exercise is quite tricky, and if you managed to solve it correctly you should be proud of yourself. A subtle requirement in the request might be overlooked or interpreted incorrectly. Observe that the request said "return orders with *total value* greater than 10,000" and not "return orders with *value* greater than 10,000." In other words, the individual order detail row shouldn't meet the requirement. Instead, the group of all order details within the order should meet the requirement. This means that the query shouldn't have a filter in the WHERE clause saying:

```
WHERE quantity * unitprice > 10000
```

Rather, the query should group the data by order ID, and have a filter in the HAVING clause saying:

```
HAVING SUM(quantity*unitprice) > 10000
```

Here's the complete solution query:

```
SELECT orderid, SUM(qty*unitprice) AS totalvalue
FROM Sales.OrderDetails
GROUP BY orderid
HAVING SUM(qty*unitprice) > 10000
ORDER BY totalvalue DESC;
```

5

Because the request involves activity in the year 2004, the query should have a WHERE clause with the appropriate date range filter (orderdate >= '20040101' AND orderdate < '20050101'). Because the request involves average freight values per shipping country and the table can have multiple rows per country, the query should group the rows by country, and calculate the average freight. To get the three countries with the highest average freights, the query should specify *TOP(3)*, based on logical order of average freight descending. Here's the complete solution query:

```
SELECT TOP(3) shipcountry, AVG(freight) AS avgfreight
FROM Sales.Orders
WHERE orderdate >= '20070101' AND orderdate < '20080101'
GROUP BY shipcountry
ORDER BY avgfreight DESC;
```

6

Because the exercise requests that the row number calculation be done for each customer separately, the expression should have PARTITION BY custid. In addition, the request was to use logical ordering by orderdate, and orderid as a tiebreaker. Therefore, the OVER clause should have ORDER BY orderdate, orderid. Here's the complete solution query:

```
SELECT custid, orderdate, orderid,
  ROW_NUMBER() OVER(PARTITION BY custid ORDER BY orderdate, orderid) AS rownum
FROM Sales.Orders
ORDER BY custid, rownum;
```

7

You can handle the conditional logic required by this exercise by using a CASE expression. Using the simple CASE expression form, you specify the titleofcourtesy attribute right after the *CASE* keyword; list each possible title of courtesy in a separate WHEN clause followed by the THEN clause and the gender; and in the ELSE clause specify 'Unknown':

```
SELECT empid, firstname, lastname, titleofcourtesy,
  CASE titleofcourtesy
    WHEN 'Ms.'  THEN 'Female'
    WHEN 'Mrs.' THEN 'Female'
    WHEN 'Mr.'  THEN 'Male'
    ELSE             'Unknown'
  END AS gender
FROM HR.Employees;
```

You can also use the searched CASE form with two predicates—one to handle all cases where the gender is female and one for all cases where the gender is male—and an ELSE clause with 'Unknown':

```
SELECT empid, firstname, lastname, titleofcourtesy,
  CASE
    WHEN titleofcourtesy IN('Ms.', 'Mrs.') THEN 'Female'
    WHEN titleofcourtesy = 'Mr.'           THEN 'Male'
    ELSE                                        'Unknown'
  END AS gender
FROM HR.Employees;
```

8

By default SQL Server sorts NULLs before non-NULL values. To get NULLs to sort last, you can use a CASE expression that returns 1 when the region column is NULL and 0 when it is not NULL. Non-NULLs get 0 back from the expression; therefore, they sort before NULLs (which get 1). This CASE expression is used as the first sort column. The region column should be specified as the second sort column. This way, non-NULLs sort correctly among themselves. Here's the complete solution query:

```
SELECT custid, region
FROM Sales.Customers
ORDER BY
  CASE WHEN region IS NULL THEN 1 ELSE 0 END, region;
```

Chapter 3
Joins

The FROM clause of a query is the first clause to be logically processed, and within the FROM clause table operators operate on input tables. Microsoft SQL Server 2008 supports four table operators—JOIN, APPLY, PIVOT, and UNPIVOT. The JOIN table operator is standard, while APPLY, PIVOT, and UNPIVOT are T-SQL extensions to the standard. These last three were introduced in SQL Server 2005. Each table operator acts on tables provided to it as input, applies a set of logical query processing phases, and returns a table result. This chapter focuses on the JOIN table operator. The APPLY operator will be covered in Chapter 5, "Table Expressions," and the PIVOT and UNPIVOT operators will be covered in Chapter 7, "Pivot, Unpivot, and Grouping Sets."

A JOIN table operator operates on two input tables. The three fundamental types of joins are cross, inner, and outer. The three types of joins differ in how they apply their logical query processing phases; each type applies a different set of phases. A cross join applies only one phase—Cartesian Product. An inner join applies two phases—Cartesian Product and Filter. An outer join applies three phases—Cartesian Product, Filter, and Add Outer Rows. This chapter explains each of the join types and the phases involved in detail.

Logical query processing describes a generic series of logical steps that for any given query produces the correct result, while physical query processing is the way the query is processed by the RDBMS engine in practice. Some phases of logical query processing of joins may sound inefficient, but the physical implementation may be optimized. It's important to stress the term *logical* in logical query processing. The steps in the process apply operations to the input tables based on relational algebra. The database engine does not have to follow logical query processing phases literally as long as it can guarantee that the result that it produces is the same as dictated by logical query processing. The SQL Server relational engine often applies many shortcuts for optimization purposes when it knows that it can still produce the correct result. Even though this book's focus is to understand the logical aspects of querying, I want to stress this point to avoid any misunderstanding and confusion.

Cross Joins

Logically, a cross join is the simplest type of join. A cross join implements only one logical query processing phase—a Cartesian Product. This phase operates on the two tables provided as inputs to the join, and produces a Cartesian product of the two. That is, each row from one input is matched with all rows from the other. So if you have m rows in one table and n rows in the other, you get $m \times n$ rows in the result.

SQL Server supports two standard syntaxes for cross joins—the ANSI SQL-92 and ANSI SQL-89 syntaxes. I recommend that you use the ANSI-SQL 92 syntax for reasons that I'll describe shortly. Therefore, ANSI-SQL 92 syntax is the main syntax that I use throughout the book. For the sake of completeness, I describe both syntaxes in this section.

ANSI SQL-92 Syntax

The following query applies a cross join between the Customers and Employees tables (using the ANSI SQL-92 syntax) in the TSQLFundamentals2008 database, and returns the custid and empid attributes in the result set:

```
USE TSQLFundamentals2008;

SELECT C.custid, E.empid
FROM Sales.Customers AS C
  CROSS JOIN HR.Employees AS E;
```

Because there are 91 rows in the Customers table and 9 rows in the Employees table, this query produces a result set with 819 rows, as shown here in abbreviated form:

```
custid      empid
----------- -----------
1           1
1           2
1           3
1           4
1           5
1           6
1           7
1           8
1           9
2           1
2           2
2           3
2           4
2           5
2           6
2           7
2           8
2           9
...

(819 row(s) affected)
```

Using the ANSI SQL-92 syntax, you specify the *CROSS JOIN* keywords between the two tables involved in the join.

Notice that in the FROM clause of the preceding query, I assigned the aliases C and E to the Customers and Employees tables, respectively. The result set produced by the cross join is a virtual table with attributes that originate from both sides of the join. Because I assigned aliases to the source tables, the names of the columns in the virtual table are prefixed by the table aliases (for example, C.custid, E.empid). If you do not assign aliases to the tables in the FROM clause, the names of the columns in the virtual table are prefixed by the full source table names (for example, Customers.custid, Employees.empid). The purpose of the prefixes is to enable the identification of columns in an unambiguous manner when the same column name appears in both tables. The aliases of the tables are assigned for brevity. Note that you are required to use column prefixes only when referring to ambiguous column names (column names that appear in more than one table); in unambiguous cases column prefixes are optional. However, some people find it a good practice to always use column prefixes for the sake of clarity. Also note that if you assign an alias to a table, it is invalid to use the full table name as a column prefix; in ambiguous cases you have to use the table alias as a prefix.

ANSI SQL-89 Syntax

SQL Server also supports an older syntax for cross joins that was introduced in ANSI SQL-89. In this syntax you simply specify a comma between the table names like so:

```
SELECT C.custid, E.empid
FROM Sales.Customers AS C, HR.Employees AS E;
```

There is no logical or performance difference between the two syntaxes. Both syntaxes are integral parts of the latest SQL standard (ANSI SQL:2006 at the time of this writing), and both are fully supported by the latest version of SQL Server (SQL Server 2008 at the time of this writing). I am not aware of any plans to deprecate the older syntax, and I don't see any reason to do so while it's an integral part of the standard. However, I recommend using the ANSI SQL-92 syntax for reasons that will become clear after inner joins are explained.

Self Cross Joins

You can join multiple instances of the same table. This capability is known as *self-join* and is supported with all fundamental join types (cross, inner, and outer). For example, the following query performs a self cross join between two instances of the Employees table:

```
SELECT
  E1.empid, E1.firstname, E1.lastname,
  E2.empid, E2.firstname, E2.lastname
FROM HR.Employees AS E1
  CROSS JOIN HR.Employees AS E2;
```

This query produces all possible combinations of pairs of employees. Because the Employees table has 9 rows, this query returns 81 rows, shown here in abbreviated form:

```
empid  firstname  lastname         empid  firstname  lastname
------ ---------- ---------------- ------ ---------- ---------
1      Sara       Davis            1      Sara       Davis
2      Don        Funk             1      Sara       Davis
3      Judy       Lew              1      Sara       Davis
4      Yael       Peled            1      Sara       Davis
5      Sven       Buck             1      Sara       Davis
6      Paul       Suurs            1      Sara       Davis
7      Russell    King             1      Sara       Davis
8      Maria      Cameron          1      Sara       Davis
9      Zoya       Dolgopyatova     1      Sara       Davis
1      Sara       Davis            2      Don        Funk
2      Don        Funk             2      Don        Funk
3      Judy       Lew              2      Don        Funk
4      Yael       Peled            2      Don        Funk
5      Sven       Buck             2      Don        Funk
6      Paul       Suurs            2      Don        Funk
7      Russell    King             2      Don        Funk
8      Maria      Cameron          2      Don        Funk
9      Zoya       Dolgopyatova     2      Don        Funk
...

(81 row(s) affected)
```

In a self-join, aliasing tables is not optional. Without table aliases, all column names in the result of the join would be ambiguous.

Producing Tables of Numbers

One situation in which cross joins can be very handy is when they are used to produce a result set with a sequence of integers (1, 2, 3, and so on). Such a sequence of numbers is an extremely powerful tool that I use for many purposes. Using cross joins you can produce the sequence of integers in a very efficient manner.

You can start by creating a table called Digits with a column called digit, and populate the table with 10 rows with the digits 0 through 9. Run the following code to create the Digits table in the tempdb database (for test purposes) and populate it with the 10 digits:

```
USE tempdb;
IF OBJECT_ID('dbo.Digits', 'U') IS NOT NULL DROP TABLE dbo.Digits;
CREATE TABLE dbo.Digits(digit INT NOT NULL PRIMARY KEY);

INSERT INTO dbo.Digits(digit)
  VALUES (0),(1),(2),(3),(4),(5),(6),(7),(8),(9);

/*
Note:
Above INSERT syntax is new in Microsoft SQL Server 2008.
```

```
In earlier versions use:

INSERT INTO dbo.Digits(digit) VALUES(0);
INSERT INTO dbo.Digits(digit) VALUES(1);
INSERT INTO dbo.Digits(digit) VALUES(2);
INSERT INTO dbo.Digits(digit) VALUES(3);
INSERT INTO dbo.Digits(digit) VALUES(4);
INSERT INTO dbo.Digits(digit) VALUES(5);
INSERT INTO dbo.Digits(digit) VALUES(6);
INSERT INTO dbo.Digits(digit) VALUES(7);
INSERT INTO dbo.Digits(digit) VALUES(8);
INSERT INTO dbo.Digits(digit) VALUES(9);
*/

SELECT digit FROM dbo.Digits;
```

This code uses a couple of syntax elements for the first time in this book, so I'll briefly explain them. Any text residing within a block starting with /* and ending with */ is treated as a block comment and is ignored by SQL Server. This code also uses an *INSERT* statement to populate the Digits table. If you're not familiar with the syntax of the *INSERT* statement, see Chapter 8, "Data Modification," for details. Note, however, that this code uses new syntax that was introduced in SQL Server 2008 for the *INSERT VALUES* statement, allowing a single statement to insert multiple rows. A block comment embedded in the code explains that in earlier versions you need to use a separate *INSERT VALUES* statement for each row.

The contents of the Digits table are shown here:

```
digit
-----------
0
1
2
3
4
5
6
7
8
9
```

Suppose you need to write a query that produces a sequence of integers in the range 1 through 1,000. You can cross three instances of the Digits table, each representing a different power of 10 (1, 10, 100). By crossing three instances of the same table, each instance with 10 rows, you get a result set with 1,000 rows. To produce the actual number, multiply the digit from each instance by the power of 10 it represents, sum the results, and add 1. Here's the complete query:

```
SELECT D3.digit * 100 + D2.digit * 10 + D1.digit + 1 AS n
FROM        dbo.Digits AS D1
  CROSS JOIN dbo.Digits AS D2
  CROSS JOIN dbo.Digits AS D3
ORDER BY n;
```

This query returns the following output, shown here in abbreviated form:

```
n
-----------
1
2
3
4
5
6
7
8
9
10
...
998
999
1000

(1000 row(s) affected)
```

This was just an example producing a sequence of 1,000 integers. If you need more, you can add more instances of the Digits table to the query. For example, if you need to produce a sequence of 1,000,000 rows, you would need to join six instances.

Inner Joins

An inner join applies two logical query processing phases—it applies a Cartesian product between the two input tables like a cross join, and then it filters rows based on a predicate that you specify. Like cross joins, inner joins have two standard syntaxes: ANSI SQL-92 and ANSI SQL-89.

ANSI SQL-92 Syntax

Using the ANSI SQL-92 syntax, you specify the *INNER JOIN* keywords between the table names. The *INNER* keyword is optional because an inner join is the default, so you can specify the *JOIN* keyword alone. You specify the predicate that is used to filter rows in a designated clause called ON. This predicate is also known as the *join condition*.

For example, the following query performs an inner join between the Employees and Orders tables in the TSQLFundamentals2008 database, matching employees and orders based on the predicate E.empid = O.empid:

```
USE TSQLFundamentals2008;

SELECT E.empid, E.firstname, E.lastname, O.orderid
FROM HR.Employees AS E
  JOIN Sales.Orders AS O
    ON E.empid = O.empid;
```

This query produces the following result set, shown here in abbreviated form:

```
empid        firstname  lastname             orderid
-----------  ---------- -------------------- -----------
1            Sara       Davis                10258
1            Sara       Davis                10270
1            Sara       Davis                10275
1            Sara       Davis                10285
1            Sara       Davis                10292
...
2            Don        Funk                 10265
2            Don        Funk                 10277
2            Don        Funk                 10280
2            Don        Funk                 10295
2            Don        Funk                 10300
...

(830 row(s) affected)
```

For most people the easiest way to think of such an inner join is as matching each employee row to all order rows that have the same employee ID as the employee's employee ID. This is a simplified way to think of the join. The more formal way to think of the join based on relational algebra is that first the join performs a Cartesian product of the two tables (9 employee rows × 830 order rows = 7,470 rows), and then filters rows based on the predicate E.empid = O.empid, eventually returning 830 rows. As mentioned earlier, that's just the logical way the join is processed; in practice, physical processing of the query by the database engine can be different.

Recall the discussion from previous chapters about the three-valued predicate logic used by SQL. Like with the WHERE and HAVING clauses, the ON clause also returns only rows for which the predicate returns TRUE, and does not return rows for which the predicate evaluates to FALSE or UNKNOWN.

In the TSQLFundamentals2008 database all employees have related orders, so all employees show up in the output. However, had there been employees with no related orders, they would have been filtered out by the filter phase.

ANSI SQL-89 Syntax

Similar to cross joins, inner joins can be expressed using the ANSI SQL-89 syntax. You specify a comma between the table names just like in a cross join, and specify the join condition in the query's WHERE clause, like so:

```
SELECT E.empid, E.firstname, E.lastname, O.orderid
FROM HR.Employees AS E, Sales.Orders AS O
WHERE E.empid = O.empid;
```

Note that the ANSI SQL-89 syntax has no ON clause.

Again, both syntaxes are standard, fully supported by SQL Server, and interpreted the same by the engine, so you shouldn't expect any performance difference between the two. But one syntax is safer, as explained in the next section.

Inner Join Safety

I strongly recommend that you stick to the ANSI SQL-92 join syntax because it is safer in several ways. Say you intend to write an inner join query, and by mistake forget to specify the join condition. With the ANSI SQL-92 syntax the query becomes invalid and the parser generates an error. For example, try to run the following code:

```
SELECT E.empid, E.firstname, E.lastname, O.orderid
FROM HR.Employees AS E
  JOIN Sales.Orders AS O;
```

You get the following error:

```
Msg 102, Level 15, State 1, Line 3
Incorrect syntax near ';'.
```

Even though it might not be obvious immediately that the error involves a missing join condition, you will figure it out eventually and fix the query. However, if you forget to specify the join condition using the ANSI SQL-89 syntax, you get a valid query that performs a cross join:

```
SELECT E.empid, E.firstname, E.lastname, O.orderid
FROM HR.Employees AS E, Sales.Orders AS O;
```

Because the query doesn't fail, the logical error might go unnoticed for a while, and users of your application might end up relying on incorrect results. It is unlikely that a programmer would forget to specify the join condition with such short and simple queries; however, most production queries are much more complicated and have multiple tables, filters, and other query elements. In those cases the likelihood of forgetting to specify a join condition increases.

If I've convinced you that it is important to use the ANSI SQL-92 syntax for inner joins, you might wonder whether the recommendation holds for cross joins. Because no join condition is involved, you might think that both syntaxes are just as good for cross joins. However, I recommend staying with the ANSI SQL-92 syntax with cross joins for a couple of reasons—one being consistency. Also, let's say you do use the ANSI SQL-89 syntax. Even if you intended to write a cross join, when other developers need to review or maintain your code, how will they know whether you intended to write a cross join or intended to write an inner join and forgot to specify the join condition?

Further Join Examples

This section covers a few join examples that are known by specific names, including composite joins, non-equi joins, and multi-table joins.

Composite Joins

A composite join is simply a join based on a predicate that involves more than one attribute from each side. A composite join is commonly required when you need to join two tables based on a primary key–foreign key relationship, and the relationship is composite: that is, based on more than one attribute. For example, suppose you have a foreign key defined on dbo.Table2, columns col1, col2, referencing dbo.Table1, columns col1, col2, and you need to write a query that joins the two based on primary key–foreign key relationship. The FROM clause of the query would look like this:

```
FROM dbo.Table1 AS T1
  JOIN dbo.Table2 AS T2
    ON T1.col1 = T2.col1
    AND T1.col2 = T2.col2
```

For a more tangible example, suppose that you need to audit updates to column values against the OrderDetails table in the TSQLFundamentals2008 database. You create a custom auditing table called OrderDetailsAudit:

```
USE TSQLFundamentals2008;
IF OBJECT_ID('Sales.OrderDetailsAudit', 'U') IS NOT NULL
  DROP TABLE Sales.OrderDetailsAudit;
CREATE TABLE Sales.OrderDetailsAudit
(
  lsn        INT NOT NULL IDENTITY,
  orderid    INT NOT NULL,
  productid  INT NOT NULL,
  dt         DATETIME NOT NULL,
  loginname  sysname NOT NULL,
  columnname sysname NOT NULL,
  oldval     SQL_VARIANT,
  newval     SQL_VARIANT,
  CONSTRAINT PK_OrderDetailsAudit PRIMARY KEY(lsn),
  CONSTRAINT FK_OrderDetailsAudit_OrderDetails
    FOREIGN KEY(orderid, productid)
    REFERENCES Sales.OrderDetails(orderid, productid)
);
```

Each audit row stores a log serial number (lsn), the key of the modified row (orderid, productid), the name of the modified column (columnname), the old value (*oldval*), new value (*newval*), when the change took place (dt), and who made the change (loginname). The table has a foreign key defined on the attributes orderid, productid, referencing the primary key of the OrderDetails table, which is defined on the attributes orderid, productid.

Suppose that you already have in place all the required processes that audit column value changes taking place in the OrderDetails table in the OrderDetailsAudit table.

You need to write a query that returns all value changes that took place against the column qty, but in each result row you need to return the current value from the OrderDetails table, and the values before and after the change from the OrderDetailsAudit table. You need to join the two tables based on primary key–foreign key relationship like so:

```
SELECT OD.orderid, OD.productid, OD.qty,
  ODA.dt, ODA.loginname, ODA.oldval, ODA.newval
FROM Sales.OrderDetails AS OD
  JOIN Sales.OrderDetailsAudit AS ODA
    ON OD.orderid = ODA.orderid
    AND OD.productid = ODA.productid
WHERE ODA.columnname = N'qty';
```

Because the relationship is based on multiple attributes, the join condition is composite.

Non-Equi Joins

When the join condition involves only an equality operator, the join is said to be an equi join. When the join condition involves any operator besides equality, the join is said to be a non-equi join. As an example of a non-equi join, the following query joins two instances of the Employees table to produce unique pairs of employees:

```
SELECT
  E1.empid, E1.firstname, E1.lastname,
  E2.empid, E2.firstname, E2.lastname
FROM HR.Employees AS E1
  JOIN HR.Employees AS E2
    ON E1.empid < E2.empid;
```

Notice the predicate specified in the ON clause. The purpose of the query is to produce unique pairs of employees. Had you used a cross join, you would have gotten self pairs (for example, 1 with 1), and also mirrored pairs (for example, 1 with 2 and also 2 with 1). Using an inner join with a join condition that says that the key in the left side must be smaller than the key in the right side eliminates the two inapplicable cases. Self pairs are eliminated because both sides are equal. With mirrored pairs, only one of the two cases qualifies because out of the two cases, only one will have a left key that is smaller than the right key. In our case, out of the 81 possible pairs of employees that a cross join would have returned, our query returns the 36 unique pairs shown here:

empid	firstname	lastname	empid	firstname	lastname
1	Sara	Davis	2	Don	Funk
1	Sara	Davis	3	Judy	Lew
2	Don	Funk	3	Judy	Lew

1	Sara	Davis	4	Yael	Peled
2	Don	Funk	4	Yael	Peled
3	Judy	Lew	4	Yael	Peled
1	Sara	Davis	5	Sven	Buck
2	Don	Funk	5	Sven	Buck
3	Judy	Lew	5	Sven	Buck
4	Yael	Peled	5	Sven	Buck
1	Sara	Davis	6	Paul	Suurs
2	Don	Funk	6	Paul	Suurs
3	Judy	Lew	6	Paul	Suurs
4	Yael	Peled	6	Paul	Suurs
5	Sven	Buck	6	Paul	Suurs
1	Sara	Davis	7	Russell	King
2	Don	Funk	7	Russell	King
3	Judy	Lew	7	Russell	King
4	Yael	Peled	7	Russell	King
5	Sven	Buck	7	Russell	King
6	Paul	Suurs	7	Russell	King
1	Sara	Davis	8	Maria	Cameron
2	Don	Funk	8	Maria	Cameron
3	Judy	Lew	8	Maria	Cameron
4	Yael	Peled	8	Maria	Cameron
5	Sven	Buck	8	Maria	Cameron
6	Paul	Suurs	8	Maria	Cameron
7	Russell	King	8	Maria	Cameron
1	Sara	Davis	9	Zoya	Dolgopyatova
2	Don	Funk	9	Zoya	Dolgopyatova
3	Judy	Lew	9	Zoya	Dolgopyatova
4	Yael	Peled	9	Zoya	Dolgopyatova
5	Sven	Buck	9	Zoya	Dolgopyatova
6	Paul	Suurs	9	Zoya	Dolgopyatova
7	Russell	King	9	Zoya	Dolgopyatova
8	Maria	Cameron	9	Zoya	Dolgopyatova

(36 row(s) affected)

If it is still not clear to you what this query does, try to process it one step at a time with a smaller set of employees. For example, suppose the Employees table contained only employees 1, 2, and 3. First, produce the Cartesian product of two instances of the table:

E1.empid	E2.empid
1	1
1	2
1	3
2	1
2	2
2	3
3	1
3	2
3	3

Next, filter the rows based on the predicate E1.empid < E2.empid, and you are left with only three rows:

```
E1.empid       E2.empid
-------------  -------------
1              2
1              3
2              3
```

Multi-Table Joins

A join table operator operates only on two tables, but a single query can have multiple joins. In general, when more than one table operator appears in the FROM clause, the table operators are logically processed from left to right. That is, the result table of the first table operator is served as the left input to the second table operator; the result of the second table operator is served as the left input to the third table operator and so on. So if there are multiple joins in the FROM clause, logically the first join operates on two base tables, but all other joins get the result of the preceding join as their left input. With cross joins and inner joins, the database engine can (and often does) internally rearrange join ordering for optimization purposes because it won't have an impact on the correctness of the result of the query.

As an example, the following query joins the Customers and Orders tables to match customers with their orders, and joins the result of the first join with the OrderDetails table to match orders with their order lines:

```
SELECT
  C.custid, C.companyname, O.orderid,
  OD.productid, OD.qty
FROM Sales.Customers AS C
  JOIN Sales.Orders AS O
    ON C.custid = O.custid
  JOIN Sales.OrderDetails AS OD
    ON O.orderid = OD.orderid;
```

This query returns the following output, shown here in abbreviated form:

```
custid       companyname         orderid      productid    qty
-----------  ------------------  -----------  -----------  ------
85           Customer ENQZT      10248        11           12
85           Customer ENQZT      10248        42           10
85           Customer ENQZT      10248        72           5
79           Customer FAPSM      10249        14           9
79           Customer FAPSM      10249        51           40
34           Customer IBVRG      10250        41           10
34           Customer IBVRG      10250        51           35
34           Customer IBVRG      10250        65           15
84           Customer NRCSK      10251        22           6
84           Customer NRCSK      10251        57           15
...

(2155 row(s) affected)
```

Outer Joins

Outer joins are usually harder for people to grasp compared to the other types of joins. First I will describe the fundamentals of outer joins. If by the end of the section "Fundamentals of Outer Joins," you feel very comfortable with the material and are ready for more advanced content, you can read an optional section describing aspects of outer joins that are beyond the fundamentals. Otherwise, feel free to skip that part and return to it when you feel comfortable with the material.

Fundamentals of Outer Joins

Outer joins were introduced in ANSI SQL-92 and unlike inner and cross joins, they only have one standard syntax—the one where you specify the *JOIN* keyword between the table names, and the join condition in the ON clause. Outer joins apply the two logical processing phases that inner joins apply (Cartesian product and the ON filter), plus a third phase called Adding Outer Rows that is unique to this type of join.

In an outer join you mark a table as a "preserved" table by using the keywords *LEFT OUTER JOIN*, *RIGHT OUTER JOIN*, or *FULL OUTER JOIN* between the table names. The *OUTER* keyword is optional. The *LEFT* keyword means that the rows of the left table are preserved, the *RIGHT* keyword means that the rows in the right table are preserved, and the *FULL* keyword means that the rows in both the left and right tables are preserved. The third logical query processing phase of an outer join identifies the rows from the preserved table that did not find matches in the other table based on the ON predicate. This phase adds those rows to the result table produced by the first two phases of the join, and uses NULLs as place holders for the attributes from the nonpreserved side of the join in those outer rows.

A good way to understand outer joins is through an example. The following query joins the Customers and Orders tables based on a match between the customer's customer ID and the order's customer ID to return customers and their orders. The join type is a left outer join; therefore, the query also returns customers who did not place any orders in the result:

```
SELECT C.custid, C.companyname, O.orderid
FROM Sales.Customers AS C
  LEFT OUTER JOIN Sales.Orders AS O
    ON C.custid = O.custid;
```

This query returns the following output, shown here in abbreviated form:

```
custid       companyname      orderid
-----------  ---------------  -----------
1            Customer NRZBB   10643
1            Customer NRZBB   10692
1            Customer NRZBB   10702
1            Customer NRZBB   10835
1            Customer NRZBB   10952
...
```

```
21        Customer KIDPX  10414
21        Customer KIDPX  10512
21        Customer KIDPX  10581
21        Customer KIDPX  10650
21        Customer KIDPX  10725
22        Customer DTDMN  NULL
23        Customer WVFAF  10408
23        Customer WVFAF  10480
23        Customer WVFAF  10634
23        Customer WVFAF  10763
23        Customer WVFAF  10789
...
56        Customer QNIVZ  10684
56        Customer QNIVZ  10766
56        Customer QNIVZ  10833
56        Customer QNIVZ  10999
56        Customer QNIVZ  11020
57        Customer WVAXS  NULL
58        Customer AHXHT  10322
58        Customer AHXHT  10354
58        Customer AHXHT  10474
58        Customer AHXHT  10502
58        Customer AHXHT  10995
...
91        Customer CCFIZ  10792
91        Customer CCFIZ  10870
91        Customer CCFIZ  10906
91        Customer CCFIZ  10998
91        Customer CCFIZ  11044

(832 row(s) affected)
```

Two customers in the Customers table did not place any orders. Their IDs are 22 and 57. Observe that in the output of the query both customers are returned with NULLs in the attributes from the Orders table. Logically, the rows for these two customers were filtered out by the second phase of the join (filter based on the ON predicate), but the third phase added those as outer rows. Had the join been an inner join, these two rows would not have been returned. These two rows are added to preserve all the rows of the left table.

You can consider two kinds of rows in the result of an outer join in respect to the preserved side—inner rows and outer rows. Inner rows are rows that have matches in the other side based on the ON predicate, and outer rows are rows that don't. An inner join returns only inner rows, while an outer join returns both inner and outer rows.

A common question when using outer joins that is the source of a lot of confusion is whether to specify a predicate in the ON or WHERE clauses of a query. You can see that with respect to rows from the preserved side of an outer join, the filter based on the ON predicate is not final. In other words, the ON predicate does not determine whether the row will show up in the output, only whether it will be matched with rows from the other side. So when you need to express a predicate that is not final—meaning a predicate that determines which rows to match from the nonpreserved side—specify the predicate in the ON clause. When you need a filter to be applied after outer rows are produced, and you want the filter to be final, specify the predicate in the WHERE clause. The WHERE clause is processed after the FROM clause—namely, after all table operators were processed and (in the case of outer joins), after all outer rows were produced. Also, the WHERE clause is final with respect to rows that it filters out, unlike the ON clause.

Suppose that you need to return only customers who did not place any orders, or more technically speaking, you need to return only outer rows. You can use the previous query as your basis, and add a WHERE clause that filters only outer rows. Remember that outer rows are identified by the NULLs in the attributes from the nonpreserved side of the join. So you can filter only the rows where one of the attributes in the nonpreserved side of the join is NULL, like so:

```
SELECT C.custid, C.companyname
FROM Sales.Customers AS C
  LEFT OUTER JOIN Sales.Orders AS O
    ON C.custid = O.custid
WHERE O.orderid IS NULL;
```

This query returns only two rows, with the customers 22 and 57:

```
custid        companyname
-----------   ---------------
22            Customer DTDMN
57            Customer WVAXS

(2 row(s) affected)
```

Notice a couple of important things about this query. Recall the discussions about NULLs earlier in the book: When looking for a NULL you should use the operator IS NULL and not an equality operator, because an equality operator comparing something with a NULL always returns UNKNOWN—even when comparing two NULLs. Also, the choice of which attribute from the nonpreserved side of the join to filter is important. You should choose an attribute that can only have a NULL when the row is an outer row and not otherwise (for example, a NULL originating from the base table). For this purpose, three cases are safe to consider—a primary key column, a join column, and a column defined as NOT NULL. A primary key column cannot be NULL; therefore, a NULL in such a column can only mean that the row is an outer row. If a row has a NULL in the join column, that row is filtered out by the second phase of the join, so a NULL in such a column can only mean that it's an outer row. And obviously a NULL in a column that is defined as NOT NULL can only mean that the row is an outer row.

To practice what you've learned and get a better grasp of outer joins, make sure that you perform the exercises for this chapter.

Beyond the Fundamentals of Outer Joins

This section covers more advanced aspects of outer joins and is provided as optional reading for when you feel very comfortable with the fundamentals of outer joins.

Including Missing Values

You can use outer joins to identify and include missing values when querying data. For example, suppose that you need to query all orders from the Orders table in the TSQLFundamentals2008 database. You need to ensure that you get at least one row in the output for each date in the range January 1, 2006 through December 31, 2008. You don't want to do anything special with dates within the range that have orders. But you do want the output to include the dates with no orders, with NULLs as placeholders in the attributes of the order.

To solve the problem, you can first write a query that returns a sequence of all dates in the requested date range. You can then perform a left outer join between that set and the Orders table. This way the result also includes the missing order dates.

To produce a sequence of dates in a given range, I usually use an auxiliary table of numbers. I create a table called Nums with a column called n, and populate it with a sequence of integers (1, 2, 3, and so on). I find that an auxiliary table of numbers is an extremely powerful general-purpose tool that I end up using to solve many problems. You need to create it only once in the database and populate it with as many numbers as you might need. Run the code in Listing 3-1 to create the Nums table in the dbo schema and populate it with 100,000 rows:

LISTING 3-1 Code to Create and Populate the Auxiliary Table Nums

```
SET NOCOUNT ON;
USE TSQLFundamentals2008;
IF OBJECT_ID('dbo.Nums', 'U') IS NOT NULL DROP TABLE dbo.Nums;
CREATE TABLE dbo.Nums(n INT NOT NULL PRIMARY KEY);

DECLARE @i AS INT = 1;
/*
Note:
The ability to declare and initialize variables in one statement
is new in Microsoft SQL Server 2008.
In earlier versions use separate DECLARE and SET statements:

DECLARE @i AS INT;
SET @i = 1;
*/
BEGIN TRAN
  WHILE @i <= 100000
  BEGIN
    INSERT INTO dbo.Nums VALUES(@i);
    SET @i = @i + 1;
  END
COMMIT TRAN
SET NOCOUNT OFF;
```

> **Note** Don't worry if you don't yet understand some parts of the code, such as using variables and loops—those are explained later in the book. For now, it's enough to understand what this code is supposed to do; how it does it is not the focus of discussion here. But in case you're curious and cannot resist, you can find details in Chapter 10, "Programmable Objects." I should point out, however, that declaring and initializing variables in the same statement is new in SQL Server 2008 as the block comment that appears in the code explains. If you're working with an earlier version, you should use separate *DECLARE* and *SET* statements.

As the first step in the solution, you need to produce a sequence of all dates in the requested range. You can achieve this by querying the Nums table, and filtering as many numbers as the number of days in the requested date range. You can use the *DATEDIFF* function to calculate that number. By adding $n - 1$ days to the starting point of the date range (January 1, 2006) you get the actual date in the sequence. Here's the solution query:

```
SELECT DATEADD(day, n-1, '20060101') AS orderdate
FROM dbo.Nums
WHERE n <= DATEDIFF(day, '20060101', '20081231') + 1
ORDER BY orderdate;
```

This query returns a sequence of all dates in the range January 1, 2006 through December 31, 2008, as shown here in abbreviated form:

```
orderdate
-----------------------
2006-01-01 00:00:00.000
2006-01-02 00:00:00.000
2006-01-03 00:00:00.000
2006-01-04 00:00:00.000
2006-01-05 00:00:00.000
...
2008-12-27 00:00:00.000
2008-12-28 00:00:00.000
2008-12-29 00:00:00.000
2008-12-30 00:00:00.000
2008-12-31 00:00:00.000

(1096 row(s) affected)
```

The next step is to extend the previous query, adding a left outer join between Nums and the Orders tables. The join condition compares the order date produced from the Nums table using the expression DATEADD(day, Nums.n - 1, '20060101') and the orderdate from the Orders table like so:

```
SELECT DATEADD(day, Nums.n - 1, '20060101') AS orderdate,
  O.orderid, O.custid, O.empid
FROM dbo.Nums
  LEFT OUTER JOIN Sales.Orders AS O
    ON DATEADD(day, Nums.n - 1, '20060101') = O.orderdate
WHERE Nums.n <= DATEDIFF(day, '20060101', '20081231') + 1
ORDER BY orderdate;
```

This query produces the following output, shown here in abbreviated form:

```
orderdate                   orderid      custid       empid
--------------------------  -----------  -----------  -----------
2006-01-01 00:00:00.000     NULL         NULL         NULL
2006-01-02 00:00:00.000     NULL         NULL         NULL
2006-01-03 00:00:00.000     NULL         NULL         NULL
2006-01-04 00:00:00.000     NULL         NULL         NULL
2006-01-05 00:00:00.000     NULL         NULL         NULL
...
2006-06-29 00:00:00.000     NULL         NULL         NULL
2006-06-30 00:00:00.000     NULL         NULL         NULL
2006-07-01 00:00:00.000     NULL         NULL         NULL
2006-07-02 00:00:00.000     NULL         NULL         NULL
2006-07-03 00:00:00.000     NULL         NULL         NULL
2006-07-04 00:00:00.000     10248        85           5
2006-07-05 00:00:00.000     10249        79           6
2006-07-06 00:00:00.000     NULL         NULL         NULL
2006-07-07 00:00:00.000     NULL         NULL         NULL
2006-07-08 00:00:00.000     10250        34           4
2006-07-08 00:00:00.000     10251        84           3
2006-07-09 00:00:00.000     10252        76           4
2006-07-10 00:00:00.000     10253        34           3
2006-07-11 00:00:00.000     10254        14           5
2006-07-12 00:00:00.000     10255        68           9
2006-07-13 00:00:00.000     NULL         NULL         NULL
2006-07-14 00:00:00.000     NULL         NULL         NULL
2006-07-15 00:00:00.000     10256        88           3
2006-07-16 00:00:00.000     10257        35           4
...
2008-12-27 00:00:00.000     NULL         NULL         NULL
2008-12-28 00:00:00.000     NULL         NULL         NULL
2008-12-29 00:00:00.000     NULL         NULL         NULL
2008-12-30 00:00:00.000     NULL         NULL         NULL
2008-12-31 00:00:00.000     NULL         NULL         NULL

(1446 row(s) affected)
```

Order dates that do not appear in the Orders table appear in the output of the query with NULLs in the order attributes.

Filtering Attributes from the Nonpreserved Side of an Outer Join

When you need to review code involving outer joins to look for logical bugs, one of the things you should examine is the WHERE clause. If the predicate in the WHERE clause refers to an attribute from the nonpreserved side of the join using an expression in the form <attribute> <operator> <value>, it's usually an indication of a bug. This is because attributes from the nonpreserved side of the join are NULLs in outer rows, and an expression in the form NULL <operator> <value> yields UNKNOWN (unless it's the IS NULL operator explicitly looking for NULLs). Recall that a WHERE clause filters UNKNOWN out. Such a predicate in the WHERE clause causes all outer rows to be filtered out, effectively nullifying the outer join. In other words, it's as if the join type logically becomes an inner join. So the programmer either made a mistake in the choice of the join type, or made a mistake in the predicate. If this is not clear yet, the following example might help. Consider the following query:

```
SELECT C.custid, C.companyname, O.orderid, O.orderdate
FROM Sales.Customers AS C
  LEFT OUTER JOIN Sales.Orders AS O
    ON C.custid = O.custid
WHERE O.orderdate >= '20070101';
```

The query performs a left outer join between the Customers and Orders tables. Prior to applying the WHERE filter, the join operator returns inner rows for customers who placed orders, and outer rows for customers who didn't place orders, with NULLs in the order attributes. The predicate O.orderdate >= '20070101' in the WHERE clause evaluates to UNKNOWN for all outer rows because those have a NULL in the O.orderdate attribute. All outer rows are eliminated by the WHERE filter, as you can see in the output of the query, shown here in abbreviated form:

```
custid      companyname         orderid      orderdate
----------- ------------------  -----------  -----------------------
19          Customer RFNQC      10400        2007-01-01 00:00:00.000
65          Customer NYUHS      10401        2007-01-01 00:00:00.000
20          Customer THHDP      10402        2007-01-02 00:00:00.000
20          Customer THHDP      10403        2007-01-03 00:00:00.000
49          Customer CQRAA      10404        2007-01-03 00:00:00.000
...
58          Customer AHXHT      11073        2008-05-05 00:00:00.000
73          Customer JMIKW      11074        2008-05-06 00:00:00.000
68          Customer CCKOT      11075        2008-05-06 00:00:00.000
9           Customer RTXGC      11076        2008-05-06 00:00:00.000
65          Customer NYUHS      11077        2008-05-06 00:00:00.000

(678 row(s) affected)
```

This means that the use of an outer join here was futile. The programmer either made a mistake in using an outer join or made a mistake in the WHERE predicate.

Using Outer Joins in a Multi-Table Join

Recall the discussion about all-at-once operations in Chapter 2, "Single Table Queries." The concept means that all expressions that appear in the same logical query processing phase are logically evaluated at the same point in time. However, this concept is not applicable to the processing of table operators in the FROM phase. Table operators are logically evaluated from left to right. Rearranging the order in which outer joins are processed might result in different output, so you cannot rearrange them at will.

Some interesting logical bugs have to do with the logical order in which outer joins are processed. For example, a common logical bug involving outer joins could be considered a variation of the bug in the previous section. Suppose that you write a multi-table join query with an outer join between two tables, followed by an inner join with a third table. If the predicate in the inner join's ON clause compares an attribute from the nonpreserved side of the outer join and an attribute from the third table, all outer rows are filtered out. Remember that outer rows have NULLs in the attributes from the nonpreserved side of the join, and comparing a NULL with anything yields UNKNOWN, and UNKNOWN is filtered out by the ON filter. In other words, such a predicate would nullify the outer join and logically it would be as if you specified an inner join. For example, consider the following query:

```
SELECT C.custid, O.orderid, OD.productid, OD.qty
FROM Sales.Customers AS C
  LEFT OUTER JOIN Sales.Orders AS O
    ON C.custid = O.custid
  JOIN Sales.OrderDetails AS OD
    ON O.orderid = OD.orderid;
```

The first join is an outer join returning customers and their orders and also customers who did not place any orders. The outer rows representing customers with no orders have NULLs in the order attributes. The second join matches order lines from the OrderDetails table with rows from the result of the first join based on the predicate O.orderid = OD.orderid; however, in the rows representing customers with no orders, the O.orderid attribute is NULL. Therefore, the predicate evaluates to UNKNOWN and those rows are filtered out. The output shown here in abbreviated form doesn't contain the customers 22 and 57, the two customers who did not place orders:

```
custid       orderid       productid    qty
-----------  -----------   -----------  ------
85           10248         11           12
85           10248         42           10
85           10248         72           5
79           10249         14           9
79           10249         51           40
...
65           11077         64           2
65           11077         66           1
65           11077         73           2
65           11077         75           4
65           11077         77           2

(2155 row(s) affected)
```

To generalize the problem: outer rows are nullified whenever any kind of outer join (left, right, or full) is followed by a subsequent inner join or right outer join. That's assuming, of course, that the join condition compares the NULLs from the left side with something from the right side.

You have several ways to get around the problem if you want to return customers with no orders in the output. One option is to use a left outer join in the second join as well:

```
SELECT C.custid, O.orderid, OD.productid, OD.qty
FROM Sales.Customers AS C
  LEFT OUTER JOIN Sales.Orders AS O
    ON C.custid = O.custid
  LEFT OUTER JOIN Sales.OrderDetails AS OD
    ON O.orderid = OD.orderid;
```

This way, the outer rows produced by the first join aren't filtered out, as you can see in the output shown here in abbreviated form:

```
custid       orderid      productid    qty
-----------  -----------  -----------  ------
85           10248        11           12
85           10248        42           10
85           10248        72           5
79           10249        14           9
79           10249        51           40
...
65           11077        64           2
65           11077        66           1
65           11077        73           2
65           11077        75           4
65           11077        77           2
22           NULL         NULL         NULL
57           NULL         NULL         NULL

(2157 row(s) affected)
```

A second option is to first join Orders and OrderDetails using an inner join, and then join to the Customers table using a right outer join:

```
SELECT C.custid, O.orderid, OD.productid, OD.qty
FROM Sales.Orders AS O
  JOIN Sales.OrderDetails AS OD
    ON O.orderid = OD.orderid
  RIGHT OUTER JOIN Sales.Customers AS C
    ON O.custid = C.custid;
```

This way, the outer rows are produced by the last join, and are not filtered out.

A third option is to use parentheses to make the inner join between Orders and OrderDetails become an independent logical phase. This way you can apply a left outer join between the Customers table and the result of the inner join between Orders and OrderDetails. The query would look like this:

```
SELECT C.custid, O.orderid, OD.productid, OD.qty
FROM Sales.Customers AS C
  LEFT OUTER JOIN
```

```
    (Sales.Orders AS O
       JOIN Sales.OrderDetails AS OD
          ON O.orderid = OD.orderid)
  ON C.custid = O.custid;
```

Using the COUNT Aggregate with Outer Joins

Another common logical bug involves using COUNT with outer joins. When you group the result of an outer join and use the *COUNT(*)* aggregate, the aggregate takes into consideration both inner rows and outer rows because it counts rows regardless of their contents. Usually, you're not supposed to take outer rows into consideration for the purposes of counting. For example, the following query is supposed to return the count of orders for each customer:

```
SELECT C.custid, COUNT(*) AS numorders
FROM Sales.Customers AS C
  LEFT OUTER JOIN Sales.Orders AS O
    ON C.custid = O.custid
GROUP BY C.custid;
```

However, the *COUNT(*)* aggregate counts rows regardless of their meaning or contents, and customers who did not place orders—like 22 and 57—each have an outer row in the result of the join. As you can see in the output of the query shown here in abbreviated form, both 22 and 57 show up with a count of 1, while the number of orders they place is actually 0:

```
custid      numorders
----------- -----------
1           6
2           4
3           7
4           13
5           18
...
22          1
...
57          1
...
87          15
88          9
89          14
90          7
91          7

(91 row(s) affected)
```

The *COUNT(*)* aggregate function cannot detect whether a row really represents an order. To fix the problem you should use COUNT(<column>) instead of *COUNT(*)*, and provide a column from the nonpreserved side of the join. This way, the *COUNT()* aggregate ignores outer rows because they have a NULL in that column. Remember to use a column that can only be NULL in case the row is an outer row—for example, the primary key column orderid:

```
SELECT C.custid, COUNT(O.orderid) AS numorders
FROM Sales.Customers AS C
  LEFT OUTER JOIN Sales.Orders AS O
    ON C.custid = O.custid
GROUP BY C.custid;
```

Notice in the output shown here in abbreviated form that the customers 22 and 57 now show up with a count of 0:

```
custid      numorders
----------- -----------
1           6
2           4
3           7
4           13
5           18
...
22          0
...
57          0
...
87          15
88          9
89          14
90          7
91          7

(91 row(s) affected)
```

Conclusion

This chapter covered the join table operator. It described the logical query processing phases involved in the three fundamental types of joins—cross, inner, and outer. The chapter also covered further join examples including composite joins, non-equi joins, and multi-table joins. The chapter concluded with an optional reading section covering more advanced aspects of outer joins. To practice what you've learned, go over the exercises for this chapter.

Exercises

This section provides exercises to help you familiarize yourself with the subjects discussed in this chapter. All exercises involve querying objects in the TSQLFundamentals2008 database.

1-1

Run the following code to create the dbo.Nums auxiliary table in the TSQLFundamentals2008 database:

```
SET NOCOUNT ON;
USE TSQLFundamentals2008;
IF OBJECT_ID('dbo.Nums', 'U') IS NOT NULL DROP TABLE dbo.Nums;
CREATE TABLE dbo.Nums(n INT NOT NULL PRIMARY KEY);

DECLARE @i AS INT = 1;
BEGIN TRAN
  WHILE @i <= 100000
  BEGIN
    INSERT INTO dbo.Nums VALUES(@i);
    SET @i = @i + 1;
  END
COMMIT TRAN
SET NOCOUNT OFF;
```

1-2

Write a query that generates five copies out of each employee row.

Tables involved: HR.Employees, and dbo.Nums tables.

Desired output:

```
empid        firstname   lastname               n
-----------  ----------  ---------------------  -----------
1            Sara        Davis                  1
2            Don         Funk                   1
3            Judy        Lew                    1
4            Yael        Peled                  1
5            Sven        Buck                   1
6            Paul        Suurs                  1
7            Russell     King                   1
8            Maria       Cameron                1
9            Zoya        Dolgopyatova           1
1            Sara        Davis                  2
2            Don         Funk                   2
3            Judy        Lew                    2
4            Yael        Peled                  2
5            Sven        Buck                   2
6            Paul        Suurs                  2
7            Russell     King                   2
8            Maria       Cameron                2
9            Zoya        Dolgopyatova           2
1            Sara        Davis                  3
2            Don         Funk                   3
3            Judy        Lew                    3
4            Yael        Peled                  3
5            Sven        Buck                   3
6            Paul        Suurs                  3
```

```
7          Russell   King            3
8          Maria     Cameron         3
9          Zoya      Dolgopyatova     3
1          Sara      Davis           4
2          Don       Funk            4
3          Judy      Lew             4
4          Yael      Peled           4
5          Sven      Buck            4
6          Paul      Suurs           4
7          Russell   King            4
8          Maria     Cameron         4
9          Zoya      Dolgopyatova     4
1          Sara      Davis           5
2          Don       Funk            5
3          Judy      Lew             5
4          Yael      Peled           5
5          Sven      Buck            5
6          Paul      Suurs           5
7          Russell   King            5
8          Maria     Cameron         5
9          Zoya      Dolgopyatova     5

(45 row(s) affected)
```

1-3 (Optional, Advanced)

Write a query that returns a row for each employee and day in the range June 12, 2009 –
June 16, 2009.

Tables involved: HR.Employees, and dbo.Nums tables.

Desired output:

```
empid       dt
----------- -----------------------
1           2009-06-12 00:00:00.000
1           2009-06-13 00:00:00.000
1           2009-06-14 00:00:00.000
1           2009-06-15 00:00:00.000
1           2009-06-16 00:00:00.000
2           2009-06-12 00:00:00.000
2           2009-06-13 00:00:00.000
2           2009-06-14 00:00:00.000
2           2009-06-15 00:00:00.000
2           2009-06-16 00:00:00.000
3           2009-06-12 00:00:00.000
3           2009-06-13 00:00:00.000
3           2009-06-14 00:00:00.000
3           2009-06-15 00:00:00.000
3           2009-06-16 00:00:00.000
4           2009-06-12 00:00:00.000
4           2009-06-13 00:00:00.000
4           2009-06-14 00:00:00.000
4           2009-06-15 00:00:00.000
4           2009-06-16 00:00:00.000
5           2009-06-12 00:00:00.000
5           2009-06-13 00:00:00.000
```

```
5              2009-06-14 00:00:00.000
5              2009-06-15 00:00:00.000
5              2009-06-16 00:00:00.000
6              2009-06-12 00:00:00.000
6              2009-06-13 00:00:00.000
6              2009-06-14 00:00:00.000
6              2009-06-15 00:00:00.000
6              2009-06-16 00:00:00.000
7              2009-06-12 00:00:00.000
7              2009-06-13 00:00:00.000
7              2009-06-14 00:00:00.000
7              2009-06-15 00:00:00.000
7              2009-06-16 00:00:00.000
8              2009-06-12 00:00:00.000
8              2009-06-13 00:00:00.000
8              2009-06-14 00:00:00.000
8              2009-06-15 00:00:00.000
8              2009-06-16 00:00:00.000
9              2009-06-12 00:00:00.000
9              2009-06-13 00:00:00.000
9              2009-06-14 00:00:00.000
9              2009-06-15 00:00:00.000
9              2009-06-16 00:00:00.000

(45 row(s) affected)
```

2

Return U.S. customers, and for each customer return the total number of orders and total quantities.

Tables involved: Sales.Customers, Sales.Orders, and Sales.OrderDetails tables.

Desired output:

```
custid       numorders    totalqty
-----------  -----------  -----------
32           11           345
36           5            122
43           2            20
45           4            181
48           8            134
55           10           603
65           18           1383
71           31           4958
75           9            327
77           4            46
78           3            59
82           3            89
89           14           1063

(13 row(s) affected)
```

3

Return customers and their orders including customers who placed no orders.
Tables involved: Sales.Customers, and Sales.Orders tables.
Desired output (abbreviated):

```
custid       companyname      orderid      orderdate
-----------  ---------------  -----------  ------------------------
85           Customer ENQZT   10248        2006-07-04 00:00:00.000
79           Customer FAPSM   10249        2006-07-05 00:00:00.000
34           Customer IBVRG   10250        2006-07-08 00:00:00.000
84           Customer NRCSK   10251        2006-07-08 00:00:00.000
...
73           Customer JMIKW   11074        2008-05-06 00:00:00.000
68           Customer CCKOT   11075        2008-05-06 00:00:00.000
9            Customer RTXGC   11076        2008-05-06 00:00:00.000
65           Customer NYUHS   11077        2008-05-06 00:00:00.000
22           Customer DTDMN   NULL         NULL
57           Customer WVAXS   NULL         NULL

(832 row(s) affected)
```

4

Return customers who placed no orders.
Tables involved: Sales.Customers, and Sales.Orders tables.
Desired output:

```
custid       companyname
-----------  ---------------
22           Customer DTDMN
57           Customer WVAXS

(2 row(s) affected)
```

5

Return customers with orders placed on Feb 12, 2007 along with their orders.
Tables involved: Sales.Customers, and Sales.Orders tables.
Desired output:

```
custid       companyname      orderid      orderdate
-----------  ---------------  -----------  ------------------------
66           Customer LHANT   10443        2007-02-12 00:00:00.000
5            Customer HGVLZ   10444        2007-02-12 00:00:00.000

(2 row(s) affected)
```

6 (Optional, Advanced)

Return customers with orders placed on Feb 12, 2007 along with their orders. Also return customers who didn't place orders on Feb 12, 2007.

Tables involved: Sales.Customers, and Sales.Orders tables.

Desired output (abbreviated):

```
custid      companyname        orderid      orderdate
----------- ------------------ ----------- -----------------------
72          Customer AHPOP     NULL         NULL
58          Customer AHXHT     NULL         NULL
25          Customer AZJED     NULL         NULL
18          Customer BSVAR     NULL         NULL
91          Customer CCFIZ     NULL         NULL
...
33          Customer FVXPQ     NULL         NULL
53          Customer GCJSG     NULL         NULL
39          Customer GLLAG     NULL         NULL
16          Customer GYBBY     NULL         NULL
4           Customer HFBZG     NULL         NULL
5           Customer HGVLZ     10444        2007-02-12 00:00:00.000
42          Customer IAIJK     NULL         NULL
34          Customer IBVRG     NULL         NULL
63          Customer IRRVL     NULL         NULL
73          Customer JMIKW     NULL         NULL
15          Customer JUWXK     NULL         NULL
...
21          Customer KIDPX     NULL         NULL
30          Customer KSLQF     NULL         NULL
55          Customer KZQZT     NULL         NULL
71          Customer LCOUJ     NULL         NULL
77          Customer LCYBZ     NULL         NULL
66          Customer LHANT     10443        2007-02-12 00:00:00.000
38          Customer LJUCA     NULL         NULL
59          Customer LOLJO     NULL         NULL
36          Customer LVJSO     NULL         NULL
64          Customer LWGMD     NULL         NULL
29          Customer MDLWA     NULL         NULL
...

(91 row(s) affected)
```

7 (Optional, Advanced)

Return all customers, and for each return a Yes/No value depending on whether the customer placed an order on Feb 12, 2007.

Tables involved: Sales.Customers, and Sales.Orders tables.

Desired output (abbreviated):

```
custid      companyname        HasOrderOn20070212
----------- ------------------ ------------------
1           Customer NRZBB     No
2           Customer MLTDN     No
3           Customer KBUDE     No
```

4	Customer	HFBZG	No
5	Customer	HGVLZ	Yes
6	Customer	XHXJV	No
7	Customer	QXVLA	No
8	Customer	QUHWH	No
9	Customer	RTXGC	No
10	Customer	EEALV	No

...

```
(91 row(s) affected)
```

Solutions

This section provides solutions to the exercises for this chapter.

1-2

Producing multiple copies of rows can be achieved with a fundamental technique that utilizes a cross join. If you need to produce five copies out of each employee row, you need to perform a cross join between the Employees table and a table that has five rows; alternatively, you can perform a cross join between Employees and a table that has more than five rows, but filter only five from that table in the WHERE clause. The Nums table is very convenient for this purpose. Simply cross Employees and Nums, and filter from Nums as many rows as the number of requested copies (five in this case). Here's the solution query:

```
SELECT E.empid, E.FirstName, E.LastName, Nums.n
FROM HR.Employees AS E
  CROSS JOIN dbo.Nums
WHERE Nums.n <= 5
ORDER BY n, empid;
```

1-3

This exercise is an extension of the previous exercise. Instead of being asked to produce a predetermined constant number of copies out of each employee row, you are asked to produce a copy for each day in a certain date range. So here you need to calculate the number of days in the requested date range using the *DATEDIFF* function, and refer to the result of that expression in the query's WHERE clause instead of referring to a constant. To produce the dates, simply add *n* - 1 days to the date that starts the requested range. Here's the solution query:

```
SELECT E.empid,
  DATEADD(day, D.n - 1, '20090612') AS dt
FROM HR.Employees AS E
  CROSS JOIN dbo.Nums AS D
WHERE D.n <= DATEDIFF(day, '20090612', '20090616') + 1
ORDER BY empid, dt;
```

The *DATEDIFF* function returns 4 because there is a four-day difference between June 12, 2009 and June 16, 2009. Add 1 to the result, and you get 5 for the five days in the range. So the WHERE clause filters five rows from Nums where *n* is smaller than or equal to 5. By adding *n* - 1 days to June 12, 2009, you get all dates in the range June 12, 2009 and June 16, 2009.

2

This exercise requires you to write a query that joins three tables: Customers, Orders, and OrderDetails. The query should filter in the WHERE clause only rows where the customer's country is USA. Because you are asked to return aggregates per customer, the query should group the rows by customer ID. You need to resolve a tricky issue here to return the right number of orders for each customer. Because of the join between Orders and OrderDetails, you don't get only one row per order—you get one row per order line. So if you use the *COUNT(*)* function in the SELECT list, you get back the number of order lines for each customer and not the number of orders. To resolve this issue, you need to take each order into consideration only once. You can do this by using COUNT(DISTINCT O.orderid) instead of *COUNT(*)*. The total quantities don't create any special issues because the quantity is associated with the order line and not the order. Here's the solution query:

```
SELECT C.custid, COUNT(DISTINCT O.orderid) AS numorders, SUM(OD.qty) AS totalqty
FROM Sales.Customers AS C
  JOIN Sales.Orders AS O
    ON O.custid = C.custid
  JOIN Sales.OrderDetails AS OD
    ON OD.orderid = O.orderid
WHERE C.country = N'USA'
GROUP BY C.custid;
```

3

To get both customers who placed orders and customers who didn't place orders in the result, you need to use an outer join like so:

```
SELECT C.custid, C.companyname, O.orderid, O.orderdate
FROM Sales.Customers AS C
  LEFT JOIN Sales.Orders AS O
    ON O.custid = C.custid;
```

This query returns 832 rows (including the customers 22 and 57, who didn't place orders). An inner join between the tables would return only 830 rows without these customers.

4

This exercise is an extension of the previous one. To return only customers who didn't place orders, you need to add a WHERE clause to the query that filters only outer rows; namely, rows that represent customers with no orders. Outer rows have NULLs in the attributes from the nonpreserved side of the join (Orders). But to make sure that the NULL is a placeholder for an outer row and not a NULL that originated from the table, it is recommended that you refer to an attribute that is the primary key, or the join column, or one defined as not allowing NULLs. Here's the solution query referring to the primary key of the Orders table in the WHERE clause:

```
SELECT C.custid, C.companyname
FROM Sales.Customers AS C
  LEFT JOIN Sales.Orders AS O
    ON O.custid = C.custid
WHERE O.orderid IS NULL;
```

This query returns only two rows for the customers 22 and 57, who didn't place orders.

5

This exercise involves writing a query that performs an inner join between Customers and Orders, and filters only rows where the order date is February 12, 2007:

```
SELECT C.custid, C.companyname, O.orderid, O.orderdate
FROM Sales.Customers AS C
  JOIN Sales.Orders AS O
    ON O.custid = C.custid
WHERE O.orderdate = '20070212';
```

The WHERE clause filtered out Customers who didn't place orders on February 12, 2007, but that was the request.

6

This exercise builds on the previous one. The trick here is to realize two things. First, you need an outer join because you are supposed to return customers who do not meet a certain criteria. Second, the filter on the order date must appear in the ON clause and not the WHERE clause. Remember that the WHERE filter is applied after outer rows are added and is final. Your goal is to match orders to customers only if the order was placed by the customer and on February 12, 2007. You still want to get customers who didn't place orders on that date in the output; in other words, the filter on the order date should only determine matches and not be considered final in regards to the customer rows. Hence the ON clause should match customers and orders based on both an equality between the customer's customer ID and the order's customer ID, and the order date being February 12, 2007. Here's the solution query:

```
SELECT C.custid, C.companyname, O.orderid, O.orderdate
FROM Sales.Customers AS C
  LEFT JOIN Sales.Orders AS O
    ON O.custid = C.custid
    AND O.orderdate = '20070212';
```

7

This exercise is an extension of the previous exercise. Here, instead of returning matching orders, you just need to return a Yes/No value indicating whether there is a matching order. Remember that in an outer join a nonmatch is identified as an outer row with NULLs in the attributes of the nonpreserved side. So you can use a simple CASE expression that checks whether the current row is an outer one, in which case it returns 'Yes'; otherwise, it returns 'No'. Because technically you can have more than one match per customer, you should add a DISTINCT clause to the SELECT list. This way you get only one row back for each customer. Here's the solution query:

```
SELECT DISTINCT C.custid, C.companyname,
  CASE WHEN O.orderid IS NOT NULL THEN 'Yes' ELSE 'No' END AS [HasOrderOn20070212]
FROM Sales.Customers AS C
  LEFT JOIN Sales.Orders AS O
    ON O.custid = C.custid
    AND O.orderdate = '20070212';
```

Chapter 4
Subqueries

SQL supports writing queries within queries, or *nesting* queries. The outermost query is a query whose result set is returned to the caller and is known as the outer query. The inner query is a query whose result is used by the outer query and is known as a subquery. The inner query acts in place of an expression that is based on constants or variables and is evaluated at run time. Unlike using constants in your expressions, the result of a subquery may change because of changes in the queried tables. By using subqueries you avoid the need for separate steps in your solutions that store intermediate query results in variables.

A subquery can be either self-contained or correlated. A self-contained subquery has no dependency on the outer query that it belongs to, while a correlated subquery does. A subquery can be single-valued, multi-valued, or table-valued. That is, a subquery can return a single value (scalar), multiple values, or a whole table result.

This chapter will focus on subqueries that return a single value (scalar subqueries) and subqueries that return multiple values (multi-valued subqueries). I'll cover subqueries that return a whole table (table subqueries) later in the book.

Both self-contained and correlated subqueries can return a scalar or multiple values. I'll first describe self-contained subqueries and demonstrate both scalar and multi-valued examples, and explicitly identify those as scalar or multi-valued subqueries. Then I'll describe correlated subqueries, but I won't explicitly identify them as scalar or multi-valued ones, assuming you already understand the difference.

Once again, exercises at the end of the chapter can help you practice what you've learned.

Self-Contained Subqueries

Every subquery has an outer query that it belongs to. Self-contained subqueries are subqueries that are independent of the outer query that they belong to. Self-contained subqueries are very convenient to debug because you can always highlight the subquery code, run it, and ensure that it does what it's supposed to do. Logically, it's as if the subquery code is evaluated only once before the outer query is evaluated, and then the outer query uses the result of the subquery. The following sections take a look at some concrete examples of self-contained subqueries.

Self-Contained Scalar Subquery Examples

A scalar subquery is a subquery that returns a single value—regardless of whether it is self-contained. Such a subquery can appear anywhere in the outer query where a single-valued expression can appear (WHERE, SELECT, and so on).

For example, suppose that you need to query the Orders table in the TSQLFundamentals2008 database, and return information about the order with the maximum order ID in the table. You could accomplish the task by using a variable. The code can retrieve the maximum order ID from the Orders table and store the result in a variable. Then the code can query the Orders table and filter the order where the order ID is equal to the value stored in the variable. The following code demonstrates this technique:

```
USE TSQLFundamentals2008;

DECLARE @maxid AS INT = (SELECT MAX(orderid)
                         FROM Sales.Orders);

SELECT orderid, orderdate, empid, custid
FROM Sales.Orders
WHERE orderid = @maxid;
```

 Note Remember that the ability to declare and initialize variables using the same statement is new in Microsoft SQL Server 2008. In earlier versions, use separate *DECLARE* and *SET* statements.

This query returns the following output:

```
orderid      orderdate                   empid        custid
------------ --------------------------- ------------ -----------
11077        2008-05-06 00:00:00.000     1            65
```

You can substitute the technique that uses a variable with an embedded subquery. You achieve this by substituting the reference to the variable with a scalar self-contained subquery that returns the maximum order ID. This way your solution has a single query instead of this two-step process:

```
SELECT orderid, orderdate, empid, custid
FROM Sales.Orders
WHERE orderid = (SELECT MAX(O.orderid)
                 FROM Sales.Orders AS O);
```

For a scalar subquery to be valid, it must return no more than one value. If a scalar subquery can return more than one value, it may fail at runtime. The following query happens to run without failure:

```
SELECT orderid
FROM Sales.Orders
WHERE empid =
  (SELECT E.empid
   FROM HR.Employees AS E
   WHERE E.lastname LIKE N'B%');
```

The purpose of this query is to return the order IDs of orders placed by any employee whose last name starts with the letter B. The subquery returns employee IDs of all employees whose last names start with the letter B, and the outer query returns order IDs of orders where the employee ID is equal to the result of the subquery. Because an equality operator expects single-valued expressions from both sides, the subquery is considered scalar. Because the subquery can potentially return more than one value, the choices of using an equality operator and a scalar subquery here are wrong. If the subquery returns more than one value, the query fails.

This query happens to run without failure because currently the Employees table contains only one employee whose last name starts with B (Sven Buck with employee ID 5). This query returns the following output, shown here in abbreviated form:

```
orderid
-----------
10248
10254
10269
10297
10320
...
10874
10899
10922
10954
11043

(42 row(s) affected)
```

Of course, if the subquery returns more than one value, the query fails. For example, try running the query with employees whose last names start with D:

```
SELECT orderid
FROM Sales.Orders
WHERE empid =
  (SELECT E.empid
   FROM HR.Employees AS E
   WHERE E.lastname LIKE N'D%');
```

Apparently two employees have a last name starting with D (Sara Davis and Zoya Dolgopyatova). Therefore, the query fails at run time with the following error:

```
Msg 512, Level 16, State 1, Line 1
Subquery returned more than 1 value. This is not permitted when the subquery follows =, !=,
<, <= , >, >= or when the subquery is used as an expression.
```

If a scalar subquery returns no values, it is converted to NULL. Recall that a comparison with a NULL yields UNKNOWN and that query filters do not return a row for which the filter expression evaluates to UNKNOWN. For example, the Employees table currently has no employees whose last names start with A; therefore, the following query returns an empty set:

```
SELECT orderid
FROM Sales.Orders
WHERE empid =
  (SELECT E.empid
   FROM HR.Employees AS E
   WHERE E.lastname LIKE N'A%');
```

Self-Contained Multi-Valued Subquery Examples

A multi-valued subquery is a subquery that returns multiple values as a single column, regardless of whether the subquery is self-contained. Some predicates, such as the IN predicate, operate on a multi-valued subquery. The form of the IN predicate is:

<scalar_expression> IN (<multi-valued subquery>)

The predicate evaluates to TRUE if scalar_expression is equal to any of the values returned by the subquery. Recall the last request discussed in the previous section—return order IDs of orders that were handled by employees with a last name starting with a certain letter. Because more than one employee can have a last name starting with the same letter, this request should be handled with the IN predicate and a multi-valued subquery, and not with an equality operator and a scalar subquery. For example, the following query returns order IDs of orders placed by employees with a last name starting with D:

```
SELECT orderid
FROM Sales.Orders
```

```
WHERE empid IN
  (SELECT E.empid
   FROM HR.Employees AS E
   WHERE E.lastname LIKE N'D%');
```

Using the IN predicate, this query is valid with any number of values returned—0, 1, or more. This query returns the following output, shown here in abbreviated form:

```
orderid
-----------
10258
10270
10275
10285
10292
...
10978
11016
11017
11022
11058

(166 row(s) affected)
```

You might wonder why you wouldn't implement this task by using a join instead of subqueries, like so:

```
SELECT O.orderid
FROM HR.Employees AS E
  JOIN Sales.Orders AS O
    ON E.empid = O.empid
WHERE E.lastname LIKE N'D%';
```

Similarly, you are likely to stumble into many other querying problems that you can solve with either subqueries or joins. In my experience there's no reliable rule of thumb that says that a subquery is better than a join. In some cases, the database engine interprets both types of queries the same way. In some cases, joins perform better than subqueries; and in some cases, the opposite is true. My approach is to first write the solution query for the given task in an intuitive form, and if performance is not satisfactory, one of my tuning approaches is to try query revisions. Such query revisions may include using joins instead of subqueries or using subqueries instead of joins.

As another example of using multi-valued subqueries, suppose that you need to write a query that returns orders placed by customers from the United States. You can write a query against the Orders table returning orders where the customer ID is in (the set of customer IDs of customers from the USA). You can implement the last part in a self-contained, multi-valued subquery. Here's the complete solution query:

```
SELECT custid, orderid, orderdate, empid
FROM Sales.Orders
```

```
WHERE custid IN
  (SELECT C.custid
   FROM Sales.Customers AS C
   WHERE C.country = N'USA');
```

This query returns the following output, shown here in abbreviated form:

```
custid       orderid      orderdate                   empid
-----------  -----------  --------------------------  -----------
65           10262        2006-07-22 00:00:00.000     8
89           10269        2006-07-31 00:00:00.000     5
75           10271        2006-08-01 00:00:00.000     6
65           10272        2006-08-02 00:00:00.000     6
65           10294        2006-08-30 00:00:00.000     4
...
32           11040        2008-04-22 00:00:00.000     4
32           11061        2008-04-30 00:00:00.000     4
71           11064        2008-05-01 00:00:00.000     1
89           11066        2008-05-01 00:00:00.000     7
65           11077        2008-05-06 00:00:00.000     1

(122 row(s) affected)
```

As with any other predicate, you can negate the IN predicate with the NOT logical operator. For example, the following query returns customers who did not place any orders:

```
SELECT custid, companyname
FROM Sales.Customers
WHERE custid NOT IN
  (SELECT O.custid
   FROM Sales.Orders AS O);
```

Note that to follow best practices the subquery should be qualified to exclude NULLs. Here, to keep the example simple, I didn't exclude NULLs , but later in the chapter, in the section "NULL Trouble," I explain this recommendation.

The self-contained, multi-valued subquery returns all customer IDs that appear in the Orders table. Naturally, only IDs of customers who did place orders appear in the Orders table. The outer query returns customers from the Customers table where the customer ID is not in the set of values returned by the subquery—in other words, customers who did not place orders. This query returns the following output:

```
custid       companyname
-----------  ----------------
22           Customer DTDMN
57           Customer WVAXS
```

You might wonder whether specifying a DISTINCT clause in the subquery can help performance, because the same customer ID can occur more than once in the Orders table. The database engine is smart enough to consider removing duplicates without you asking it to do so explicitly, so this isn't something you need to worry about.

The last example in this section demonstrates using multiple, self-contained subqueries in the same query—both single-valued and multi-valued. Before I describe the task at hand, run the following code to create a table called Orders in the tempdb database (for test purposes), and populate it with orders from the Orders table in the TSQLFundamentals2008 database that have even-numbered order IDs:

```
USE tempdb;

SELECT *
INTO dbo.Orders
FROM TSQLFundamentals2008.Sales.Orders
WHERE orderid % 2 = 0;
```

I describe the *SELECT INTO* statement in more detail in Chapter 8, "Data Modification," but for now, suffice it to say that this statement is used to create a target table and populate it with the result set of the query.

The task at hand is to return all individual order IDs that are missing between the minimum and maximum in the table. It can be quite complicated to solve this problem with a query without any helper tables. You may find the Nums table used in Chapter 3, "Joins," very useful here. (If you don't have the Nums table in your database, you can use the code in Listing 3-1 from Chapter 3 to create and populate it.) The Nums table contains a sequence of integers, from 1 and onward, with no gaps. To return all missing order IDs from the Orders table, query the Nums table, and filter only numbers that are between the minimum and maximum in the Orders table and that do not appear in the set of order IDs in the Orders table. You can use scalar, self-contained subqueries to return the minimum and maximum order IDs, and a multi-valued, self-contained subquery to return the set of all existing order IDs. Here's the complete solution query:

```
SELECT n
FROM dbo.Nums
WHERE n BETWEEN (SELECT MIN(O.orderid) FROM dbo.Orders AS O)
           AND (SELECT MAX(O.orderid) FROM dbo.Orders AS O)
  AND n NOT IN (SELECT O.orderid FROM dbo.Orders AS O);
```

Because the code that populated the Orders table in tempdb filtered only even-numbered order IDs, this query returns all odd-numbered values between the minimum and maximum order IDs in the Orders table. The output of this query is shown here in abbreviated form:

```
n
-----------
10249
10251
10253
10255
10257
...
11067
11069
```

```
11071
11073
11075
```

```
(414 row(s) affected)
```

When you're done, run the following code for cleanup:

```
DROP TABLE tempdb.dbo.Orders;
```

Correlated Subqueries

Correlated subqueries are subqueries that refer to attributes from the table that appears in the outer query. This means that the subquery is dependent on the outer query, and cannot be invoked independently. Logically, it's as if the subquery is evaluated separately for each outer row. For example, the query in Listing 4-1 returns orders with the maximum order ID for each customer:

LISTING 4-1 Correlated Subquery

```
USE TSQLFundamentals2008;

SELECT custid, orderid, orderdate, empid
FROM Sales.Orders AS O1
WHERE orderid =
  (SELECT MAX(O2.orderid)
   FROM Sales.Orders AS O2
   WHERE O2.custid = O1.custid);
```

The outer query is against an instance of the Orders table called O1; it filters orders where the order ID is equal to the value returned by the subquery. The subquery filters orders from a second instance of the Orders table called O2, where the inner customer ID is equal to the outer customer ID, and returns the maximum order ID out of the filtered orders. In simpler terms, for each row in O1, the subquery is in charge of returning the maximum order ID for the current customer. If the order ID in O1 and the order ID returned by the subquery match, the order ID in O1 is the maximum for the current customer, in which case the row from O1 is returned by the query. This query returns the following output, shown here in abbreviated form:

```
custid       orderid      orderdate                   empid
-----------  -----------  --------------------------  -----------
91           11044        2008-04-23 00:00:00.000     4
90           11005        2008-04-07 00:00:00.000     2
89           11066        2008-05-01 00:00:00.000     7
```

```
88          10935       2008-03-09 00:00:00.000    4
87          11025       2008-04-15 00:00:00.000    6
...
5           10924       2008-03-04 00:00:00.000    3
4           11016       2008-04-10 00:00:00.000    9
3           10856       2008-01-28 00:00:00.000    3
2           10926       2008-03-04 00:00:00.000    4
1           11011       2008-04-09 00:00:00.000    3
```

```
(89 row(s) affected)
```

Correlated subqueries are usually much harder to figure out than self-contained subqueries. To better understand the concept of correlated subqueries, I find it useful to focus attention on a single row in the outer table and understand the logical processing that takes place for that row. For example, focus your attention on the order in the Orders table with order ID 10248:

```
custid      orderid     orderdate                  empid
----------- ----------- -------------------------- -----------
85          10248       2006-07-04 00:00:00.000    5
```

With respect to this outer row, when the subquery is evaluated, the correlation or reference to O1.custid means 85. After substituting the correlation with 85, you get the following:

```
SELECT MAX(O2.orderid)
FROM Sales.Orders AS O2
WHERE O2.custid = 85;
```

This query returns the order ID 10274. The outer row's order ID—10248—is compared with the inner one—10274—and because there's no match in this case, the outer row is filtered out. The subquery returns the same value for all rows in O1 with the same customer ID, and only in one case is there a match—when the outer row's order ID is the maximum for the current customer. Thinking in such terms will make it easier for you to grasp the concept of correlated subqueries.

The fact that correlated subqueries are dependent on the outer query makes them harder to debug than self-contained subqueries. You can't just highlight the subquery portion and run it. For example, if you try to highlight and run the subquery portion in Listing 4-1 you get the following error:

```
Msg 4104, Level 16, State 1, Line 1
The multi-part identifier "O1.custid" could not be bound.
```

This error indicates that the identifier O1.custid cannot be bound to an object in the query, because O1 is not defined in the query. It is only defined in the context of the outer query. To debug correlated subqueries you need to substitute the correlation with a constant, and after ensuring that the code is correct, substitute the constant with the correlation.

As another example of a correlated subquery, suppose that you need to query the Sales.OrderValues view, and return for each order the percentage of the current order value out of the customer total value. In Chapter 2, "Single-Table Queries," I provided a solution to this problem using the OVER clause; here I'll explain how to solve the problem using subqueries. It's always a good idea to try to come up with several solutions to each problem because the different solutions will usually vary in complexity and performance.

You can write an outer query against one instance of the OrderValues view called O1; in the SELECT list divide the current value by the result of a correlated subquery that returns (the total value from a second instance of OrderValues called O2 for the current customer). Here's the complete solution query:

```
SELECT orderid, custid, val,
  CAST(100. * val / (SELECT SUM(O2.val)
                     FROM Sales.OrderValues AS O2
                     WHERE O2.custid = O1.custid)
       AS NUMERIC(5,2)) AS pct
FROM Sales.OrderValues AS O1
ORDER BY custid, orderid;
```

The *CAST* function is used to convert the datatype of the expression to NUMERIC with a precision 5 (total number of digits) and a scale 2 (number of digits after the decimal point).

This query returns the following output:

```
orderid     custid      val         pct
----------- ----------- ----------- ------
10643       1           814.50      19.06
10692       1           878.00      20.55
10702       1           330.00      7.72
10835       1           845.80      19.79
10952       1           471.20      11.03
11011       1           933.50      21.85
10308       2           88.80       6.33
10625       2           479.75      34.20
10759       2           320.00      22.81
10926       2           514.40      36.67
...
```

The EXISTS Predicate

T-SQL supports a predicate called EXISTS that accepts a subquery as input, and returns TRUE if the subquery returns any rows and FALSE otherwise. For example, the following query returns customers from Spain who placed orders:

```
SELECT custid, companyname
FROM Sales.Customers AS C
```

```
WHERE country = N'Spain'
  AND EXISTS
    (SELECT * FROM Sales.Orders AS O
     WHERE O.custid = C.custid);
```

The outer query against the Customers table filters only customers from Spain for whom the EXISTS predicate returns TRUE. The EXISTS predicate returns TRUE if the current customer has related orders in the Orders table.

One of the benefits of using the EXISTS predicate is that it allows you to intuitively phrase English-like queries. For example, this query can be read just as you would say it in ordinary English: select the customer ID and company name attributes from the Customers table, where the country is equal to Spain, and at least one order exists in the Orders table with the same customer ID as the customer's customer ID.

This query returns the following output:

```
custid      companyname
----------- ----------------
8           Customer QUHWH
29          Customer MDLWA
30          Customer KSLQF
69          Customer SIUIH
```

As with other predicates, you can negate the EXISTS predicate with the NOT logical operator. For example, the following query returns customers from Spain who did not place orders:

```
SELECT custid, companyname
FROM Sales.Customers AS C
WHERE country = N'Spain'
  AND NOT EXISTS
    (SELECT * FROM Sales.Orders AS O
     WHERE O.custid = C.custid);
```

This query returns the following output:

```
custid      companyname
----------- ----------------
22          Customer DTDMN
```

Even though this book's focus is logical query processing and not performance, I thought you might be interested to know that the EXISTS predicate lends itself to good optimization. That is, the SQL Server engine knows that it is enough to determine whether the subquery returns at least one row or none, and it doesn't need to process all qualifying rows. You can think of this capability as a kind of short-circuit.

Unlike most other cases, logically it's not a bad practice to use an asterisk (*) in the SELECT list of the subquery in the context of the EXISTS predicate. The EXISTS predicate only cares about existence of matching rows regardless of the attributes specified in the SELECT list, as if the whole SELECT clause were superfluous. The SQL Server database engine knows this, and in terms of optimization, ignores the subquery's SELECT list. So in terms of optimization, specifying the column wildcard * has no negative impact compared to alternatives such as specifying a constant. However, some minor extra cost is involved in the resolution process that needs to expand * to the full column list to ensure that you have permissions to access all columns. In this sense, using a constant instead of * does not involve this cost. But this extra resolution cost is so minor that you will probably barely notice it. My opinion on this matter is that queries should be natural and intuitive, unless there's a very compelling reason to sacrifice this aspect of the code. I find the form EXISTS(SELECT * FROM …) much more intuitive than EXISTS(SELECT 1 FROM …). Saving the minor extra cost associated with the resolution of * is something that is not worthwhile at the cost of sacrificing the readability of the code.

Finally, another aspect of the EXISTS predicate that is interesting to note is that unlike most predicates in T-SQL, EXISTS uses two-valued logic and not three-valued logic. If you think about it, there's no situation where it is unknown whether a query returns rows.

Beyond the Fundamentals of Subqueries

This section covers aspects of subqueries that you might consider to be beyond the fundamentals. I provide it as optional reading in case you feel very comfortable with the material covered so far in this chapter.

Returning Previous or Next Values

Suppose that you need to query the Orders table in the TSQLFundamentals2008 database and return, for each order, information about the current order, and also the previous order ID. The concept *previous* implies logical ordering, but because you know that the rows in a table have no order, you need to come up with a logical equivalent to the concept of "previous" that can be phrased with a T-SQL expression. One example of such a logical equivalent is "the maximum value that is smaller than the current." This phrase can be expressed in T-SQL with a correlated subquery like so:

```
SELECT orderid, orderdate, empid, custid,
  (SELECT MAX(O2.orderid)
   FROM Sales.Orders AS O2
   WHERE O2.orderid < O1.orderid) AS prevorderid
FROM Sales.Orders AS O1;
```

This query produces the following output, shown here in abbreviated form:

```
orderid     orderdate                   empid        custid       prevorderid
----------- --------------------------- ------------ ------------ -----------
10248       2006-07-04 00:00:00.000     5            85           NULL
10249       2006-07-05 00:00:00.000     6            79           10248
10250       2006-07-08 00:00:00.000     4            34           10249
```

10251	2006-07-08 00:00:00.000	3	84	10250
10252	2006-07-09 00:00:00.000	4	76	10251
...				
11073	2008-05-05 00:00:00.000	2	58	11072
11074	2008-05-06 00:00:00.000	7	73	11073
11075	2008-05-06 00:00:00.000	8	68	11074
11076	2008-05-06 00:00:00.000	4	9	11075
11077	2008-05-06 00:00:00.000	1	65	11076

(830 row(s) affected)

Notice that because there's no order before the first, the subquery returned a NULL for the first order.

Similarly, you can phrase the concept *next* as "the minimum value that is greater than the current." Here's the T-SQL query that returns for each order the next order ID:

```
SELECT orderid, orderdate, empid, custid,
  (SELECT MIN(O2.orderid)
   FROM Sales.Orders AS O2
   WHERE O2.orderid > O1.orderid) AS nextorderid
FROM Sales.Orders AS O1;
```

This query produces the following output, shown here in abbreviated form:

orderid	orderdate	empid	custid	nextorderid
10248	2006-07-04 00:00:00.000	5	85	10249
10249	2006-07-05 00:00:00.000	6	79	10250
10250	2006-07-08 00:00:00.000	4	34	10251
10251	2006-07-08 00:00:00.000	3	84	10252
10252	2006-07-09 00:00:00.000	4	76	10253
...				
11073	2008-05-05 00:00:00.000	2	58	11074
11074	2008-05-06 00:00:00.000	7	73	11075
11075	2008-05-06 00:00:00.000	8	68	11076
11076	2008-05-06 00:00:00.000	4	9	11077
11077	2008-05-06 00:00:00.000	1	65	NULL

(830 row(s) affected)

Notice that because there's no order after the last, the subquery returned a NULL for the last order.

Running Aggregates

Running aggregates are aggregates that accumulate values over time. I will use the view Sales.OrderTotalsByYear to demonstrate the technique to calculate running aggregates. The view has total order quantities by year. Query the view to examine its contents:

```
SELECT orderyear, qty
FROM Sales.OrderTotalsByYear;
```

You get the following output:

```
orderyear    qty
-----------  -----------
2007         25489
2008         16247
2006         9581
```

Suppose you get a task to return for each year the order year, quantity, and running total quantity over the years. That is, for each year, return the sum of quantity up to that year. So for the earliest year recorded in the view (2006), the running total is equal to that year's quantity. For the second year (2007), the running total is the sum of the first plus second years, and so on.

You can achieve this task by querying one instance of the view (call it O1) returning for each year the order year and quantity, and using a correlated subquery against a second instance of the view (call it O2) to calculate the running total quantity. The subquery should filter all years in O2 that are smaller than or equal to the current year in O1, and sum the quantities from O2. Here's the solution query:

```
SELECT orderyear, qty,
  (SELECT SUM(O2.qty)
   FROM Sales.OrderTotalsByYear AS O2
   WHERE O2.orderyear <= O1.orderyear) AS runqty
FROM Sales.OrderTotalsByYear AS O1
ORDER BY orderyear;
```

This query returns the following output:

```
orderyear    qty          runqty
-----------  -----------  -----------
2006         9581         9581
2007         25489        35070
2008         16247        51317
```

Misbehaving Subqueries

This section introduces cases where subqueries might behave counter to your expectations and best practices that you can follow to avoid logical bugs in your code that are associated with those cases.

NULL Trouble

Remember that T-SQL uses three-valued logic. In this section, I will demonstrate problems that can evolve with subqueries when NULLs are involved, and you do not take into consideration the three-valued logic.

Consider the following seemingly intuitive query that is supposed to return customers who did not place orders:

```
SELECT custid, companyname
FROM Sales.Customers AS C
WHERE custid NOT IN(SELECT O.custid
                    FROM Sales.Orders AS O);
```

With the current sample data in the Orders table in the TSQLFundamentals2008 database the query seems to work the way you expect it to, and indeed it returns two rows for the two customers who did not place orders:

```
custid       companyname
-----------  ----------------
22           Customer DTDMN
57           Customer WVAXS
```

Next, run the following code to insert a new order to the Orders table with a NULL customer ID:

```
INSERT INTO Sales.Orders
  (custid, empid, orderdate, requireddate, shippeddate, shipperid,
   freight, shipname, shipaddress, shipcity, shipregion,
   shippostalcode, shipcountry)
  VALUES(NULL, 1, '20090212', '20090212',
         '20090212', 1, 123.00, N'abc', N'abc', N'abc',
         N'abc', N'abc', N'abc');
```

Run the query that is supposed to return customers who did not place orders again:

```
SELECT custid, companyname
FROM Sales.Customers AS C
WHERE custid NOT IN(SELECT O.custid
                    FROM Sales.Orders AS O);
```

This time the query returns an empty set. Keeping in mind what you've read in the section about NULLs in Chapter 2, try to explain why the query returns an empty set. Also try to think of ways to get customers 22 and 57 in the output, and in general, to figure out best practices you can follow to avoid such problems, assuming there is a problem here.

Obviously, the culprit in this story is the NULL customer ID that was added to the Orders table and is now returned by the subquery among the known customer IDs.

Let's start with the part that behaves the way you expect it to. The IN predicate returns TRUE for a customer who placed orders (for example, customer 85) because such a customer is returned by the subquery. The NOT operator is used to negate the IN predicate; hence, the NOT TRUE becomes FALSE, and the customer is not returned by the outer query. This means that when a customer ID appears in the Orders table, you can tell for sure that the customer placed orders, and therefore you don't want to see it in the output. However, having a NULL customer ID in the Orders table, you can't tell for sure whether a certain customer ID does not appear in Orders, as explained shortly.

The IN predicate returns UNKNOWN (the truth value UNKNOWN like the truth values TRUE and FALSE) for a customer such as 22 that does not appear in the set of known customer IDs in Orders. The IN predicate returns UNKNOWN for such a customer because comparing it with all known customer IDs yields FALSE, and comparing it with the NULL in the set yields UNKNOWN. FALSE OR UNKNOWN yields UNKNOWN. As a more tangible example, consider the expression 22 NOT IN (1, 2, NULL). This expression can be rephrased as NOT 22 IN (1, 2, NULL). You can expand the last expression to NOT (22 = 1 OR 22 = 2 OR 22 = NULL). Evaluate each individual expression in the parentheses to its truth value and you get NOT (FALSE OR FALSE OR UNKNOWN), which translates to NOT UNKNOWN, which evaluates to UNKNOWN.

The logical meaning of UNKNOWN here before you apply the NOT operator is that you can't tell for sure whether the customer ID appears in the set, because the NULL could represent that customer ID as well as anything else. The tricky part is that negating the UNKNOWN with the NOT operator still yields UNKNOWN, and UNKNOWN in a query filter is filtered out. This means that in a case where it is unknown whether a customer ID appears in a set, it is also unknown whether it doesn't appear in the set.

In short, when you use the NOT IN predicate against a subquery that returns at least one NULL, the outer query always returns an empty set. Values from the outer table that are known to appear in the set are not returned because the outer query is supposed to return values that do not appear in the set. Values that do not appear in the set of known values are not returned because you can never tell for sure that the value is not in the set that includes the NULL.

So, what practices can you follow to avoid such trouble?

First, when a column is not supposed to allow NULLs, it is important to define it as NOT NULL. Enforcing data integrity is much more important than many people realize.

Second, in all queries that you write you should consider all three possible truth values of a three-valued logic (TRUE, FALSE, and UNKNOWN). Think explicitly about whether the query might process NULLs, and if so, whether the default treatment of NULLs is suitable for your needs. When it isn't, you need to intervene. For example, in our case the outer query returns an empty set because of the comparison with NULL. If you want to check whether a customer ID appears in the set of known values and ignore the NULLs, you should exclude the NULLs—either explicitly or implicitly. An example of explicitly excluding the NULLs is by adding the predicate O.custid IS NOT NULL to the subquery, like so:

```
SELECT custid, companyname
FROM Sales.Customers AS C
WHERE custid NOT IN(SELECT O.custid
                    FROM Sales.Orders AS O
                    WHERE O.custid IS NOT NULL);
```

An example of excluding the NULLs implicitly is using the NOT EXISTS predicate instead of NOT IN, like so:

```
SELECT custid, companyname
FROM Sales.Customers AS C
WHERE NOT EXISTS
  (SELECT *
   FROM Sales.Orders AS O
   WHERE O.custid = C.custid);
```

Recall that unlike IN, EXISTS uses two-valued predicate logic. EXISTS always returns TRUE or FALSE and never UNKNOWN. When the subquery stumbles into a NULL in O.custid, the expression evaluates to UNKNOWN and the row is filtered out. As far as the EXISTS predicate is concerned, the NULL cases are eliminated naturally, as though they weren't there. So EXISTS ends up handling only known customer IDs. Therefore, it's safer to use NOT EXISTS than NOT IN.

When you're done experimenting, run the following code for cleanup:

```
DELETE FROM Sales.Orders WHERE custid IS NULL;
DBCC CHECKIDENT('Sales.Orders', RESEED, 11077);
```

Substitution Error in a Subquery Column Name

Logical bugs in your code can sometimes be very elusive. In this section, I describe an elusive bug that has to do with an innocent substitution error in a subquery column name. After explaining the bug, I'll provide best practices that can help you avoid such bugs in the future.

The examples in this section query a table called MyShippers in the Sales schema. Run the following code to create and populate this table:

```
IF OBJECT_ID('Sales.MyShippers', 'U') IS NOT NULL
  DROP TABLE Sales.MyShippers;

CREATE TABLE Sales.MyShippers
(
  shipper_id  INT          NOT NULL,
  companyname NVARCHAR(40) NOT NULL,
  phone       NVARCHAR(24) NOT NULL,
  CONSTRAINT PK_MyShippers PRIMARY KEY(shipper_id)
);

INSERT INTO Sales.MyShippers(shipper_id, companyname, phone)
  VALUES(1, N'Shipper GVSUA', N'(503) 555-0137');
INSERT INTO Sales.MyShippers(shipper_id, companyname, phone)
  VALUES(2, N'Shipper ETYNR', N'(425) 555-0136');
INSERT INTO Sales.MyShippers(shipper_id, companyname, phone)
  VALUES(3, N'Shipper ZHISN', N'(415) 555-0138');
```

Consider the following query, which is supposed to return shippers who shipped orders to the customer 43:

```
SELECT shipper_id, companyname
FROM Sales.MyShippers
WHERE shipper_id IN
  (SELECT shipper_id
   FROM Sales.Orders
   WHERE custid = 43);
```

This query produces the following output:

```
shipper_id  companyname
----------- ---------------
1           Shipper GVSUA
2           Shipper ETYNR
3           Shipper ZHISN
```

Apparently, only shippers 2 and 3 shipped orders to the customer 43, but for some reason, this query returned all shippers from the table MyShippers. Examine the query carefully and also the schemas of the tables involved, and see if you can explain why.

It turns out that the column name in the Orders table holding the shipper ID is not called shipper_id; it is called shipperid (no underscore). The column in the MyShippers table is called shipper_id with an underscore. The resolution of nonprefixed column names works in the context of a subquery from the current/inner scope outward. In our example, SQL Server first looks for the column shipper_id in the Orders table. Such a column is not found there, so SQL Server looks for it in the outer table in the query, MyShippers. Because one is found, it is the one used.

You can see that what was supposed to be a self-contained subquery unintentionally became a correlated subquery. As long as the Orders table has at least one row, all rows from the table MyShippers find a match when comparing the outer shipper ID with a query that returns the very same outer shipper ID for each row from the Orders table.

Some may argue that this behavior is a design flaw in standard SQL. However, it's not that the designers of this behavior in the ANSI SQL committee thought that it would be difficult to detect the "error;" rather, it's an intentional behavior designed to allow you to refer to column names from the outer table without needing to prefix them with the table name as long as those column names are unambiguous (appear only in one of the tables).

This problem is more common in environments that do not use consistent attribute names across tables. Sometimes the names are only slightly different like in our case—shipperid in one table and shipper_id in another. That's enough for the bug to manifest itself.

You can follow a couple of best practices to avoid such problems—one to implement in the long run, and one that you can implement in the short run.

In the long run, your organization should as a policy not underestimate the importance of using consistent attribute names across tables. In the short run, of course, you don't want to start changing existing column names, which could break application code.

In the short run, you can adopt a very simple practice—prefix column names in subqueries with the source table alias. This way, the resolution process only looks for the column in the specified table, and if no such column is there, you get a resolution error. For example, try running the following code:

```
SELECT shipper_id, companyname
FROM Sales.MyShippers
WHERE shipper_id IN
  (SELECT O.shipper_id
   FROM Sales.Orders AS O
   WHERE O.custid = 43);
```

You get the following resolution error:

```
Msg 207, Level 16, State 1, Line 4
Invalid column name 'shipper_id'.
```

After getting this error, you of course can identify the problem and correct the query:

```
SELECT shipper_id, companyname
FROM Sales.MyShippers
WHERE shipper_id IN
  (SELECT O.shipperid
   FROM Sales.Orders AS O
   WHERE O.custid = 43);
```

This time the query returns the expected result:

```
shipper_id  companyname
----------- ---------------
2           Shipper ETYNR
3           Shipper ZHISN
```

When you're done, run the following code for cleanup:

```
IF OBJECT_ID('Sales.MyShippers', 'U') IS NOT NULL
  DROP TABLE Sales.MyShippers;
```

Conclusion

This chapter covered subqueries. It discussed self-contained subqueries, which are independent of the outer query, and correlated subqueries, which are dependent on the outer query. Regarding the result of the subquery, I discussed scalar and multi-valued subqueries. I also provided a more advanced section as optional reading in which I covered returning previous and next values, running aggregates, and misbehaving subqueries.

Remember to always think about the three-valued logic and the importance of prefixing column names in subqueries with the source table alias.

The next chapter focuses on table subqueries, also known as table expressions.

Exercises

This section provides exercises to help you familiarize yourself with the subjects discussed in this chapter. The sample database TSQLFundamentals2008 is used in all exercises in this chapter.

1

Write a query that returns all orders placed on the last day of activity that can be found in the Orders table.

Tables involved: Sales.Orders table.

Desired output:

```
orderid      orderdate                    custid        empid
-----------  --------------------------   -----------   -----------
11077        2008-05-06 00:00:00.000      65            1
11076        2008-05-06 00:00:00.000      9             4
11075        2008-05-06 00:00:00.000      68            8
11074        2008-05-06 00:00:00.000      73            7
```

2 (Optional, Advanced)

Write a query that returns all orders placed by the customer(s) who placed the highest number of orders. Note that more than one customer may have the same number of orders.

Tables involved: Sales.Orders table.

Desired output (abbreviated):

```
custid       orderid      orderdate                    empid
-----------  -----------  --------------------------   -----------
71           10324        2006-10-08 00:00:00.000      9
71           10393        2006-12-25 00:00:00.000      1
71           10398        2006-12-30 00:00:00.000      2
71           10440        2007-02-10 00:00:00.000      4
71           10452        2007-02-20 00:00:00.000      8
71           10510        2007-04-18 00:00:00.000      6
71           10555        2007-06-02 00:00:00.000      6
71           10603        2007-07-18 00:00:00.000      8
71           10607        2007-07-22 00:00:00.000      5
71           10612        2007-07-28 00:00:00.000      1
```

71	10627	2007-08-11 00:00:00.000	8
71	10657	2007-09-04 00:00:00.000	2
71	10678	2007-09-23 00:00:00.000	7
71	10700	2007-10-10 00:00:00.000	3
71	10711	2007-10-21 00:00:00.000	5
71	10713	2007-10-22 00:00:00.000	1
71	10714	2007-10-22 00:00:00.000	5
71	10722	2007-10-29 00:00:00.000	8
71	10748	2007-11-20 00:00:00.000	3
71	10757	2007-11-27 00:00:00.000	6
71	10815	2008-01-05 00:00:00.000	2
71	10847	2008-01-22 00:00:00.000	4
71	10882	2008-02-11 00:00:00.000	4
71	10894	2008-02-18 00:00:00.000	1
71	10941	2008-03-11 00:00:00.000	7
71	10983	2008-03-27 00:00:00.000	2
71	10984	2008-03-30 00:00:00.000	1
71	11002	2008-04-06 00:00:00.000	4
71	11030	2008-04-17 00:00:00.000	7
71	11031	2008-04-17 00:00:00.000	6
71	11064	2008-05-01 00:00:00.000	1

```
(31 row(s) affected)
```

3

Write a query that returns employees who did not place orders on or after May 1, 2008.

Tables involved: HR.Employees, and Sales.Orders tables.

Desired output:

```
empid        FirstName      lastname
-----------  -------------  --------------------
3            Judy           Lew
5            Sven           Buck
6            Paul           Suurs
9            Zoya           Dolgopyatova
```

4

Write a query that returns countries where there are customers but not employees.

Tables involved: Sales.Customers, and HR.Employees tables.

Desired output:

```
country
---------------
Argentina
Austria
Belgium
```

```
Brazil
Canada
Denmark
Finland
France
Germany
Ireland
Italy
Mexico
Norway
Poland
Portugal
Spain
Sweden
Switzerland
Venezuela

(19 row(s) affected)
```

5

Write a query that returns for each customer all orders placed on the customer's last day of activity.

Tables involved: Sales.Orders table.

Desired output:

```
custid      orderid     orderdate               empid
----------- ----------- ----------------------- -----------
1           11011       2008-04-09 00:00:00.000 3
2           10926       2008-03-04 00:00:00.000 4
3           10856       2008-01-28 00:00:00.000 3
4           11016       2008-04-10 00:00:00.000 9
5           10924       2008-03-04 00:00:00.000 3
...
87          11025       2008-04-15 00:00:00.000 6
88          10935       2008-03-09 00:00:00.000 4
89          11066       2008-05-01 00:00:00.000 7
90          11005       2008-04-07 00:00:00.000 2
91          11044       2008-04-23 00:00:00.000 4

(90 row(s) affected)
```

6

Write a query that returns customers who placed orders in 2007 but not in 2008.

Tables involved: Sales.Customers, and Sales.Orders tables.

Desired output:

```
custid      companyname
----------- ----------------
21          Customer KIDPX
23          Customer WVFAF
33          Customer FVXPQ
36          Customer LVJSO
43          Customer UISOJ
51          Customer PVDZC
85          Customer ENQZT

(7 row(s) affected)
```

7 (Optional, Advanced)

Write a query that returns customers who ordered product 12.

Tables involved: Sales.Customers, Sales.Orders, and Sales.OrderDetails tables.

Desired output:

```
custid      companyname
----------- ----------------
48          Customer DVFMB
39          Customer GLLAG
71          Customer LCOUJ
65          Customer NYUHS
44          Customer OXFRU
51          Customer PVDZC
86          Customer SNXOJ
20          Customer THHDP
90          Customer XBBVR
46          Customer XPNIK
31          Customer YJCBX
87          Customer ZHYOS

(12 row(s) affected)
```

8 (Optional, Advanced)

Write a query that calculates a running total quantity for each customer and month.

Tables involved: Sales.CustOrders view.

Desired output:

```
custid      ordermonth                  qty         runqty
----------- --------------------------- ----------- -----------
1           2007-08-01 00:00:00.000     38          38
1           2007-10-01 00:00:00.000     41          79
1           2008-01-01 00:00:00.000     17          96
```

1	2008-03-01 00:00:00.000	18	114
1	2008-04-01 00:00:00.000	60	174
2	2006-09-01 00:00:00.000	6	6
2	2007-08-01 00:00:00.000	18	24
2	2007-11-01 00:00:00.000	10	34
2	2008-03-01 00:00:00.000	29	63
3	2006-11-01 00:00:00.000	24	24
3	2007-04-01 00:00:00.000	30	54
3	2007-05-01 00:00:00.000	80	134
3	2007-06-01 00:00:00.000	83	217
3	2007-09-01 00:00:00.000	102	319
3	2008-01-01 00:00:00.000	40	359

```
...

(636 row(s) affected)
```

Solutions

This section provides solutions to the exercises in the preceding section.

1

You can write a self-contained subquery that returns the maximum order date from the Orders table. You can refer to the subquery in the WHERE clause of the outer query to return all orders that were placed on the last day of activity. Here's the solution query:

```
USE TSQLFundamentals2008;

SELECT orderid, orderdate, custid, empid
FROM Sales.Orders
WHERE orderdate =
  (SELECT MAX(O.orderdate) FROM Sales.Orders AS O);
```

2

This problem is best solved in multiple steps. First, you can write a query that returns the customer or customers who placed the highest number of orders. You can achieve this by grouping the orders by customer, ordering the customers by COUNT(*) descending, and using the TOP(1) WITH TIES option to return the IDs of the customers who placed the highest number of orders. If you don't remember how to use the TOP option, please refer to Chapter 2, "Single-Table Queries." Here's the query that solves the first step:

```
SELECT TOP (1) WITH TIES O.custid
FROM Sales.Orders AS O
GROUP BY O.custid
ORDER BY COUNT(*) DESC;
```

This query returns the value 71, which is the customer ID of the customer who placed the highest number of orders, 31. With the sample data stored in the Orders table, only one customer placed the maximum number of orders. But the query uses the WITH TIES option to return all IDs of customers who placed the maximum number of orders in case there's more than one.

The next step is to write a query against the Orders table, returning all orders where the customer ID is in the set of customer IDs returned by the solution query for the first step:

```
SELECT custid, orderid, orderdate, empid
FROM Sales.Orders
WHERE custid IN
  (SELECT TOP (1) WITH TIES O.custid
   FROM Sales.Orders AS O
   GROUP BY O.custid
   ORDER BY COUNT(*) DESC);
```

3

You can write a self-contained subquery against the Orders table that filters orders placed on or after May 1, 2008, and returns only the employee IDs from those orders. Write an outer query against the Employees table returning employees whose IDs appear in the set of employee IDs returned by the subquery. Here's the complete solution query:

```
SELECT empid, FirstName, lastname
FROM HR.Employees
WHERE empid NOT IN
  (SELECT O.empid
   FROM Sales.Orders AS O
   WHERE O.orderdate >= '20080501');
```

4

You can write a self-contained subquery against the Employees table returning the country attribute from each employee row. Write an outer query against the Customers table that filters only customer rows where the country attribute appears in the set of countries returned by the subquery. In the SELECT list of the outer query, specify DISTINCT country to return only distinct occurrences of countries, because the same country can have more than one query. Here's the complete solution query:

```
SELECT DISTINCT country
FROM Sales.Customers
WHERE country NOT IN
  (SELECT E.country FROM HR.Employees AS E);
```

5

This exercise is similar to Exercise 4-1, except that in that exercise you were asked to return orders placed on the last day of activity in general, and in this exercise you were asked to return orders placed on the last day of activity for the customer. The solutions for both exercises are similar, but here you need to correlate the subquery matching the inner customer ID with the outer customer ID, like so:

```
SELECT custid, orderid, orderdate, empid
FROM Sales.Orders AS O1
WHERE orderdate =
  (SELECT MAX(O2.orderdate)
   FROM Sales.Orders AS O2
   WHERE O2.custid = O1.custid)
ORDER BY custid;
```

You're not comparing the outer row's order date with the general maximum order date, but instead with the maximum order date for the current customer.

6

You can solve this problem by querying the Customers table and using EXISTS and NOT EXISTS predicates with correlated subqueries to ensure that the customer placed orders in 2007 but not in 2008. The EXISTS predicate returns TRUE only if at least one row exists in the Orders table with the same customer ID as in the outer row, within the date range representing the year 2007. The NOT EXISTS predicate returns TRUE only if no row exists in the Orders table with the same customer ID as in the outer row, within the date range representing the year 2008. Here's the complete solution query:

```
SELECT custid, companyname
FROM Sales.Customers AS C
WHERE EXISTS
  (SELECT *
   FROM Sales.Orders AS O
   WHERE O.custid = C.custid
     AND O.orderdate >= '20070101'
     AND O.orderdate < '20080101')
  AND NOT EXISTS
  (SELECT *
   FROM Sales.Orders AS O
   WHERE O.custid = C.custid
     AND O.orderdate >= '20080101'
     AND O.orderdate < '20090101');
```

7

You can solve this exercise by nesting EXISTS predicates with correlated subqueries. You write the outermost query against the Customers table. In the WHERE clause of the outer query you can use the EXISTS predicate with a correlated subquery against the Orders table to filter only the current customer's orders. In the filter of the subquery against the Orders table you can use a nested EXISTS predicate with a subquery against the OrderDetails table that filters only order details with product ID 12. This way, only customers who placed orders that contain product 12 in their order details are returned. Here's the complete solution query:

```
SELECT custid, companyname
FROM Sales.Customers AS C
WHERE EXISTS
  (SELECT *
   FROM Sales.Orders AS O
   WHERE O.custid = C.custid
     AND EXISTS
       (SELECT *
        FROM Sales.OrderDetails AS OD
        WHERE OD.orderid = O.orderid
          AND OD.ProductID = 12));
```

8

When I need to solve querying problems I often find it useful to rephrase the original request in a more technical way so that it will be more convenient to translate the request to a T-SQL query. To solve the current exercise, you can first try to express the request "return a running total quantity for each customer and month" differently—in a more technical manner. For each customer, return the customer id, month, the sum of the quantity for that month, and the sum of all months less than or equal to the current month. The rephrased request can be translated to the following T-SQL query quite literally:

```
SELECT custid, ordermonth, qty,
  (SELECT SUM(O2.qty)
   FROM Sales.CustOrders AS O2
   WHERE O2.custid = O1.custid
     AND O2.ordermonth <= O1.ordermonth) AS runqty
FROM Sales.CustOrders AS O1
ORDER BY custid, ordermonth;
```

Table Expressions

Table expressions are named query expressions that represent a valid relational table. You can use them in data manipulation statements similar to other tables. Microsoft SQL Server supports four types of table expressions: derived tables, common table expressions (CTEs), views, and inline table-valued functions (inline TVFs), each of which I will describe in detail in this chapter. The focus of this chapter is SELECT queries against table expressions; Chapter 8, "Data Modification," covers modifications against table expressions.

Table expressions are not physically materialized anywhere—they are virtual. A query against a table expression is internally translated to a query against the underlying objects. The benefits of using table expressions are typically related to logical aspects of your code and not to performance. For example, table expressions help you simplify your solutions by using a modular approach. Table expressions also help you circumvent certain restrictions in the language, such as the inability to refer to column aliases assigned in the SELECT clause in query clauses that are logically processed prior to the SELECT clause.

This chapter also introduces the APPLY table operator used in conjunction with a table expression. I will explain how to use this operator to apply a table expression to each row of another table.

Derived Tables

Derived tables (also known as table subqueries) are defined in the FROM clause of an outer query. Their scope of existence is the outer query. As soon as the outer query is finished, the derived table is gone.

You specify the query defining the derived table within parentheses, followed by the AS clause and the derived table name. For example, the following code defines a derived table called USACusts based on a query that returns all customers from the United States, and the outer query selects all rows from the derived table:

```
USE TSQLFundamentals2008;

SELECT *
FROM (SELECT custid, companyname
      FROM Sales.Customers
      WHERE country = N'USA') AS USACusts;
```

In this particular case, which is a simple example of the basic syntax, a derived table is not needed because the outer query doesn't apply any manipulation.

The code in this basic example returns the following output:

```
custid       companyname
-----------  ----------------
32           Customer YSIQX
36           Customer LVJSO
43           Customer UISOJ
45           Customer QXPPT
48           Customer DVFMB
55           Customer KZQZT
65           Customer NYUHS
71           Customer LCOUJ
75           Customer XOJYP
77           Customer LCYBZ
78           Customer NLTYP
82           Customer EYHKM
89           Customer YBQTI
```

A query must meet three requirements to be valid to define a table expression of any kind:

1. **Order is not guaranteed.**   A table expression is supposed to represent a relational table, and the rows in a relational table have no guaranteed order. Recall that this aspect of a relation stems from set theory. For this reason, ANSI SQL disallows an ORDER BY clause in queries that are used to define table expressions. T-SQL follows this restriction for the most part, with one exception—when TOP is also specified. In the context of a query with the TOP option, the ORDER BY clause serves a logical purpose: defining for the TOP option which rows to filter. If you use a query with TOP and ORDER BY to define a table expression, ORDER BY is only guaranteed to serve the logical filtering purpose for the TOP option and not the usual presentation purpose. If the outer query against the table expression does not have a presentation ORDER BY, the output is not guaranteed to be returned in any particular order. The section "Views and the ORDER BY Clause," later in this chapter, provides more detail on this item.

2. **All columns must have names.**   All columns in a table must have names; therefore, you must assign column aliases to all expressions in the SELECT list of the query that is used to define a table expression.

3. **All column names must be unique.**   All column names in a table must be unique; therefore, a table expression that has multiple columns with the same name is invalid. This might happen when the query defining the table expression joins two tables, and both tables have a column with the same name. If you need to incorporate both columns in your table expression, they must have different column names. You can resolve this by assigning the two columns with different column aliases.

Assigning Column Aliases

One of the benefits of using table expressions is that in any clause of the outer query you can refer to column aliases that were assigned in the SELECT clause of the inner query. This helps you get around the fact that you can't refer to column aliases assigned in the SELECT clause in query clauses that are logically processed prior to the SELECT clause (for example, WHERE or GROUP BY).

For example, suppose that you need to write a query against the Sales.Orders table and return the number of distinct customers handled in each order year. The following attempt is invalid because the GROUP BY clause refers to a column alias that was assigned in the SELECT clause, and the GROUP BY clause is logically processed prior to the SELECT clause:

```
SELECT
  YEAR(orderdate) AS orderyear,
  COUNT(DISTINCT custid) AS numcusts
FROM Sales.Orders
GROUP BY orderyear;
```

You could solve the problem by referring to the expression YEAR(orderdate) in both the GROUP BY and the SELECT clauses, but this is an example with a short expression. What if the expression were much longer? Maintaining two copies of the same expression might hurt code readability and maintainability and is more prone to errors. To solve the problem in a way that requires only one copy of the expression, you can use a table expression like so:

LISTING 5-1 Query with a Derived Table Using Inline Aliasing Form

```
SELECT orderyear, COUNT(DISTINCT custid) AS numcusts
FROM (SELECT YEAR(orderdate) AS orderyear, custid
      FROM Sales.Orders) AS D
GROUP BY orderyear;
```

This query returns the following output:

```
orderyear   numcusts
----------- -----------
2006        67
2007        86
2008        81
```

This code defines a derived table called D based on a query against the Orders table that returns the order year and customer ID from all rows. The SELECT list of the inner query uses inline aliasing format to assign the alias orderyear to the expression YEAR(orderdate). The outer query can refer to the orderyear column alias in both the GROUP BY and SELECT clauses, because as far as the outer query is concerned, it queries a table called D with columns called orderyear and custid.

As I mentioned earlier, SQL Server expands the definition of the table expression and accesses the underlying objects directly. After expansion, the query in Listing 5-1 looks like this:

```
SELECT YEAR(orderdate) AS orderyear, COUNT(DISTINCT custid) AS numcusts
FROM Sales.Orders
GROUP BY YEAR(orderdate);
```

This is just to emphasize that you use table expressions for logical (not performance-related) reasons. Generally speaking, table expressions have neither positive nor negative performance impact.

The code in Listing 5-1 uses the inline aliasing format to assign column aliases to expressions. The syntax for inline aliasing is <expression> [AS] <alias>. Note that the word AS is optional in the syntax for inline aliasing; however, I find that it helps the readability of the code and recommend using it.

In some cases, you might prefer to use a second supported form for assigning column aliases, which you can think of as an external form. With this form you do not assign column aliases following the expressions in the SELECT list—you specify all target column names in parentheses following the table expression's name like so:

```
SELECT orderyear, COUNT(DISTINCT custid) AS numcusts
FROM (SELECT YEAR(orderdate), custid
      FROM Sales.Orders) AS D(orderyear, custid)
GROUP BY orderyear;
```

It is generally recommended that you use the inline form for a couple of reasons. If you need to debug the code when using the inline form, when you highlight the query defining the table expression and run it, the columns in the result appear with the aliases you assigned. With the external form, you cannot include the target column names when you highlight the table expression query, so the result appears with no column names in the case of the unnamed expressions. Also, when the table expression query is lengthy, using the external form it can be quite difficult to figure out which column alias belongs to which expression.

Even though it's a best practice to use the inline aliasing form, in some cases you may find the external form more convenient to work with. For example, when the query defining the table expression isn't going to undergo any further revisions and you want to treat it like a "black box"—you want to focus your attention on the table expression name followed by the target column list when you look at the outer query.

Using Arguments

In the query defining a derived table, you can refer to arguments. The arguments can be local variables and input parameters to a routine such as a stored procedure or function. For example, the following code declares and initializes a local variable called *@empid*, and the query in the code that is used to define the derived table D refers to the local variable in the WHERE clause:

```
DECLARE @empid AS INT = 3;

/*
-- Prior to SQL Server 2008 use separate DECLARE and SET statements:
DECLARE @empid AS INT;
SET @empid = 3;
*/

SELECT orderyear, COUNT(DISTINCT custid) AS numcusts
FROM (SELECT YEAR(orderdate) AS orderyear, custid
      FROM Sales.Orders
      WHERE empid = @empid) AS D
GROUP BY orderyear;
```

This query returns the number of distinct customers per year that handled the orders of the input employee (the employee whose ID is stored in the variable *@empid*). Here's the output of this query:

```
orderyear   numcusts
----------- -----------
2006        16
2007        46
2008        30
```

Nesting

If you need to define a derived table using a query that by itself refers to a derived table, you end up nesting derived tables. Nesting of derived tables is a result of the fact that a derived table is defined in the FROM clause of the outer query and not separately. Nesting is a problematic aspect of programming in general as it tends to complicate the code and reduce its readability.

For example, the code in Listing 5-2 returns order years and the number of customers handled in each year only for years in which more than 70 customers were handled:

LISTING 5-2 Query with Nested Derived Tables

```
SELECT orderyear, numcusts
FROM (SELECT orderyear, COUNT(DISTINCT custid) AS numcusts
      FROM (SELECT YEAR(orderdate) AS orderyear, custid
            FROM Sales.Orders) AS D1
      GROUP BY orderyear) AS D2
WHERE numcusts > 70;
```

This code returns the following output:

```
orderyear   numcusts
----------- -----------
2007        86
2008        81
```

The purpose of the innermost derived table, D1, is to assign the column alias orderyear to the expression YEAR(orderdate). The query against D1 refers to orderyear in both the GROUP BY and SELECT clauses, and assigns the column alias numcusts to the expression COUNT(DISTINCT custid). The query against D1 is used to define the derived table D2. The query against D2 refers to numcusts in the WHERE clause to filter order years in which more than 70 customers were handled.

The whole purpose of using table expressions in this example was to simplify the solution by reusing column aliases instead of repeating expressions. However, with the complexity added by the nesting aspect of derived tables, I'm not sure that the solution is simpler than the alternative, which does not make any use of derived tables but instead repeats expressions:

```
SELECT YEAR(orderdate) AS orderyear, COUNT(DISTINCT custid) AS numcusts
FROM Sales.Orders
GROUP BY YEAR(orderdate)
HAVING COUNT(DISTINCT custid) > 70;
```

In short, nesting is a problematic aspect of derived tables.

Multiple References

Another problematic aspect of derived tables stems from the fact that derived tables are defined in the FROM clause of the outer query and not prior to the outer query. As far as the FROM clause of the outer query is concerned, the derived table doesn't exist yet; therefore, if you need to refer to multiple instances of the derived table, you can't. Instead, you have to define multiple derived tables based on the same query. The query in Listing 5-3 provides an example:

LISTING 5-3 Multiple Derived Tables Based on the Same Query

```
SELECT Cur.orderyear,
  Cur.numcusts AS curnumcusts, Prv.numcusts AS prvnumcusts,
  Cur.numcusts - Prv.numcusts AS growth
FROM (SELECT YEAR(orderdate) AS orderyear,
        COUNT(DISTINCT custid) AS numcusts
     FROM Sales.Orders
     GROUP BY YEAR(orderdate)) AS Cur
  LEFT OUTER JOIN
    (SELECT YEAR(orderdate) AS orderyear,
        COUNT(DISTINCT custid) AS numcusts
     FROM Sales.Orders
     GROUP BY YEAR(orderdate)) AS Prv
  ON Cur.orderyear = Prv.orderyear + 1;
```

This query joins two instances of a table expression to create two derived tables: the first derived table, Cur, represents current years, and the second derived table, Prv, represents previous years. The join condition Cur.orderyear = Prv.orderyear + 1 ensures that each row from the first derived table matches with the previous year of the second. By making it a LEFT outer join, the first year that has no previous year is also returned from the Cur table. The SELECT clause of the outer query calculates the difference between the number of customers handled in the current and previous years.

The code in Listing 5-3 produces the following output:

```
orderyear   curnumcusts prvnumcusts growth
----------- ----------- ----------- -----------
2006        67          NULL        NULL
2007        86          67          19
2008        81          86          -5
```

The fact that you cannot refer to multiple instances of the same derived table forces you to maintain multiple copies of the same query definition. This leads to lengthy code that is hard to maintain and is prone to errors.

Common Table Expressions

Common table expressions (CTEs) are another form of table expression very similar to derived tables, yet with a couple of important advantages. CTEs were introduced in SQL Server 2005 and are part of ANSI SQL:1999 and later standards.

CTEs are defined using a *WITH* statement and have the following general form:

```
WITH <CTE_Name>[(<target_column_list>)]
AS
(
  <inner_query_defining_CTE>
)
<outer_query_against_CTE>;
```

The inner query defining the CTE must follow all requirements mentioned earlier to be valid to define a table expression. As a simple example, the following code defines a CTE called USACusts based on a query that returns all customers from the United States, and the outer query selects all rows from the CTE:

```
WITH USACusts AS
(
  SELECT custid, companyname
  FROM Sales.Customers
  WHERE country = N'USA'
)
SELECT * FROM USACusts;
```

As with derived tables, as soon as the outer query finishes, the CTE gets out of scope.

> **Note** The WITH clause is used in T-SQL for several different purposes. To avoid ambiguity, when the WITH clause is used to define a CTE, the preceding statement in the same batch—if one exists—must be terminated with a semicolon. And oddly enough, the semicolon for the entire CTE is not required, though I still recommend specifying it.

Assigning Column Aliases

CTEs also support two forms of column aliasing—inline and external. For the inline form, specify <expression> AS <column_alias>; for the external form, specify the target column list in parentheses immediately after the CTE name.

Here's an example of the inline form:

```
WITH C AS
(
  SELECT YEAR(orderdate) AS orderyear, custid
  FROM Sales.Orders
)
SELECT orderyear, COUNT(DISTINCT custid) AS numcusts
FROM C
GROUP BY orderyear;
```

And here's an example of the external form:

```
WITH C(orderyear, custid) AS
(
  SELECT YEAR(orderdate), custid
  FROM Sales.Orders
)
SELECT orderyear, COUNT(DISTINCT custid) AS numcusts
FROM C
GROUP BY orderyear;
```

The motivations for using one form or the other are similar to those described in the context of derived tables.

Using Arguments

As with derived tables, you can also use arguments in the query used to define a CTE. Here's an example:

```
DECLARE @empid AS INT = 3;

/*
-- Prior to SQL Server 2008 use separate DECLARE and SET statements:
DECLARE @empid AS INT;
SET @empid = 3;
*/
```

```
WITH C AS
(
  SELECT YEAR(orderdate) AS orderyear, custid
  FROM Sales.Orders
  WHERE empid = @empid
)
SELECT orderyear, COUNT(DISTINCT custid) AS numcusts
FROM C
GROUP BY orderyear;
```

Defining Multiple CTEs

On the surface, the difference between derived tables and CTEs might seem to be merely semantic. However, the fact that you first define a CTE and then use it gives it several important advantages over derived tables. One of those advantages is that if you need to refer to one CTE from another, you don't end up nesting them like derived tables. Instead, you simply define multiple CTEs separated by commas under the same *WITH* statement. Each CTE can refer to all previously defined CTEs, and the outer query can refer to all CTEs. For example, the following code is the CTE alternative to the nested derived tables approach in Listing 5-2:

```
WITH C1 AS
(
  SELECT YEAR(orderdate) AS orderyear, custid
  FROM Sales.Orders
),
C2 AS
(
  SELECT orderyear, COUNT(DISTINCT custid) AS numcusts
  FROM C1
  GROUP BY orderyear
)
SELECT orderyear, numcusts
FROM C2
WHERE numcusts > 70;
```

Because you define a CTE before you use it, you don't end up nesting CTEs. Each CTE appears separately in the code in a modular manner. This modular approach substantially improves the readability and maintainability of the code compared to the nested derived table approach.

Technically you cannot nest CTEs, nor can you define a CTE within the parentheses of a derived table. However, nesting is a problematic practice; therefore, think of these restrictions as aids to code clarity rather than obstacles.

Multiple References

The fact that a CTE is defined first and then queried has another advantage: As far as the FROM clause of the outer query is concerned, the CTE already exists; therefore, you can refer to multiple instances of the same CTE. For example, the following code is the logical equivalent of the code shown earlier in Listing 5-3, using CTEs instead of derived tables:

```
WITH YearlyCount AS
(
  SELECT YEAR(orderdate) AS orderyear,
    COUNT(DISTINCT custid) AS numcusts
  FROM Sales.Orders
  GROUP BY YEAR(orderdate)
)
SELECT Cur.orderyear,
  Cur.numcusts AS curnumcusts, Prv.numcusts AS prvnumcusts,
  Cur.numcusts - Prv.numcusts AS growth
FROM YearlyCount AS Cur
  LEFT OUTER JOIN YearlyCount AS Prv
    ON Cur.orderyear = Prv.orderyear + 1;
```

As you can see, the CTE YearlyCount is defined once and accessed twice in the FROM clause of the outer query—once as Cur and once as Prv. You need to maintain only one copy of the CTE query and not multiple copies as you would with derived tables.

If you're curious about performance, recall that earlier I mentioned that typically table expressions have no performance impact because they are not physically materialized anywhere. Both references to the CTE here are going to be expanded. Internally, this query has a self join between two instances of the Orders table, each of which involves scanning the table data and aggregating it before the join—the same physical processing that takes place with the derived table approach.

Recursive CTEs

This section is optional because it covers subjects that are beyond the fundamentals.

CTEs are unique among table expressions because they have recursive capabilities. A recursive CTE is defined by at least two queries (more are possible)—at least one query known as the *anchor member* and at least one query known as the *recursive member*. The general form of a basic recursive CTE looks like this:

```
WITH <CTE_Name>[(<target_column_list>)]
AS
(
  <anchor_member>
  UNION ALL
  <recursive_member>
)
<outer_query_against_CTE>;
```

The anchor member is a query that returns a valid relational result table—like a query that is used to define a nonrecursive table expression. The anchor member query is invoked only once.

The recursive member is a query that has a reference to the CTE name. The reference to the CTE name represents what is logically the previous result set in a sequence of executions. The first time that the recursive member is invoked, the previous result set represents whatever the anchor member returned. In each subsequent invocation of the recursive member, the reference to the CTE name represents the result set returned by the previous invocation of the recursive member. The recursive member has no explicit recursion termination check—the termination check is implicit. The recursive member is invoked repeatedly until it returns an empty set, or exceeds some limit.

Both queries must be compatible in terms of the number of columns they return and the data types of the corresponding columns.

The reference to the CTE name in the outer query represents the unified result sets of the invocation of the anchor member and all invocations of the recursive member.

If this is your first encounter with recursive CTEs, you might find this explanation hard to understand. They are best explained with an example. The following code demonstrates how to use a recursive CTE to return information about an employee (Don Funk, employee ID 2) and all of the employee's subordinates in all levels (direct or indirect):

```
WITH EmpsCTE AS
(
  SELECT empid, mgrid, firstname, lastname
  FROM HR.Employees
  WHERE empid = 2

  UNION ALL

  SELECT C.empid, C.mgrid, C.firstname, C.lastname
  FROM EmpsCTE AS P
    JOIN HR.Employees AS C
      ON C.mgrid = P.empid
)
SELECT empid, mgrid, firstname, lastname
FROM EmpsCTE;
```

The anchor member queries the HR.Employees table and simply returns the row for employee 2:

```
  SELECT empid, mgrid, firstname, lastname
  FROM HR.Employees
  WHERE empid = 2
```

The recursive member joins the CTE—representing the previous result set—with the Employees table to return the direct subordinates of the employees returned in the previous result set:

```
  SELECT C.empid, C.mgrid, C.firstname, C.lastname
  FROM EmpsCTE AS P
    JOIN HR.Employees AS C
      ON C.mgrid = P.empid
```

In other words, the recursive member is invoked repeatedly, and in each invocation it returns the next level of subordinates. The first time the recursive member is invoked it returns the direct subordinates of employee 2—employees 3 and 5. The second time the recursive member is invoked, it returns the direct subordinates of employees 3 and 5—employees 4, 6, 7, 8, and 9. The third time the recursive member is invoked, there are no more subordinates; the recursive member returns an empty set and therefore recursion stops.

The reference to the CTE name in the outer query represents the unified result sets; in other words, employee 2 and all of the employee's subordinates.

Here's the output of this code:

```
empid        mgrid        firstname  lastname
-----------  -----------  ---------- --------------------
2            1            Don        Funk
3            2            Judy       Lew
5            2            Sven       Buck
6            5            Paul       Suurs
7            5            Russell    King
9            5            Zoya       Dolgopyatova
4            3            Yael       Peled
8            3            Maria      Cameron
```

In the event of a logical error in the join predicate in the recursive member, or problems with the data resulting in cycles, the recursive member can potentially be invoked an infinite number of times. As a safety measure, by default SQL Server restricts the number of times that the recursive member can be invoked to 100. The code will fail upon the 101st invocation of the recursive member. You can change the default maximum recursion limit by specifying the hint OPTION(MAXRECURSION n) at the end of the outer query, where n is an integer in the range 0 through 32,767 representing the maximum recursion limit you want to set. If you want to remove the restriction altogether, specify MAXRECURSION 0. Note that SQL Server stores the intermediate result sets returned by the anchor and recursive members in a work table in tempdb; if you remove the restriction and have a runaway query, the work table will quickly get very large. If tempdb can't grow anymore—for example, when you run out of disk space—the query will fail.

Views

The two types of table expressions discussed so far—derived tables and CTEs—have a very limited scope, which is the single statement scope. As soon as the outer query against those table expressions is finished, they are gone. This means that derived tables and CTEs are not reusable.

Views and inline table-valued functions (inline TVFs) are two reusable types of table expressions; their definition is stored as a database object. Once created, those objects are permanent parts of the database and are only removed from the database if explicitly dropped.

In most other respects, views and inline TVFs are treated like derived tables and CTEs. For example, when querying a view or an inline TVF, SQL Server expands the definition of the table expression and queries the underlying objects directly, as with derived tables and CTEs.

In this section, I'll describe views; in the next section, I'll describe inline TVFs. As I mentioned earlier, a view is a reusable table expression whose definition is stored in the database. For example, the following code creates a view called USACusts in the Sales schema in the TSQLFundamentals2008 database, representing all customers from the United States:

```
USE TSQLFundamentals2008;
IF OBJECT_ID('Sales.USACusts') IS NOT NULL
  DROP VIEW Sales.USACusts;
GO
CREATE VIEW Sales.USACusts
AS

SELECT
  custid, companyname, contactname, contacttitle, address,
  city, region, postalcode, country, phone, fax
FROM Sales.Customers
WHERE country = N'USA';
GO
```

Note that just as with derived tables and CTEs, instead of using inline column aliasing as shown in the preceding code, you can use external column aliasing by specifying the target column names in parentheses immediately after the view name.

Once you create this view, you can query it much like you query other tables in the database:

```
SELECT custid, companyname
FROM Sales.USACusts;
```

Because a view is an object in the database, you can control access to the view with permissions just like other objects that can be queried (for example, SELECT, INSERT, UPDATE, and DELETE permissions). For example, you can deny direct access to the underlying objects while granting access to the view.

Note that the general recommendation to avoid using SELECT * has specific relevance in the context of views. The columns are enumerated in the compiled form of the view and new table columns will not be automatically added to the view. For example, suppose you define a view based on the query SELECT * FROM dbo.T1, and at the view creation time the table T1 has the columns col1 and col2. SQL Server stores information only on those two columns in the view's metadata. If you alter the definition of the table adding new columns, those new columns will not be added to the view. You can refresh the view's metadata using a stored procedure called sp_refreshview, but to avoid confusion, the best practice is to explicitly list the column names that you need in the definition of the view. If columns are added to the underlying tables and you need them in the view, use the *ALTER VIEW* statement to revise the view definition accordingly.

Views and the ORDER BY Clause

The query that you use to define a view must meet all requirements mentioned earlier with respect to table expressions in the context of derived tables. The view should not guarantee any order to the rows, all view columns must have names, and all column names must be unique. In this section, I'll elaborate a bit about the ordering issue, which is a fundamental point that is crucial to understand.

Remember that a presentation ORDER BY clause is not allowed in the query defining a table expression because there's no order among the rows of a relational table. An attempt to create an ordered view is absurd because it violates fundamental properties of a relation as defined by the relational model. If you need to return rows from a view sorted for presentation purposes, you shouldn't try to make the view something it shouldn't be. Instead, you should specify a presentation ORDER BY clause in the outer query against the view, like so:

```
SELECT custid, companyname, region
FROM Sales.USACusts
ORDER BY region;
```

Try running the following code to create a view with a presentation ORDER BY clause:

```
ALTER VIEW Sales.USACusts
AS

SELECT
  custid, companyname, contactname, contacttitle, address,
  city, region, postalcode, country, phone, fax
FROM Sales.Customers
WHERE country = N'USA'
ORDER BY region;
GO
```

This attempt fails and you get the following error:

```
Msg 1033, Level 15, State 1, Procedure USACusts, Line 9
The ORDER BY clause is invalid in views, inline functions, derived tables, subqueries, and
common table expressions, unless TOP or FOR XML is also specified.
```

The error message indicates that SQL Server allows the ORDER BY clause in two exceptional cases—when the TOP or FOR XML options are used. Neither case follows the SQL standard, and in both cases the ORDER BY clause serves a purpose beyond the usual presentation purpose.

Because T-SQL allows an ORDER BY clause in a view when TOP is also specified, some people think that they can create "ordered views" by using TOP (100) PERCENT like so:

```
ALTER VIEW Sales.USACusts
AS

SELECT TOP (100)
  custid, companyname, contactname, contacttitle, address,
  city, region, postalcode, country, phone, fax
```

```
FROM Sales.Customers
WHERE country = N'USA'
ORDER BY region;
GO
```

Even though the code is technically valid and the view is created, you should be aware that because the query is used to define a table expression, the ORDER BY clause here is only guaranteed to serve the logical filtering purpose for the TOP option. If you query the view and don't specify an ORDER BY clause in the outer query, presentation order is not guaranteed.

For example, run the following query against the view:

```
SELECT custid, companyname, region
FROM Sales.USACusts;
```

Here is the output from one of my executions showing that the rows are not sorted by region:

```
custid       companyname               region
-----------  ------------------------  ---------------
32           Customer YSIQX            OR
36           Customer LVJSO            OR
43           Customer UISOJ            WA
45           Customer QXPPT            CA
48           Customer DVFMB            OR
55           Customer KZQZT            AK
65           Customer NYUHS            NM
71           Customer LCOUJ            ID
75           Customer XOJYP            WY
77           Customer LCYBZ            OR
78           Customer NLTYP            MT
82           Customer EYHKM            WA
89           Customer YBQTI            WA
```

In some cases a query that is used to define a table expression has the TOP option with an ORDER BY clause, and the query against the table expression doesn't have an ORDER BY clause. In those cases, therefore, the output might or might not be returned in the specified order. If the results happen to be ordered, it may be due to optimization reasons, especially when you use values other than TOP (100) PERCENT. The point I'm trying to make is that any order of the rows in the output is considered valid, and no specific order is guaranteed; therefore, when querying a table expression, you should not assume any order unless you specify an ORDER BY clause in the outer query.

Do not confuse the behavior of a query that is used to define a table expression with a query that isn't. A query with TOP and ORDER BY does not guarantee presentation order only in the context of a table expression. In the context of a query that is not used to define a table expression, the ORDER BY clause serves both the logical filtering purpose for the TOP option and the presentation purpose.

View Options

When you create or alter a view, you can specify view attributes and options as part of the view definition. In the header of the view under the WITH clause you can specify attributes such as ENCRYPTION and SCHEMABINDING, and at the end of the query you can specify WITH CHECK OPTION. The following sections describe the purpose of these options.

The ENCRYPTION Option

The ENCRYPTION option is available when you create or alter views, stored procedures, triggers, and user-defined functions (UDFs). The ENCRYPTION option indicates that SQL Server will internally store the text with the definition of the object in an obfuscated format. The obfuscated text is not directly visible to users through any of the catalog objects—only to privileged users through special means.

Before you look at the ENCRYPTION option, run the following code to alter the definition of the USACusts view to its original version:

```
ALTER VIEW Sales.USACusts
AS

SELECT
  custid, companyname, contactname, contacttitle, address,
  city, region, postalcode, country, phone, fax
FROM Sales.Customers
WHERE country = N'USA';
GO
```

To get the definition of the view, invoke the *OBJECT_DEFINITION* function like so:

```
SELECT OBJECT_DEFINITION(OBJECT_ID('Sales.USACusts'));
```

The text with the definition of the view is available because the view was created without the ENCRYPTION option. You get the following output:

```
CREATE VIEW Sales.USACusts
AS

SELECT
  custid, companyname, contactname, contacttitle, address,
  city, region, postalcode, country, phone, fax
FROM Sales.Customers
WHERE country = N'USA';
```

Next, alter the view definition—only this time, include the ENCRYPTION option:

```
ALTER VIEW Sales.USACusts WITH ENCRYPTION
AS

SELECT
  custid, companyname, contactname, contacttitle, address,
  city, region, postalcode, country, phone, fax
```

```
FROM Sales.Customers
WHERE country = N'USA';
GO
```

Try again to get the text with the definition of the view:

```
SELECT OBJECT_DEFINITION(OBJECT_ID('Sales.USACusts'));
```

This time you get a NULL back.

As an alternative to the *OBJECT_DEFINITION* function, you can use the sp_helptext stored procedure to get object definitions. The *OBJECT_DEFINITION* function was added in SQL Server 2005 while sp_helptext was also available in earlier versions. For example, the following code requests the object definition of the USACusts view:

```
EXEC sp_helptext 'Sales.USACusts';
```

Because in our case the view was created with the ENCRYPTION option, you will not get the object definition back, but the following message:

```
The text for object 'Sales.USACusts' is encrypted.
```

The SCHEMABINDING Option

The SCHEMABINDING option is available to views and UDFs, and it binds the schema of referenced objects and columns to the schema of the referencing object. It indicates that referenced objects cannot be dropped and that referenced columns cannot be dropped or altered.

For example, alter the USACusts view with the SCHEMABINDING option:

```
ALTER VIEW Sales.USACusts WITH SCHEMABINDING
AS

SELECT
  custid, companyname, contactname, contacttitle, address,
  city, region, postalcode, country, phone, fax
FROM Sales.Customers
WHERE country = N'USA';
GO
```

Now try to drop the Address column from the Customers table:

```
ALTER TABLE Sales.Customers DROP COLUMN address;
```

You get the following error:

```
Msg 5074, Level 16, State 1, Line 1
The object 'USACusts' is dependent on column 'address'.
Msg 4922, Level 16, State 9, Line 1
ALTER TABLE DROP COLUMN address failed because one or more objects access this column.
```

Without the SCHEMABINDING option, such a schema change would have been allowed, as well as dropping the Customers table altogether. This can lead to errors at run time when you try to query the view, and referenced objects or columns that do not exist. If you create the view with the SCHEMABINDING option, you can avoid these errors.

The object definition must meet a couple of technical requirements to support the SCHEMABINDING option. The query is not allowed to use * in the SELECT clause; instead, you have to explicitly list column names. Also, you must use schema-qualified two-part names when referring to objects. Both requirements are actually good practices in general.

As you can imagine, creating your objects with the SCHEMABINDING option is a good practice.

The Option CHECK OPTION

The purpose of CHECK OPTION is to prevent modifications through the view that conflict with the view's filter—assuming that one exists in the query defining the view.

The query defining the view USACusts filters customers where the country attribute is equal to N'USA'. The view is currently defined without CHECK OPTION. This means that you can currently insert rows through the view with customers from countries other than the United States, and you can update existing customers through the view, changing their country to one other than the United States. For example, the following code successfully inserts a customer with company name Customer ABCDE from the United Kingdom through the view:

```
INSERT INTO Sales.USACusts(
  companyname, contactname, contacttitle, address,
  city, region, postalcode, country, phone, fax)
 VALUES(
  N'Customer ABCDE', N'Contact ABCDE', N'Title ABCDE', N'Address ABCDE',
  N'London', NULL, N'12345', N'UK', N'012-3456789', N'012-3456789');
```

The row was inserted through the view into the Customers table. However, because the view filters only customers from the United States, if you query the view looking for the new customer you get an empty set back:

```
SELECT custid, companyname, country
FROM Sales.USACusts
WHERE companyname = N'Customer ABCDE';
```

Query the Customers table directly looking for the new customer:

```
SELECT custid, companyname, country
FROM Sales.Customers
WHERE companyname = N'Customer ABCDE';
```

You get the customer information in the output, because the new row made it to the Customers table:

```
custid      companyname         country
----------- ------------------- ---------------
92          Customer ABCDE      UK
```

Similarly, if you update a customer row through the view, changing the country attribute to a country other than the United States, the update makes it to the table. But that customer doesn't show up anymore in the view because it doesn't qualify to the view's query filter.

If you want to prevent modifications that conflict with the view's filter, add WITH CHECK OPTION at the end of the query defining the view:

```
ALTER VIEW Sales.USACusts WITH SCHEMABINDING
AS

SELECT
  custid, companyname, contactname, contacttitle, address,
  city, region, postalcode, country, phone, fax
FROM Sales.Customers
WHERE country = N'USA'
WITH CHECK OPTION;
GO
```

Now try to insert a row that conflicts with the view's filter:

```
INSERT INTO Sales.USACusts(
  companyname, contactname, contacttitle, address,
  city, region, postalcode, country, phone, fax)
  VALUES(
  N'Customer FGHIJ', N'Contact FGHIJ', N'Title FGHIJ', N'Address FGHIJ',
  N'London', NULL, N'12345', N'UK', N'012-3456789', N'012-3456789');
```

You get the following error:

```
Msg 550, Level 16, State 1, Line 1
The attempted insert or update failed because the target view either specifies WITH CHECK
OPTION or spans a view that specifies WITH CHECK OPTION and one or more rows resulting from
the operation did not qualify under the CHECK OPTION constraint.
The statement has been terminated.
```

When you're done, run the following code for cleanup:

```
DELETE FROM Sales.Customers
WHERE custid > 91;

DBCC CHECKIDENT('Sales.Customers', RESEED, 91);

IF OBJECT_ID('Sales.USACusts') IS NOT NULL DROP VIEW Sales.USACusts;
```

Inline Table-Valued Functions

Inline TVFs are reusable table expressions that support input parameters. In all respects except for the support for input parameters, inline TVFs are similar to views. For this reason, I like to think of inline TVFs as parameterized views, even though they are not called this formally.

For example, the following code creates an inline TVF called *fn_GetCustOrders* in the TSQLFundamentals2008 database:

```
USE TSQLFundamentals2008;
IF OBJECT_ID('dbo.fn_GetCustOrders') IS NOT NULL
  DROP FUNCTION dbo.fn_GetCustOrders;
GO
CREATE FUNCTION dbo.fn_GetCustOrders
  (@cid AS INT) RETURNS TABLE
AS
RETURN
  SELECT orderid, custid, empid, orderdate, requireddate,
    shippeddate, shipperid, freight, shipname, shipaddress, shipcity,
    shipregion, shippostalcode, shipcountry
  FROM Sales.Orders
  WHERE custid = @cid;
GO
```

This inline TVF accepts an input parameter called *@cid* representing a customer ID, and returns all orders that were placed by the input customer. You query inline TVFs like you query other tables with DML statements. If the function accepts input parameters, you specify those in parentheses following the function's name. Also, make sure you provide an alias to the table expression. Providing a table expression with an alias is not always a requirement but is a good practice because it makes your code more readable and less prone to errors. For example, the following code queries the function requesting all orders that were placed by customer 1:

```
SELECT orderid, custid
FROM dbo.fn_GetCustOrders(1) AS CO;
```

This code returns the following output:

```
orderid     custid
----------- -----------
10643       1
10692       1
10702       1
10835       1
10952       1
11011       1
```

As with other tables, you can refer to an inline TVF as part of a join. For example, the following query joins the inline TVF returning customer 1's orders with the Sales.OrderDetails table, matching customer 1's orders with the related order lines:

```
SELECT CO.orderid, CO.custid, OD.productid, OD.qty
FROM dbo.fn_GetCustOrders(1) AS CO
  JOIN Sales.OrderDetails AS OD
    ON CO.orderid = OD.orderid;
```

This code returns the following output:

```
orderid      custid      productid    qty
-----------  ----------- -----------  ------
10643        1           28           15
10643        1           39           21
10643        1           46            2
10692        1           63           20
10702        1            3            6
10702        1           76           15
10835        1           59           15
10835        1           77            2
10952        1            6           16
10952        1           28            2
11011        1           58           40
11011        1           71           20
```

When you're done, run the following code for cleanup:

```
IF OBJECT_ID('dbo.fn_GetCustOrders') IS NOT NULL
  DROP FUNCTION dbo.fn_GetCustOrders;
```

The APPLY Operator

The APPLY operator is a nonstandard table operator that was introduced in SQL Server 2005. This operator is used in the FROM clause of a query like all table operators. The two supported types of the APPLY operator are CROSS APPLY and OUTER APPLY. CROSS APPLY implements only one logical query processing phase, while OUTER APPLY implements two.

The APPLY operator operates on two input tables, the second of which may be a table expression; I'll refer to them as the left and right tables. The right table is usually a derived table or an inline TVF. The CROSS APPLY operator implements one logical query processing phase—it applies the right table expression to each row from the left table, and produces a result table with the unified result sets.

So far it might sound like the CROSS APPLY operator is very similar to a cross join, and in a sense that's true. For example, the following two queries return the same result sets:

```
SELECT S.shipperid, E.empid
FROM Sales.Shippers AS S
  CROSS JOIN HR.Employees AS E;

SELECT S.shipperid, E.empid
FROM Sales.Shippers AS S
  CROSS APPLY HR.Employees AS E;
```

However, with the CROSS APPLY operator the right table expression can represent a different set of rows per each row from the left table, unlike in a join. You can achieve this when you use a derived table in the right side, and in the derived table query refer to attributes from the left side. Or when you use an inline TVF, you can pass attributes from the left side as input arguments.

For example, the following code uses the CROSS APPLY operator to return the three most recent orders for each customer:

```
SELECT C.custid, A.orderid, A.orderdate
FROM Sales.Customers AS C
  CROSS APPLY
    (SELECT TOP(3) orderid, empid, orderdate, requireddate
     FROM Sales.Orders AS O
     WHERE O.custid = C.custid
     ORDER BY orderdate DESC, orderid DESC) AS A;
```

You can think of the table expression A as a correlated table subquery. In terms of logical query processing, the right table expression (derived table in our case) is applied to each row from the Customers table. Notice the reference to the attribute C.custid from the left table in the derived table's query filter. The derived table returns the three most recent orders for the customer from the current left row. Because the derived table is applied to each row from the left side, the CROSS APPLY operator returns the three most recent orders for each customer.

Here's the output of this query, shown here in abbreviated form:

```
custid       orderid      orderdate
----------- ----------- -----------------------
1            11011        2008-04-09 00:00:00.000
1            10952        2008-03-16 00:00:00.000
1            10835        2008-01-15 00:00:00.000
2            10926        2008-03-04 00:00:00.000
2            10759        2007-11-28 00:00:00.000
2            10625        2007-08-08 00:00:00.000
3            10856        2008-01-28 00:00:00.000
3            10682        2007-09-25 00:00:00.000
3            10677        2007-09-22 00:00:00.000
...

(263 row(s) affected)
```

If the right table expression returns an empty set, the CROSS APPLY operator does not return the corresponding left row. For example, customers 22 and 57 did not place orders. In both cases the derived table is an empty set; therefore, those customers are not returned in the output. If you want to return rows from the left table for which the right table expression returns an empty set, use the OUTER APPLY operator instead of CROSS APPLY. The OUTER APPLY operator adds a second logical phase that identifies rows from the left side for which the right table expression returns an empty set, and adds those rows to the result table as outer rows with NULLs in the right side's attributes as place holders. In a sense, this phase is similar to the phase that adds outer rows in a left outer join.

For example, run the following code to return the three most recent orders for each customer, and include in the output customers with no orders as well:

```
SELECT C.custid, A.orderid, A.orderdate
FROM Sales.Customers AS C
  OUTER APPLY
```

```
  (SELECT TOP(3) orderid, empid, orderdate, requireddate
   FROM Sales.Orders AS O
   WHERE O.custid = C.custid
   ORDER BY orderdate DESC, orderid DESC) AS A;
```

This time, customers 22 and 57, who did not place orders, are included in the output, which is shown here in abbreviated form:

```
custid       orderid      orderdate
-----------  -----------  -----------------------
1            11011        2008-04-09 00:00:00.000
1            10952        2008-03-16 00:00:00.000
1            10835        2008-01-15 00:00:00.000
2            10926        2008-03-04 00:00:00.000
2            10759        2007-11-28 00:00:00.000
2            10625        2007-08-08 00:00:00.000
3            10856        2008-01-28 00:00:00.000
3            10682        2007-09-25 00:00:00.000
3            10677        2007-09-22 00:00:00.000
...
22           NULL         NULL
...
57           NULL         NULL
...

(265 row(s) affected)
```

For encapsulation purposes you may find it more convenient to work with inline TVFs instead of derived tables. This way your code will be simpler to follow and maintain. For example, the following code creates an inline TVF called *fn_TopOrders* that accepts as inputs a customer ID (*@custid*) and a number (*@n*), and returns the *@n* most recent orders for customer *@custid*:

```
IF OBJECT_ID('dbo.fn_TopOrders') IS NOT NULL
  DROP FUNCTION dbo.fn_TopOrders;
GO
CREATE FUNCTION dbo.fn_TopOrders
  (@custid AS INT, @n AS INT)
  RETURNS TABLE
AS
RETURN
  SELECT TOP(@n) orderid, empid, orderdate, requireddate
  FROM Sales.Orders
  WHERE custid = @custid
  ORDER BY orderdate DESC, orderid DESC;
GO
```

You can now substitute the use of the derived table from the previous examples with the new function:

```
SELECT
  C.custid, C.companyname,
  A.orderid, A.empid, A.orderdate, A.requireddate
FROM Sales.Customers AS C
  CROSS APPLY dbo.fn_TopOrders(C.custid, 3) AS A;
```

The code is much more readable and easier to maintain. In terms of physical processing, nothing really changed because, as I stated earlier, the definition of table expressions is expanded, and SQL Server will in any case end up querying the underlying objects directly.

Conclusion

Table expressions can help you simplify your code, improve its maintainability, and encapsulate querying logic. When you need to use table expressions and are not planning to reuse their definitions, use derived tables or CTEs. CTEs have a couple of advantages over derived tables; you do not nest CTEs as you do derived tables, making CTEs more modular and easier to maintain. Also, you can refer to multiple instances of the same CTE, which you cannot do with derived tables.

When you need to define reusable table expressions, use views or inline TVFs. When you do not need to support input parameters, use views; otherwise, use inline TVFs.

Use the APPLY operator when you want to apply a table expression to each row from a source table, and unify all result sets into one result table.

Exercises

This section provides exercises to help you familiarize yourself with the subjects discussed in this chapter. All the exercises in this chapter require your session to be connected to the database TSQLFundamentals2008.

1-1

Write a query that returns the maximum order date for each employee.

Tables involved: TSQLFundamentals2008 database, Sales.Orders table.

Desired output:

```
empid       maxorderdate
----------- -----------------------
3           2008-04-30 00:00:00.000
6           2008-04-23 00:00:00.000
9           2008-04-29 00:00:00.000
7           2008-05-06 00:00:00.000
1           2008-05-06 00:00:00.000
4           2008-05-06 00:00:00.000
2           2008-05-05 00:00:00.000
5           2008-04-22 00:00:00.000
8           2008-05-06 00:00:00.000

(9 row(s) affected)
```

1-2

Encapsulate the query from Exercise 1-1 in a derived table. Write a join query between the derived table and the Orders table to return the orders with the maximum order date for each employee.

Tables involved: Sales.Orders.

Desired output:

```
empid       orderdate                 orderid     custid
----------- ------------------------- ----------- -----------
9           2008-04-29 00:00:00.000   11058       6
8           2008-05-06 00:00:00.000   11075       68
7           2008-05-06 00:00:00.000   11074       73
6           2008-04-23 00:00:00.000   11045       10
5           2008-04-22 00:00:00.000   11043       74
4           2008-05-06 00:00:00.000   11076       9
3           2008-04-30 00:00:00.000   11063       37
2           2008-05-05 00:00:00.000   11073       58
2           2008-05-05 00:00:00.000   11070       44
1           2008-05-06 00:00:00.000   11077       65

(10 row(s) affected)
```

2-1

Write a query that calculates a row number for each order based on orderdate, orderid ordering.

Tables involved: Sales.Orders.

Desired output (abbreviated):

```
orderid     orderdate                 custid      empid       rownum
----------- ------------------------- ----------- ----------- -------
10248       2006-07-04 00:00:00.000   85          5           1
10249       2006-07-05 00:00:00.000   79          6           2
10250       2006-07-08 00:00:00.000   34          4           3
10251       2006-07-08 00:00:00.000   84          3           4
10252       2006-07-09 00:00:00.000   76          4           5
10253       2006-07-10 00:00:00.000   34          3           6
10254       2006-07-11 00:00:00.000   14          5           7
10255       2006-07-12 00:00:00.000   68          9           8
10256       2006-07-15 00:00:00.000   88          3           9
10257       2006-07-16 00:00:00.000   35          4           10
...

(830 row(s) affected)
```

2-2

Write a query that returns rows with row numbers 11 through 20 based on the row number definition in Exercise 2-1. Use a CTE to encapsulate the code from Exercise 2-1.

Tables involved: Sales.Orders.

Desired output:

```
orderid      orderdate                   custid        empid         rownum
-----------  --------------------------  -----------   -----------   -------
10258        2006-07-17 00:00:00.000     20            1             11
10259        2006-07-18 00:00:00.000     13            4             12
10260        2006-07-19 00:00:00.000     56            4             13
10261        2006-07-19 00:00:00.000     61            4             14
10262        2006-07-22 00:00:00.000     65            8             15
10263        2006-07-23 00:00:00.000     20            9             16
10264        2006-07-24 00:00:00.000     24            6             17
10265        2006-07-25 00:00:00.000     7             2             18
10266        2006-07-26 00:00:00.000     87            3             19
10267        2006-07-29 00:00:00.000     25            4             20

(10 row(s) affected)
```

3

Write a solution using a recursive CTE that returns the management chain leading to Zoya Dolgopyatova (employee ID 9).

Tables involved: HR.Employees.

Desired output:

```
empid        mgrid        firstname   lastname
-----------  -----------  ----------  --------------------
9            5            Zoya        Dolgopyatova
5            2            Sven        Buck
2            1            Don         Funk
1            NULL         Sara        Davis

(4 row(s) affected)
```

4-1

Create a view that returns the total quantity for each employee and year.

Tables involved: Sales.Orders and Sales.OrderDetails.

When running the following code:

```
SELECT * FROM Sales.VEmpOrders ORDER BY empid, orderyear;
```

The desired output is:

```
empid       orderyear    qty
----------- ------------ -----------
1           2006         1620
1           2007         3877
1           2008         2315
2           2006         1085
2           2007         2604
2           2008         2366
3           2006         940
3           2007         4436
3           2008         2476
4           2006         2212
4           2007         5273
4           2008         2313
5           2006         778
5           2007         1471
5           2008         787
6           2006         963
6           2007         1738
6           2008         826
7           2006         485
7           2007         2292
7           2008         1877
8           2006         923
8           2007         2843
8           2008         2147
9           2006         575
9           2007         955
9           2008         1140

(27 row(s) affected)
```

4-2 (Optional, Advanced)

Write a query against Sales.VEmpOrders that returns the running total quantity for each employee and year.

Tables involved: Sales.VEmpOrders view.

Desired output:

```
empid       orderyear    qty          runqty
----------- ------------ ------------ -----------
1           2006         1620         1620
1           2007         3877         5497
1           2008         2315         7812
2           2006         1085         1085
2           2007         2604         3689
2           2008         2366         6055
3           2006         940          940
```

3	2007	4436	5376
3	2008	2476	7852
4	2006	2212	2212
4	2007	5273	7485
4	2008	2313	9798
5	2006	778	778
5	2007	1471	2249
5	2008	787	3036
6	2006	963	963
6	2007	1738	2701
6	2008	826	3527
7	2006	485	485
7	2007	2292	2777
7	2008	1877	4654
8	2006	923	923
8	2007	2843	3766
8	2008	2147	5913
9	2006	575	575
9	2007	955	1530
9	2008	1140	2670

```
(27 row(s) affected)
```

5-1

Create an inline function that accepts as inputs a supplier ID (*@supid* AS *INT*) and a requested number of products (*@n* AS *INT*). The function should return *@n* products with the highest unit prices that are supplied by the given supplier ID.

Tables involved: Production.Products.

When issuing the following query:

```
SELECT * FROM Production.fn_TopProducts(5, 2);
```

Desired output:

```
productid   productname         unitprice
----------- ------------------- ---------------
12          Product OSFNS       38.00
11          Product QMVUN       21.00

(2 row(s) affected)
```

5-2

Using the CROSS APPLY operator and the function you created in Exercise 4-1, return, for each supplier, the two most expensive products.

Desired output:

```
supplierid  companyname       productid   productname       unitprice
----------- ----------------- ----------- ----------------- ----------
8           Supplier BWGYE    20          Product QHFFP     81.00
8           Supplier BWGYE    68          Product TBTBL     12.50
20          Supplier CIYNM    43          Product ZZZHR     46.00
20          Supplier CIYNM    44          Product VJIEO     19.45
23          Supplier ELCRN    49          Product FPYPN     20.00
23          Supplier ELCRN    76          Product JYGFE     18.00
5           Supplier EQPNC    12          Product OSFNS     38.00
5           Supplier EQPNC    11          Product QMVUN     21.00
...

(55 row(s) affected)
```

Solutions

This section provides solutions to the exercises in the preceding section.

1-1

This exercise is just a preliminary step to the next exercise. This step involves writing a query that returns the maximum order date for each employee:

```
USE TSQLFundamentals2008;

SELECT empid, MAX(orderdate) AS maxorderdate
FROM Sales.Orders
GROUP BY empid;
```

1-2

This exercise requires you to use the query from the previous step to define a derived table, and join this derived table with the Orders table to return the orders with the maximum order date for each employee, like so:

```
SELECT O.empid, O.orderdate, O.orderid, O.custid
FROM Sales.Orders AS O
  JOIN (SELECT empid, MAX(orderdate) AS maxorderdate
        FROM Sales.Orders
        GROUP BY empid) AS D
    ON O.empid = D.empid
    AND O.orderdate = D.maxorderdate;
```

2-1

This exercise is a preliminary step to the next exercise. It requires you to query the Orders table and calculate row numbers based on orderdate, orderid ordering, like so:

```
SELECT orderid, orderdate, custid, empid,
  ROW_NUMBER() OVER(ORDER BY orderdate, orderid) AS rownum
FROM Sales.Orders;
```

2-2

This exercise requires you to define a CTE based on the query from the previous step, and filter only rows with row numbers in the range 11 through 20 from the CTE, like so:

```
WITH OrdersRN AS
(
  SELECT orderid, orderdate, custid, empid,
    ROW_NUMBER() OVER(ORDER BY orderdate, orderid) AS rownum
  FROM Sales.Orders
)
SELECT * FROM OrdersRN WHERE rownum BETWEEN 11 AND 20;
```

You might wonder why you need a table expression here. Remember that calculations based on the OVER clause (such as the *ROW_NUMBER* function) are only allowed in the SELECT and ORDER BY clauses of a query, and not directly in the WHERE clause. By using a table expression you can invoke the *ROW_NUMBER* function in the SELECT clause, assign an alias to the result column, and refer to the result column in the WHERE clause of the outer query.

3

You can think of this exercise as the inverse of the request to return an employee and all subordinates in all levels. Here, the anchor member is a query that returns the row for employee 9. The recursive member joins the CTE (call it C)—representing the subordinate/child from the previous level—with the Employees table (call it P)—representing the manager/parent in the next level. This way, each invocation of the recursive member returns the manager from the next level, until no next level manager is found (in the case of the CEO).

Here's the complete solution query:

```
WITH EmpsCTE AS
(
  SELECT empid, mgrid, firstname, lastname
  FROM HR.Employees
  WHERE empid = 9

  UNION ALL
```

```
  SELECT P.empid, P.mgrid, P.firstname, P.lastname
  FROM EmpsCTE AS C
    JOIN HR.Employees AS P
      ON C.mgrid = P.empid
)
SELECT empid, mgrid, firstname, lastname
FROM EmpsCTE;
```

4-1

This exercise is a preliminary step to the next exercise. Here you are required to define a view based on a query that joins the Orders and OrderDetails tables, group the rows by employee ID and order year, and return the total quantity for each group. The view definition should look like this:

```
USE TSQLFundamentals2008;
IF OBJECT_ID('Sales.VEmpOrders') IS NOT NULL
  DROP VIEW Sales.VEmpOrders;
GO
CREATE VIEW  Sales.VEmpOrders
AS

SELECT
  empid,
  YEAR(orderdate) AS orderyear,
  SUM(qty) AS qty
FROM Sales.Orders AS O
  JOIN Sales.OrderDetails AS OD
    ON O.orderid = OD.orderid
GROUP BY
  empid,
  YEAR(orderdate);
GO
```

4-2

In this exercise, you query the VEmpOrders view and return the running total quantity for each employee and order year. To achieve this, you can write a query against the VEmpOrders view (call it V1) that returns from each row the employee ID, order year, and quantity. In the SELECT list you can incorporate a subquery against a second instance of VEmpOrders (call it V2), that returns the sum of all quantities from the rows where the employee ID is equal to the one in V1, and the order year is smaller than or equal to the one in V1. The complete solution query looks like this:

```
SELECT empid, orderyear, qty,
  (SELECT SUM(qty)
   FROM  Sales.VEmpOrders AS V2
   WHERE V2.empid = V1.empid
     AND V2.orderyear <= V1.orderyear) AS runqty
FROM  Sales.VEmpOrders AS V1
ORDER BY empid, orderyear;
```

5-1

This exercise requires you to define a function called *fn_TopProducts* that accepts a supplier ID (*@supid*) and a number (*@n*), and is supposed to return the *@n* most expensive products supplied by the input supplier ID. Here's how the function definition should look:

```
USE TSQLFundamentals2008;
IF OBJECT_ID('Production.fn_TopProducts') IS NOT NULL
  DROP FUNCTION Production.fn_TopProducts;
GO
CREATE FUNCTION Production.fn_TopProducts
  (@supid AS INT, @n AS INT)
  RETURNS TABLE
AS
RETURN
  SELECT TOP(@n) productid, productname, unitprice
  FROM Production.Products
  WHERE supplierid = @supid
  ORDER BY unitprice DESC;
GO
```

5-2

In this exercise, you write a query against the Production.Suppliers table, and use the CROSS APPLY operator to apply the function you defined by the previous step to each supplier. Your query is supposed to return the two most expensive products for each supplier. Here's the solution query:

```
SELECT S.supplierid, S.companyname, P.productid, P.productname, P.unitprice
FROM Production.Suppliers AS S
  CROSS APPLY Production.fn_TopProducts(S.supplierid, 2) AS P;
```

Chapter 6
Set Operations

Set operations are operations between two input sets—or more accurately, multisets—resulting from two input queries. Remember, a multiset is not a true set because it can contain duplicates. When I use the term *multiset* in this chapter, I'm referring to the intermediate result sets from two input queries that may contain duplicates. Although there are two multisets as inputs to a SQL set operation, the final output is still one result set that may also be a multiset.

T-SQL supports three set operations: UNION, INTERSECT, and EXCEPT. INTERSECT and EXCEPT were introduced in Microsoft SQL Server 2005. In this chapter, I'll first introduce the general form and requirements of set operations, and then describe each set operation in detail.

The general form of a set operation is:

```
Input Query1
<set_operation>
Input Query2
[ORDER BY ...]
```

A set operation compares complete rows between the result sets of the two input queries involved. Whether a row will be returned in the result of the set operation depends upon the outcome of the comparison and the set operation used. Because by definition, a set operation is an operation between two sets (or multisets), and a set has no guaranteed order, the two queries involved cannot have ORDER BY clauses. Remember that a query with an ORDER BY clause guarantees presentation order, and therefore does not return a set—it returns a cursor. However, while the queries involved cannot have ORDER BY clauses, you can optionally add an ORDER BY clause that is applied to the result of the entire set operation.

In terms of logical query processing, each of the individual queries can have all logical query processing phases except for a presentation ORDER BY, as I just explained. The set operation is applied between the results of the two queries, and the outer ORDER BY clause (if one exists) is applied to the result of the set operation.

The two queries involved in a set operation must produce result sets with the same number of columns, and corresponding columns must have compatible data types. By "compatible data types," I mean that the data type that is lower in terms of data type precedence must be implicitly convertible to the higher data type.

The names of the columns in the result of a set operation are determined by the first query; therefore, if you need to assign aliases to result columns, you should assign those in the first query.

An interesting aspect of set operations is that when comparing rows, a set operation considers two NULLs as equal. I'll demonstrate the importance of this point later in the chapter.

ANSI SQL supports two "flavors" of each set operation—DISTINCT (default) and ALL. DISTINCT logically eliminates duplicates from the two input multisets—making them sets— and returns a set. ALL operates on two multisets without eliminating duplicates, and it returns a multiset that can have duplicates. SQL Server 2008 supports DISTINCT for all three set operations, but it supports ALL only with UNION. In terms of syntax, you cannot explicitly specify the DISTINCT clause. Instead, it is implied when you don't specify ALL explicitly. I'll provide alternatives to the missing INTERSECT ALL and EXCEPT ALL in the sections "The INTERSECT Set Operation" and "The EXCEPT Set Operation."

The UNION Set Operation

In set theory, the *union* of two sets (call them A and B) is the set containing all elements of both A and B. In other words, if an element belongs to any of the input sets, it belongs to the result set. Figure 6-1 shows a set diagram (also known as a Venn diagram) with a graphical depiction of the union of two sets. The area marked with diagonal lines represents the result of the set operation.

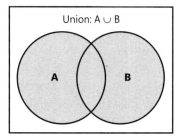

FIGURE 6-1 Union of two sets

In T-SQL, the UNION set operation unifies the result sets of two input queries. If a row appears in any of the input sets, it will appear in the result of the UNION operation. T-SQL supports both the UNION ALL and UNION (implicit DISTINCT) flavors of the UNION set operation.

The UNION ALL Set Operation

The UNION ALL set operation returns all rows that appear in any of the input multisets resulting from the two input queries of the operation, without really comparing rows and without eliminating duplicates. Assuming that Query1 returns m rows and Query2 returns n rows, Query1 UNION ALL Query2 returns $m + n$ rows.

For example, the following code performs a UNION ALL set operation between the result multiset of a query that selects the location attributes (country, region, city) from the HR.Employees table in the TSQLFundamentals2008 database and the result multiset of a query that selects the location attributes from the Sales.Customers table:

```
USE TSQLFundamentals2008;

SELECT country, region, city FROM HR.Employees
UNION ALL
SELECT country, region, city FROM Sales.Customers;
```

The result has 100 rows—nine from the Employees table and 91 from the Customers table—and is shown here in abbreviated form:

```
country          region           city
---------------  ---------------  ---------------
USA              WA               Seattle
USA              WA               Tacoma
USA              WA               Kirkland
USA              WA               Redmond
UK               NULL             London
...
Finland          NULL             Oulu
Brazil           SP               Resende
USA              WA               Seattle
Finland          NULL             Helsinki
Poland           NULL             Warszawa

(100 row(s) affected)
```

Because UNION ALL doesn't eliminate duplicates, the result is a multiset and not a set. The same row can appear multiple times in the result, as is the case with (UK, NULL, London) in the result of our set operation query.

The UNION DISTINCT Set Operation

The UNION (implicit DISTINCT) set operation acts at the logical level as though it turns the two input multisets to sets by eliminating duplicates, and it returns a set with all rows that appear in any of the input sets. Note that if a row appears in both input sets, it will appear only once in the result; in other words, the result is also a set and not a multiset.

In terms of physical processing, SQL Server doesn't necessarily first eliminate duplicates from the input multisets and then apply the set operation—instead, it may first unify the two multisets and then eliminate duplicates.

For example, the following code returns distinct locations that are either employee locations or customer locations:

```
SELECT country, region, city FROM HR.Employees
UNION
SELECT country, region, city FROM Sales.Customers;
```

The difference between this example and the previous one with the UNION ALL operation is that in this example the set operation removed duplicates, while in the previous example it didn't. Hence, the result of this query has distinct rows, as shown here in abbreviated form:

```
country          region           city
---------------  ---------------  ---------------
Argentina        NULL             Buenos Aires
Austria          NULL             Graz
Austria          NULL             Salzburg
Belgium          NULL             Bruxelles
Belgium          NULL             Charleroi
...
USA              WY               Lander
Venezuela        DF               Caracas
Venezuela        Lara             Barquisimeto
Venezuela        Nueva Esparta    I. de Margarita
Venezuela        Táchira          San Cristóbal

(71 row(s) affected)
```

So when should you use UNION ALL and when should you use UNION? If a potential exists for duplicates after unifying the two inputs of the set operation, and you need to return the duplicates, use UNION ALL. If a potential exists for duplicates but you need to return distinct rows, use UNION. If no potential exists for duplicates after unifying the two inputs, UNION and UNION ALL are logically equivalent. However, in such a case I'd recommend that you use UNION ALL because adding ALL removes the overhead of SQL Server checking for duplicates.

The INTERSECT Set Operation

In set theory, the *intersection* of two sets (call them A and B) is the set of all elements that belong to A and also belong to B (and the reverse is also true). Figure 6-2 shows a graphical depiction of the intersection of two sets.

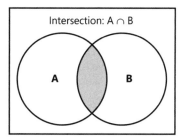

FIGURE 6-2 Intersection of two sets

In T-SQL, the INTERSECT set operation intersects the result sets of two input queries and returns only rows that appear in both inputs. After I describe INTERSECT (implicit DISTINCT), I'll provide an alternative solution to the INTERSECT ALL operation that has not yet been implemented as of SQL Server 2008.

The INTERSECT DISTINCT Set Operation

The INTERSECT set operation logically first eliminates duplicate rows from the two input multisets—turning them to sets—and then returns only rows that appear in both sets. In other words, a row is returned provided that it appears at least once in both input multisets.

For example, the following code returns distinct locations that are both employee locations and customer locations:

```
SELECT country, region, city FROM HR.Employees
INTERSECT
SELECT country, region, city FROM Sales.Customers;
```

This query returns the following output:

```
country          region           city
---------------- ---------------- ---------------
UK               NULL             London
USA              WA               Kirkland
USA              WA               Seattle
```

It doesn't matter exactly how many occurrences there are of an employee or customer location—if the location appears at least once in the Employees table and also at least once in the Customers table, the location is returned. The output of this query shows that three locations are both customer and employee locations.

Remember that earlier I mentioned that when comparing rows, a set operation considers two NULLs as equal. There are both customers and employees with the location (UK, NULL, London), but it's not trivial that this row should appear in the output. Except for the country and city attributes, when comparing the NULL region in the employee row and the NULL region in the customer row, the set operation considers the two equal, and that's why it returns the row.

When this is the desired behavior of NULL comparison—as it is in our case—set operations have a powerful advantage over alternatives. For example, one alternative to using the INTERSECT set operation is to use an inner join, and another is to use the EXISTS predicate. In both cases, when the NULL in the region attribute of an employee is compared with the NULL in the region attribute of a customer, the comparison yields UNKNOWN, and such a row is filtered out. This means that unless you add extra logic that handles NULLs in a special manner, neither the inner join nor the EXISTS alternative return the row (UK, NULL, London), even though it does appear in both sides.

The INTERSECT ALL Set Operation

I provide this section as optional reading in case you feel very comfortable with the material covered so far in this chapter. ANSI SQL supports an ALL flavor of the INTERSECT set operation, but this flavor has not yet been implemented as of SQL Server 2008. After I describe the meaning of INTERSECT ALL in ANSI SQL, I'll provide an alternative in T-SQL.

Remember the meaning of the *ALL* keyword in the UNION ALL set operation: it returns all duplicate rows. Similarly, the keyword *ALL* in the INTERSECT ALL set operation means that duplicate intersections will not be removed. INTERSECT ALL is different from UNION ALL in that the former does not return all duplicates but only returns the number of duplicate rows matching the lower of the counts in both multisets. Another way to look at it is that the INTERSECT ALL operation doesn't only care about the existence of a row in both sides—it also cares about the number of occurrences of the row in each side. It's as if this set operation looks for matches per occurrence of each row. If there are *x* occurrences of a row *R* in the first input multiset and y occurrences of *R* in the second, *R* appears minimum(x, y) times in the result of the operation. For example, the location (UK, NULL, London) appears four times in Employees and six times in Customers; hence, an INTERSECT ALL operation between the employee locations and the customer locations should return four occurrences of (UK, NULL, London), because at the logical level, four occurrences can be intersected.

Even though SQL Server does not support a built-in INTERSECT ALL operator, you can provide a solution that produces the same result. You can use the *ROW_NUMBER* function to number the occurrences of each row in each input query. To achieve this, specify all participating attributes in the PARTITION BY clause of the function, and (SELECT <constant>) in the ORDER BY clause of the function to indicate that order doesn't matter.

> **Tip** Using ORDER BY (SELECT <constant>) in the ranking function's OVER clause is one of several ways to tell SQL Server that order doesn't matter. SQL Server is smart enough to realize that the same constant will be assigned to all rows, and therefore it's not necessary to actually sort the data and pay the associated cost.

Then apply the INTERSECT set operation between the two queries with the *ROW_NUMBER* function. Because the occurrences of each row are numbered, the intersection is based on the row numbers in addition to the original attributes. For example, in the Employees table, which has four occurrences of the location (UK, NULL, London), those occurrences would be numbered 1 through 4. In the Customers table, which has six occurrences of the location (UK, NULL, London) those occurrences would be numbered 1 through 6. Occurrences 1 through 4 would all be intersected between the two.

Here's the complete solution code:

```
SELECT
  ROW_NUMBER()
    OVER(PARTITION BY country, region, city
         ORDER     BY (SELECT 0)) AS rownum,
  country, region, city
FROM HR.Employees

INTERSECT

SELECT
  ROW_NUMBER()
    OVER(PARTITION BY country, region, city
         ORDER     BY (SELECT 0)),
  country, region, city
FROM Sales.Customers;
```

This code produces the following output:

```
rownum               country          region           city
-------------------- ---------------- ---------------- ---------------
1                    UK               NULL             London
1                    USA              WA               Kirkland
1                    USA              WA               Seattle
2                    UK               NULL             London
3                    UK               NULL             London
4                    UK               NULL             London
```

Of course, the INTERSECT ALL operation is not supposed to return any row numbers; rather those are used to support the solution. If you don't want to return those in the output, you can define a table expression (for example, a CTE) based on this query and select only the original attributes from the table expression. Here's an example of how you can use INTERSECT ALL to return occurrences of employee and customer locations that intersect:

```
WITH INTERSECT_ALL
AS
(
  SELECT
    ROW_NUMBER()
      OVER(PARTITION BY country, region, city
           ORDER     BY (SELECT 0)) AS rownum,
    country, region, city
  FROM HR.Employees
```

```
INTERSECT

SELECT
  ROW_NUMBER()
    OVER(PARTITION BY country, region, city
         ORDER      BY (SELECT 0)),
    country, region, city
  FROM Sales.Customers
)
SELECT country, region, city
FROM INTERSECT_ALL;
```

Here's the output of this query, which is equivalent to what the standard INTERSECT ALL would have returned:

```
country          region           city
---------------- ---------------- ----------------
UK               NULL             London
USA              WA               Kirkland
USA              WA               Seattle
UK               NULL             London
UK               NULL             London
UK               NULL             London
```

The EXCEPT Set Operation

In set theory, the *difference* of sets A, B (A - B) is the set of elements that belong to A and do not belong to B. You can think of the set difference A - B as A less the members of B also in A. Figure 6-3 shows a graphical depiction of the set difference A - B.

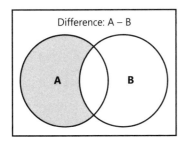

FIGURE 6-3 Set difference

In T-SQL, set difference is implemented with the EXCEPT set operation. EXCEPT operates on the result sets of two input queries and returns rows that appear in the first input but not the second. After I describe the EXCEPT (implicit DISTINCT) operation, I'll describe EXCEPT ALL that has not yet been implemented as of SQL Server 2008, and how to provide an alternative to this operation.

The EXCEPT DISTINCT Set Operation

The EXCEPT set operation logically first eliminates duplicate rows from the two input multisets—turning them to sets—and then returns only rows that appear in the first set but not the second. In other words, a row is returned provided that it appears at least once in the first input multiset and zero times in the second. Note that unlike the other two operations, EXCEPT is asymmetric; that is, with the other set operations it doesn't matter which input query appears first and which second—with EXCEPT, it does.

For example, the following code returns distinct locations that are employee locations but not customer locations:

```
SELECT country, region, city FROM HR.Employees
EXCEPT
SELECT country, region, city FROM Sales.Customers;
```

This query returns the following two locations:

```
country          region           city
---------------- ---------------- ----------------
USA              WA               Redmond
USA              WA               Tacoma
```

The following query returns distinct locations that are customer locations but not employee locations:

```
SELECT country, region, city FROM Sales.Customers
EXCEPT
SELECT country, region, city FROM HR.Employees;
```

This query returns 66 locations, shown here in abbreviated form:

```
country          region           city
---------------- ---------------- ----------------
Argentina        NULL             Buenos Aires
Austria          NULL             Graz
Austria          NULL             Salzburg
Belgium          NULL             Bruxelles
Belgium          NULL             Charleroi
...
USA              WY               Lander
Venezuela        DF               Caracas
Venezuela        Lara             Barquisimeto
Venezuela        Nueva Esparta    I. de Margarita
Venezuela        Táchira          San Cristóbal

(66 row(s) affected)
```

You can also use alternatives to the EXCEPT operation. One alternative is an outer join that filters only outer rows, which are rows that appear in one side but not the other. Another alternative is to use the NOT EXISTS predicate. However, if you want to consider two

NULLs as equal, set operations give you this behavior by default with no need for special treatment, while the alternatives don't.

The EXCEPT ALL Set Operation

I provide this section as optional reading in case you feel very comfortable with the material covered so far in this chapter. The EXCEPT ALL operation is very similar to the EXCEPT operation, but it also takes into account the number of occurrences of each row. Provided that a row R appears x times in the first multiset and y times in the second, and $x > y$, R will appear $x - y$ times in Query1 EXCEPT ALL Query2. In other words, at the logical level EXCEPT ALL returns only occurrences of a row from the first multiset that do not have a corresponding occurrence in the second.

SQL Server does not provide a built-in EXCEPT ALL operator, but you can provide an alternative with a very similar solution to the one provided for INTERSECT ALL. Namely, add a ROW_NUMBER calculation to each of the input queries to number the occurrences of each row, and use the EXCEPT operation between them. Only occurrences that don't find matches will be returned.

The following example shows how you can use EXCEPT ALL to return occurrences of employee locations that have no corresponding occurrences of customer locations:

```
WITH EXCEPT_ALL
AS
(
  SELECT
    ROW_NUMBER()
      OVER(PARTITION BY country, region, city
           ORDER     BY (SELECT 0)) AS rownum,
    country, region, city
    FROM HR.Employees

  EXCEPT

  SELECT
    ROW_NUMBER()
      OVER(PARTITION BY country, region, city
           ORDER     BY (SELECT 0)),
    country, region, city
  FROM Sales.Customers
)
SELECT country, region, city
FROM EXCEPT_ALL;
```

This query returns the following output:

```
country          region           city
---------------- ---------------- ----------------
USA              WA               Redmond
USA              WA               Tacoma
USA              WA               Seattle
```

Precedence

SQL defines precedence among set operations. The INTERSECT operation precedes UNION and EXCEPT, while UNION and EXCEPT are considered equal. In a query that contains multiple set operations, first INTERSECT operations are evaluated, and then operations with the same precedence are evaluated based on appearance order.

Consider the following query which shows how INTERSECT precedes EXCEPT:

```
SELECT country, region, city FROM Production.Suppliers
EXCEPT
SELECT country, region, city FROM HR.Employees
INTERSECT
SELECT country, region, city FROM Sales.Customers;
```

Because INTERSECT precedes EXCEPT, the INTERSECT operation is evaluated first, even though it appears second. Therefore, the meaning of this query is: "locations that are supplier locations but not (locations that are both employee and customer locations)."

This query returns the following output:

```
country          region           city
---------------  ---------------  ---------------
Australia        NSW              Sydney
Australia        Victoria         Melbourne
Brazil           NULL             Sao Paulo
Canada           Québec           Montréal
Canada           Québec           Ste-Hyacinthe
Denmark          NULL             Lyngby
Finland          NULL             Lappeenranta
France           NULL             Annecy
France           NULL             Montceau
France           NULL             Paris
Germany          NULL             Berlin
Germany          NULL             Cuxhaven
Germany          NULL             Frankfurt
Italy            NULL             Ravenna
Italy            NULL             Salerno
Japan            NULL             Osaka
Japan            NULL             Tokyo
Netherlands      NULL             Zaandam
Norway           NULL             Sandvika
Singapore        NULL             Singapore
Spain            Asturias         Oviedo
Sweden           NULL             Göteborg
Sweden           NULL             Stockholm
UK               NULL             Manchester
USA              LA               New Orleans
USA              MA               Boston
USA              MI               Ann Arbor
USA              OR               Bend

(28 row(s) affected)
```

To control the order of evaluation of set operations, use parentheses, which have the highest precedence. For example, if you want to return "(locations that are supplier locations but not employee locations) and are also customer locations," use the following code:

```
(SELECT country, region, city FROM Production.Suppliers
 EXCEPT
 SELECT country, region, city FROM HR.Employees)
INTERSECT
SELECT country, region, city FROM Sales.Customers;
```

This query returns the following output:

```
country          region           city
---------------  ---------------  ---------------
Canada           Québec           Montréal
France           NULL             Paris
Germany          NULL             Berlin
```

Circumventing Unsupported Logical Phases

This section may be considered advanced for the book's target audience and is provided here as optional reading. The individual queries that participate in a set operation support all logical query processing phases (table operators, WHERE, GROUP BY, HAVING, and so on) except for ORDER BY. However, only the ORDER BY phase is allowed on the result of the set operation. What if you need to apply other logical phases besides ORDER BY to the result of the set operation? This is not supported as part of the set operation query itself, but you can easily circumvent this restriction by using table expressions. Define a table expression based on a query with a set operation, and apply any logical query processing phases that you like in the outer query against the table expression. For example, the following query returns the number of distinct locations that are either employee or customer locations in each country:

```
SELECT country, COUNT(*) AS numlocations
FROM (SELECT country, region, city FROM HR.Employees
      UNION
      SELECT country, region, city FROM Sales.Customers) AS U
GROUP BY country;
```

This query returns the following output:

```
country          numlocations
---------------  ------------
Argentina        1
Austria          2
Belgium          2
Brazil           4
Canada           3
Denmark          2
Finland          2
France           9
Germany          11
```

```
Ireland         1
Italy           3
Mexico          1
Norway          1
Poland          1
Portugal        1
Spain           3
Sweden          2
Switzerland     2
UK              2
USA            14
Venezuela       4
```

(21 row(s) affected)

This query demonstrates how to apply the GROUP BY logical query processing phase to the result of a UNION set operation; similarly, you could of course apply any logical query processing phase in the outer query.

The fact that you cannot specify ORDER BY with the individual queries involved in the set operation might also cause logical problems. What if you need to restrict the number of rows in those queries with the TOP option? Again, you can resolve this problem with table expressions. Recall that an ORDER BY clause is allowed in a TOP query that is used to define a table expression, and that in this case, the ORDER BY clause serves only a logical meaning for TOP and not a presentation meaning.

So if you need a TOP query with an ORDER BY clause to participate in a set operation, simply define a table expression based on the TOP query, and have an outer query against the table expression participate in the set operation. For example, the following code returns the two most recent orders for those employees with employee ID of 3 or 5:

```
SELECT empid, orderid, orderdate
FROM (SELECT TOP (2) empid, orderid, orderdate
      FROM Sales.Orders
      WHERE empid = 3
      ORDER BY orderdate DESC, orderid DESC) AS D1

UNION ALL

SELECT empid, orderid, orderdate
FROM (SELECT TOP (2) empid, orderid, orderdate
      FROM Sales.Orders
      WHERE empid = 5
      ORDER BY orderdate DESC, orderid DESC) AS D2;
```

This query returns the following output:

```
empid       orderid     orderdate
----------- ----------- -----------------------
3           11063       2008-04-30 00:00:00.000
3           11057       2008-04-29 00:00:00.000
5           11043       2008-04-22 00:00:00.000
5           10954       2008-03-17 00:00:00.000
```

Conclusion

This chapter covered set operations, including the general syntax and requirements of set operations, and describing in detail each supported set operation—UNION, INTERSECT, and EXCEPT. I explained that ANSI SQL supports two flavors of each set operation—DISTINCT and ALL—and that as of SQL Server 2008, SQL Server implements the ALL flavor only with the UNION operation. I provided alternatives to the missing INTERSECT ALL and EXCEPT ALL that make use of the *ROW_NUMBER* function and table expressions. Finally, I introduced precedence among set operations, and explained how to circumvent unsupported logical query processing phases by using table expressions.

Exercises

This section provides exercises to help you familiarize yourself with the subjects discussed in Chapter 6. All exercises besides the first require you to be connected to the sample database TSQLFundamentals2008.

1

Write a query that generates a virtual auxiliary table of 10 numbers in the range 1 through 10 without using a looping construct. You do not need to guarantee any order of the rows in the output of your solution.

Tables involved: no table.

Desired output:

```
n
-----------
1
2
3
4
5
6
7
8
9
10

(10 row(s) affected)
```

2

Write a query that returns customer and employee pairs that had order activity in January 2008 but not in February 2008.

Tables involved: TSQLFundamentals2008 database, Sales.Orders table.

Desired output:

```
custid       empid
-----------  -----------
1            1
3            3
5            8
5            9
6            9
7            6
9            1
12           2
16           7
17           1
20           7
24           8
25           1
26           3
32           4
38           9
39           3
40           2
41           2
42           2
44           8
47           3
47           4
47           8
49           7
55           2
55           3
56           6
59           8
63           8
64           9
65           3
65           8
66           5
67           5
70           3
71           2
75           1
76           2
76           5
80           1
81           1
81           3
81           4
82           6
84           1
84           3
84           4
88           7
89           4

(50 row(s) affected)
```

3

Write a query that returns customer and employee pairs that had order activity in both January 2008 and February 2008.

Tables involved: Sales.Orders.

Desired output:

```
custid      empid
----------- -----------
20          3
39          9
46          5
67          1
71          4

(5 row(s) affected)
```

4

Write a query that returns customer and employee pairs that had order activity in both January 2008 and February 2008 but not in 2007.

Tables involved: Sales.Orders.

Desired output:

```
custid      empid
----------- -----------
67          1
46          5

(2 row(s) affected)
```

5 (Optional, Advanced)

You are given the following query:

```
SELECT country, region, city
FROM HR.Employees

UNION ALL

SELECT country, region, city
FROM Production.Suppliers;
```

You are asked to add logic to the query so that it guarantees that the rows from Employees are returned in the output before the rows from Customers, and within each segment, the rows should be sorted by country, region, and city.

Tables involved: HR. Employees and Production.Suppliers.

Desired output:

```
country           region            city
---------------   ---------------   ---------------
UK                NULL              London
UK                NULL              London
UK                NULL              London
UK                NULL              London
USA               WA                Kirkland
USA               WA                Redmond
USA               WA                Seattle
USA               WA                Seattle
USA               WA                Tacoma
Australia         NSW               Sydney
Australia         Victoria          Melbourne
Brazil            NULL              Sao Paulo
Canada            Québec            Montréal
Canada            Québec            Ste-Hyacinthe
Denmark           NULL              Lyngby
Finland           NULL              Lappeenranta
France            NULL              Annecy
France            NULL              Montceau
France            NULL              Paris
Germany           NULL              Berlin
Germany           NULL              Cuxhaven
Germany           NULL              Frankfurt
Italy             NULL              Ravenna
Italy             NULL              Salerno
Japan             NULL              Osaka
Japan             NULL              Tokyo
Netherlands       NULL              Zaandam
Norway            NULL              Sandvika
Singapore         NULL              Singapore
Spain             Asturias          Oviedo
Sweden            NULL              Göteborg
Sweden            NULL              Stockholm
UK                NULL              London
UK                NULL              Manchester
USA               LA                New Orleans
USA               MA                Boston
USA               MI                Ann Arbor
USA               OR                Bend

(38 row(s) affected)
```

Solutions

This section provides solutions to the Chapter 6 exercises.

1

T-SQL supports a *SELECT* statement based on constants with no FROM clause. Such a *SELECT* statement returns a table with a single row. For example, the following statement returns a row with a single column called n with the value 1:

SELECT 1 AS n;

Here's the output of this statement:

```
n
-----------
1

(1 row(s) affected)
```

Using the UNION ALL set operation, you can unify the result sets of multiple such statements, each returning a row with a different number in the range 1 through 10, like so:

```
SELECT 1 AS n
UNION ALL SELECT 2
UNION ALL SELECT 3
UNION ALL SELECT 4
UNION ALL SELECT 5
UNION ALL SELECT 6
UNION ALL SELECT 7
UNION ALL SELECT 8
UNION ALL SELECT 9
UNION ALL SELECT 10;
```

> **Tip** As an aside, SQL Server 2008 enhances the VALUES clause that you may be familiar with in the context of the *INSERT* statement in two ways. Instead of restricting it to representing a single row, now a single VALUES can represent multiple rows. Also, instead of restricting it to *INSERT* statements, the VALUES clause can now be used to define a table expression with rows based on constants. As an example, here's how you can use the VALUES clause to provide a solution to this exercise instead of using set operations:
>
> ```
> SELECT n
> FROM (VALUES(1),(2),(3),(4),(5),(6),(7),(8),(9),(10)) AS Nums(n);
> ```
>
> I will provide details about the VALUES clause and row value constructors in Chapter 8 as part of the discussion of the *INSERT* statement.

2

You can solve this exercise by using the EXCEPT set operation. The left input is a query that returns customer and employee pairs that had order activity in January 2008. The right input is a query that returns customer and employee pairs that had order activity in February 2008. Here's the solution query:

```
USE TSQLFundamentals2008;

SELECT custid, empid
FROM Sales.Orders
WHERE orderdate >= '20080101' AND orderdate < '20080201'

EXCEPT

SELECT custid, empid
FROM Sales.Orders
WHERE orderdate >= '20080201' AND orderdate < '20080301';
```

3

While Exercise 2 requested customer and employee pairs that had activity in one period but not another, this exercise concerns customer and employee pairs that had activity in both periods. So this time, instead of using the EXCEPT set operation, you need to use the INTERSECT set operation, like so:

```
SELECT custid, empid
FROM Sales.Orders
WHERE orderdate >= '20080101' AND orderdate < '20080201'

INTERSECT

SELECT custid, empid
FROM Sales.Orders
WHERE orderdate >= '20080201' AND orderdate < '20080301';
```

4

This exercise requires you to combine set operations. To return customer and employee pairs that had order activity in both January 2008 and February 2008 you need to use the INTERSECT set operation, as in Exercise 3. To exclude customer and employee pairs that had order activity in 2007 from the result, you need to use the EXCEPT set operation between the result and a third query. The solution query looks like this:

```
SELECT custid, empid
FROM Sales.Orders
WHERE orderdate >= '20080101' AND orderdate < '20080201'
```

```
INTERSECT

SELECT custid, empid
FROM Sales.Orders
WHERE orderdate >= '20080201' AND orderdate < '20080301'

EXCEPT

SELECT custid, empid
FROM Sales.Orders
WHERE orderdate >= '20070101' AND orderdate < '20080101';
```

Keep in mind that the INTERSECT set operation precedes EXCEPT. In our case, the default precedence is also the desired precedence, so you don't need to intervene by using parentheses. But you may prefer to add those for clarity:

```
(SELECT custid, empid
 FROM Sales.Orders
 WHERE orderdate >= '20080101' AND orderdate < '20080201'

 INTERSECT

 SELECT custid, empid
 FROM Sales.Orders
 WHERE orderdate >= '20080201' AND orderdate < '20080301')

EXCEPT

SELECT custid, empid
FROM Sales.Orders
WHERE orderdate >= '20070101' AND orderdate < '20080101';
```

5

The problem here is that the individual queries are not allowed to have ORDER BY clauses, and for a good reason. You can solve the problem by adding a result column based on a constant to each of the queries involved in the set operation (call it sortcol). In the query against Employees, specify a smaller constant than the one you specify in the query against Suppliers. Define a table expression based on the query with the set operation, and in the ORDER BY clause of the outer query, specify sortcol as the first sort column, followed by country, region, and city. Here's the complete solution query:

```
SELECT country, region, city
FROM (SELECT 1 AS sortcol, country, region, city
      FROM HR.Employees

      UNION ALL

      SELECT 2, country, region, city
      FROM Production.Suppliers) AS D
ORDER BY sortcol, country, region, city;
```

Chapter 7
Pivot, Unpivot, and Grouping Sets

This chapter covers techniques for pivoting and unpivoting data and handling grouping sets. *Pivoting* means rotating data from a state of rows to a state of columns. *Unpivoting* means rotating data from a state of columns to a state of rows. *Grouping sets* are sets of attributes that you group by, and this chapter will cover techniques for requesting multiple grouping sets in the same query.

Note that all subjects covered in this chapter may be considered advanced for readers who are new to T-SQL; therefore, the chapter is optional reading. If you already feel comfortable with the material discussed in the book so far, you may want to tackle this chapter; otherwise, feel free to skip it at this point and return to it later after you've gained more experience.

Pivoting Data

Pivoting data involves rotating data from a state of rows to a state of columns, possibly aggregating values along the way. Don't worry that this description isn't enough to clarify exactly what pivoting data means; this is a subject best explained through examples.

Throughout this chapter, I will use a sample Orders table that you create in tempdb (for demonstration purposes) and populate it with sample data by running the code in Listing 7-1.

LISTING 7-1 Code to Create and Populate the Orders Table

```
USE tempdb;

IF OBJECT_ID('dbo.Orders', 'U') IS NOT NULL DROP TABLE dbo.Orders;

CREATE TABLE dbo.Orders
```

```
(
  orderid   INT         NOT NULL,
  orderdate DATE        NOT NULL,
  empid     INT         NOT NULL,
  custid    VARCHAR(5)  NOT NULL,
  qty       INT         NOT NULL,
  CONSTRAINT PK_Orders PRIMARY KEY(orderid)
);

INSERT INTO dbo.Orders(orderid, orderdate, empid, custid, qty)
VALUES
  (30001, '20070802', 3, 'A', 10),
  (10001, '20071224', 2, 'A', 12),
  (10005, '20071224', 1, 'B', 20),
  (40001, '20080109', 2, 'A', 40),
  (10006, '20080118', 1, 'C', 14),
  (20001, '20080212', 2, 'B', 12),
  (40005, '20090212', 3, 'A', 10),
  (20002, '20090216', 1, 'C', 20),
  (30003, '20090418', 2, 'B', 15),
  (30004, '20070418', 3, 'C', 22),
  (30007, '20090907', 3, 'D', 30);

SELECT * FROM dbo.Orders;
```

Note The *DATE* data type and the ability to use a single VALUES clause to insert multiple rows to a table are new in Microsoft SQL Server 2008. If you're working with an earlier version of SQL Server, use the *DATETIME* data type instead of *DATE*, and substitute the single *INSERT* statement in Listing 7-1 with an *INSERT* statement per each row. For details about date and time data types, please refer to Chapter 2, "Single-Table Queries." For details about the VALUES clause, please refer to Chapter 8, "Data Modification."

The query at the end of the code in Listing 7-1 produces the following output showing the contents of the Orders table:

```
orderid     orderdate                   empid           custid    qty
----------- --------------------------- --------------- --------- -----------
10001       2007-12-24 00:00:00.000     2               A         12
10005       2007-12-24 00:00:00.000     1               B         20
10006       2008-01-18 00:00:00.000     1               C         14
20001       2008-02-12 00:00:00.000     2               B         12
20002       2009-02-16 00:00:00.000     1               C         20
30001       2007-08-02 00:00:00.000     3               A         10
30003       2009-04-18 00:00:00.000     2               B         15
30004       2007-04-18 00:00:00.000     3               C         22
30007       2009-09-07 00:00:00.000     3               D         30
40001       2008-01-09 00:00:00.000     2               A         40
40005       2009-02-12 00:00:00.000     3               A         10
```

Before I further explain what pivoting is, consider a request to produce a report with the total order quantity for each employee and customer. The request is satisfied with the following simple query:

```
SELECT empid, custid, SUM(qty) AS sumqty
FROM dbo.Orders
GROUP BY empid, custid;
```

This query generates the following output:

```
empid        custid    sumqty
-----------  --------- -----------
2            A         52
3            A         20
1            B         20
2            B         27
1            C         34
3            C         22
3            D         30
```

Suppose, however, that you have a requirement to produce the output in the form shown in Table 7-1.

TABLE 7-1 Pivoted View of Total Quantity per Employee (On Rows) and Customer (On Columns)

empid	A	B	C	D
1	NULL	20	34	NULL
2	52	27	NULL	NULL
3	20	NULL	22	30

What you see in Table 7-1 is an aggregated and pivoted view of the data from the Orders table, and the technique for generating this view of the data is called pivoting.

Every pivoting request involves three logical processing phases, each with associated elements: a grouping phase with an associated grouping or *on rows* element, a spreading phase with an associated spreading or *on cols* element, and an aggregation phase with an associated aggregation element and aggregate function.

In our example, you need to produce a single row in the result for each unique employee ID. This means that the rows from the Orders table need to be grouped by the empid attribute, and therefore the grouping element in our case is the empid attribute.

The Orders table has a single column holding all customer ID values, and a single column holding their ordered quantities. The pivoting process is supposed to produce a different result column for each unique customer ID, and each column contains the aggregated quantities for that customer. You can think of this process as "spreading" quantities by customer IDs. The spreading element in our case is the custid attribute.

Finally, because pivoting involves grouping, you will need to aggregate data to produce the result values in the "intersection" of the grouping and spreading elements. You will need to identify the aggregate function (*SUM* in our case), and the aggregation element (qty attribute in our case).

To recap, pivoting involves grouping, spreading, and aggregating. In our case, we group by empid, spread (quantities) by custid, and aggregate SUM(qty). After you have identified the elements involved in pivoting, the rest is just a matter of incorporating those elements in the right places in a generic query template for pivoting.

I'll present two solutions for pivoting—a standard solution and a solution that uses a T-SQL-specific PIVOT operator.

Pivoting with Standard SQL

The standard solution for pivoting handles all three phases involved in a very straightforward manner.

The grouping phase is achieved with a GROUP BY clause; in our case, GROUP BY empid.

The spreading phase is achieved in the SELECT clause with a CASE expression for each target column. You need to know the spreading element values ahead of time and specify a separate expression for each. Because in our case we need to "spread" the quantities of four customers (A, B, C, and D), there are four CASE expressions. For example, here's the CASE expression for customer A:

```
CASE WHEN custid = 'A' THEN qty END
```

This expression returns the quantity from the current row only when the current row represents an order for customer A; otherwise the expression returns a NULL. Remember that if an ELSE clause is not specified in a CASE expression, the default is ELSE NULL. This means that in the target column for customer A, only quantities associated with customer A appear as column values, and in all other cases the column values are NULL.

If you don't know the values that you need to spread by ahead of time (the distinct customer IDs in our case), and you want to query them from the data, you need to use dynamic SQL to construct the query string and execute it. Dynamic pivoting is demonstrated in Chapter 10, "Programmable Objects."

Finally, the aggregation phase is achieved by applying the relevant aggregate function (*SUM* in our case) to the result of each CASE expression. For example, here's the expression that produces the result column for customer A:

```
SUM(CASE WHEN custid = 'A' THEN qty END) AS A
```

Of course, depending on the request, you might need to use another aggregate function (*MAX, MIN, COUNT,* and so on).

Here's the complete solution query pivoting order data, returning the total quantity for each employee (on rows) and customer (on cols):

```
SELECT empid,
  SUM(CASE WHEN custid = 'A' THEN qty END) AS A,
  SUM(CASE WHEN custid = 'B' THEN qty END) AS B,
  SUM(CASE WHEN custid = 'C' THEN qty END) AS C,
  SUM(CASE WHEN custid = 'D' THEN qty END) AS D
FROM dbo.Orders
GROUP BY empid;
```

This query produces the output shown earlier in Table 7-1.

Pivoting with the Native T-SQL PIVOT Operator

SQL Server 2005 introduced a T-SQL–specific table operator called PIVOT. The PIVOT operator operates in the context of the FROM clause of a query like other table operators (for example, JOIN). It operates on some source table or table expression, pivots the data, and returns a result table. The PIVOT operator involves the same logical processing phases as described earlier (grouping, spreading, and aggregating) with the same pivoting elements, but uses different, native syntax.

The general form of a query with the PIVOT operator is:

```
SELECT ...
FROM <source_table_or_table_expression>
  PIVOT(<agg_func>(<aggregation_element>)
        FOR <spreading_element>
          IN (<list_of_target_columns>)) AS <result_table_alias>
...;
```

In the parentheses of the PIVOT operator you specify the aggregate function (*SUM* in our example), aggregation element (qty), spreading element (custid), and the list of target column names (A, B, C, D). Following the parentheses of the PIVOT operator you specify an alias for the result table.

It is important to note that with the PIVOT operator, you do not explicitly specify the grouping elements, removing the need for a GROUP BY in the query. The PIVOT operator figures out the grouping elements implicitly as all attributes from the source table (or table expression) that were not specified as either the spreading element or the aggregation element. You need to ensure that the source table for the PIVOT operator has no attributes besides the grouping, spreading, and aggregation elements, so that after specifying the spreading and aggregation elements, the only attributes left are those you intend as grouping elements. You achieve this is by not applying the PIVOT operator to the original table directly (Orders in our case), but instead to a table expression that includes only the attributes representing the pivoting elements and no others. For example, here's the solution query to our original pivoting request, using the native PIVOT operator:

```
SELECT empid, A, B, C, D
FROM (SELECT empid, custid, qty
      FROM dbo.Orders) AS D
  PIVOT(SUM(qty) FOR custid IN(A, B, C, D)) AS P;
```

Instead of operating directly on the Orders table, the PIVOT operator operates on a derived table called D that includes only the pivoting elements empid, custid, and qty. Besides the spreading element, which is custid, and the aggregation element, which is qty, what's left is empid, considered the grouping element.

This query returns the output shown earlier in Table 7-1.

To understand why you're required to use a table expression here, consider the following query that applies the PIVOT operator directly to the Orders table:

```
SELECT empid, A, B, C, D
FROM dbo.Orders
  PIVOT(SUM(qty) FOR custid IN(A, B, C, D)) AS P;
```

The Orders table contains the attributes orderid, orderdate, empid, custid, and qty. Because we specified custid as the spreading element and qty as the aggregation element, the remaining attributes (orderid, orderdate, and empid) are all considered the grouping elements. This query, therefore returns the following output:

```
empid       A             B             C             D
----------- ------------  ------------  ------------  -----------
2           12            NULL          NULL          NULL
1           NULL          20            NULL          NULL
1           NULL          NULL          14            NULL
2           NULL          12            NULL          NULL
1           NULL          NULL          20            NULL
3           10            NULL          NULL          NULL
2           NULL          15            NULL          NULL
3           NULL          NULL          22            NULL
3           NULL          NULL          NULL          30
2           40            NULL          NULL          NULL
3           10            NULL          NULL          NULL

(11 row(s) affected)
```

Because orderid is part of the grouping elements, you get a row per order instead of a row per employee. The logical equivalent of this query using the standard solution for pivoting has orderid, orderdate, and empid listed in the GROUP BY list as follows:

```
SELECT empid,
  SUM(CASE WHEN custid = 'A' THEN qty END) AS A,
  SUM(CASE WHEN custid = 'B' THEN qty END) AS B,
```

```
    SUM(CASE WHEN custid = 'C' THEN qty END) AS C,
    SUM(CASE WHEN custid = 'D' THEN qty END) AS D
FROM dbo.Orders
GROUP BY orderid, orderdate, empid;
```

I strongly recommend that you never operate on the base table directly, even when the table contains only columns used as pivoting elements. You never know whether new columns will be added to the table in the future, rendering your queries incorrect. I recommend considering the use of a table expression as the input table to the PIVOT operator as if it were part of the requirement of the operator's syntax.

As another example for a pivoting request, suppose that instead of returning employees on rows and customers on columns, you want it the other way around: the grouping element is custid, the spreading element is empid, and the aggregation element and aggregate function remain *SUM*(qty). After you learn the "template" for a pivoting solution (standard or native), it's just a matter of fitting those elements in the right places. The following solution query uses the native PIVOT operator:

```
SELECT custid, [1], [2], [3]
FROM (SELECT empid, custid, qty
      FROM dbo.Orders) AS D
  PIVOT(SUM(qty) FOR empid IN([1], [2], [3])) AS P;
```

The employee IDs 1, 2, and 3 are values in the empid column in the source table, but in terms of the result, these values become target column names. Therefore, in the PIVOT IN clause you must refer to them as identifiers. When identifiers are irregular (for example, when they start with a digit), you need to delimit them—hence the use of square brackets.

This query returns the following output:

```
custid    1            2            3
--------  -----------  -----------  -----------
A         NULL         52           20
B         20           27           NULL
C         34           NULL         22
D         NULL         NULL         30
```

Unpivoting Data

Unpivoting is a technique to rotate data from a state of columns to a state of rows. Usually it involves querying a pivoted state of the data, producing out of each source row multiple result rows, each with a different source column value. In other words, each source row of the pivoted table becomes potentially many rows, one row for each of the specified source column values. This may be difficult to understand at first, but it should be much easier to understand by looking at an example.

Run the following code to create and populate a table called EmpCustOrders in tempdb (for demo purposes):

```
IF OBJECT_ID('dbo.EmpCustOrders', 'U') IS NOT NULL DROP TABLE dbo.EmpCustOrders;

SELECT empid, A, B, C, D
INTO dbo.EmpCustOrders
FROM (SELECT empid, custid, qty
        FROM dbo.Orders) AS D
  PIVOT(SUM(qty) FOR custid IN(A, B, C, D)) AS P;

SELECT * FROM dbo.EmpCustOrders;
```

Here's the output of the query against EmpCustOrders showing its contents:

empid	A	B	C	D
1	NULL	20	34	NULL
2	52	27	NULL	NULL
3	20	NULL	22	30

The table has a row for each employee, a column for each of the four customers A, B, C, and D, and the order quantity per each employee and customer in the employee-customer intersections. Notice that irrelevant intersections (employee-customer combination that had no order activity together) are represented by NULLs. You get a request to unpivot the data, returning a row for each employee and customer, along with the order quantity. The desired output should look like this:

empid	custid	qty
1	B	20
1	C	34
2	A	52
2	B	27
3	A	20
3	C	22
3	D	30

In the following sections, I'll discuss two techniques to solve this problem—a technique that follows the SQL standard and a technique using a T-SQL–specific UNPIVOT operator.

Unpivoting with Standard SQL

The standard solution to unpivoting involves implementing three logical processing phases in a very explicit manner: producing copies, extracting elements, and eliminating irrelevant intersections.

The first step in the solution involves producing multiple copies out of each source row—one per each column that you need to unpivot. In our case, you need to produce a copy for each of the columns A, B, C, and D, which represent customer IDs. In relational algebra and in SQL, the operation used to produce multiple copies of each row is a Cartesian product (cross join). You need apply a cross join between the EmpCustOrders table and a table that has a row for each customer.

As of SQL Server 2008 you can use a table value constructor in the form of a VALUES clause to create a virtual table with a row for each customer. The query implementing the first step in the solution looks like this:

```
SELECT *
FROM dbo.EmpCustOrders
  CROSS JOIN (VALUES('A'),('B'),('C'),('D')) AS Custs(custid);
```

However, in versions prior to SQL Server 2008, you need to substitute the VALUES clause with a series of *SELECT* statements, each constructing a single row based on constants with UNION ALL set operations between them like so:

```
SELECT *
FROM dbo.EmpCustOrders
  CROSS JOIN (SELECT 'A' AS custid
              UNION ALL SELECT 'B'
              UNION ALL SELECT 'C'
              UNION ALL SELECT 'D') AS Custs;
```

This form, however, is not standard—the standard form requires a FROM clause in a SELECT query.

In our example, the query implementing the first step in the solution returns the following output:

```
empid       A            B            C            D            custid
----------- ------------ ------------ ------------ ------------ ------
1           NULL         20           34           NULL         A
1           NULL         20           34           NULL         B
1           NULL         20           34           NULL         C
1           NULL         20           34           NULL         D
2           52           27           NULL         NULL         A
2           52           27           NULL         NULL         B
2           52           27           NULL         NULL         C
2           52           27           NULL         NULL         D
3           20           NULL         22           30           A
3           20           NULL         22           30           B
3           20           NULL         22           30           C
3           20           NULL         22           30           D
```

As you can see, four copies were produced for each source row—one each for customers A, B, C, and D.

The second step in the solution is to produce a column (call it qty in our case) that returns the value from the column that corresponds to the customer represented by the current copy. More specifically in our case, if the current custid value is A, the qty column should return the value from column A, if custid is B, qty should return the value from column B, and so on. You can implement this step with a simple CASE expression like so:

```
SELECT empid, custid,
  CASE custid
    WHEN 'A' THEN A
    WHEN 'B' THEN B
    WHEN 'C' THEN C
    WHEN 'D' THEN D
  END AS qty
FROM dbo.EmpCustOrders
  CROSS JOIN (VALUES('A'),('B'),('C'),('D')) AS Custs(custid);
```

This query returns the following output:

```
empid        custid    qty
-----------  --------- -----------
1            A         NULL
1            B         20
1            C         34
1            D         NULL
2            A         52
2            B         27
2            C         NULL
2            D         NULL
3            A         20
3            B         NULL
3            C         22
3            D         30
```

Recall that in the original table, NULLs represent irrelevant intersections. To eliminate irrelevant intersections, define a table expression based on the query implementing step 2 in the solution, and in the outer query filter out NULLs. Here's the complete solution query:

```
SELECT *
FROM (SELECT empid, custid,
        CASE custid
          WHEN 'A' THEN A
          WHEN 'B' THEN B
          WHEN 'C' THEN C
          WHEN 'D' THEN D
        END AS qty
      FROM dbo.EmpCustOrders
        CROSS JOIN (VALUES('A'),('B'),('C'),('D')) AS Custs(custid)) AS D
WHERE qty IS NOT NULL;
```

This query returns the following output:

```
empid        custid    qty
-----------  --------- -----------
1            B         20
1            C         34
2            A         52
```

2	B	27
3	A	20
3	C	22
3	D	30

Unpivoting with the Native T-SQL UNPIVOT Operator

Unpivoting data involves producing two result columns out of any number of source columns that you unpivot. In our example, you need to unpivot the source columns A, B, C and D, producing two result columns called custid and qty. The former will hold the source column names ('A', 'B', 'C', and 'D'), and the latter will hold the source column values (quantities in our case). SQL Server 2005 introduced a very elegant, minimalistic native UNPIVOT table operator. The general form of a query with the UNPIVOT operator is:

```
SELECT ...
FROM <source_table_or_table_expression>
  UNPIVOT(<target_col_to_hold_source_col_values>
    FOR <target_col_to_hold_source_col_names> IN(<list_of_source_columns>)) AS
<result_table_alias>
...;
```

Like the PIVOT operator, UNPIVOT was also implemented as a table operator in the context of the FROM clause. It operates on a source table or table expression (EmpCustOrders in this case). Within the parentheses of the UNPIVOT operator you specify the name you want to assign to the column that will hold the source column values (qty here), the name you want to assign to the column that will hold the source column names (custid), and list the source column names (A, B, C, and D). Following the parentheses, you provide an alias to the table resulting from the table operator.

Here's the complete solution query to the unpivoting request in our example using the UNPIVOT operator:

```
SELECT empid, custid, qty
FROM dbo.EmpCustOrders
  UNPIVOT(qty FOR custid IN(A, B, C, D)) AS U;
```

Note that the UNPIVOT operator implements the same logical processing phases described earlier—generating copies, extracting elements, and eliminating NULL intersections. The last phase is not an optional phase as in the solution based on standard SQL.

Also note that unpivoting a pivoted table cannot bring back the original table. Rather, unpivoting is just a rotation of the pivoted values into a new format. However, the table that has been unpivoted can be pivoted back to its original pivoted state. In other words, the aggregation results in a loss of detail information in the original pivoting. After the initial pivot, all the aggregations can be preserved between the operations, provided that the unpivot does not lose information.

Grouping Sets

This section describes both what grouping sets are and the features in SQL Server that support grouping sets.

A grouping set is simply a set of attributes that you group by. Traditionally in SQL, a single aggregate query defines a single grouping set. For example, each of the following four queries defines a single grouping set:

```
SELECT empid, custid, SUM(qty) AS sumqty
FROM dbo.Orders
GROUP BY empid, custid;

SELECT empid, SUM(qty) AS sumqty
FROM dbo.Orders
GROUP BY empid;

SELECT custid, SUM(qty) AS sumqty
FROM dbo.Orders
GROUP BY custid;

SELECT SUM(qty) AS sumqty
FROM dbo.Orders;
```

The first query defines the grouping set (empid, custid); the second (empid), third (custid), and last query defines what's known as the empty grouping set (). This code returns four result sets—one for each of the four queries.

Suppose that instead of four separate result sets, you wanted a single unified result set with the aggregated data for all four grouping sets. You could achieve this by using the UNION ALL set operation to unify the result sets of all four queries. Because set operations require all result sets to have compatible schemas with the same number of columns, you need to adjust the queries by adding placeholders (for example, NULLs) instead of missing columns. Here's what the code would look like:

```
SELECT empid, custid, SUM(qty) AS sumqty
FROM dbo.Orders
GROUP BY empid, custid

UNION ALL

SELECT empid, NULL, SUM(qty) AS sumqty
FROM dbo.Orders
GROUP BY empid

UNION ALL

SELECT NULL, custid, SUM(qty) AS sumqty
FROM dbo.Orders
GROUP BY custid
```

```
UNION ALL

SELECT NULL, NULL, SUM(qty) AS sumqty
FROM dbo.Orders;
```

This code generates a single result set, with the aggregates for all four grouping sets unified:

```
empid        custid     sumqty
-----------  ---------  -----------
2            A          52
3            A          20
1            B          20
2            B          27
1            C          34
3            C          22
3            D          30
1            NULL       54
2            NULL       79
3            NULL       72
NULL         A          72
NULL         B          47
NULL         C          56
NULL         D          30
NULL         NULL       205

(15 row(s) affected)
```

Even though you managed to get what you were after, this solution has two main problems—the length of code and performance. This solution requires you to specify a whole GROUP BY query for each grouping set. With a large number of grouping sets, the query can get quite long. Also, to process the query, SQL Server will scan the source table separately for each query, which is inefficient.

SQL Server 2008 introduced a number of features following standard SQL that address the need to define multiple grouping sets in the same query. Those are the GROUPING SETS, CUBE, and ROLLUP subclauses of the GROUP BY clause, and the *GROUPING_ID* function.

The GROUPING SETS Subclause

The GROUPING SETS subclause is a powerful enhancement to the GROUP BY clause that is used mainly in reporting and data warehousing. Using this subclause you can define multiple grouping sets in the same query. Simply list the grouping sets that you want to define, separated by commas within the parentheses of the GROUPING SETS subclause, and for each grouping set list the members separated by commas within parentheses. For example, the following query defines four grouping sets: (empid, custid), (empid), (custid) and ():

```
SELECT empid, custid, SUM(qty) AS sumqty
FROM dbo.Orders
GROUP BY
  GROUPING SETS
```

```
(
  (empid, custid),
  (empid),
  (custid),
  ()
);
```

This query is a logical equivalent of the previous solution that unified the result sets of four aggregate queries, returning the same output. This query, though, has two main advantages over the previous solution—obviously it requires much less code, and SQL Server will optimize the number of times it scans the source table and won't necessarily scan it separately for each grouping set.

There is no logical equivalent to the GROUPING SETS subclause prior to SQL Server 2008 other than explicitly unifying the result sets of multiple aggregate queries. As mentioned, SQL Server 2008 implementation follows the SQL standard.

The CUBE Subclause

The CUBE subclause of the GROUP BY clause provides an abbreviated way to define multiple grouping sets. In the parentheses of the CUBE subclause you provide a list of members separated by commas, and you get all possible grouping sets that can be defined based on the input members. For example, CUBE(a, b, c) is equivalent to GROUPING SETS((a, b, c), (a, b), (a, c), (b, c), (a), (b), (c), ()). In set theory, the set of all subsets of elements that can be produced from a given set is called the *power set*. You can think of the CUBE subclause as producing the power set of grouping sets that can be formed from the given set of elements.

Instead of the GROUPING SETS subclause used in the previous query to define the four grouping sets (empid, custid), (empid), (custid), and (), you can simply use CUBE(empid, custid). Here's the complete query:

```
SELECT empid, custid, SUM(qty) AS sumqty
FROM dbo.Orders
GROUP BY CUBE(empid, custid);
```

The CUBE subclause of the GROUP BY clause was introduced in SQL Server 2008 and it was implemented following the SQL standard. Earlier versions of SQL Server supported a nonstandard CUBE option that wasn't implemented as a subclause of the GROUP BY clause but as an option in a separate WITH clause. Here's a logical equivalent of the previous query using the older CUBE option:

```
SELECT empid, custid, SUM(qty) AS sumqty
FROM dbo.Orders
GROUP BY empid, custid
WITH CUBE;
```

I recommend that you always use the grouping sets features that conform to the SQL standard because the nonstandard ones will be removed in a future version of SQL Server.

The ROLLUP Subclause

The ROLLUP subclause of the GROUP BY clause also provides an abbreviated way to define multiple grouping sets. However, unlike the CUBE subclause, ROLLUP doesn't produce all possible grouping sets that can be defined based on the input members—it produces a subset of those. ROLLUP assumes a hierarchy among the input members, and produces all grouping sets that make sense considering the hierarchy. In other words, while CUBE(a, b, c) produces all eight possible grouping sets out of the three input members, ROLLUP(a, b, c) produces only four grouping sets assuming the hierarchy a>b>c, and is the equivalent of specifying GROUPING SETS((a, b, c), (a, b), (a), ()).

For example, suppose that you want to return total quantities for all grouping sets that can be defined based on the time hierarchy order year > order month > order day. You could use the GROUPING SETS subclause and explicitly list all four possible grouping sets:

```
GROUPING SETS(
  (YEAR(orderdate), MONTH(orderdate), DAY(orderdate)),
  (YEAR(orderdate), MONTH(orderdate)),
  (YEAR(orderdate)),
  () )
```

The logical equivalent using the ROLLUP subclause is much more economical:

```
ROLLUP(YEAR(orderdate), MONTH(orderdate), DAY(orderdate))
```

Here's the complete query that you need to run in the tempdb database:

```
SELECT
  YEAR(orderdate) AS orderyear,
  MONTH(orderdate) AS ordermonth,
  DAY(orderdate) AS orderday,
  SUM(qty) AS sumqty
FROM dbo.Orders
GROUP BY ROLLUP(YEAR(orderdate), MONTH(orderdate), DAY(orderdate));
```

This query produces the following output:

```
orderyear    ordermonth      orderday     sumqty
-----------  --------------  -----------  -----------
2007         4               18           22
2007         4               NULL         22
2007         8               2            10
2007         8               NULL         10
2007         12              24           32
2007         12              NULL         32
2007         NULL            NULL         64
```

2008	1	9	40
2008	1	18	14
2008	1	NULL	54
2008	2	12	12
2008	2	NULL	12
2008	NULL	NULL	66
2009	2	12	10
2009	2	16	20
2009	2	NULL	30
2009	4	18	15
2009	4	NULL	15
2009	9	7	30
2009	9	NULL	30
2009	NULL	NULL	75
NULL	NULL	NULL	205

```
(22 row(s) affected)
```

As with the CUBE subclause, the standard ROLLUP subclause introduced in SQL Server 2008 had a nonstandard predecessor in earlier versions of SQL Server in the form of an option in a separate WITH clause. Here's the logical equivalent of the previous query using the nonstandard WITH ROLLUP option:

```
SELECT
  YEAR(orderdate) AS orderyear,
  MONTH(orderdate) AS ordermonth,
  DAY(orderdate) AS orderday,
  SUM(qty) AS sumqty
FROM dbo.Orders
GROUP BY YEAR(orderdate), MONTH(orderdate), DAY(orderdate)
WITH ROLLUP;
```

Again, I recommend that you always use the standard features in new development work because the nonstandard features will be removed in a future version of SQL Server.

The standard GROUPING SETS, CUBE, and ROLLUP subclauses are more flexible than the nonstandard CUBE and ROLLUP options. You can combine multiple standard subclauses in the same GROUP BY clause, giving you all sorts of interesting capabilities. With the nonstandard options, you are restricted to using only one per query.

The GROUPING and GROUPING_ID Functions

When you have a single query that defines multiple grouping sets, you may need to be able to associate result rows and grouping sets—that is, to identify for each result row the grouping set it is associated with. As long as all grouping elements are defined as NOT NULL, this is easy. For example, consider the following query:

```
SELECT empid, custid, SUM(qty) AS sumqty
FROM dbo.Orders
GROUP BY CUBE(empid, custid);
```

This query produces the following output:

```
empid        custid     sumqty
-----------  ---------  -----------
2            A          52
3            A          20
NULL         A          72
1            B          20
2            B          27
NULL         B          47
1            C          34
3            C          22
NULL         C          56
3            D          30
NULL         D          30
NULL         NULL       205
1            NULL       54
2            NULL       79
3            NULL       72

(15 row(s) affected)
```

Because both the empid and custid columns were defined in the Orders table as NOT NULL, a NULL in those columns can only represent a placeholder, indicating that the column did not participate in the current grouping set. So, for example, all rows where empid is not NULL and custid is not NULL are associated with the grouping set (empid, custid). All rows where empid is not NULL and custid is NULL are associated with the grouping set (empid), and so on. Some people override the presentation of NULLs with "ALL" or a similar designator, provided that the original columns are not nullable. This helps for reporting.

However, if a grouping column is defined as allowing NULLs in the table, you cannot tell for sure whether a NULL in the result set originated from the data or is a placeholder for a nonparticipating member in a grouping set. One way to determine grouping set association in a deterministic manner, even when grouping columns allow NULLs, is to use the *GROUPING* function. This function accepts a name of a column and returns 0 if it is a member of the current grouping set and 1 otherwise. For example, the following query invokes the *GROUPING* function for each of the grouping elements:

```
SELECT
  GROUPING(empid) AS grpemp,
  GROUPING(custid) AS grpcust,
  empid, custid, SUM(qty) AS sumqty
FROM dbo.Orders
GROUP BY CUBE(empid, custid);
```

This query returns the following output:

```
grpemp     grpcust     empid        custid     sumqty
---------  ----------  -----------  ---------  -----------
0          0           2            A          52
0          0           3            A          20
```

1	0	NULL	A	72
0	0	1	B	20
0	0	2	B	27
1	0	NULL	B	47
0	0	1	C	34
0	0	3	C	22
1	0	NULL	C	56
0	0	3	D	30
1	0	NULL	D	30
1	1	NULL	NULL	205
0	1	1	NULL	54
0	1	2	NULL	79
0	1	3	NULL	72

```
(15 row(s) affected)
```

Now you don't need to rely on the NULLs anymore to figure out the association between result rows and grouping sets. For example, all rows where empid is 0 and custid is 0 are associated with the grouping set (empid, custid). All rows where empid is 0 and custid 1 are associated with the grouping set (empid), and so on.

The *GROUPING* function was available prior to SQL Server 2008 and could be used in conjunction with the nonstandard WITH CUBE and WITH ROLLUP options. SQL Server 2008 introduces a new function called *GROUPING_ID* that can further simplify the process of associating result rows and grouping sets. You provide the function with all elements that participate in any grouping set as inputs—for example, *GROUPING_ID*(a, b, c, d)—and the function returns an integer bitmap where each bit represents a different input element—rightmost element represented by rightmost bit. For example, the grouping set (a, b, c, d) is represented by the integer 0 (0×8 + 0×4 + 0×2 + 0×1). The grouping set (a, c) is represented by the integer 10 (1×8 + 0×4 + 1×2 + 0×1), and so on.

Instead of calling the *GROUPING* function for each grouping element as you did in the previous query, you can call the *GROUPING_ID* function once and provide it with all grouping elements as input as follows:

```
SELECT
  GROUPING_ID(empid, custid) AS groupingset,
  empid, custid, SUM(qty) AS sumqty
FROM dbo.Orders
GROUP BY CUBE(empid, custid);
```

This query produces the following output:

groupingset	empid	custid	sumqty
0	2	A	52
0	3	A	20
2	NULL	A	72
0	1	B	20

0	2	B	27
2	NULL	B	47
0	1	C	34
0	3	C	22
2	NULL	C	56
0	3	D	30
2	NULL	D	30
3	NULL	NULL	205
1	1	NULL	54
1	2	NULL	79
1	3	NULL	72

```
(15 row(s) affected)
```

Now you can easily figure out which grouping set each row is associated with. The integer 0 (binary 00) represents the grouping set (empid, custid); the integer 1 (binary 01) represents (empid); the integer 2 (binary 10) represents (custid); and the integer 3 (binary (11) represents ().

Conclusion

This chapter covered pivoting and unpivoting data and features related to grouping sets.

I provided both standard and nonstandard techniques to achieve pivoting and unpivoting. The nonstandard techniques use the T-SQL specific PIVOT and UNPIVOT operators; the main advantage is that they require less code than standard techniques.

SQL Server 2008 introduces several important features that make handling of grouping sets flexible and efficient: the GROUPING SETS, CUBE, and ROLLUP subclauses and the *GROUPING_ID* function. Refrain from using the old nonstandard WITH CUBE and WITH ROLLUP options, which will be removed in a future version of SQL Server.

Exercises

This section provides exercises to help you familiarize yourself with the subjects discussed in Chapter 7.

All exercises for this chapter involve querying the Orders table in the tempdb database that you created and populated earlier by running the code in Listing 7-1.

1

Write a query against the Orders table that returns a row for each employee, a column for each order year, and the count of orders for each employee and order year.

Tables involved: tempdb database, Orders table.

Desired output:

```
empid        cnt2007      cnt2008      cnt2009
-----------  -----------  -----------  -----------
1            1            1            1
2            1            2            1
3            2            0            2
```

2

Run the following code to create and populate the EmpYearOrders table:

```
USE tempdb;

IF OBJECT_ID('dbo.EmpYearOrders', 'U') IS NOT NULL DROP TABLE dbo.EmpYearOrders;

SELECT empid, [2007] AS cnt2007, [2008] AS cnt2008, [2009] AS cnt2009
INTO dbo.EmpYearOrders
FROM (SELECT empid, YEAR(orderdate) AS orderyear
      FROM dbo.Orders) AS D
  PIVOT(COUNT(orderyear)
        FOR orderyear IN([2007], [2008], [2009])) AS P;

SELECT * FROM dbo.EmpYearOrders;
```

Output:

```
empid        cnt2007      cnt2008      cnt2009
-----------  -----------  -----------  -----------
1            1            1            1
2            1            2            1
3            2            0            2
```

Write a query against the EmpYearOrders table that unpivots the data, returning a row for each employee and order year with the number of orders. Exclude rows where the number of orders is 0 (in our example, employee 3 in year 2008).

Desired output:

```
empid        orderyear    numorders
-----------  -----------  -----------
1            2007         1
1            2008         1
1            2009         1
2            2007         1
2            2008         2
```

2	2009	1
3	2007	2
3	2009	2

3

Write a query against the Orders table that returns the total quantities for each: (employee, customer, and order year), (employee and order year), (customer and order year). Include a result column in the output that uniquely identifies the grouping set with which the current row is associated.

Tables involved: tempdb database, Orders table.

Desired output:

groupingset	empid	custid	orderyear	sumqty
0	2	A	2007	12
0	3	A	2007	10
4	NULL	A	2007	22
0	2	A	2008	40
4	NULL	A	2008	40
0	3	A	2009	10
4	NULL	A	2009	10
0	1	B	2007	20
4	NULL	B	2007	20
0	2	B	2008	12
4	NULL	B	2008	12
0	2	B	2009	15
4	NULL	B	2009	15
0	3	C	2007	22
4	NULL	C	2007	22
0	1	C	2008	14
4	NULL	C	2008	14
0	1	C	2009	20
4	NULL	C	2009	20
0	3	D	2009	30
4	NULL	D	2009	30
2	1	NULL	2007	20
2	2	NULL	2007	12
2	3	NULL	2007	32
2	1	NULL	2008	14
2	2	NULL	2008	52
2	1	NULL	2009	20
2	2	NULL	2009	15
2	3	NULL	2009	40

(29 row(s) affected)

Solutions

This section provides solutions to the Chapter 7 exercises.

1

Solving a pivoting problem is all about identifying the elements involved: the grouping element, the spreading element, the aggregation element, and the aggregate function. After you identify the elements involved, you simply fit them in the "template" query for pivoting—whether it is the standard solution or the solution using the native PIVOT operator.

In this exercise, the grouping element is the employee (empid), the spreading element is order year (YEAR(orderdate)), and the aggregate function is *COUNT;* however, identifying the aggregation element is not that straightforward. You want the *COUNT* aggregate function to count matching rows and orders—you don't really care which attribute it will count. In other words, you can use any attribute that you like, as long as the attribute does not allow NULLs, because aggregate functions ignore NULLs, and counting an attribute allowing NULLs would result in incorrect count of orders.

If it doesn't really matter which attribute you use as the input to the COUNT aggregate, why not use the same attribute that you already use as the spreading element? In our case, you can use the order year as both the spreading and aggregation element.

Now that you've identified all pivoting elements, you're ready to write the complete solution. Here's the solution query without using the PIVOT operator:

```
USE tempdb;

SELECT empid,
  COUNT(CASE WHEN orderyear = 2007 THEN orderyear END) AS cnt2007,
  COUNT(CASE WHEN orderyear = 2008 THEN orderyear END) AS cnt2008,
  COUNT(CASE WHEN orderyear = 2009 THEN orderyear END) AS cnt2009
FROM (SELECT empid, YEAR(orderdate) AS orderyear
      FROM dbo.Orders) AS D
GROUP BY empid;
```

Recall that if you do not specify an ELSE clause in a CASE expression, an implicit ELSE NULL is assumed. Thus the CASE expression produces non-NULL values only for matching orders (orders placed by the current employee in the current order year), and only those matching orders are taken into consideration by the COUNT aggregate.

Notice that even though the standard solution does not require using a table expression, I used one here to alias the YEAR(orderdate) expression as orderyear to avoid repeating the expression YEAR(orderdate) multiple times in the outer query.

Here's the solution query that uses the native PIVOT operator:

```
SELECT empid, [2007] AS cnt2007, [2008] AS cnt2008, [2009] AS cnt2009
FROM (SELECT empid, YEAR(orderdate) AS orderyear
      FROM dbo.Orders) AS D
  PIVOT(COUNT(orderyear)
        FOR orderyear IN([2007], [2008], [2009])) AS P;
```

As you can see, it's just a matter of fitting the pivoting elements in the right places.

If you prefer to use your own target column names and not the ones based on the actual data, of course you can provide your own aliases in the SELECT list. In this query I aliased the result columns [2007], [2008], and [2009] as cnt2007, cnt2008, and cnt2009, respectively.

2

This exercise involves a request to unpivot the source columns cnt2007, cnt2008, and cnt2009 to two target columns—orderyear to hold the year that the source column name represents and numorders to hold the source column value. You can use the solutions that I showed in the chapter as the basis for solving this exercise with a couple of small revisions.

In the examples I used in the chapter, NULLs in the table represented irrelevant column values. The unpivoting solutions I presented filtered out rows with NULLs. The EmpYearOrders table has no NULLS, but rather zeros in some cases, and the request is to filter out rows with zero number of orders. With the standard solution, simply use the predicate numorders <> 0 instead of using IS NOT NULL. Here's the version using the VALUES clause supported as of SQL Server 2008:

```
SELECT *
FROM (SELECT empid, orderyear,
        CASE orderyear
          WHEN 2007 THEN cnt2007
          WHEN 2008 THEN cnt2008
          WHEN 2009 THEN cnt2009
        END AS numorders
      FROM dbo.EmpYearOrders
        CROSS JOIN (VALUES(2007),(2008),(2009)) AS Years (orderyear)) AS D
WHERE numorders <> 0;
```

And here is a T-SQL version that does not use the UNPIVOT operator:

```
SELECT *
FROM (SELECT empid, orderyear,
        CASE orderyear
          WHEN 2007 THEN cnt2007
          WHEN 2008 THEN cnt2008
          WHEN 2009 THEN cnt2009
        END AS numorders
```

```
    FROM dbo.EmpYearOrders
      CROSS JOIN (SELECT 2007 AS orderyear
                    UNION ALL SELECT 2008
                    UNION ALL SELECT 2009) AS Years) AS D
WHERE numorders <> 0;
```

As for the solution that uses the native UNPIVOT operator and is supported as of SQL Server 2005, remember that it eliminates NULLs as an integral part of its logic. However, it does not eliminate zeros—you have to take care of eliminating zeros yourself by adding a WHERE clause like so:

```
SELECT empid, CAST(RIGHT(orderyear, 4) AS INT) AS orderyear, numorders
FROM dbo.EmpYearOrders
  UNPIVOT(numorders FOR orderyear IN(cnt2007, cnt2008, cnt2009)) AS U
WHERE numorders <> 0;
```

Notice the expression used in the SELECT list to produce the orderyear result column: CAST(RIGHT(orderyear, 4) AS INT). The original column names that the query unpivots are cnt2007, cnt2008, and cnt2009. These column names become the values 'cnt2007', 'cnt2008', and 'cnt2009', respectively, in the orderyear column in the result of the UNPIVOT operator. The purpose of this expression is to extract the four rightmost characters representing the order year, and convert the value to an integer. This manipulation was not required in the standard solution because the constants used to construct the table expression Years were specified as the integer order years to begin with.

3

If you understand the concept of grouping sets, this exercise should be straightforward for you. You can use the GROUPING SETS subclause to list the requested grouping sets and the *GROUPING_ID* function to produce a unique identifier for the grouping set with which each row is associated. Here's the complete solution query:

```
SELECT
  GROUPING_ID(empid, custid, YEAR(Orderdate)) AS groupingset,
  empid, custid, YEAR(Orderdate) AS orderyear, SUM(qty) AS sumqty
FROM dbo.Orders
GROUP BY
  GROUPING SETS
  (
    (empid, custid, YEAR(orderdate)),
    (empid, YEAR(orderdate)),
    (custid, YEAR(orderdate))
  );
```

The requested grouping sets are neither a power set nor a rollup of some set of attributes. Therefore, you cannot use either the CUBE or the ROLLUP subclause to further abbreviate the code.

Chapter 8
Data Modification

SQL has a set of statements known as Data Manipulation Language (DML) that deals with, well, data manipulation. Some people think that DML involves only statements that modify data, but in fact it also involves data retrieval. DML includes the statements *SELECT*, *INSERT*, *UPDATE*, *DELETE*, and *MERGE*. Up to this point in the book I've focused on the *SELECT* statement. This chapter focuses on data modification statements. In addition to covering standard aspects of data modification, in this chapter I'll also cover T-SQL–specific aspects.

To avoid changing data in your existing sample databases, for demonstration purposes most of the examples in this chapter will create, populate, and operate against tables in the tempdb database that use the dbo schema.

Inserting Data

T-SQL provides several statements to insert data into tables: *INSERT VALUES*, *INSERT SELECT*, *INSERT EXEC*, *SELECT INTO*, and *BULK INSERT*. I'll first describe those statements and then I'll talk about a column property called *IDENTITY* that automatically generates numeric values in the target column upon insert.

The INSERT VALUES Statement

You use the *INSERT VALUES* statement to insert rows into a table based on specified values. To demonstrate this statement and others, you will work with a table called Orders in the dbo schema in the tempdb database. Run the following code to create the Orders table:

```
USE tempdb;

IF OBJECT_ID('dbo.Orders', 'U') IS NOT NULL DROP TABLE dbo.Orders;

CREATE TABLE dbo.Orders
(
  orderid    INT        NOT NULL
    CONSTRAINT PK_Orders PRIMARY KEY,
  orderdate DATE        NOT NULL
    CONSTRAINT DFT_orderdate DEFAULT(CURRENT_TIMESTAMP),
  empid     INT        NOT NULL,
  custid     VARCHAR(10) NOT NULL
)
```

The following example demonstrates how to use the *INSERT VALUES* statement to insert a single row into the Orders table:

```
INSERT INTO dbo.Orders(orderid, orderdate, empid, custid)
  VALUES(10001, '20090212', 3, 'A');
```

Specifying the target column names right after the table name is optional, but by doing so you control the value-column associations instead of relying on the order in which the columns appeared when the table was defined (or the table structure was last altered).

If you specify a value for a column, Microsoft SQL Server will use that value. If you don't, SQL Server will check whether a default value is defined for the column, and if so, the default will be used. If a default value isn't defined and the column allows NULLs, a NULL will be used. If you do not specify a value for a column that does not somehow get its value automatically, your *INSERT* statement will fail. As an example of relying on a default value or expression, the following statement inserts a row into the Orders table without specifying a value for the orderdate column, but because this column has a default expression defined for it (CURRENT_TIMESTAMP), that default will be used:

```
INSERT INTO dbo.Orders(orderid, empid, custid)
  VALUES(10002, 5, 'B');
```

SQL Server 2008 enhances the VALUES clause by allowing you to specify multiple rows separated by commas. For example, the following statement inserts four rows into the Orders table:

```
INSERT INTO dbo.Orders
  (orderid, orderdate, empid, custid)
```

```
VALUES
  (10003, '20090213', 4, 'B'),
  (10004, '20090214', 1, 'A'),
  (10005, '20090213', 1, 'C'),
  (10006, '20090215', 3, 'C');
```

This statement is processed as an atomic operation, meaning that if any row fails to enter the table, none of the rows in the statement enters the table.

There's more to this enhancement than meets the eye. Not only was the *INSERT VALUES* statement enhanced, but the VALUES clause itself was also enhanced so that you can use it to construct a virtual table. This feature, called Row Value Constructor and also Table Value Constructor, is standard. This means that you can define a table expression based on the VALUES clause. Here's an example of a query against a derived table that is defined based on the VALUES clause:

```
SELECT *
FROM ( VALUES
        (10003, '20090213', 4, 'B'),
        (10004, '20090214', 1, 'A'),
        (10005, '20090213', 1, 'C'),
        (10006, '20090215', 3, 'C') )
    AS O(orderid, orderdate, empid, custid);
```

Following the parentheses that contain the table value constructor, you assign an alias to the table (O in our case), and following the table alias you assign aliases to the target columns in parentheses. This query generates the following output:

```
orderid     orderdate    empid        custid
----------- ------------ ------------ ------
10003       20090213     4            B
10004       20090214     1            A
10005       20090213     1            C
10006       20090215     3            C
```

The INSERT SELECT Statement

The *INSERT SELECT* statement inserts a set of rows returned by a SELECT query into a target table. The syntax is very similar to that of an *INSERT VALUES* statement, but instead of the VALUES clause you specify a SELECT query. For example, the following code inserts into the dbo.Orders table in tempdb the result of a query against the Sales.Orders table in TSQLFundamentals2008 returning orders that were shipped to the UK:

```
USE tempdb;

INSERT INTO dbo.Orders(orderid, orderdate, empid, custid)
  SELECT orderid, orderdate, empid, custid
  FROM TSQLFundamentals2008.Sales.Orders
  WHERE shipcountry = 'UK';
```

The *INSERT SELECT* statement also optionally allows you to specify the target column names, and the recommendations I gave earlier regarding specifying those names remain the same.

The requirement to provide values for all columns that do not somehow get their values automatically and the implicit use of default values/NULLs when a value is not provided also behave the same way as with the *INSERT VALUES* statement. The *INSERT SELECT* statement is performed as an atomic operation, so if any row fails to enter the target table, none of the rows enters the table.

If you wanted to construct a virtual table based on values prior to SQL Server 2008, you had to use multiple *SELECT* statements, each returning a single row based on values, and unify the rows with UNION ALL set operations. In the context of an *INSERT SELECT* statement, you could use this technique to insert multiple rows based on values in a single statement that is considered an atomic operation. For example, the following statement inserts four rows based on values into the Orders table:

```
INSERT INTO dbo.Orders(orderid, orderdate, empid, custid)
  SELECT 10007, '20090215', 2, 'B' UNION ALL
  SELECT 10008, '20090215', 1, 'C' UNION ALL
  SELECT 10009, '20090216', 2, 'C' UNION ALL
  SELECT 10010, '20090216', 3, 'A';
```

As I mentioned earlier, SQL Server 2008 supports table value constructors, so you don't really need this technique anymore.

Almost all *INSERT SELECT* operations were fully logged (that is, fully written to the database's transaction log) prior to SQL Server 2008, and compared to minimally logged operations, fully logged operations can be substantially slower. SQL Server 2008 supports minimal logging in more scenarios than in previous versions, including with the *INSERT SELECT* statement. Performance discussions are outside the scope of this book, but if you're interested in learning more, you can find details in the SQL Server Books Online article "Operations That Can Be Minimally Logged."

The INSERT EXEC Statement

You use the *INSERT EXEC* statement to insert a result set returned from a stored procedure or a dynamic SQL batch into a target table. You'll find information about stored procedures, batches, and dynamic SQL in Chapter 10, "Programmable Objects." The *INSERT EXEC* statement is very similar in syntax and concept to the *INSERT SELECT* statement, but instead of a *SELECT* statement, you specify an *EXEC* statement.

For example, the following code creates a stored procedure called Sales.usp_getorders in the TSQLFundamentals2008 database, returning orders that were shipped to a given input country (*@country* parameter):

```
USE TSQLFundamentals2008;

IF OBJECT_ID('Sales.usp_getorders', 'P') IS NOT NULL
  DROP PROC Sales.usp_getorders;
GO
```

```
CREATE PROC Sales.usp_getorders
  @country AS NVARCHAR(40)
AS

SELECT orderid, orderdate, empid, custid
FROM Sales.Orders
WHERE shipcountry = @country;
GO
```

To test the stored procedure, execute it with the input country France:

```
EXEC Sales.usp_getorders @country = 'France';
```

You get the following output:

```
orderid     orderdate                  empid       custid
----------- -------------------------- ----------- -----------
10248       2006-07-04 00:00:00.000    5           85
10251       2006-07-08 00:00:00.000    3           84
10265       2006-07-25 00:00:00.000    2           7
10274       2006-08-06 00:00:00.000    6           85
10295       2006-09-02 00:00:00.000    2           85
10297       2006-09-04 00:00:00.000    5           7
10311       2006-09-20 00:00:00.000    1           18
10331       2006-10-16 00:00:00.000    9           9
10334       2006-10-21 00:00:00.000    8           84
10340       2006-10-29 00:00:00.000    1           9
...

(77 row(s) affected)
```

Using an *INSERT EXEC* statement, you can direct the result set returned from the procedure to the dbo.Orders table in the tempdb database:

```
USE tempdb;

INSERT INTO dbo.Orders(orderid, orderdate, empid, custid)
  EXEC TSQLFundamentals2008.Sales.usp_getorders @country = 'France';
```

The SELECT INTO Statement

The *SELECT INTO* statement is a nonstandard T-SQL statement that creates a target table and populates it with the result set of a query. By "nonstandard," I mean not part of the ANSI SQL standard. You cannot use this statement to insert data into an existing table. In terms of syntax, simply add INTO *<target_table_name>* right before the FROM clause of the SELECT query that you want to use to produce the result set. For example, the following code creates a table called dbo.Orders in tempdb and populates it with all rows from the Sales.Orders table from TSQLFundamentals2008:

```
USE tempdb;

IF OBJECT_ID('dbo.Orders', 'U') IS NOT NULL DROP TABLE dbo.Orders;
```

```
SELECT orderid, orderdate, empid, custid
INTO dbo.Orders
FROM TSQLFundamentals2008.Sales.Orders;
```

The target table's structure and data are based on the source table. The *SELECT INTO* statement copies from the source the base structure (column names, types, NULLability, IDENTITY property) and the data. There are three things that the statement does not copy from the source: constraints, indexes, and triggers. If you need those in the target, you will need to create them yourself.

One of the advantages of the *SELECT INTO* statement is that as long as a database property called *Recovery Model* is not set to FULL, the SELECT INTO operation is performed in a minimally logged mode. This translates to a very fast operation compared to a fully logged one.

If you need to use a *SELECT INTO* statement with set operations, you specify the INTO clause right in front of the FROM clause of the first query. For example, the following *SELECT INTO* statement creates a table called Locations and populates it with the result of an EXCEPT set operation, returning locations where there are customers but not employees:

```
USE tempdb;

IF OBJECT_ID('dbo.Locations', 'U') IS NOT NULL DROP TABLE dbo.Locations;

SELECT country, region, city
INTO dbo.Locations
FROM TSQLFundamentals2008.Sales.Customers

EXCEPT

SELECT country, region, city
FROM TSQLFundamentals2008.HR.Employees;
```

The BULK INSERT Statement

You use the *BULK INSERT* statement to insert into an existing table data originating from a file. In the statement, you specify the target table, the source file, and options. You can specify many options, including the data file type (for example, char or native), the field terminator, the row terminator, and others—all of which are fully documented.

For example, the following code bulk inserts the contents of the file 'c:\temp\orders.txt' into the table dbo.Orders in tempdb, specifying that the data file type is char, the field terminator is a comma, and the row terminator is newline:

```
USE tempdb;

BULK INSERT dbo.Orders FROM 'c:\temp\orders.txt'
  WITH
    (
       DATAFILETYPE    = 'char',
       FIELDTERMINATOR = ',',
       ROWTERMINATOR   = '\n'
    );
```

Note that if you want to actually run this statement you need to place the orders.txt file provided along with the source code for this book in the c:\temp folder.

You can run the *BULK INSERT* statement in a fast, minimally logged mode in certain scenarios provided that certain requirements are met. For details, please see "Prerequisites for Minimal Logging in Bulk Import" in SQL Server Books Online.

The IDENTITY Property

SQL Server allows you to define a property called *IDENTITY* for a column with any numeric type with a scale of 0 (no fraction). This property generates values automatically upon *INSERT* based on seed (first value) and increment (step value) that are provided in the column's definition. Typically you would use this property to generate *surrogate keys*, which are keys that are produced by the system and are not derived from the application data.

For example, the following code creates a table called dbo.T1 in tempdb:

```
USE tempdb;

IF OBJECT_ID('dbo.T1', 'U') IS NOT NULL DROP TABLE dbo.T1;

CREATE TABLE dbo.T1
(
  keycol  INT        NOT NULL IDENTITY(1, 1)
    CONSTRAINT PK_T1 PRIMARY KEY,
  datacol VARCHAR(10) NOT NULL
    CONSTRAINT CHK_T1_datacol CHECK(datacol LIKE '[A-Za-z]%')
);
```

The table contains a column called keycol which is defined with an *IDENTITY* property using 1 as the seed and 1 as the increment. The table also contains a character string column called datacol whose data is restricted with a CHECK constraint to strings starting with an alpha character.

In your *INSERT* statements, you should completely ignore the identity column, pretending as though it isn't in the table. For example, the following code inserts three rows into the table, specifying values only for the column datacol:

```
INSERT INTO dbo.T1(datacol) VALUES('AAAAA');
INSERT INTO dbo.T1(datacol) VALUES('CCCCC');
INSERT INTO dbo.T1(datacol) VALUES('BBBBB');
```

SQL Server produced the values for keycol automatically. To see the values that SQL Server produced, query the table:

```
SELECT * FROM dbo.T1;
```

You get the following output:

```
keycol      datacol
----------- ----------
1           AAAAA
2           CCCCC
3           BBBBB
```

When you query the table, naturally you can refer to the identity column by its name (keycol in our case). SQL Server also provides a way to refer to the identity column using the more generic form $identity. This form is supported as of SQL Server 2005, replacing the deprecated form IDENTITYCOL. The deprecated form is still supported for backward compatibility, but will be removed from the product in a future version.

For example, the following query selects the identity column from T1 using the generic form:

```
SELECT $identity FROM dbo.T1;
```

This query returns the following output:

```
keycol
-----------
1
2
3
```

When you insert a new row into the table, SQL Server generates a new identity value based on the current identity value in the table and the increment. If you need to obtain the newly generated identity value—for example, to insert child rows into a referencing table—you query one of two functions called @@identity and SCOPE_IDENTITY(). The @@identity function is a legacy feature (predating even SQL Server 2000), and it returns the last identity value generated by the session, regardless of scope. SCOPE_IDENTITY() returns the last identity value generated by the session in the current scope (for example, the same procedure). Except for very special cases when you don't really care about scope, you should use the SCOPE_IDENTITY function.

For example, the following code inserts a row into the table T1, obtains the newly generated identity value into a variable by querying the SCOPE_IDENTITY function, and queries the variable:

```
DECLARE @new_key AS INT;

INSERT INTO dbo.T1(datacol) VALUES('AAAAA');

SET @new_key = SCOPE_IDENTITY();

SELECT @new_key AS new_key
```

If you ran all previous code samples provided in this section, this code returns the following output:

```
new_key
-----------
4
```

Remember that both *@@identity* and *SCOPE_IDENTITY* return the last identity value produced by the current session. Neither is affected by inserts issued by other sessions. However, if you want to know the current identity value in a table (last value produced) regardless of session, you should use the *IDENT_CURRENT* function and provide the table name as input. For example, run the following code from a new session (not the one where you ran the previous *INSERT* statements):

```
SELECT
  SCOPE_IDENTITY() AS [SCOPE_IDENTITY],
  @@identity AS [@@identity],
  IDENT_CURRENT('dbo.T1') AS [IDENT_CURRENT];
```

You get the following output:

```
SCOPE_IDENTITY    @@identity    IDENT_CURRENT
----------------- ------------- -------------
NULL              NULL          4
```

Both *@@identity* and *SCOPE_IDENTITY* returned NULLs because no identity values were created in the session where this query ran. *IDENT_CURRENT* returned the value 4 because it returns the current identity value in the table, regardless of the session in which it was produced.

Note the following important details regarding the identity property.

The change to the current identity value in a table is not undone if the *INSERT* that generated the change fails or the transaction in which the statement runs is rolled back. For example, run the following *INSERT* statement, which contradicts the CHECK constraint defined in the table:

```
INSERT INTO dbo.T1(datacol) VALUES('12345');
```

The insert fails, and you get the following error:

```
Msg 547, Level 16, State 0, Line 1
The INSERT statement conflicted with the CHECK constraint "CHK_T1_datacol". The conflict
occurred in database "tempdb", table "dbo.T1", column 'datacol'.
The statement has been terminated.
```

Even though the insert failed, the current identity value in the table changed from 4 to 5, and this change was not undone because of the failure. This means that the next insert will produce the value 6:

```
INSERT INTO dbo.T1(datacol) VALUES('EEEEE');
```

Query the table:

```
SELECT * FROM dbo.T1;
```

Notice a gap between the values 4 and 6 in the output:

```
keycol       datacol
-----------  ----------
1            AAAAA
2            CCCCC
3            BBBBB
4            AAAAA
6            EEEEE
```

Of course, this means that you should only rely on the identity property to auto-generate values when you don't care about having gaps. Otherwise, you should consider using your own alternative mechanism.

Another important aspect of the identity property is that you cannot add it to an existing column or remove it from an existing column; you can only define the property along with a column as part of a *CREATE TABLE* statement or an *ALTER TABLE* statement that adds a new column. However, SQL Server does allow you to explicitly specify your own values for the identity column in *INSERT* statements, provided that you set a session option called *IDENTITY_INSERT* against the table involved. No option allows you to update an identity column, though.

For example, the following code demonstrates how to insert a row to T1 with the explicit value 5 in keycol:

```
SET IDENTITY_INSERT dbo.T1 ON;
INSERT INTO dbo.T1(keycol, datacol) VALUES(5, 'FFFFF');
SET IDENTITY_INSERT dbo.T1 OFF;
```

Interestingly, SQL Server changes the current identity value in the table only if the explicit value provided for the identity column is higher than the current identity value in the table. Because the current identity value in the table prior to running the preceding code was 6, and the *INSERT* statement in this code used the lower explicit value 5, the current identity value in the table did not change. So if at this point, after running the preceding code, you query the *IDENT_CURRENT* function for this table, you will get 6 and not 5. This way the next *INSERT* statement against the table will produce the value 7:

```
INSERT INTO dbo.T1(datacol) VALUES('GGGGG');
```

Query the current contents of the table T1:

```
SELECT * FROM dbo.T1;
```

You get the following output:

```
keycol       datacol
-----------  ----------
1            AAAAA
2            CCCCC
```

```
3          BBBBB
4          AAAAA
5          FFFFF
6          EEEEE
7          GGGGG
```

It is important to understand that the identity property itself does not enforce uniqueness in the column. I already explained that you can provide your own explicit values after setting the *IDENTITY_INSERT* option to ON, and those values can be ones that already exist in rows in the table. Also, you can reseed the current identity value in the table by using the *DBCC CHECKIDENT* command. For details about the syntax of the *DBCC CHECKIDENT* command please refer to "*DBCC CHECKIDENT* (Transact-SQL)" at SQL Server Books Online. In short, the identity property does not enforce uniqueness. If you need to guarantee uniqueness in an identity column, make sure you also define a primary key or a unique constraint on that column.

Deleting Data

T-SQL provides two statements for deleting rows from a table—*DELETE* and *TRUNCATE*. In this section, I'll describe those statements. The examples I provide in this section are against copies of the Customers and Orders tables from the TSQLFundamentals2008 database created in the tempdb database. Run the following code to create and populate those tables:

```
USE tempdb;

IF OBJECT_ID('dbo.Orders', 'U') IS NOT NULL DROP TABLE dbo.Orders;
IF OBJECT_ID('dbo.Customers', 'U') IS NOT NULL DROP TABLE dbo.Customers;

SELECT * INTO dbo.Customers FROM TSQLFundamentals2008.Sales.Customers;
SELECT * INTO dbo.Orders FROM TSQLFundamentals2008.Sales.Orders;

ALTER TABLE dbo.Customers ADD
  CONSTRAINT PK_Customers PRIMARY KEY(custid);
ALTER TABLE dbo.Orders ADD
  CONSTRAINT PK_Orders PRIMARY KEY(orderid),
  CONSTRAINT FK_Orders_Customers FOREIGN KEY(custid)
    REFERENCES dbo.Customers(custid);
```

The DELETE Statement

The *DELETE* statement is a standard statement used to delete data from a table based on a predicate. The standard statement has only two clauses—the FROM clause, in which you specify the target table name, and a WHERE clause, in which you specify a predicate. Only the subset of rows for which the predicate evaluates to TRUE will be deleted.

For example, the following statement deletes, from the dbo.Orders table in tempdb, all orders that were placed prior to 2007:

```
USE tempdb;

DELETE FROM dbo.Orders
WHERE orderdate < '20070101';
```

Run this statement and SQL Server will report that it deleted 152 rows:

```
(152 row(s) affected)
```

Note that the message indicating how many rows were affected only appears if the session option NOCOUNT is OFF, which it is by default. If it is ON, SQL Server Management Studio will only state that the command completed successfully.

The *DELETE* statement is fully logged. Therefore, you should expect it to run for a while when you delete a large number of rows.

The TRUNCATE Statement

The *TRUNCATE* statement is a nonstandard statement that deletes all rows from a table. Unlike the *DELETE* statement, *TRUNCATE* has no filter. For example, to delete all rows from a table called dbo.T1, you run the following code:

```
TRUNCATE TABLE dbo.T1;
```

The advantage that *TRUNCATE* has over *DELETE* is that the former is minimally logged while the latter is fully logged, resulting in significant performance differences. For example, if you use the *TRUNCATE* statement to delete all rows from a table with millions of rows, the operation will finish in a matter of seconds. If you use the *DELETE* statement, the operation can take minutes or even hours.

TRUNCATE and *DELETE* also have a functional difference when the table has an identity column. *TRUNCATE* resets the identity value back to the original seed, while *DELETE* doesn't.

The *TRUNCATE* statement is not allowed when the target table is referenced by a foreign key constraint, even if the referencing table is empty and even if the foreign key is disabled. The only way to allow a *TRUNCATE* statement is to drop all foreign keys referencing the table.

Because the *TRUNCATE* statement is so fast, it can also be dangerous. Accidents such as truncating or dropping the incorrect table can happen. For example, let's say you have connections open against both the production and the development environments, and you submit your code in the wrong connection. Both the *TRUNCATE* and *DROP* statements are so fast that before you realize your mistake, the transaction is committed. To prevent such accidents, you can protect a production table by simply creating a dummy table with a foreign key pointing to the production table. You can even disable the foreign key so that it won't have any impact on performance. As I mentioned earlier, even when disabled, this foreign key prevents truncating or dropping the referenced table.

DELETE Based on a Join

T-SQL supports a nonstandard DELETE syntax based on joins. The join itself serves a filtering purpose because it has a filter based on a predicate (the ON clause). The join also gives you access to attributes of related rows from another table that you can refer to in the WHERE clause. This means that you can delete rows from one table based on a filter against attributes in related rows from another table.

For example, the following statement deletes orders placed by customers from the USA:

```
USE tempdb;

DELETE FROM O
FROM dbo.Orders AS O
  JOIN dbo.Customers AS C
    ON O.custid = C.custid
WHERE C.country = N'USA';
```

Very much like in a *SELECT* statement, the first clause that is logically processed in a *DELETE* statement is the FROM clause (the second one that appears in this statement). Then the WHERE clause is processed, and finally the DELETE clause. The way to "read" or interpret this query is: "The query joins the Orders table (aliased as O) with the Customers table (aliased as C) based on a match between the order's customer ID and the customer's customer ID. The query then filters only orders placed by customers from the USA. Finally, the query deletes all qualifying rows from O (the alias representing the Orders table)."

The two FROM clauses in a *DELETE* statement based on a join might be confusing. But when you develop the code, develop it as if it were a *SELECT* statement with a join. That is, start with the FROM clause with the joins, move on to the WHERE clause, and finally, instead of specifying a SELECT clause, specify a DELETE clause with the alias of the side of the join that is supposed to be the target for the delete.

As I mentioned earlier, a *DELETE* statement based on a join is nonstandard. If you want to stick to standard code, you can use subqueries instead of joins. For example, the following *DELETE* statement uses a subquery to achieve the same task:

```
DELETE FROM dbo.Orders
WHERE EXISTS
  (SELECT *
  FROM dbo.Customers AS C
  WHERE Orders.Custid = C.Custid
    AND C.Country = 'USA');
```

This code deletes all rows from the Orders table where a related customer in the customers table from the USA exists.

SQL Server will most likely process the two queries the same way; therefore you shouldn't expect any performance difference between the two. So why do people even consider using the nonstandard syntax? Some people feel more comfortable with joins while others feel more comfortable with subqueries. I usually recommend sticking to the standard as much as possible unless you have a very compelling reason to do otherwise—for example, in the case of a big performance difference.

Updating Data

T-SQL supports a standard *UPDATE* statement that allows you to update rows in a table. T-SQL also supports nonstandard uses of the *UPDATE* statement with joins and with variables. This section describes the various uses of the *UPDATE* statement.

The examples I provide in this section are against copies of the Orders and OrderDetails tables from the TSQLFundamentals2008 database created in the tempdb database. Run the following code to create and populate those tables:

```
USE tempdb;

IF OBJECT_ID('dbo.OrderDetails', 'U') IS NOT NULL DROP TABLE dbo.OrderDetails;
IF OBJECT_ID('dbo.Orders', 'U') IS NOT NULL DROP TABLE dbo.Orders;

SELECT * INTO dbo.Orders FROM TSQLFundamentals2008.Sales.Orders;
SELECT * INTO dbo.OrderDetails FROM TSQLFundamentals2008.Sales.OrderDetails;

ALTER TABLE dbo.Orders ADD
  CONSTRAINT PK_Orders PRIMARY KEY(orderid);
ALTER TABLE dbo.OrderDetails ADD
  CONSTRAINT PK_OrderDetails PRIMARY KEY(orderid, productid),
  CONSTRAINT FK_OrderDetails_Orders FOREIGN KEY(orderid)
    REFERENCES dbo.Orders(orderid);
```

The UPDATE Statement

The *UPDATE* statement is a standard statement that allows you to update a subset of rows in a table. To identify the subset of rows that are the target of the update, you specify a predicate in a WHERE clause. You specify the assignment of values or expressions to columns in a SET clause, separated by commas.

For example, the following *UPDATE* statement increases the discount of all order details with product 51 by 5 percent:

```
USE tempdb;

UPDATE dbo.OrderDetails
  SET discount = discount + 0.05
WHERE productid = 51;
```

Of course you can run a *SELECT* statement with the same filter before and after the update to see the changes. Later in the chapter, I'll show you another way to see the changes using a clause called OUTPUT that you can add to modification statements.

SQL Server 2008 introduces support for compound assignment operators: += (plus equal), −= (minus equal), *= (multiplication equal), /= (division equal,) and %= (modulo equal), allowing you to shorten assignment expressions such as the one in the preceding query. Instead of the expression discount = discount + 0.05, you can use the shorter form: discount += 0.05. The full *UPDATE* statement looks like this:

```
UPDATE dbo.OrderDetails
  SET discount += 0.05
WHERE productid = 51;
```

All-at-once operations are an important aspect of SQL that you should keep in mind when writing *UPDATE* statements. I explained the concept in Chapter 2, "Single-Table Queries," in the context of *SELECT* statements, but it's just as applicable with *UPDATE* statements. Remember the concept that says that all expressions in the same logical phase are evaluated as if at the same point in time. To understand the relevance of this concept, consider the following *UPDATE* statement:

```
UPDATE dbo.T1
  SET col1 = col1 + 10, col2 = col1 + 10;
```

Suppose that one row in the table has the values 100 in col1 and 200 in col2 prior to the update. Can you determine the values of those columns after the update?

If you do not consider the all-at-once concept, you would think that col1 will be set to 110 and col2 to 120, as if the assignments were performed from left to right. However, the assignments take place as if all at once, meaning that both assignments use the same value of col1—the value before the update. The result of this update is that both col1 and col2 will end up with the value 110.

With the concept of all-at-once in mind, can you figure out how to write an *UPDATE* statement that swaps the values in the columns col1 and col2? In most programming languages where expressions and assignments are evaluated in some order (typically left to right), you need a temporary variable. However, because in SQL all assignments take place as if at the same point in time, the solution is very simple:

```
UPDATE dbo.T1
  SET col1 = col2, col2 = col1;
```

In both assignments the source column values used are those prior to the update, so you don't need a temporary variable.

UPDATE Based on a Join

Similar to the *DELETE* statement, T-SQL also supports a nonstandard syntax for *UPDATE* statements based on joins. As with *DELETE* statements, the join serves a filtering purpose.

The syntax is very similar to a *SELECT* statement based on a join; that is, the FROM and WHERE clauses are the same, but instead of the SELECT clause you specify an UPDATE clause. The *UPDATE* keyword is followed by the alias of the table that is the target of the update (you can't update more than one table in the same statement), followed by the SET clause with the column assignments.

For example, the *UPDATE* statement in Listing 8-1 increases the discount of all order details of orders placed by customer 1 by 5 percent:

LISTING 8-1 UPDATE Based on a Join

```
UPDATE OD
  SET discount = discount + 0.05
FROM dbo.OrderDetails AS OD
  JOIN dbo.Orders AS O
    ON OD.orderid = O.orderid
WHERE custid = 1;
```

To "read" or interpret the query, start with the FROM clause, move on to the WHERE clause, and finally go to the UPDATE clause. The query joins the OrderDetails table (aliased as OD) with the Orders table (aliased as O) based on a match between the order detail's order ID and the order's order ID. The query then filters only the rows where the order's customer ID is 1. The query then specifies in the UPDATE clause that OD (the alias of the OrderDetails table) is the target of the update, and increases the discount by 5 percent.

If you want to achieve the same task using standard code you would need to use a subquery instead of a join, like so:

```
UPDATE dbo.OrderDetails
  SET discount = discount + 0.05
WHERE EXISTS
  (SELECT * FROM dbo.Orders AS O
   WHERE O.orderid = OrderDetails.orderid
     AND custid = 1);
```

The query's WHERE clause filters only order details in which a related order is placed by customer 1. With this particular task, SQL Server will most likely interpret both versions the same way; therefore, you shouldn't expect performance differences between the two. Again, the version you feel more comfortable with probably depends on whether you feel more comfortable with joins or subqueries. But as I mentioned earlier in regards to the *DELETE* statement, I recommend sticking to standard code unless you have a compelling reason to do otherwise. With our current task, I do not see a compelling reason.

However, in some cases, the join version will have a performance advantage over the subquery version. In addition to filtering, the join also gives you access to attributes from other tables that you can use in the column assignments in the SET clause. The same access to the other table can serve both the filtering purpose and obtaining attribute values from the other table for the assignments. However, with the subquery approach, each subquery involves separate access to the other table—that's at least the way subqueries are processed today by SQL Server's engine.

For example, consider the following nonstandard *UPDATE* statement based on a join:

```
UPDATE T1
  SET col1 = T2.col1,
      col2 = T2.col2,
      col3 = T2.col3
FROM dbo.T1 JOIN dbo.T2
  ON T2.keycol = T1.keycol
WHERE T2.col4 = 'ABC';
```

This statement joins the tables T1 and T2 based on a match between T1.keycol and T2.keycol. The WHERE clause filters only rows where T2.col4 is equal to 'ABC'. The *UPDATE* statement marks the T1 table as the target for the UPDATE, and the SET clause sets the values of the columns col1, col2, and col3 in T1 to the values of the corresponding columns from T2.

An attempt to express this task using standard code with subqueries yields the following lengthy query:

```
UPDATE dbo.T1
  SET col1 = (SELECT col1
                FROM dbo.T2
                WHERE T2.keycol = T1.keycol),

      col2 = (SELECT col2
                FROM dbo.T2
                WHERE T2.keycol = T1.keycol),

      col3 = (SELECT col3
                FROM dbo.T2
                WHERE T2.keycol = T1.keycol)
WHERE EXISTS
  (SELECT *
   FROM dbo.T2
   WHERE T2.keycol = T1.keycol
     AND T2.col4 = 'ABC');
```

Not only is this version convoluted (unlike the join version), but each subquery also involves separate access to table T2. So this version is less efficient than the join version.

ANSI SQL has support for row constructors (also known as vector expressions) that were only implemented partially in SQL Server 2008 as I explained earlier. Still, many aspects of row constructors have not yet been implemented in SQL Server, including the ability to use those in the SET clause of an *UPDATE* statement like so:

```
UPDATE dbo.T1

  SET (col1, col2, col3) =

      (SELECT col1, col2, col3
       FROM dbo.T2
       WHERE T2.keycol = T1.keycol)

WHERE EXISTS
  (SELECT *
   FROM dbo.T2
   WHERE T2.keycol = T1.keycol
     AND T2.col4 = 'ABC');
```

But as you can see, this version would still be more complicated than the join version because it requires separate subqueries for the filtering part and for obtaining the attributes from the other table for the assignments.

Assignment UPDATE

T-SQL supports a proprietary UPDATE syntax that both updates data in a table and assigns values to variables at the same time. This syntax saves you the need to use separate *UPDATE* and *SELECT* statements to achieve the same task.

One of the common cases where you can use this syntax is in maintaining a custom sequence/auto-numbering mechanism when, for whatever reason, the identity column property doesn't work for you. The idea is to keep the last used value in a table, and to use this special UPDATE syntax to increment the value in the table and assign the new value to a variable.

Run the following code to first create the Sequence table with the column val, and then populate it with a single row with the value 0—one less than the first value that you want to use:

```
USE tempdb;
IF OBJECT_ID('dbo.Sequence', 'U') IS NOT NULL DROP TABLE dbo.Sequence;
CREATE TABLE dbo.Sequence(val INT NOT NULL);
INSERT INTO dbo.Sequence VALUES(0);
```

Now, whenever you need to obtain a new sequence value use the following code:

```
DECLARE @nextval AS INT;
UPDATE Sequence SET @nextval = val = val + 1;
SELECT @nextval;
```

The code declares a local variable called *@nextval*. Then it uses the special UPDATE syntax to increment the column value by 1, assigns the updated column value to the variable, and presents the value in the variable. The assignments in the SET clause take place from right to left. That is, first val is set to val + 1, then the result (val + 1) is set to the variable @*nextval*.

The specialized UPDATE syntax is run as an atomic operation, and it is more efficient than using separate *UPDATE* and *SELECT* statements because it accesses the data only once.

Merging Data

SQL Server 2008 introduces a statement called *MERGE* that allows you to modify data, applying different actions (*INSERT, UPDATE, DELETE*) based on conditional logic. The *MERGE* statement is part of the SQL standard, although the T-SQL version adds a few nonstandard extensions to the statement.

Because *MERGE* is new, you must use SQL Server 2008 for the code samples in this section. A task achieved by a single *MERGE* statement will typically translate to a combination of several other DML statements (*INSERT, UPDATE, DELETE*) in earlier versions of SQL Server. The benefit to using *MERGE* over the alternatives is that it allows you to express the request with less code and more efficiently because it requires fewer accesses to the tables involved.

To demonstrate the *MERGE* statement, I'll use tables called Customers and CustomersStage. Run the code in Listing 8-2 to create those tables in tempdb and populate them with sample data:

LISTING 8-2 Code that Creates and Populates Customers and CustomersStage

```
USE tempdb;

IF OBJECT_ID('dbo.Customers', 'U') IS NOT NULL DROP TABLE dbo.Customers;
GO

CREATE TABLE dbo.Customers
(
  custid       INT         NOT NULL,
  companyname  VARCHAR(25) NOT NULL,
  phone        VARCHAR(20) NOT NULL,
  address      VARCHAR(50) NOT NULL,
  CONSTRAINT PK_Customers PRIMARY KEY(custid)
);

INSERT INTO dbo.Customers(custid, companyname, phone, address)
VALUES
  (1, 'cust 1', '(111) 111-1111', 'address 1'),
  (2, 'cust 2', '(222) 222-2222', 'address 2'),
  (3, 'cust 3', '(333) 333-3333', 'address 3'),
  (4, 'cust 4', '(444) 444-4444', 'address 4'),
  (5, 'cust 5', '(555) 555-5555', 'address 5');
```

```
IF OBJECT_ID('dbo.CustomersStage', 'U') IS NOT NULL DROP TABLE dbo.CustomersStage;
GO

CREATE TABLE dbo.CustomersStage
(
  custid      INT         NOT NULL,
  companyname VARCHAR(25) NOT NULL,
  phone       VARCHAR(20) NOT NULL,
  address     VARCHAR(50) NOT NULL,
  CONSTRAINT PK_CustomersStage PRIMARY KEY(custid)
);

INSERT INTO dbo.CustomersStage(custid, companyname, phone, address)
VALUES
  (2, 'AAAAA', '(222) 222-2222', 'address 2'),
  (3, 'cust 3', '(333) 333-3333', 'address 3'),
  (5, 'BBBBB', 'CCCCC', 'DDDDD'),
  (6, 'cust 6 (new)', '(666) 666-6666', 'address 6'),
  (7, 'cust 7 (new)', '(777) 777-7777', 'address 7');
```

Run the following query to examine the contents of the Customers table:

```
SELECT * FROM dbo.Customers;
```

This query returns the following output:

custid	companyname	phone	address
1	cust 1	(111) 111-1111	address 1
2	cust 2	(222) 222-2222	address 2
3	cust 3	(333) 333-3333	address 3
4	cust 4	(444) 444-4444	address 4
5	cust 5	(555) 555-5555	address 5

Run the following query to examine the contents of the CustomersStage table:

```
SELECT * FROM dbo.CustomersStage;
```

This query returns the following output:

custid	companyname	phone	address
2	AAAAA	(222) 222-2222	address 2
3	cust 3	(333) 333-3333	address 3
5	BBBBB	CCCCC	DDDDD
6	cust 6 (new)	(666) 666-6666	address 6
7	cust 7 (new)	(777) 777-7777	address 7

The purpose of the first example of the *MERGE* statement that I'll demonstrate is to merge the contents of the CustomersStage table (the source) into the Customers table (the target). More specifically, you are supposed to add customers that do not exist, and to update the attributes of customers that already exist.

If you already feel comfortable with the sections that covered deletes and updates based on joins, you should feel pretty much at home with *MERGE*, which is based on join semantics. You specify the target table name in the MERGE clause and the source table name in the USING clause. You define a merge condition by specifying a predicate in the ON clause, very much as you do in a join. The merge condition defines which rows in the source table have matches in the target and which don't. You define both the action to take when a match is found in a clause called WHEN MATCHED THEN, and the action to take when a match is not found in the WHEN NOT MATCHED THEN clause.

Here's our first example for the *MERGE* statement: adding nonexisting customers and updating existing ones:

```
MERGE INTO dbo.Customers AS TGT
USING dbo.CustomersStage AS SRC
  ON TGT.custid = SRC.custid
WHEN MATCHED THEN
  UPDATE SET
    TGT.companyname = SRC.companyname,
    TGT.phone = SRC.phone,
    TGT.address = SRC.address
WHEN NOT MATCHED THEN
  INSERT (custid, companyname, phone, address)
  VALUES (SRC.custid, SRC.companyname, SRC.phone, SRC.address);
```

 Note It is mandatory to terminate the *MERGE* statement with a semicolon, whereas in most other statements in T-SQL, it is optional. But if you follow best practices (which I mentioned early in the book) to terminate all statements with a semicolon, this shouldn't concern you.

This *MERGE* statement defines the Customers table as the target (MERGE clause) and the CustomersStage table as the source (USING clause). Notice that you can assign aliases to the target and source tables for brevity (TGT and SRC in our case). The predicate TGT.custid = SRC.custid is used to define what is considered a match and what is considered a nonmatch. In our case, if a customer ID that exists in the source also exists in the target, that's a match. If a customer ID in the source does not exist in the target, that's a nonmatch.

The *MERGE* statement defines an UPDATE action when a match is found, setting the target *companyname*, *phone*, and *address* values to those of the corresponding row from the source. Notice that the syntax of the UPDATE action is similar to a normal *UPDATE* statement, except that you don't need to provide the name of the table that is the target of the update because it was already defined in the MERGE clause.

The *MERGE* statement defines an INSERT action when a match is not found, inserting the row from the source to the target. Again, the syntax of the INSERT action is similar to a normal *INSERT* statement, except that you don't need to provide the name of the table that is the target of the activity because it was already defined in the MERGE clause.

Our *MERGE* statement reports that five rows were modified:

```
(5 row(s) affected)
```

This includes three rows that were updated (customers 2, 3, and 5), and two that were inserted (customers 6 and 7). Query the Customers table to get the new contents:

```
SELECT * FROM dbo.Customers;
```

This query returns the following output:

```
custid       companyname          phone                address
-----------  -------------------  -------------------- ----------
1            cust 1               (111) 111-1111       address 1
2            AAAAA                (222) 222-2222       address 2
3            cust 3               (333) 333-3333       address 3
4            cust 4               (444) 444-4444       address 4
5            BBBBB                CCCCC                DDDDD
6            cust 6 (new)         (666) 666-6666       address 6
7            cust 7 (new)         (777) 777-7777       address 7
```

The WHEN MATCHED clause defines what action to take when a source row is matched by a target row. The WHEN NOT MATCHED clause defines what action to take when a source row is not matched by a target row. T-SQL also supports a third clause that defines what action to take when a target row is not matched by a source row; this clause is called WHEN NOT MATCHED BY SOURCE. For example, suppose that you want to add logic to our MERGE example to delete rows from the target when the target is not matched by a source row. All you need to do is add the WHEN NOT MATCHED BY SOURCE clause with a DELETE action, like so:

```
MERGE dbo.Customers AS TGT
USING dbo.CustomersStage AS SRC
  ON TGT.custid = SRC.custid
WHEN MATCHED THEN
  UPDATE SET
    TGT.companyname = SRC.companyname,
    TGT.phone = SRC.phone,
    TGT.address = SRC.address
WHEN NOT MATCHED THEN
  INSERT (custid, companyname, phone, address)
  VALUES (SRC.custid, SRC.companyname, SRC.phone, SRC.address)
WHEN NOT MATCHED BY SOURCE THEN
  DELETE;
```

Query the Customers table to see the result of this *MERGE* statement:

```
SELECT * FROM dbo.Customers;
```

This query returns the following output, showing that customers 1 and 4 were deleted:

```
custid       companyname          phone                address
-----------  -------------------  -------------------- ----------
2            AAAAA                (222) 222-2222       address 2
3            cust 3               (333) 333-3333       address 3
```

5	BBBBB	CCCCC	DDDDD
6	cust 6 (new)	(666) 666-6666	address 6
7	cust 7 (new)	(777) 777-7777	address 7

Going back to our first MERGE example, which updates existing customers and adds nonexisting ones, we can see that it is not written in the most efficient way. The statement doesn't check whether column values actually changed before overwriting the attributes of an existing customer. This means that a customer row is modified even when the source and target rows are identical. You can add predicates to the different action clauses using the AND option; except for the original condition, action will take place only if the additional predicate evaluates to TRUE. In our case, you need to add a predicate under the WHEN MATCHED AND clause that checks whether at least one of the attributes changed to justify the UPDATE action. The complete *MERGE* statement looks like this:

```
MERGE dbo.Customers AS TGT
USING dbo.CustomersStage AS SRC
  ON TGT.custid = SRC.custid
WHEN MATCHED AND
     (   TGT.companyname <> SRC.companyname
      OR TGT.phone       <> SRC.phone
      OR TGT.address      <> SRC.address) THEN
  UPDATE SET
    TGT.companyname = SRC.companyname,
    TGT.phone = SRC.phone,
    TGT.address = SRC.address
WHEN NOT MATCHED THEN
  INSERT (custid, companyname, phone, address)
  VALUES (SRC.custid, SRC.companyname, SRC.phone, SRC.address);
```

As you can see, the *MERGE* statement is very powerful, allowing you to express modification logic with less code and more efficiently than the alternatives.

Modifying Data Through Table Expressions

SQL Server doesn't limit the actions against table expressions (derived tables, CTEs, views, and inline table-valued UDFs) to SELECT only, but also allows other DML statements against those (*INSERT, UPDATE, DELETE*, and *MERGE*). Think about it: a table expression doesn't really contain data—it's a reflection of underlying data in base tables. With this in mind, think of a modification against a table expression as modifying the data in the underlying tables through the table expression. Just as with a *SELECT* statement against a table expression, and also with a data modification statement, the definition of the table expression gets expanded, so in practice the activity is done against the underlying tables.

Modifying data through table expressions has a few logical restrictions. For example:

- If the query defining the table expression joins tables, you're only allowed to impact one of the sides of the join and not both in the same modification statement.

- You cannot update a column that is a result of a calculation; SQL Server doesn't try to reverse engineer the values.

■ You cannot insert a row through the table expression if the table expression doesn't include at least one column that doesn't somehow get its value automatically (has a default value, allows NULLs, has an *IDENTITY* property).

You can find other requirements in SQL Server Books Online, but as you can see, the requirements make sense.

Now that you know that you can modify data through table expressions, the question is, why would you want to? One reason is for better debugging and troubleshooting. For example, Listing 8-1 contained the following *UPDATE* statement:

```
USE tempdb;

UPDATE OD
  SET discount = discount + 0.05
FROM dbo.OrderDetails AS OD
  JOIN dbo.Orders AS O
    ON OD.orderid = O.orderid
WHERE custid = 1;
```

Suppose that for troubleshooting purposes you first want to see which rows would be modified by this statement without actually modifying them. One option is to revise the code to a *SELECT* statement, and after troubleshooting the code, change it back to an *UPDATE* statement. But instead of making such revisions back and forth between *SELECT* and *UPDATE* statements, you can simply use a table expression. That is, you can define a table expression based on a *SELECT* statement with the join query, and have an *UPDATE* statement against the table expression. The following example uses a CTE (supported as of SQL Server 2005):

```
WITH C AS
(
  SELECT custid, OD.orderid,
    productid, discount, discount + 0.05 AS newdiscount
  FROM dbo.OrderDetails AS OD
    JOIN dbo.Orders AS O
      ON OD.orderid = O.orderid
  WHERE custid = 1
)
UPDATE C
  SET discount = newdiscount;
```

And here's an example using a derived table (supported prior to SQL Server 2005):

```
UPDATE D
  SET discount = newdiscount
FROM ( SELECT custid, OD.orderid,
         productid, discount, discount + 0.05 AS newdiscount
       FROM dbo.OrderDetails AS OD
         JOIN dbo.Orders AS O
           ON OD.orderid = O.orderid
       WHERE custid = 1 ) AS D;
```

With the table expression, troubleshooting is simpler because you can always highlight just the *SELECT* statement that defines the table expression and run it without making any data changes. With this example, the use of table expressions is for convenience purposes. However, with some problems using a table expression is not really an option. To demonstrate such a problem I'll use a table called T1 that you create and populate by running the following code:

```
USE tempdb;

IF OBJECT_ID('dbo.T1', 'U') IS NOT NULL DROP TABLE dbo.T1;

CREATE TABLE dbo.T1(col1 INT, col2 INT);
GO

INSERT INTO dbo.T1(col1) VALUES(10);
INSERT INTO dbo.T1(col1) VALUES(20);
INSERT INTO dbo.T1(col1) VALUES(30);

SELECT * FROM dbo.T1;
```

The last query returns the following output showing the current contents of the table T1:

```
col1         col2
-----------  -----------
10           NULL
20           NULL
30           NULL
```

Suppose that you want to update the table, setting col2 to the result of an expression with the *ROW_NUMBER* function. The problem is that the *ROW_NUMBER* function is not allowed in the SET clause of an *UPDATE* statement. Try running the following code:

```
UPDATE dbo.T1
  SET col2 = ROW_NUMBER() OVER(ORDER BY col1);
```

You get the following error:

```
Msg 4108, Level 15, State 1, Line 2
Windowed functions can only appear in the SELECT or ORDER BY clauses.
```

To get around this problem, define a table expression that returns both the column that you need to update (col2) and a result column based on an expression with the *ROW_NUMBER* function (call it rownum). The outer statement against the table expression would then be an *UPDATE* statement setting col2 to rownum. Here's how the code would look using a CTE:

```
WITH C AS
(
  SELECT col1, col2, ROW_NUMBER() OVER(ORDER BY col1) AS rownum
  FROM dbo.T1
)
UPDATE C
  SET col2 = rownum;
```

Query the table to see the result of the update:

```
SELECT * FROM dbo.T1;
```

You get the following output:

```
col1        col2
----------- -----------
10          1
20          2
30          3
```

Note that you must have SQL Server 2005 or SQL Server 2008 to run these examples because both CTEs and the *ROW_NUMBER* function were introduced in SQL Server 2005.

Modifications with the TOP Option

SQL Server 2005 introduced the ability to use the TOP option with modification statements *INSERT*, *UPDATE*, and *DELETE*. SQL Server 2008 extends this support for the new *MERGE* statement. When you use the TOP option, SQL Server stops processing the modification statement as soon as the specified number or percentage of rows are processed. Unfortunately, unlike with the *SELECT* statement, you cannot specify a logical ORDER BY clause for the TOP option with modification statements. Essentially, whichever rows SQL Server happens to access first will be the rows affected by the modification.

I'll demonstrate modifications with TOP using an Orders table that you create in tempdb and populate with sample data by running the following code:

```
USE tempdb;

IF OBJECT_ID('dbo.OrderDetails', 'U') IS NOT NULL DROP TABLE dbo.OrderDetails;
IF OBJECT_ID('dbo.Orders', 'U') IS NOT NULL DROP TABLE dbo.Orders;

SELECT * INTO dbo.Orders FROM TSQLFundamentals2008.Sales.Orders;
```

The following example demonstrates using a *DELETE* statement with the TOP option to delete 50 rows from the Orders table:

```
DELETE TOP(50) FROM dbo.Orders;
```

Because you are not allowed to specify a logical ORDER BY for the TOP option in a modification statement, this query is problematic in the sense that you can't control which 50 rows will be deleted. They will be the first 50 rows from the table that SQL Server happens to access first. This problem demonstrates the limited use cases for modifications with TOP.

Similarly, you can use the TOP option with *UPDATE* and *INSERT* statements, but again, an ORDER BY is not allowed. As an example of an *UPDATE* statement with TOP, the following code updates 50 rows from the Orders table, increasing their *freight* values by 10:

```
UPDATE TOP(50) dbo.Orders
  SET freight = freight + 10.00;
```

Again, you cannot control which 50 rows will be updated; they are the first 50 rows that SQL Server happens to access first.

In practice, of course, you would usually care which rows are affected and you wouldn't want them to be chosen arbitrarily. To get around this problem, you can rely on the fact that you can modify data through table expressions. You can define a table expression based on a SELECT query with the TOP option based on a logical ORDER BY clause that defines precedence among rows. You can then issue the modification statement against the table expression.

For example, the following code deletes the 50 orders with the lowest order ID values rather than just any 50 rows:

```
WITH C AS
(
  SELECT TOP(50) *
  FROM dbo.Orders
  ORDER BY orderid
)
DELETE FROM C;
```

Similarly, the following code updates the 50 orders with the highest order ID values, increasing their *freight* values by 10:

```
WITH C AS
(
  SELECT TOP(50) *
  FROM dbo.Orders
  ORDER BY orderid DESC
)
UPDATE C
  SET freight = freight + 10.00;
```

To achieve the same effect prior to SQL Server 2005, use derived tables instead of CTEs.

The OUTPUT Clause

Normally you would not expect a modification statement to do more than modify data. That is, you would not expect a modification statement to return any output. However, in some scenarios, being able to get back data from the modified rows can be useful.

For example, think about the ability to request from an *UPDATE* statement that besides modifying data, it also returns the old and new values of the updated columns. This can be useful for troubleshooting, auditing, and other purposes.

SQL Server 2005 introduced this capability via a clause called OUTPUT that you add to the modification statement. In this OUTPUT clause, you specify the attributes and expressions that you want to return from the modified rows. SQL Server 2008 also supports the OUTPUT clause with the new *MERGE* statement.

You should think of the OUTPUT clause in very similar terms to the way you think about the SELECT clause. That is, you list the attributes and expressions based on existing attributes that you want to return. What's special in terms of the OUTPUT clause syntax is that you need to prefix the attribute names with either the inserted or the deleted keywords. In an *INSERT* statement you refer to *inserted*, in a *DELETE* statement you refer to *deleted*, and in an *UPDATE* statement you refer to *deleted* when you're after the image of the row before the change and *inserted* when you're after the image of the row after the change.

The OUTPUT clause will return the requested attributes from the modified rows as a result set, very much like a *SELECT* statement does. If you want to direct the result set to a table, add an INTO clause with the target table name. If you want to return modified rows back to the caller and also to direct a copy to a table, specify two OUTPUT clauses—one with the INTO clause and one without it.

The following sections will provide examples for using the OUTPUT clause with the different modification statements.

INSERT with OUTPUT

An example of an *INSERT* statement where the OUTPUT clause can be useful is when you need to insert a row set into a table with an identity column, and you need to get back all identity values that were generated. The *SCOPE_IDENTITY* function returns only the very last identity value that was generated by your session; it doesn't help you much in obtaining all identity values that were generated by an insert of a row set. The OUTPUT clause makes the task very simple to solve. To demonstrate the technique, first create a table called T1 with an identity column called keycol and another column called datacol by running the following code:

```
USE tempdb;

IF OBJECT_ID('dbo.T1', 'U') IS NOT NULL DROP TABLE dbo.T1;

CREATE TABLE dbo.T1
(
  keycol  INT          NOT NULL IDENTITY(1, 1) CONSTRAINT PK_T1 PRIMARY KEY,
  datacol NVARCHAR(40) NOT NULL
);
```

Suppose you want to insert into T1 the result of a query against the HR.Employees table in TSQLFundamentals2008. To return all newly generated identity values from the *INSERT* statement, simply add the OUTPUT clause and specify the attributes you want to return:

```
INSERT INTO dbo.T1(datacol)
  OUTPUT inserted.keycol, inserted.datacol
    SELECT lastname
    FROM TSQLFundamentals2008.HR.Employees
    WHERE country = N'USA';
```

This statement returns the following result set:

```
keycol       datacol
-----------  ---------
1            Davis
2            Funk
3            Lew
4            Peled
5            Cameron

(5 row(s) affected)
```

As I mentioned earlier, you can also direct the result set into a table. The table can be a real table, a temporary table, or a table variable. When the result set is stored in the target table, you can manipulate the data by querying that table. For example, the following code declares a table variable called *@NewRows*, inserts another result set into T1, and directs the result set returned by the OUTPUT clause into the table variable. The code then queries the table variable just to show the data that was stored in it:

```
DECLARE @NewRows TABLE(keycol INT, datacol NVARCHAR(40));

INSERT INTO dbo.T1(datacol)
  OUTPUT inserted.keycol, inserted.datacol
  INTO @NewRows
    SELECT lastname
    FROM TSQLFundamentals2008.HR.Employees
    WHERE country = N'UK';

SELECT * FROM @NewRows;
```

This code returns the following output showing the contents of the table variable:

```
keycol       datacol
-----------  -------------
6            Buck
7            Suurs
8            King
9            Dolgopyatova

(4 row(s) affected)
```

DELETE with OUTPUT

The next example demonstrates using the OUTPUT clause with a *DELETE* statement. First, run the following code to create a copy of the Orders table from TSQLFundamentals2008 in tempdb:

```
USE tempdb;
IF OBJECT_ID('dbo.Orders', 'U') IS NOT NULL DROP TABLE dbo.Orders;
SELECT * INTO dbo.Orders FROM TSQLFundamentals2008.Sales.Orders;
```

The following code deletes all orders that were placed prior to 2008 and, using the OUTPUT clause, returns attributes from the deleted rows:

```
DELETE FROM dbo.Orders
  OUTPUT
    deleted.orderid,
    deleted.orderdate,
    deleted.empid,
    deleted.custid
WHERE orderdate < '20080101';
```

This *DELETE* statement returns the following result set:

```
orderid     orderdate                empid       custid
----------- ------------------------ ----------- -----------
10248       2006-07-04 00:00:00.000  5           85
10249       2006-07-05 00:00:00.000  6           79
10250       2006-07-08 00:00:00.000  4           34
10251       2006-07-08 00:00:00.000  3           84
10252       2006-07-09 00:00:00.000  4           76
...
10400       2007-01-01 00:00:00.000  1           19
10401       2007-01-01 00:00:00.000  1           65
10402       2007-01-02 00:00:00.000  8           20
10403       2007-01-03 00:00:00.000  4           20
10404       2007-01-03 00:00:00.000  2           49
...

(560 row(s) affected)
```

If you want to archive the rows that are deleted, simply add an INTO clause and specify the archive table name as the target.

UPDATE with OUTPUT

Using the OUTPUT clause with an *UPDATE* statement, you can refer to both the image of the modified row before the change by prefixing the attributes with the keyword deleted, and to the image after the change by prefixing the attribute names with the keyword inserted. This way you can return both old and new images of the updated attributes.

Before demonstrating how to use the OUTPUT clause in an *UPDATE* statement, first run the following code to create a copy of the Sales.OrderDetails table from TSQLFundamentals2008 in the dbo schema in tempdb:

```
USE tempdb;
IF OBJECT_ID('dbo.OrderDetails', 'U') IS NOT NULL DROP TABLE dbo.OrderDetails;
SELECT * INTO dbo.OrderDetails FROM TSQLFundamentals2008.Sales.OrderDetails;
```

The following *UPDATE* statement increases the discount of all order details with product 51 by 5 percent, and using the OUTPUT clause returns the product ID, old discount, and new discount from the modified rows:

```
UPDATE dbo.OrderDetails
  SET discount = discount + 0.05
OUTPUT
  inserted.productid,
  deleted.discount AS olddiscount,
  inserted.discount AS newdiscount
WHERE productid = 51;
```

This statement returns the following output:

```
productid   olddiscount   newdiscount
----------- ------------- -----------
51          0.000         0.050
51          0.150         0.200
51          0.100         0.150
51          0.200         0.250
51          0.000         0.050
51          0.150         0.200
51          0.000         0.050
51          0.000         0.050
51          0.000         0.050
51          0.000         0.050
...

(39 row(s) affected)
```

MERGE with OUTPUT

You can also use the OUTPUT clause with the *MERGE* statement, but remember that a single *MERGE* statement can invoke multiple, different DML actions based on conditional logic. This means that a single *MERGE* statement might return through the OUTPUT clause rows produced by different DML actions. To identify which DML action produced the output row, you can invoke a function called *$action* in the OUTPUT clause, and it will return a string representing the action ('INSERT,' 'UPDATE,' or 'DELETE'). To demonstrate using the OUTPUT clause with the *MERGE* statement, I'll use one of the examples from the "Merging Data" section earlier in the chapter. To run this example, make sure you rerun Listing 8-2 to re-create the Customers and CustomersStage tables in tempdb and populate them with sample data.

The following code merges the contents of CustomersStage into Customers, updating the attributes of customers who already exist in the target and adding customers who don't:

```
MERGE INTO dbo.Customers AS TGT
USING dbo.CustomersStage AS SRC
  ON TGT.custid = SRC.custid
WHEN MATCHED THEN
  UPDATE SET
    TGT.companyname = SRC.companyname,
    TGT.phone = SRC.phone,
    TGT.address = SRC.address
WHEN NOT MATCHED THEN
  INSERT (custid, companyname, phone, address)
  VALUES (SRC.custid, SRC.companyname, SRC.phone, SRC.address)
OUTPUT $action, inserted.custid,
  deleted.companyname AS oldcompanyname,
  inserted.companyname AS newcompanyname,
  deleted.phone AS oldphone,
  inserted.phone AS newphone,
  deleted.address AS oldaddress,
  inserted.address AS newaddress;
```

This *MERGE* statement uses the OUTPUT clause to return the old and new values of the modified rows. Of course, with INSERT actions there were no old values, so all references to deleted attributes return NULLs. The *$action* function tells you whether an UPDATE or an INSERT action produced the output row. Here's the output of this *MERGE* statement:

$action	custid	oldcompany name	newcompany name	oldphone	newphone	oldaddress	newaddress
UPDATE	2	cust 2	AAAAA	(222) 222-2222	(222) 222-2222	address 2	address 2
UPDATE	3	cust 3	cust 3	(333) 333-3333	(333) 333-3333	address 3	address 3
UPDATE	5	cust 5	BBBBB	(555) 555-5555	CCCCC	address 5	DDDDD
INSERT	6	NULL	cust 6 (new)	NULL	(666) 666-6666	NULL	address 6
INSERT	7	NULL	cust 7 (new)	NULL	(777) 777-7777	NULL	address 7

```
(5 row(s) affected)
```

Composable DML

The OUTPUT clause returns an output row for every modified row. But what if you need to direct only a subset of the modified rows to a table, say for auditing purposes? In SQL Server 2005 you had to direct all rows to a staging table and then copy the subset of rows that you needed from the staging table to the audit table. SQL Server 2008 introduces a feature called composable DML that allows you to skip the phase with the staging table and directly insert into the final target table only the subset of rows that you need from the full set of modified rows.

To demonstrate this capability, first create a copy of the Production.Products table from TSQLFundamentals2008 in the dbo schema in tempdb, and the ProductsAudit table, by running the following code:

```
USE tempdb;
IF OBJECT_ID('dbo.ProductsAudit', 'U') IS NOT NULL DROP TABLE dbo.ProductsAudit;
IF OBJECT_ID('dbo.Products', 'U') IS NOT NULL DROP TABLE dbo.Products;

SELECT * INTO dbo.Products FROM TSQLFundamentals2008.Production.Products;

CREATE TABLE dbo.ProductsAudit
(
  LSN INT NOT NULL IDENTITY PRIMARY KEY,
  TS  DATETIME NOT NULL DEFAULT(CURRENT_TIMESTAMP),
  productid INT NOT NULL,
  colname SYSNAME NOT NULL,
  oldval SQL_VARIANT NOT NULL,
  newval SQL_VARIANT NOT NULL
);
```

Suppose that you now need to update all products that are supplied by supplier 1, increasing their price by 15 percent. You also need to audit the old and new values of updated products, but only those with an old price that was less than 20 and a new price that is greater than or equal to 20.

You can achieve this by using composable DML. You write an *UPDATE* statement with an OUTPUT clause, and define a derived table based on the *UPDATE* statement. You write an *INSERT SELECT* statement that queries the derived table, filtering only the subset of rows that is needed. Here's the complete solution code:

```
INSERT INTO dbo.ProductsAudit(productid, colname, oldval, newval)
  SELECT productid, N'unitprice', oldval, newval
  FROM (UPDATE dbo.Products
          SET unitprice *= 1.15
          OUTPUT
            inserted.productid,
            deleted.unitprice AS oldval,
            inserted.unitprice AS newval
        WHERE SupplierID = 1) AS D
  WHERE oldval < 20.0 AND newval >= 20.0;
```

Recall earlier discussions in the book about logical query processing and table expressions—the multiset output of one query can be used as input to subsequent SQL statements. Here, the output of the OUTPUT clause is a multiset input for the *SELECT* statement, and then the output of the *SELECT* statement is inserted into a table.

Run the following code to query the ProductsAudit table:

```
SELECT * FROM dbo.ProductsAudit;
```

You get the following output:

```
LSN TS                       ProductID  ColName      OldVal   NewVal
--- ------------------------ ---------- ------------ -------- ------
1   2008-08-05 18:56:04.793  1          unitprice    18.00    20.70
2   2008-08-05 18:56:04.793  2          unitprice    19.00    21.85
```

Three products were updated, but only two were filtered by the outer query; therefore, only those two were audited.

Conclusion

In this chapter, I covered various aspects of data modification. I described inserting, updating, deleting, and merging data. I also discussed modifying data through table expressions, using TOP with modification statements, and returning modified rows using the OUTPUT clause. The next section provides exercises so that you can practice what you've learned in this chapter.

Exercises

This section provides exercises so you can practice the subjects discussed in this chapter. Unless explicitly mentioned otherwise, the database assumed in the exercise is tempdb.

1-1

Run the following code to create the Customers table in the tempdb database:

```
USE tempdb;

IF OBJECT_ID('dbo.Customers', 'U') IS NOT NULL DROP TABLE dbo.Customers;

CREATE TABLE dbo.Customers
(
  custid      INT          NOT NULL PRIMARY KEY,
  companyname NVARCHAR(40) NOT NULL,
  country     NVARCHAR(15) NOT NULL,
  region      NVARCHAR(15) NULL,
  city        NVARCHAR(15) NOT NULL
);
```

1-2

Insert into the Customers table a row with:

custid: 100

companyname: Company ABCDE

country: USA

region: WA

city: Redmond

1-3

Insert into the Customers table in tempdb all customers from TSQLFundamentals2008.Sales.Customers who placed orders.

1-4

Use a *SELECT INTO* statement to create and populate an Orders table in the dbo schema in tempdb, with orders from the Sales.Orders table in TSQLFundamentals2008 that were placed in the years 2006 through 2008.

2

Delete orders that were placed before August 2006. Use the OUTPUT clause to return the orderid and orderdate of the deleted orders.

Desired output:

```
orderid     orderdate
----------- -----------------------
10248       2006-07-04 00:00:00.000
10249       2006-07-05 00:00:00.000
10250       2006-07-08 00:00:00.000
10251       2006-07-08 00:00:00.000
10252       2006-07-09 00:00:00.000
10253       2006-07-10 00:00:00.000
10254       2006-07-11 00:00:00.000
10255       2006-07-12 00:00:00.000
10256       2006-07-15 00:00:00.000
10257       2006-07-16 00:00:00.000
10258       2006-07-17 00:00:00.000
10259       2006-07-18 00:00:00.000
10260       2006-07-19 00:00:00.000
10261       2006-07-19 00:00:00.000
10262       2006-07-22 00:00:00.000
10263       2006-07-23 00:00:00.000
10264       2006-07-24 00:00:00.000
10265       2006-07-25 00:00:00.000
10266       2006-07-26 00:00:00.000
10267       2006-07-29 00:00:00.000
10268       2006-07-30 00:00:00.000
10269       2006-07-31 00:00:00.000

(22 row(s) affected)
```

3

Delete orders placed by customers from Brazil.

4-1

Run the following query against Customers, and notice that some rows have a NULL in the region column:

```
SELECT * FROM dbo.Customers;
```

Output:

```
custid      companyname       country          region      city
----------- ----------------- ---------------- ----------- ----------------
1           Customer NRZBB     Germany          NULL        Berlin
2           Customer MLTDN     Mexico           NULL        México D.F.
3           Customer KBUDE     Mexico           NULL        México D.F.
4           Customer HFBZG     UK               NULL        London
5           Customer HGVLZ     Sweden           NULL        Luleå
6           Customer XHXJV     Germany          NULL        Mannheim
7           Customer QXVLA     France           NULL        Strasbourg
8           Customer QUHWH     Spain            NULL        Madrid
9           Customer RTXGC     France           NULL        Marseille
10          Customer EEALV     Canada           BC          Tsawassen
...


(90 row(s) affected)
```

4-2

Update the Customers table and change all NULL region values to '<None>'. Use the OUTPUT clause to show the custid, old region, and new region.

Desired output:

```
custid      oldregion        newregion
----------- ---------------- ----------------
1           NULL             <None>
2           NULL             <None>
3           NULL             <None>
4           NULL             <None>
5           NULL             <None>
6           NULL             <None>
7           NULL             <None>
8           NULL             <None>
9           NULL             <None>
11          NULL             <None>
12          NULL             <None>
13          NULL             <None>
```

```
14          NULL          <None>
16          NULL          <None>
17          NULL          <None>
18          NULL          <None>
19          NULL          <None>
20          NULL          <None>
23          NULL          <None>
24          NULL          <None>
25          NULL          <None>
26          NULL          <None>
27          NULL          <None>
28          NULL          <None>
29          NULL          <None>
30          NULL          <None>
39          NULL          <None>
40          NULL          <None>
41          NULL          <None>
44          NULL          <None>
49          NULL          <None>
50          NULL          <None>
52          NULL          <None>
53          NULL          <None>
54          NULL          <None>
56          NULL          <None>
58          NULL          <None>
59          NULL          <None>
60          NULL          <None>
63          NULL          <None>
64          NULL          <None>
66          NULL          <None>
68          NULL          <None>
69          NULL          <None>
70          NULL          <None>
72          NULL          <None>
73          NULL          <None>
74          NULL          <None>
76          NULL          <None>
79          NULL          <None>
80          NULL          <None>
83          NULL          <None>
84          NULL          <None>
85          NULL          <None>
86          NULL          <None>
87          NULL          <None>
90          NULL          <None>
91          NULL          <None>

(58 row(s) affected)
```

5

Update all orders placed by UK customers and set their *shipcountry*, *shipregion*, and *shipcity* values to the *country*, *region*, and *city* values of the corresponding customers.

Solutions

This section provides solutions to the preceding exercises.

1-2

Make sure that you are connected to the tempdb database:

```
USE tempdb;
```

Use the following *INSERT VALUES* statement to insert a row into the Customers table with the values provided in the exercise:

```
INSERT INTO dbo.Customers(custid, companyname, country, region, city)
  VALUES(100, N'Company ABCDE', N'USA', N'WA', N'Redmond');
```

1-3

One way to identify customers who placed orders is to use the EXISTS predicate, as the following query shows:

```
  SELECT custid, companyname, country, region, city
  FROM TSQLFundamentals2008.Sales.Customers AS C
  WHERE EXISTS
    (SELECT * FROM TSQLFundamentals2008.Sales.Orders AS O
     WHERE O.custid = C.custid);
```

To insert the rows returned from this query into the Customers table in tempdb you can use an *INSERT SELECT* statement as follows:

```
INSERT INTO dbo.Customers(custid, companyname, country, region, city)
  SELECT custid, companyname, country, region, city
  FROM TSQLFundamentals2008.Sales.Customers AS C
  WHERE EXISTS
    (SELECT * FROM TSQLFundamentals2008.Sales.Orders AS O
     WHERE O.custid = C.custid);
```

1-4

The following code first ensures that the session is connected to the tempdb database, then it drops the Orders table if it already exists, and then it uses the *SELECT INTO* statement to create a new Orders table and populate it with orders placed in the years 2006 through 2008 from the TSQLFundamentals2008 database:

```
USE tempdb;

IF OBJECT_ID('dbo.Orders', 'U') IS NOT NULL DROP TABLE dbo.Orders;
```

```
SELECT *
INTO dbo.Orders
FROM TSQLFundamentals2008.Sales.Orders
WHERE orderdate >= '20060101'
  AND orderdate < '20090101';
```

2

To delete orders placed before August 2006 you need a *DELETE* statement with a filter based on the predicate: orderdate < '20060801'. As requested, use the OUTPUT clause to return attributes from the deleted rows:

```
DELETE FROM dbo.Orders
  OUTPUT deleted.orderid, deleted.orderdate
WHERE orderdate < '20060801';
```

3

This exercise requires you to write a *DELETE* statement that deletes rows from one table (Orders) based on an existence of a matching row in another table (Customers). One way to solve the problem is to use a standard *DELETE* statement with an EXISTS predicate in the WHERE clause, like so:

```
DELETE FROM dbo.Orders
WHERE EXISTS
  (SELECT *
   FROM dbo.Customers AS C
   WHERE Orders.custid = C.custid
     AND C.country = N'Brazil');
```

This *DELETE* statement deletes the rows from the Orders table where a related row exists in the Customers table with the same customer ID as the order's customer ID and the customer's country is Brazil.

Another way to solve this problem is to use the T-SQL–specific DELETE syntax based on a join, like so:

```
DELETE FROM O
FROM dbo.Orders AS O
  JOIN dbo.Customers AS C
    ON O.custid = C.custid
WHERE country = N'Brazil';
```

Note that there are no matched rows, of course, if the previous DELETE is executed.

The join between the Orders and Customers tables serves a filtering purpose. The join matches each order with the customer who placed the order. The WHERE clause filters only rows where the customer's country is Brazil. The DELETE FROM clause refers to the alias O representing the table Orders, indicating that Orders is the target of the DELETE operation.

If you are working with SQL Server 2008, you can use the *MERGE* statement to solve this problem. Even though you would normally think of using *MERGE* when you need to apply different actions based on conditional logic, you can also use it when you need to apply one action when a certain predicate is TRUE. In other words, you can use the *MERGE* statement with the WHEN MATCHED clause alone; you don't have to have a WHEN NOT MATCHED clause as well. The following *MERGE* statement handles the request in the exercise:

```
MERGE INTO dbo.Orders AS O
USING dbo.Customers AS C
  ON O.custid = C.custid
  AND country = N'Brazil'
WHEN MATCHED THEN DELETE;
```

Again, note that there are no matched rows if either of the previous DELETEs is executed.

This *MERGE* statement defines the Orders table as the target and the Customers table as the source. An order is deleted from the target (Orders) when a matching row is found in the source (Customers) with the same customer ID and the country Brazil.

4-2

This exercise involves writing an *UPDATE* statement that filters only rows where the region attribute is NULL. Make sure you use the IS NULL predicate and not an equality operator when looking for NULLs. Use the OUTPUT clause to return the requested information. Here's the complete *UPDATE* statement:

```
UPDATE dbo.Customers
  SET region = '<None>'
OUTPUT
  deleted.custid,
  deleted.region AS oldregion,
  inserted.region AS newregion
WHERE region IS NULL;
```

5

One way to solve this exercise is to use the T-SQL–specific UPDATE syntax based on a join. You can join Orders and Customers based on a match between the order's customer ID and the customers customer ID. In the WHERE clause you can filter only the rows where the customer's country is the UK. In the UPDATE clause specify the alias you assigned to the Orders table to indicate that it's the target of the modification. In the SET clause assign the values of the shipping location attributes of the order to the location attributes of the corresponding customer. Here's the complete *UPDATE* statement:

```
UPDATE O
  SET shipcountry = C.country,
      shipregion = C.region,
      shipcity = C.city
```

```
FROM dbo.Orders AS O
  JOIN dbo.Customers AS C
    ON O.custid = C.custid
WHERE C.country = 'UK';
```

Another solution to this exercise uses CTEs, which are supported as of SQL Server 2005. You can define a CTE based on a SELECT query that joins Orders and Customers and returns both the target location attributes from Orders and the source location attributes from Customers. The outer query would then be an *UPDATE* statement modifying the target attributes with the values of the source attributes. Here's the complete solution statement:

```
WITH CTE_UPD AS
(
  SELECT
    O.shipcountry AS ocountry, C.country AS ccountry,
    O.shipregion  AS oregion,  C.region  AS cregion,
    O.shipcity    AS ocity,    C.city    AS ccity
  FROM dbo.Orders AS O
    JOIN dbo.Customers AS C
      ON O.custid = C.custid
  WHERE C.country = 'UK'
)
UPDATE CTE_UPD
  SET ocountry = ccountry, oregion = cregion, ocity = ccity;
```

As of SQL Server 2008 you can use the *MERGE* statement to achieve this task. As explained earlier, even though in a *MERGE* statement you usually want to specify both the WHEN MATCHED and the WHEN NOT MATCHED clauses, the statement supports specifying only one of the clauses. Having only a WHEN MATCHED clause with an UPDATE action, you can write a solution that is logically equivalent to the last two solutions. Here's the complete solution statement:

```
MERGE INTO dbo.Orders AS O
USING dbo.Customers AS C
  ON O.custid = C.custid
  AND C.country = 'UK'
WHEN MATCHED THEN
  UPDATE SET shipcountry = C.country,
             shipregion = C.region,
             shipcity = C.city;
```

Chapter 9
Transactions and Concurrency

This chapter covers transactions and their properties, and describes how Microsoft SQL Server handles concurrent users trying to access the same data. The chapter explains how SQL Server uses locks to isolate inconsistent data, how to troubleshoot blocking situations, and how to control the level of consistency you get when querying data with isolation levels. The chapter also covers deadlocks and ways to mitigate their occurrence.

Note that this chapter is just an introduction to these topics, many of which can become quite complex. You can find more information on these topics in SQL Server Books Online and in the forthcoming book *Inside Microsoft SQL Server 2008: T-SQL Programming* (Microsoft Press, 2009).

Transactions

A transaction is a unit of work that may include multiple activities that query and modify data and that possibly change data definition.

You can define transaction boundaries either explicitly or implicitly. You define the beginning of a transaction explicitly with a *BEGIN TRAN* statement. You define the end of a transaction explicitly with a *COMMIT TRAN* statement if you want to confirm it and with a *ROLLBACK TRAN* statement if you do not want to confirm it (undo its changes). Here's an example of marking the boundaries of a transaction with two *INSERT* statements:

```
BEGIN TRAN;
  INSERT INTO dbo.T1(keycol, col1, col2) VALUES(4, 101, 'C');
  INSERT INTO dbo.T2(keycol, col1, col2) VALUES(4, 201, 'X');
COMMIT TRAN;
```

If you do not mark the boundaries of a transaction explicitly, by default SQL Server treats each individual statement as a transaction; in other words, by default SQL Server automatically commits the transaction at the end of each individual statement. You can change the way SQL Server handles implicit transactions with a session option called *IMPLICIT_TRANSACTIONS*. This option is off by default. When this option is on, you do not have to specify the *BEGIN TRAN* statement to mark the beginning of a transaction, but you have to mark the transaction's end with a *COMMIT TRAN* or a *ROLLBACK TRAN* statement.

Transactions have four properties—Atomicity, Consistency, Isolation, and Durability—abbreviated with the acronym ACID.

- **Atomicity** A transaction is an atomic unit of work. Either all changes in the transaction take place, or none do. If the system fails before the transaction is completed (before the commit instruction is recorded in the transaction log), upon restart, SQL Server undoes the changes that took place. Also, if errors are encountered during the transaction, normally SQL Server automatically rolls back the transaction, with a few exceptions. Some errors are not considered severe enough to justify an automatic rollback of the transaction, such as primary key violation, lock expiration time-out (discussed later in the chapter), and so on. You can use error handling code to capture such errors and apply some course of action (for example, log the error and roll back the transaction). Chapter 10, "Programmable Objects," provides an overview of error handling.

> **Tip** At any point in your code you can tell programmatically whether you are in an open transaction by querying a function called @@*TRANCOUNT*. This function returns 0 if you're not in an open transaction, and a value greater than 0 if you are.

- **Consistency** The term *consistency* refers to the state of the data that the RDBMS gives you access to as concurrent transactions modify and query it. As you can probably imagine, consistency is a subjective term, and depends on your application's needs. The section "Isolation Levels" later in the chapter explains what level of consistency you get in SQL Server by default, and how you can control consistency if the default behavior is not suitable for your application.

- **Isolation** Isolation is a mechanism used to control access to data and ensure that transactions access data only if it is in the level of consistency that those transactions expect. SQL Server uses locks to isolate data that is modified and queried by one transaction from other transactions. The section "Locks" later in the chapter provides more details about isolation.

- **Durability** Data changes are always written to the database's transaction log on disk before they are written to the data portion of the database on disk. After the commit instruction is recorded in the transaction log on disk, the transaction is considered durable even if the change hasn't yet made it to the data portion on disk.

When the system starts, either normally or after a system failure, SQL Server inspects the transaction log of each database and runs a recovery process with two phases—redo and undo. The redo phase involves rolling forward (replaying) all changes of transactions whose commit instruction is written to the log but whose changes haven't yet made it to the data portion. The undo phase involves rolling back (undoing) changes of transactions whose commit instruction was not recorded in the log.

For example, the following code defines a transaction that records information about a new order in the TSQLFundamentals2008 database:

```
USE TSQLFundamentals2008;

-- Start a new transaction
BEGIN TRAN;

  -- Declare a variable
  DECLARE @neworderid AS INT;

  -- Insert a new order into the Sales.Orders table
  INSERT INTO Sales.Orders
      (custid, empid, orderdate, requireddate, shippeddate,
       shipperid, freight, shipname, shipaddress, shipcity,
       shippostalcode, shipcountry)
    VALUES
      (85, 5, '20090212', '20090301', '20090216',
       3, 32.38, N'Ship to 85-B', N'6789 rue de l''Abbaye', N'Reims',
       N'10345', N'France');

  -- Save the new order ID in a variable
  SET @neworderid = SCOPE_IDENTITY();

  -- Return the new order ID
  SELECT @neworderid AS neworderid;

  -- Insert order lines for new order into Sales.OrderDetails
  INSERT INTO Sales.OrderDetails
      (orderid, productid, unitprice, qty, discount)
    VALUES(@neworderid, 11, 14.00, 12, 0.000);
  INSERT INTO Sales.OrderDetails
      (orderid, productid, unitprice, qty, discount)
    VALUES(@neworderid, 42, 9.80, 10, 0.000);
  INSERT INTO Sales.OrderDetails
      (orderid, productid, unitprice, qty, discount)
    VALUES(@neworderid, 72, 34.80, 5, 0.000);

-- Commit the transaction
COMMIT TRAN;
```

The transaction's code inserts a row with the order header information into the Sales.Orders table and a few rows with the order lines information into the Sales.OrderDetails table. The new order ID is produced automatically by SQL Server because the column orderid has an identity property. Immediately after the code inserts the new row into the Sales.Orders table, it stores the newly generated order ID in a local variable, and then uses that local variable when inserting rows into the Sales.OrderDetails table. For test purposes I added a *SELECT* statement that returns the order ID of the newly generated order. Here's the output from the *SELECT* statement after the code runs:

```
neworderid
-----------
11078
```

Note that this example has no error handling and does not provision for a ROLLBACK in case of an error. To handle errors, transactions can be encased in a TRY/CATCH construct. You can find an overview of error handling in Chapter 10; for more advanced coverage of error handling please refer to *Inside Microsoft SQL Server 2008: T-SQL Programming* (Microsoft Press, 2009).

When you're done, run the following code for cleanup:

```
DELETE FROM Sales.OrderDetails
WHERE orderid > 11077;

DELETE FROM Sales.Orders
WHERE orderid > 11077;

DBCC CHECKIDENT ('Sales.Orders', RESEED, 11077);
```

Locks and Blocking

SQL Server uses locks to enforce the isolation property of transactions. The following sections provide details about locking, and explain how to troubleshoot blocking situations that are caused by conflicting lock requests.

Locks

Locks are control resources obtained by a transaction to guard data resources, preventing conflicting, or incompatible, access by other transactions. I'll first cover the important lock modes supported by SQL Server and their compatibility and then describe the lockable resource types.

Lock Modes and Compatibility

As you start learning about transactions and concurrency, you should first familiarize yourself with two main lock modes—exclusive and shared. The other lock modes (update, intent, and schema locks) are more advanced and will not be covered in this book.

When you try to modify data, your transaction requests an exclusive lock on the data resource, and if granted, the exclusive lock is held until the end of the transaction. Exclusive locks are called exclusive because you cannot obtain an exclusive lock on a resource if another transaction is holding any lock mode on the resource, and no lock mode can be obtained on a resource if another transaction is holding an exclusive lock on the resource. This is the way modifications behave by default, and this default behavior cannot be changed—not in terms of the lock mode required to modify a data resource (exclusive) and not in terms of the duration of the lock (until the end of the transaction).

When you try to read data, by default your transaction requests a shared lock on the data resource and releases the lock as soon as the read statement is done with that resource. This lock mode is called shared because multiple transactions can hold shared locks on the same data resource simultaneously. Although you cannot change the lock mode and duration required when modifying data, you can control the way locking is handled when reading data. The section "Isolation Levels" later in the chapter elaborates on this.

This lock interaction between transactions is known as lock compatibility. Table 9-1 shows lock compatibility of exclusive and shared locks. The columns represent granted lock modes and the rows represent requested lock modes.

TABLE 9-1 **Lock Compatibility of Exclusive and Shared Locks**

Requested Mode	Granted Exclusive (X)	Granted Shared (S)
Grant Request for Exclusive?	No	No
Grant Request for Shared?	No	Yes

A No in the intersection means that the requested mode is denied, meaning that the requested mode is incompatible with the granted mode. A Yes in the intersection means that the requested mode is accepted, meaning that the requested mode is compatible with the granted mode. For a more comprehensive lock compatibility table, see "Lock Compatibility" in SQL Server Books Online.

To summarize lock interaction between transactions in simple terms, data that was modified by one transaction can neither be modified nor read (at least by default) by another transaction until the first transaction finishes. While data is being read by one transaction it cannot be modified by another (at least by default).

Lockable Resource Types

SQL Server can lock different resource types, or granularities. The resource types that can be locked include RID or key (row), page, object (for example, table), database, and others. Rows reside within pages and pages are the physical data blocks that contain table or index data. You should first familiarize yourself with these resource types, and at a more advanced stage you may want to familiarize yourself with other lockable resource types such as extents, allocation units, and heap or B-tree.

To obtain a lock on a certain resource type, your transaction must first obtain intent locks of the same mode on higher levels of granularity. For example, to get an exclusive lock on a row, your transaction must first acquire an intent exclusive lock on the page where the row resides and an intent exclusive lock on the object that owns the page. Similarly, to get a shared lock on a certain level of granularity, your transaction first needs to acquire intent shared locks on higher levels of granularity. The purpose of intent locks is to efficiently detect incompatible lock requests on higher levels of granularity and prevent granting those. For example, if one transaction holds a lock on a row and another asks for an incompatible lock mode on the whole page or table where that row resides, it is easy for SQL Server to identify the conflict because of the intent locks that the first transaction acquired on the page and table. Intent locks do not interfere with requests for locks on lower levels of granularity. For example, an intent lock on a page doesn't prevent other transactions from acquiring incompatible lock modes on rows within the page. Table 9-2 expands on the lock compatibility table shown in Table 9-1, adding intent exclusive and intent shared locks.

TABLE 9-2 Lock Compatibility Including Intent Locks

Requested Mode	Granted Exclusive (X)	Granted Shared (S)	Granted Intent Exclusive (IX)	Granted Intent Shared (IS)
Grant Request for Exclusive?	No	No	No	No
Grant Request for Shared?	No	Yes	No	Yes
Grant Request for Intent Exclusive?	No	No	Yes	Yes
Grant Request for Intent Shared?	No	Yes	Yes	Yes

SQL Server determines dynamically which resource types to lock. Naturally, for ideal concurrency it is best to lock only what needs to be locked, namely only the affected rows. However, locks require memory resources and internal management overhead. So SQL Server considers both concurrency and system resources when choosing which resource types to lock.

SQL Server may first acquire fine-grained locks (for example, row or page), and in certain circumstances try to escalate the fine-grained locks to more coarse-grained locks (for example, table). For example, lock escalation is triggered when a single statement acquires at least 5,000 locks and then every 1,250 new locks if previous attempts for lock escalation were unsuccessful.

Prior to SQL Server 2008 you could not explicitly disable lock escalation, and escalation always happened to a table granularity. In SQL Server 2008, you can set a table option called LOCK_ESCALATION using the *ALTER TABLE* statement to control the way lock escalation behaves. You can disable lock escalation if you like, or determine whether escalation takes place at a table level (default) or partition level. A table can be physically organized as multiple smaller units called partitions.

Troubleshooting Blocking

When one transaction holds a lock on a data resource and another transaction requests an incompatible lock on the same resource, the request is blocked and the requester enters a wait state. By default, the blocked request keeps waiting until the blocker releases the interfering lock. Later in the chapter I'll explain how you can define a lock expiration time-out in your session if you want to restrict the amount of time that a blocked request waits before it times out.

Blocking is normal in a system as long as requests are satisfied within a reasonable amount of time. However, if some requests end up waiting too long, you may need to troubleshoot the blocking situation and see whether you can do something to prevent such long latencies. For example, long running transactions result in locks being held for long periods. You can try and shorten such transactions, moving activities that are not supposed to be part of the unit of work outside the transaction. A bug in the application might result in a transaction that remains open in certain circumstances. If you identify such a bug you can fix it and ensure that the transaction is closed in all circumstances.

This section demonstrates a blocking situation and walks you through the process of troubleshooting it. Open three separate query windows in SQL Server Management Studio. (For this example, we will refer to them as Connection 1, Connection 2, and Connection 3.) Make sure that in all of them you are connected to the sample database TSQLFundamentals2008:

```
USE TSQLFundamentals2008;
```

Run the following code in Connection 1 to update a row in the table Production.Products, adding 1.00 to the current unit price 19.00 of product 2:

```
BEGIN TRAN;

  UPDATE Production.Products
    SET unitprice = unitprice + 1.00
  WHERE productid = 2;
```

To update the row, your session had to acquire an exclusive lock, and if the update was successful, SQL Server granted your session with the lock. Recall that exclusive locks are kept until the end of the transaction, and because the transaction remains open, the lock is still held.

Run the following code in Connection 2 to try to query the same row:

```
SELECT productid, unitprice
FROM Production.Products
WHERE productid = 2;
```

By default, your session needs a shared lock to read data, but because the row is exclusively locked by the other session, and a shared lock is incompatible with an exclusive lock, your session is blocked and has to wait.

Assuming that such a blocking situation happens in your system, and the blocked session ends up waiting for a long time, you probably want to troubleshoot the situation. I'll provide queries against dynamic management objects, including views and functions, that you should run from Connection 3 when you troubleshoot the blocking situation.

To get lock information, including both locks that are currently granted to sessions and locks that sessions are waiting for, query the dynamic management view (DMV) sys.dm_tran_locks in Connection 3:

```
SELECT -- use * to explore other available attributes
  request_session_id            AS spid,
  resource_type                 AS restype,
  resource_database_id          AS dbid,
  DB_NAME(resource_database_id) AS dbname,
  resource_description          AS res,
  resource_associated_entity_id AS resid,
  request_mode                  AS mode,
  request_status                AS status
FROM sys.dm_tran_locks;
```

When I run this code in my system (with no other query window open) I get the following output:

spid	restype	dbid	dbname	res	resid	mode	status
53	DATABASE	8	TSQLFundamentals2008		0	S	GRANT
52	DATABASE	8	TSQLFundamentals2008		0	S	GRANT
51	DATABASE	8	TSQLFundamentals2008		0	S	GRANT
54	DATABASE	8	TSQLFundamentals2008		0	S	GRANT
53	PAGE	8	TSQLFundamentals2008	1:127	72057594038845440	IS	GRANT
52	PAGE	8	TSQLFundamentals2008	1:127	72057594038845440	IX	GRANT
53	OBJECT	8	TSQLFundamentals2008		133575514	IS	GRANT
52	OBJECT	8	TSQLFundamentals2008		133575514	IX	GRANT
52	KEY	8	TSQLFundamentals2008	(020068e8b274)	72057594038845440	X	GRANT
53	KEY	8	TSQLFundamentals2008	(020068e8b274)	72057594038845440	S	WAIT

Each session is identified by a unique server process ID (SPID). You can determine your session's SPID by querying the function @@SPID. If you're working with SQL Server Management Studio, you will find the session SPID in parentheses to the right of the login name in the status bar at the bottom of the screen, and also in the caption of the connected query window. For example, Figure 9-1 shows a screenshot of SQL Server Management Studio, where the SPID 53 appears to the right of the logon name QUANTUM\Gandalf.

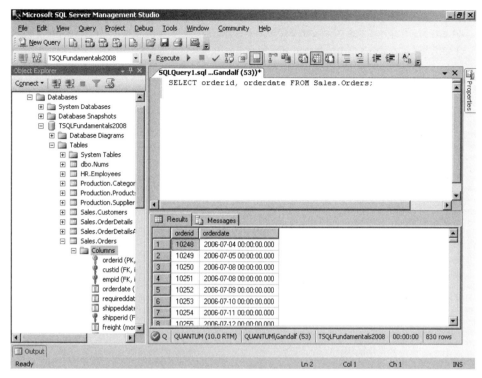

FIGURE 9-1 SQL Server Management Studio

As you can see in the output of the query against sys.dm_tran_locks, four sessions (51, 52, 53, and 54) are currently holding locks. You can see the following:

- The resource type that is locked (for example, KEY for row in an index)
- The ID of the database in which it is locked, which you can translate to the database name by using the *DB_NAME* function
- The resource and resource ID
- The lock mode
- Whether the lock was granted or the session is waiting for it

Note that this is only a subset of the view's attributes; I recommend that you explore the other attributes of the view to learn what other information about locks is available.

In the output from my query, you can observe that process 53 is waiting for a shared lock on a row in the sample database TSQLFundamentals2008. (The database name is obtained with the *DB_NAME* function.) Notice that process 52 is holding an exclusive lock on the same row. You can realize this by observing that both processes lock a row with the same *res* and *resid* values. You can figure out which table is involved by moving upward in the lock hierarchy for either process 52 or 53 and inspecting the intent locks on the page and the object (table) where the row resides. You can use the *OBJECT_NAME* function to translate the object ID (133575514 in this example) that appears under the resid attribute in the object lock to the object name. You will find that the table involved is Production.Product.

The sys.dm_tran_locks view only gives you information about the IDs of the processes involved in the blocking chain and nothing else. To get information about the connections associated with the processes involved in the blocking chain, query a view called sys.dm_exec_connections, and filter only the SPIDs that are involved:

```
SELECT -- use * to explore
  session_id AS spid,
  connect_time,
  last_read,
  last_write,
  most_recent_sql_handle
FROM sys.dm_exec_connections
WHERE session_id IN(52, 53);
```

Note that the process IDs that were involved in the blocking chain in my system were 52 and 53. Depending on what else you are doing in your system, you may get different process IDs. When you run the queries that I demonstrate here in your system, make sure that you substitute the process IDs with those you find involved in your blocking chain.

This query returns the following output (split into several parts for display purposes here):

```
spid   connect_time            last_read
------ ----------------------- -----------------------
52     2008-06-25 15:20:03.360 2008-06-25 15:20:15.750
53     2008-06-25 15:20:07.300 2008-06-25 15:20:20.950

spid   last_write              most_recent_sql_handle
------ ----------------------- --------------------------------------------------
52     2008-06-25 15:20:15.817 0x01000800DE2DB71FB0936F05000000000000000000000000
53     2008-06-25 15:20:07.327 0x0200000063FC7D052E09844778CDD615CFE7A2D1FB411802

spid   most_recent_sql_handle
------ --------------------------------------------------
52     0x01000800DE2DB71FB0936F05000000000000000000000000
53     0x0200000063FC7D052E09844778CDD615CFE7A2D1FB411802
```

The information that this query gives you about the connections includes:

- The time they connected.

- The time of their last read and write.

- A binary value holding a handle to the most recent SQL batch run by the connection. You provide this handle as an input parameter to a table function called *sys.dm_exec_sql_text*, and the function returns the batch of code represented by the handle. You can query the table function passing the binary handle explicitly, but you will probably find it more convenient to use the APPLY table operator described in Chapter 5, "Table Expressions," to apply the table function to each connection row like so (run in Connection 3):

```
SELECT session_id, text
FROM sys.dm_exec_connections
  CROSS APPLY sys.dm_exec_sql_text(most_recent_sql_handle) AS ST
WHERE session_id IN(52, 53);
```

When I run this query I get the following output showing the last batch of code invoked by each connection involved in the blocking chain:

```
session_id  text
-----------  ------------------------------------
52          BEGIN TRAN;

            UPDATE Production.Products
              SET unitprice = unitprice + 1.00
            WHERE productid = 2;

53          (@1 tinyint)
            SELECT [productid],[unitprice]
            FROM [Production].[Products]
            WHERE [productid]=@1
```

The blocked process—53—shows the query that is waiting because that's the last thing that the process ran. As for the blocker, in this example you can see the statement that caused the problem, but keep in mind that the blocker may continue work and that the last thing you see in the code isn't necessarily the statement that caused the trouble.

You can also find lots of useful information about the sessions involved in a blocking situation in the DMV sys.dm_exec_sessions. The following query returns only a small subset of the attributes available about those sessions:

```
SELECT -- use * to explore
  session_id AS spid,
  login_time,
  host_name,
  program_name,
  login_name,
  nt_user_name,
  last_request_start_time,
  last_request_end_time
FROM sys.dm_exec_sessions
WHERE session_id IN(52, 53);
```

This query returns the following output in this example, split here into several parts:

```
spid login_time               host_name
---- ------------------------ ---------
52   2008-06-25 15:20:03.407  QUANTUM
53   2008-06-25 15:20:07.303  QUANTUM
```

```
spid    program_name                                          login_name
------  ----------------------------------------------------  ---------------
52      Microsoft SQL Server Management Studio - Query        QUANTUM\Gandalf
53      Microsoft SQL Server Management Studio - Query        QUANTUM\Gandalf


spid    nt_user_name    last_request_start_time    last_request_end_time
------  --------------  -------------------------  -----------------------
52      Gandalf         2008-06-25 15:20:15.703    2008-06-25 15:20:15.750
53      Gandalf         2008-06-25 15:20:20.693    2008-06-25 15:20:07.320
```

This output contains information such as the session's login time, host name, program name, login name, NT user name, time that the last request started, and time that the last request ended. This kind of information gives you a good idea of what those sessions are doing.

Another DMV that you will probably find very useful for troubleshooting blocking situations is sys.dm_exec_requests. This view has a row for each active request, including blocked requests. In fact, you can easily isolate blocked requests because the attribute blocking_session_id is greater than zero. For example, the following query filters only blocked requests:

```
SELECT -- use * to explore
  session_id AS spid,
  blocking_session_id,
  command,
  sql_handle,
  database_id,
  wait_type,
  wait_time,
  wait_resource
FROM sys.dm_exec_requests
WHERE blocking_session_id > 0;
```

This query returns the following output, split across several lines:

```
spid    blocking_session_id    command
------  ---------------------  -------
53      52                     SELECT


spid    sql_handle                                                  database_id
------  ----------------------------------------------------------  -----------
53      0x0200000063FC7D052E09844778CDD615CFE7A2D1FB411802          8


spid    wait_type    wait_time    wait_resource
------  -----------  -----------  -------------------------------------
53      LCK_M_S      1383760      KEY: 8:72057594038845440 (020068e8b274)
```

You can easily identify the sessions that participate in the blocking chain, the resource in dispute, how long the blocked session is waiting in milliseconds, and more.

If you need to terminate the blocker—for example, if you realize that as a result of a bug in the application the transaction remained open and nothing in the application can close it—you can do so by using the *KILL* <spid> command. (Don't do so yet.)

Earlier I mentioned that by default the session has no lock time-out set. If you want to restrict the amount of time your session waits for a lock, you can set a session option called LOCK_TIMEOUT. You specify a value in milliseconds—5000 for 5 seconds, 0 for immediate time-out, -1 for indefinite (default), and so on. To demonstrate this option, first stop the query in Connection 2 by choosing Cancel Executing Query from the Query menu (or using ALT+BREAK). Next cancel the blocked query in Connection 2, and then run the following code to set the lock time-out to 5 seconds, and run the query again:

```
SET LOCK_TIMEOUT 5000;

SELECT productid, unitprice
FROM Production.Products
WHERE productid = 2;
```

The query is still blocked because Connection 1 hasn't yet ended the update transaction, but if after 5 seconds the lock request is not satisfied, SQL Server terminates the query and you get the following error:

```
Msg 1222, Level 16, State 51, Line 3
Lock request time out period exceeded.
```

Note that lock timeouts do not roll back transactions.

To remove the lock time-out value, set it back to the default (indefinite), and issue the query again, run the following code in Connection 2:

```
SET LOCK_TIMEOUT -1;

SELECT productid, unitprice
FROM Production.Products
WHERE productid = 2;
```

To demonstrate terminating the update transaction in Connection 1, run the following code from Connection 3:

```
KILL 52;
```

This statement causes a rollback of the transaction in Connection 1, meaning that the price change of product 2 from 19.00 to 20.00 is undone, and the exclusive lock is released. Go to Connection 2. Notice that you get the data after the change is undone—namely, before the price change:

```
productid   unitprice
----------- --------------------
2           19.00
```

Isolation Levels

Isolation levels determine the behavior of concurrent users that read or write data. A *reader* is any statement selecting data, using a shared lock by default. A *writer* means any statement making a modification to a table and requiring an exclusive lock. You cannot control the way writers behave in terms of the locks that they acquire and the duration of the locks, but you can control the way readers behave. Also, as a result of controlling the behavior of readers, you can have an implicit influence on the behavior of writers. You do so by setting the *isolation level* either at the session level with a session option, or at the query level with a table hint.

You can set six isolation levels: READ UNCOMMITTED, READ COMMITTED (default), REPEATABLE READ, SERIALIZABLE, SNAPSHOT, and READ COMMITTED SNAPSHOT. The last two are available only as of SQL Server 2005. You can set the isolation level of the whole session by using the following command:

```
SET TRANSACTION ISOLATION LEVEL <isolation name>;
```

You can use a table hint to set the isolation level of a query:

```
SELECT ... FROM <table> WITH (<isolationname>);
```

Note that with the session option you specify a space between the words in case the name of the isolation level is made of more than one word, such as REPEATABLE READ. With the query hint, you don't specify a space between the words—for example, WITH (REPEATABLEREAD). Also, some of the isolation level names used as table hints have synonyms. For example, NOLOCK is the equivalent of specifying READUNCOMMITTED; HOLDLOCK is the equivalent of specifying REPEATABLEREAD.

The default isolation level is READ COMMITTED. If you chose to override the default isolation level, your choice impacts both the concurrency of the database users and the consistency they get from the data. With the four isolation levels available prior to SQL Server 2005, the higher the isolation level, the tougher the locks that readers request and the longer their duration; therefore, the higher the isolation level, the higher the consistency and the lower the concurrency. The converse is also true, of course. With the two snapshot-based isolation levels, SQL Server is able to store previous committed versions of rows aside in tempdb. Instead of requesting shared locks, readers can get the consistency level that they expect without waiting by getting previous row versions if the current version is not consistent with their expectations.

The following sections describe each of the six supported isolation levels and demonstrate their behavior.

The READ UNCOMMITTED Isolation Level

READ UNCOMMITTED is the lowest available isolation level. In this isolation level, a reader doesn't ask for a shared lock. A reader that doesn't ask for a shared lock can never be in conflict with a writer that is holding an exclusive lock. This means that that reader can read uncommitted changes (also known as *dirty reads*). It also means that the reader won't interfere with a writer that asks for an exclusive lock. In other words, a writer can change data while a reader that is running under the READ UNCOMMITTED isolation level reads data.

To demonstrate an uncommitted read (dirty read), open two query windows (we will refer to them as Connection 1 and Connection 2). Make sure that in all connections your database context is that of the sample database TSQLFundamentals2008.

Run the following code in Connection 1 to open a transaction, update the unit price of product 2 by adding 1.00 to its current price (19.00), and then query the product's row:

```
BEGIN TRAN;

  UPDATE Production.Products
    SET unitprice = unitprice + 1.00
  WHERE productid = 2;

  SELECT productid, unitprice
  FROM Production.Products
  WHERE productid = 2;
```

Note that the transaction remains open, meaning that the product's row is locked exclusively by Connection 1. The code in Connection 1 returns the following output showing the product's new price:

```
productid    unitprice
----------- --------------------
2            20.00
```

In Connection 2, run the following code to set the isolation level to READ UNCOMMITTED and query the row for product 2:

```
SET TRANSACTION ISOLATION LEVEL READ UNCOMMITTED;

SELECT productid, unitprice
FROM Production.Products
WHERE productid = 2;
```

Because the query did not request a shared lock, it was in no conflict with the other transaction. This query returned the state of the row after the change, even though the change was not committed:

```
productid    unitprice
----------- --------------------
2            20.00
```

Keep in mind that Connection 1 may apply further changes to the row later in the transaction or even roll back at some point. For example, run the following code in Connection 1 to roll back the transaction:

```
ROLLBACK TRAN;
```

This rollback undoes the update of product 2, changing its price back to 19.00. The value 20.00 that the reader got was never committed. That's an example of a dirty read.

The READ COMMITTED Isolation Level

If you want to prevent reading uncommitted changes, you need to use a stronger isolation level. The lowest isolation level that prevents dirty reads is READ COMMITTED, which is also the default isolation level of all versions of SQL Server. As the name indicates, this isolation level allows reading only committed changes. It prevents uncommitted reads by requiring a reader to obtain a shared lock. This means that if a writer is holding an exclusive lock, the reader's shared lock request will be in conflict with the writer, and it has to wait. As soon as the writer commits the transaction, the reader can get its shared lock, but what it reads are necessarily only committed changes.

The following example demonstrates that a reader can only read committed changes in this isolation level.

Run the following code in Connection 1 to open a transaction, update the price of product 2, and query the row to show the new price:

```
BEGIN TRAN;

  UPDATE Production.Products
    SET unitprice = unitprice + 1.00
  WHERE productid = 2;

  SELECT productid, unitprice
  FROM Production.Products
  WHERE productid = 2;
```

This code returns the following output:

```
productid    unitprice
-----------  ---------------------
2            20.00
```

Connection 1 now locks the row for product 2 exclusively.

Run the following code in Connection 2 to set the session's isolation level to READ COMMITTED and query the row for product 2:

```
SET TRANSACTION ISOLATION LEVEL READ COMMITTED;

SELECT productid, unitprice
FROM Production.Products
WHERE productid = 2;
```

Keep in mind that this isolation level is the default, so unless you previously changed the session's isolation level, you don't need to set it explicitly. The *SELECT* statement is currently blocked because it needs a shared lock to be able to read, and this shared lock request is in conflict with the exclusive lock held by the writer in Connection 1.

Next, run the following code in Connection 1 to commit the transaction:

```
COMMIT TRAN;
```

Now go to Connection 2 and notice that you get the following output:

```
productid   unitprice
----------- --------------------
2           20.00
```

Unlike in READ UNCOMMITTED, in the READ COMMITTED isolation level you don't get dirty reads. Instead, you can only read committed changes.

In terms of the duration of locks, in the READ COMMITTED isolation level, a reader only holds the shared lock until it is done with the resource. It doesn't keep the lock until the end of the transaction; in fact, it doesn't even keep the lock until the end of the statement. This means that in between two reads of the same data resource taking place in the same transaction, no lock is held on the resource. Therefore, another transaction can modify the resource in between those two reads, and the reader might get different values in each read. This phenomenon is called *non-repeatable reads* or *inconsistent analysis*. For many applications, this phenomenon is acceptable, but for some it isn't.

When you are done, run the following code for cleanup in any of the open connections:

```
UPDATE Production.Products
  SET unitprice = 19.00
WHERE productid = 2;
```

The REPEATABLE READ Isolation Level

If you want to ensure that no one can change values in between reads that take place in the same transaction, you need to move up in the isolation levels to REPEATABLE READ. In this isolation level not only does a reader need a shared lock to be able to read, but it also holds the lock until the end of the transaction. This means that as soon as you acquired a shared lock on a data resource to read it, no one can obtain an exclusive lock to modify that resource until the reader ends the transaction. This way you're guaranteed to get repeatable reads, or consistent analysis.

The following example demonstrates getting repeatable reads.

Run the following code in Connection 1 to set the session's isolation level to REPEATABLE READ, open a transaction, and read the row for product 2:

```
SET TRANSACTION ISOLATION LEVEL REPEATABLE READ;

BEGIN TRAN;

  SELECT productid, unitprice
  FROM Production.Products
  WHERE productid = 2;
```

This code returns the following output showing the current price of product 2:

```
productid   unitprice
----------- ---------------------
2           19.00
```

Connection 1 still holds a shared lock on the row for product 2 because in REPEATABLE READ shared locks are held until the end of the transaction. Run the following code from Connection 2 to try to modify the row for product 2:

```
UPDATE Production.Products
  SET unitprice = unitprice + 1.00
WHERE productid = 2;
```

Notice that the attempt is blocked because the modifier's request for an exclusive lock is in conflict with the reader's granted shared lock. If the reader was running under the READ UNCOMMITTED or READ COMMITTED isolation level, it wouldn't have held the shared lock at this point, and the attempt to modify the row would have been successful.

Back in Connection 1, run the following code to read the row for product 2 a second time and commit the transaction:

```
  SELECT productid, unitprice
  FROM Production.Products
  WHERE productid = 2;

COMMIT TRAN;
```

This code returns the following output:

```
productid   unitprice
----------- ---------------------
2           19.00
```

Notice that the second read got the same unit price for product 2 as the first read. Now that the reader's transaction is committed, and the shared lock is released, the modifier in Connection 2 managed to obtain the exclusive lock it was waiting for and update the row.

Another phenomenon prevented by REPEATABLE READ but not by lower isolation levels is called a *lost update*. A lost update happens when two transactions read a value, make calculations based on what they read, and then update the value. Because in isolation levels lower than REPEATABLE READ no lock is held on the resource after the read, both transactions can update the value, and whichever transaction updates the value last "wins," overwriting the other transaction's update. In REPEATABLE READ, both sides keep their shared locks after the first read, so neither can acquire an exclusive lock later in order to update. The situation results in a deadlock and the update conflict is prevented. I'll provide more details on deadlocks later in the chapter.

When you're done, run the following code for cleanup:

```
UPDATE Production.Products
  SET unitprice = 19.00
WHERE productid = 2;
```

The SERIALIZABLE Isolation Level

Running under the REPEATABLE READ isolation level, readers keep shared locks until the end of the transaction. Therefore, you are guaranteed to get a repeatable read of the rows that you read the first time in the transaction. However, your transaction locks resources (for example, rows) that the query found the first time it ran, not rows that weren't there when the query ran. Therefore, a second read in the same transaction might return new rows as well. Those new rows are called phantoms, and such reads are called phantom reads. This happens if in between the reads, another transaction adds new rows that qualify to the reader's query filter.

To prevent phantom reads you need to move up in the isolation levels to SERIALIZABLE. For the most part, the SERIALIZABLE isolation level behaves similarly to REPEATABLE READ: namely, it requires a reader to obtain a shared lock to be able to read, and keeps the lock until the end of the transaction. But SERIALIZABLE isolation level adds another facet—logically, this isolation level causes a reader to lock the whole range of keys that qualify to the query's filter. This means that the reader locks not only the existing rows that qualify to the query's filter, but also future ones. Or more accurately, it blocks attempts made by other transactions to add rows that qualify to the reader's query filter.

The following example demonstrates that the SERIALIZABLE isolation level prevents phantom reads. Run the following code in Connection 1 to set the transaction isolation level to SERIALIZABLE, open a transaction, and query all products with category 1:

```
SET TRANSACTION ISOLATION LEVEL SERIALIZABLE;

BEGIN TRAN

  SELECT productid, productname, categoryid, unitprice
  FROM Production.Products
  WHERE categoryid = 1;
```

You get the following output, showing 12 products in category 1:

```
productid     productname       categoryid     unitprice
-----------   ---------------   -----------    --------------------
1             Product HHYDP     1              18.00
2             Product RECZE     1              19.00
24            Product QOGNU     1              4.50
34            Product SWNJY     1              14.00
35            Product NEVTJ     1              18.00
38            Product QDOMO     1              263.50
39            Product LSOFL     1              18.00
43            Product ZZZHR     1              46.00
67            Product XLXQF     1              14.00
70            Product TOONT     1              15.00
75            Product BWRLG     1              7.75
76            Product JYGFE     1              18.00

(12 row(s) affected)
```

From Connection 2, run the following code in an attempt to insert a new product with category 1:

```
INSERT INTO Production.Products
    (productname, supplierid, categoryid,
     unitprice, discontinued)
  VALUES('Product ABCDE', 1, 1, 20.00, 0);
```

In all isolation levels that are lower than SERIALIZABLE, such an attempt would have been successful. In SERIALIZABLE isolation level, the attempt is blocked.

Back in Connection 1, run the following code to query products with category 1 a second time and commit the transaction:

```
  SELECT productid, productname, categoryid, unitprice
  FROM Production.Products
  WHERE categoryid = 1;

COMMIT TRAN;
```

You get the same output as before, with no phantoms. Now that the reader's transaction is committed, and the shared key-range lock is released, the modifier in Connection 2 managed to obtain the exclusive lock it was waiting for and insert the row.

When you're done, run the following code for cleanup:

```
DELETE FROM Production.Products
WHERE productid > 77;

DBCC CHECKIDENT ('Production.Products', RESEED, 77);
```

Run the following code in all open connections to set the isolation level back to the default:

```
SET TRANSACTION ISOLATION LEVEL READ COMMITTED;
```

Snapshot Isolation Levels

SQL Server 2005 introduced the capability to store previous versions of committed rows in tempdb. Based on this row-versioning technology, SQL Server added support for two new isolation levels called SNAPSHOT and READ COMMITTED SNAPSHOT. SNAPSHOT isolation level is similar logically to SERIALIZABLE isolation level in terms of the types of consistency problems that can or cannot happen; READ COMMITTED SNAPSHOT isolation level is similar to READ COMMITTED isolation level. However, readers using snapshot-based isolation levels do not issue shared locks, so readers don't wait when the requested data is exclusively locked. Readers still get levels of consistency similar to SERIALIZABLE and READ COMMITTED. Readers get the version of the row they expect to see by pulling it from the version store in tempdb if the current version of the row is not the one they expect.

Note that if you enable any of the snapshot-based isolation levels, the *DELETE* and *UPDATE* statements need to copy to tempdb the version of the row before the change; *INSERT* statements don't need to be versioned in tempdb because no earlier version of the row existed. But it is important to be aware that enabling any of the snapshot-based isolation levels may have a negative impact on the performance of data updates and deletes. The performance of readers usually improves because they do not acquire shared locks and don't need to wait when data is exclusively locked or its version is not the expected one. The next sections cover snapshot-based isolation levels and demonstrate their behavior.

The SNAPSHOT Isolation Level

Under the SNAPSHOT isolation level, when reading data, the reader is guaranteed to get the last committed version of the row that was available when the transaction started. This means that you are guaranteed to get committed reads and repeatable reads, and also guaranteed not to get phantom reads—just as in the SERIALIZABLE isolation level. But instead of using shared locks, this isolation level relies on row versioning. As mentioned, snapshot isolation levels incur a performance penalty, mainly when updating and deleting data, regardless of whether the modification is executed from a session running under one of the snapshot-based isolation levels. For this reason, to allow working with the SNAPSHOT isolation level you need to first enable the option at the database level by running the following code in any open query window:

```
ALTER DATABASE TSQLFundamentals2008 SET ALLOW_SNAPSHOT_ISOLATION ON;
```

The following example demonstrates the behavior of the SNAPSHOT isolation level. Run the following code from Connection 1 to open a transaction, update the price of product 2 by adding 1.00 to its current price 19.00, and query the product's row to show the new price:

```
BEGIN TRAN;

  UPDATE Production.Products
    SET unitprice = unitprice + 1.00
  WHERE productid = 2;
```

```
SELECT productid, unitprice
FROM Production.Products
WHERE productid = 2;
```

Here the output of this code shows that the product's price was updated to 20.00:

```
productid   unitprice
----------- --------------------
2           20.00
```

Note that even though the transaction in Connection 1 ran under the default READ COMMITTED isolation level, SQL Server had to copy the version of the row before the update (with price 19.00) to tempdb. That's because SNAPSHOT isolation level is enabled at the database level. If someone begins a transaction using the SNAPSHOT isolation level, they may request the version before the update. For example, run the following code from Connection 2 to set the isolation level to SNAPSHOT, open a transaction, and query the row for product 2:

```
SET TRANSACTION ISOLATION LEVEL SNAPSHOT;

BEGIN TRAN;

  SELECT productid, unitprice
  FROM Production.Products
  WHERE productid = 2;
```

If your transaction had been under the SERIALIZABLE isolation level, the query would have been blocked. But because it is running under SNAPSHOT, you get the last committed version of the row that was available when the transaction started. That version (with price 19.00) is not the current version (price 20.00), so SQL Server pulls the appropriate version from the version store, and the code returns the following output:

```
productid   unitprice
----------- --------------------
2           19.00
```

Go back to Connection 1 and commit the transaction that modified the row:

```
COMMIT TRAN;
```

At this point the current version of the row with price 20.00 is a committed version. However, if you read the data again in Connection 2, you should still get the last committed version of the row that was available when the transaction started (with price 19.00). Run the following code in Connection 2 to read the data again, and then commit the transaction:

```
  SELECT productid, unitprice
  FROM Production.Products
  WHERE productid = 2;

COMMIT TRAN;
```

As expected, you get the following output with price 19.00:

```
productid   unitprice
----------- ---------------------
2           19.00
```

Run the following code in Connection 2 to open a new transaction, query the data, and commit the transaction:

```
BEGIN TRAN

  SELECT productid, unitprice
  FROM Production.Products
  WHERE productid = 2;

COMMIT TRAN;
```

This time, the last committed version of the row that was available when the transaction started is the one with price 20.00. Therefore, you get the following output:

```
productid   unitprice
----------- ---------------------
2           20.00
```

Now that no transaction needs the version of the row with price 19.00, a cleanup thread that runs once a minute can remove it from tempdb next time it runs.

When you're done, run the following code for cleanup:

```
UPDATE Production.Products
  SET unitprice = 19.00
WHERE productid = 2;
```

Conflict Detection

The SNAPSHOT isolation level prevents update conflicts, but unlike the REPEATABLE READ and SERIALIZABLE isolation levels that do so by generating a deadlock, the SNAPSHOT isolation level fails the transaction, indicating that an update conflict was detected. SNAPSHOT isolation level can detect update conflicts by examining the version store. It can figure out whether another transaction modified the data between a read and a write that took place in your transaction.

The following example demonstrates a scenario with no update conflict, followed by an example of a scenario with an update conflict.

Run the following code in Connection 1 to set the transaction isolation level to SNAPSHOT, open a transaction, and read the row for product 2:

```
SET TRANSACTION ISOLATION LEVEL SNAPSHOT;
```

```
BEGIN TRAN;

  SELECT productid, unitprice
  FROM Production.Products
  WHERE productid = 2;
```

You get the following output:

```
productid    unitprice
-----------  --------------------
2            19.00
```

Assuming you made some calculations based on what you read, run the following code while still in Connection 1 to update the price of the product you queried previously to 20.00, and commit the transaction:

```
  UPDATE Production.Products
    SET unitprice = 20.00
  WHERE productid = 2;
```

```
COMMIT TRAN;
```

No other transaction modified the row between your read, calculation, and write; therefore, there was no update conflict and SQL Server allowed the update to take place.

Run the following code to modify the price of product 2 back to 19.00:

```
UPDATE Production.Products
  SET unitprice = 19.00
WHERE productid = 2;
```

Next, run the following code in Connection 1, again, to open a transaction, and read the row for product 2:

```
BEGIN TRAN;

  SELECT productid, unitprice
  FROM Production.Products
  WHERE productid = 2;
```

You get the following output indication that the price of the product is 19.00:

```
productid    unitprice
-----------  --------------------
2            19.00
```

This time, run the following code in Connection 2 to update the price of product 2 to 25.00:

```
UPDATE Production.Products
  SET unitprice = 25.00
WHERE productid = 2;
```

Assuming you made calculations in Connection 1 based on the price 19.00 that you read, and based on your calculations, try to update the price of the product to 20.00 in Connection 1:

```
UPDATE Production.Products
  SET unitprice = 20.00
WHERE productid = 2;
```

SQL Server detected that this time another transaction modified the data between your read and write; therefore, it fails your transaction with the following error:

```
Msg 3960, Level 16, State 2, Line 1
Snapshot isolation transaction aborted due to update conflict. You cannot use snapshot
isolation to access table 'Production.Products' directly or indirectly in database
'TSQLFundamentals2008' to update, delete, or insert the row that has been modified or
deleted by another transaction. Retry the transaction or change the isolation level for the
update/delete statement.
```

Of course, you can use error handling code to retry the whole transaction when an update conflict is detected.

When you're done, run the following code for cleanup:

```
UPDATE Production.Products
  SET unitprice = 19.00
WHERE productid = 2;
```

Close all connections. Note that if all connections aren't closed, results may not match the chapter.

The READ COMMITTED SNAPSHOT Isolation Level

The READ COMMITTED SNAPSHOT isolation level is also based on row versioning. It differs from the SNAPSHOT isolation level in that instead of providing a reader with the last committed version of the row that was available when the transaction started, a reader gets the last committed version of the row that was available when the statement started. READ COMMITTED SNAPSHOT isolation level also does not detect update conflicts. This results in logical behavior very similar to READ COMMITTED isolation level except that readers do not acquire shared locks, and do not wait when the requested resource is exclusively locked.

To enable the use of READ COMMITTED SNAPSHOT isolation level in the database, you need to turn on a different database flag than the one required to enable SNAPSHOT isolation level. Run the following code to enable the use of READ COMMITTED SNAPSHOT isolation level in the TSQLFundamentals2008 database:

```
ALTER DATABASE TSQLFundamentals2008 SET READ_COMMITTED_SNAPSHOT ON;
```

Note that for this code to run successfully, this connection must be the only connection open to the TSQLFundamentals2008 database.

An interesting aspect of enabling this database flag is that unlike with the SNAPSHOT isolation level, this flag actually changes the meaning of the default READ COMMITTED isolation level to READ COMMITTED SNAPSHOT. This means that when this database flag is turned on, unless you explicitly change the session's isolation level, READ COMMITTED SNAPSHOT becomes the default.

For a demonstration of using READ COMMITTED SNAPSHOT isolation level, open two connections.

Run the following code in Connection 1 to open a transaction, update the row for product 2, and read the row, leaving the transaction open:

```
USE TSQLFundamentals2008;

BEGIN TRAN;

  UPDATE Production.Products
    SET unitprice = unitprice + 1.00
  WHERE productid = 2;

  SELECT productid, unitprice
  FROM Production.Products
  WHERE productid = 2;
```

You get the following output indicating that the product's price was changed to 20.00:

```
productid   unitprice
----------- ---------------------
2           20.00
```

In Connection 2, open a transaction and read the row for product 2, leaving the transaction open:

```
BEGIN TRAN;

  SELECT productid, unitprice
  FROM Production.Products
  WHERE productid = 2;
```

You get the last committed version of the row that was available when the statement started (19.00):

```
productid   unitprice
----------- ---------------------
2           19.00
```

Run the following code in Connection 1 to commit the transaction:

```
COMMIT TRAN;
```

Now run the code in Connection 2 to read the row for product 2 again, and commit the transaction:

```
SELECT productid, unitprice
FROM Production.Products
WHERE productid = 2;
```

```
COMMIT TRAN;
```

If this code had been running under the SNAPSHOT isolation level, you would have gotten the price 19.00; however, because the code is running under the READ COMMITTED SNAPSHOT isolation level, you get the last committed version of the row that was available when the statement started (20.00) and not when the transaction started (19.00):

```
productid    unitprice
-----------  --------------------
2            20.00
```

Recall that this phenomenon is called a non-repeatable read, or inconsistent analysis.

When you're done, run the following code for cleanup:

```
UPDATE Production.Products
  SET unitprice = 19.00
WHERE productid = 2;
```

Close all connections, and then in a new connection run the following code to disable the snapshot-based isolation levels in the TSQLFundamentals2008 database:

```
ALTER DATABASE TSQLFundamentals2008 SET ALLOW_SNAPSHOT_ISOLATION OFF;
ALTER DATABASE TSQLFundamentals2008 SET READ_COMMITTED_SNAPSHOT OFF;
```

Summary of Isolation Levels

Table 9-3 provides a summary of the logical consistency problems that can or cannot happen in each isolation level and indicates whether the isolation level detects update conflicts for you and whether the isolation level uses row versioning.

TABLE 9-3 Summary of Isolation Levels

Isolation Level	Uncommitted Reads?	Non Repeatable Reads?	Lost Updates?	Phantom Reads?	Detects Update Conflicts?	Uses Row Versioning?
READ UNCOMMITTED	Yes	Yes	Yes	Yes	No	No
READ COMMITTED	No	Yes	Yes	Yes	No	No

TABLE 9-3 **Summary of Isolation Levels**

Isolation Level	Uncommitted Reads?	Non Repeatable Reads?	Lost Updates?	Phantom Reads?	Detects Update Conflicts?	Uses Row Versioning?
READ COMMITTED SNAPSHOT	No	Yes	Yes	Yes	No	Yes
REPEATABLE READ	No	No	No	Yes	No	No
SERIALIZABLE	No	No	No	No	No	No
SNAPSHOT	No	No	No	No	Yes	Yes

Deadlocks

A deadlock is a situation where processes end up blocking each other. A deadlock can involve two or more processes. An example of a two-process deadlock is when process A blocks process B and process B blocks process A. An example of a deadlock involving more than two processes is when process A blocks process B, process B blocks process C, and process C blocks process A. In either case, SQL Server detects the deadlock and intervenes by terminating one of the transactions. If SQL Server does not intervene, the processes involved would remain deadlocked forever.

Unless otherwise specified, SQL Server chooses to terminate the transaction that did the least work, because it is cheapest to roll that transaction's work back. However, as of SQL Server 2005, if you like you can set a session option called DEADLOCK_PRIORITY to one of 21 values in the range -10 through 10. Prior to SQL Server 2005 only two priorities were available—LOW and NORMAL. The process with the lowest deadlock priority is chosen as the deadlock victim regardless of how much work is done, and in the event of a tie, the amount of work is used as a tiebreaker.

The following example demonstrates a simple deadlock. Then I'll explain how you can mitigate deadlock occurrences in the system.

Open two connections and make sure that you are connected to the TSQLFundamentals2008 database in both. Run the following code in Connection 1 to open a new transaction, update a row in the Production.Products table for product 2, and leave the transaction open:

```
USE TSQLFundamentals2008;

BEGIN TRAN;

  UPDATE Production.Products
    SET unitprice = unitprice + 1.00
  WHERE productid = 2;
```

Run the following code in Connection 2 to open a new transaction, update a row in the Sales.OrderDetails table for product 2, and leave the transaction open:

```
BEGIN TRAN;

  UPDATE Sales.OrderDetails
    SET unitprice = unitprice + 1.00
  WHERE productid = 2;
```

At this point the transaction in Connection 1 is holding an exclusive lock on the row for product 2 in the Production.Products table, and the transaction in Connection 2 is now holding a lock on the row for product 2 in the Sales.OrderDetails table. Both queries succeed, and no blocking has occurred yet.

Run the following code in Connection 1 to attempt to query the row for product 2 in the Sales.OrderDetails table and commit the transaction:

```
SELECT orderid, productid, unitprice
FROM Sales.OrderDetails
WHERE productid = 2;
```

```
COMMIT TRAN;
```

The code is running under the default READ COMMITTED isolation level; therefore, the transaction in Connection 1 needs a shared lock to be able to read. Because the other transaction holds an exclusive lock on the same resource, the transaction in Connection 1 is blocked. At this point you have a blocking situation, not yet a deadlock. Of course, a chance remains that Connection 2 will end the transaction, releasing all locks and allowing the transaction in Connection 1 to get the requested locks.

Next, run the following code in Connection 2 to attempt to query the row for product 2 in the Product.Production table and commit the transaction:

```
SELECT productid, unitprice
FROM Production.Products
WHERE productid = 2;
```

```
COMMIT TRAN;
```

The transaction in Connection 2 needs a shared lock on the row for product 2 in the Product.Production table to be able to read, so this request is now in conflict with the exclusive lock held on the same resource by Connection 1. Each of the processes blocks the other—you have a deadlock. SQL Server identifies the deadlock—typically within a few seconds, chooses one of the two processes as the deadlock victim, and terminates its transaction with the following error:

```
Msg 1205, Level 13, State 51, Line 1
Transaction (Process ID 52) was deadlocked on lock resources with another process and has
been chosen as the deadlock victim. Rerun the transaction.
```

In this example, SQL Server chose to terminate the transaction in Connection 1 (shown here as process ID 52). Because I didn't set a deadlock priority and both transactions did a similar amount of work, either transaction could have been terminated.

Deadlocks are expensive because they involve undoing work that has already been done. You can follow a few practices to mitigate deadlock occurrences in your system.

Obviously, the longer the transactions are, the longer locks are kept, increasing the probability of deadlocks. You should try to keep transactions as short as possible, taking activities out of the transaction that aren't logically supposed to be part of the same unit of work.

A deadlock happens when transactions access resources in inverse order. For example, in our case, Connection 1 first accessed a row in Production.Products and then accessed a row in Sales.OrderDetails, while Connection 2 first accessed a row in Sales.OrderDetails and then accessed a row in Production.Products. This type of deadlock can't happen if both transactions access resources in the same order. By swapping the order in one of the transactions you can prevent this type of deadlock from happening—assuming that it makes no logical difference to your application.

Our deadlock example has a real logical conflict because both sides try to access the same rows. However, deadlocks often happen when there is no real logical conflict because of a lack of good indexing to support query filters. For example, suppose that both statements in the transaction in Connection 2 were to filter product 5. Now that the statements in Connection 1 handle product 2 and the statements in Connection 2 handle product 5, there shouldn't be any conflict. However, if no indexes on the productid column in the tables support the filter, SQL Server has to scan (and lock) all rows in the table. This, of course, can lead to a deadlock. In short, good index design can help mitigate the occurrences of deadlocks that have no real logical conflict.

When you're done, run the following code for cleanup in any connection:

```
UPDATE Production.Products
  SET unitprice = 19.00
WHERE productid = 2;

UPDATE Sales.OrderDetails
  SET unitprice = 19.00
WHERE productid = 2
  AND orderid >= 10500;

UPDATE Sales.OrderDetails
  SET unitprice = 15.20
WHERE productid = 2
  AND orderid < 10500;
```

Conclusion

This chapter introduced you to transactions and concurrency. I described what transactions are and how SQL Server manages them. I explained how SQL Server isolates data accessed by one transaction from inconsistent use by other transactions, and how to troubleshoot blocking scenarios. I described how you can control the level of consistency that you get from the data by choosing an isolation level, and the impact that your choice has on concurrency. I described four isolation levels that do not rely on row versioning and two that do. Finally, I covered deadlocks and explained practices that you can follow to reduce the frequency of their occurrences.

To practice what you've learned, perform the practice exercises.

Exercises

This section provides exercises so you can practice the subjects covered in this chapter. The exercises for most of the previous chapters involve requests for which you have to figure out a solution in the form of a T-SQL query or statement. The exercises for this chapter are different: You will be provided with instructions to follow to troubleshoot blocking and deadlock situations, and to observe the behavior of different isolation levels. Therefore, this chapter's exercises have no separate Solutions section, as in other chapters.

In all exercises in this chapter, make sure you are connected to the TSQLFundamentals2008 sample database by running the following code:

```
USE TSQLFundamentals2008;
```

Exercises 1-1 through 1-6 deal with blocking.

1-1

Open three connections in SQL Server Management Studio (we will refer to them as Connection 1, Connection 2, and Connection 3). Run the following code in Connection 1 to update rows in Sales.OrderDetails:

```
BEGIN TRAN;

  UPDATE Sales.OrderDetails
    SET discount = 0.05
  WHERE orderid = 10249;
```

1-2

Run the following code in Connection 2 to query Sales.OrderDetails; Connection 2 will be blocked:

```
SELECT orderid, productid, unitprice, qty, discount
FROM Sales.OrderDetails
WHERE orderid = 10249;
```

1-3

Run the following code in Connection 3 and identify the locks and process IDs involved in the blocking chain:

```
SELECT -- use * to explore
  request_session_id            AS spid,
  resource_type                 AS restype,
  resource_database_id          AS dbid,
  resource_description          AS res,
  resource_associated_entity_id AS resid,
  request_mode                  AS mode,
  request_status                AS status
FROM sys.dm_tran_locks;
```

1-4

Replace the process IDs 52 and 53 with the ones you found to be involved in the blocking chain in the previous exercise. Run the following code to obtain connection, session, and blocking information about the processes involved in the blocking chain:

```
-- Connection info:
SELECT -- use * to explore
  session_id AS spid,
  connect_time,
  last_read,
  last_write,
  most_recent_sql_handle
FROM sys.dm_exec_connections
WHERE session_id IN(52, 53);

-- Session info
SELECT -- use * to explore
  session_id AS spid,
  login_time,
  host_name,
  program_name,
  login_name,
  nt_user_name,
  last_request_start_time,
  last_request_end_time
FROM sys.dm_exec_sessions
WHERE session_id IN(52, 53);
```

```
-- Blocking
SELECT -- use * to explore
  session_id AS spid,
  blocking_session_id,
  command,
  sql_handle,
  database_id,
  wait_type,
  wait_time,
  wait_resource
FROM sys.dm_exec_requests
WHERE blocking_session_id > 0;
```

1-5

Run the following code to obtain the SQL text of the connections involved in the blocking chain:

```
SELECT session_id, text
FROM sys.dm_exec_connections
  CROSS APPLY sys.dm_exec_sql_text(most_recent_sql_handle) AS ST
WHERE session_id IN(52, 53);
```

1-6

Run the following code in Connection 1 to roll back the transaction:

```
ROLLBACK TRAN;
```

Observe in Connection 2 that the SELECT query returned the two order detail rows, and that those rows were not modified.

Remember that if you need to terminate the blocker's transaction, you can use the *KILL* command.

Close all connections.

Exercises 2-1 through 2-6 deal with isolation levels.

2-1

2-1a

Open two new connections (we will refer to them as Connection 1 and Connection 2).

2-1b

Run the following code in Connection 1 to update rows in Sales.OrderDetails and query it:

```
BEGIN TRAN;

  UPDATE Sales.OrderDetails
    SET discount = discount + 0.05
  WHERE orderid = 10249;
```

```
SELECT orderid, productid, unitprice, qty, discount
FROM Sales.OrderDetails
WHERE orderid = 10249;
```

2-1c

Run the following code in Connection 2 to set the isolation level to READ UNCOMMITTED and query Sales.OrderDetails:

```
SET TRANSACTION ISOLATION LEVEL READ UNCOMMITTED;

SELECT orderid, productid, unitprice, qty, discount
FROM Sales.OrderDetails
WHERE orderid = 10249;
```

Notice that you get the modified, uncommitted version of the rows.

2-1d

Run the following code in Connection 1 to roll back the transaction:

```
ROLLBACK TRAN;
```

2-2

2-2a

Run the following code in Connection 1 to update rows in Sales.OrderDetails and query it:

```
BEGIN TRAN;

  UPDATE Sales.OrderDetails
    SET discount = discount + 0.05
  WHERE orderid = 10249;

  SELECT orderid, productid, unitprice, qty, discount
  FROM Sales.OrderDetails
  WHERE orderid = 10249;
```

2-2b

Run the following code in Connection 2 to set the isolation level to READ COMMITTED (default) and query Sales.OrderDetails:

```
SET TRANSACTION ISOLATION LEVEL READ COMMITTED;

SELECT orderid, productid, unitprice, qty, discount
FROM Sales.OrderDetails
WHERE orderid = 10249;
```

Notice that you are now blocked.

2-2c

Run the following code in Connection 1 to commit the transaction:

```
COMMIT TRAN;
```

2-2d

Go to Connection 2 and notice that you get the modified, committed version of the rows.

2-2e

Run the following code for cleanup:

```
UPDATE Sales.OrderDetails
  SET discount = 0.00
WHERE orderid = 10249;
```

2-3

2-3a

Run the following code in Connection 1 to set the isolation level to REPEATABLE READ, open a transaction, and read data from Sales.OrderDetails:

```
SET TRANSACTION ISOLATION LEVEL REPEATABLE READ;

BEGIN TRAN;

  SELECT orderid, productid, unitprice, qty, discount
  FROM Sales.OrderDetails
  WHERE orderid = 10249;
```

You get two rows with discount values 0.00.

2-3b

Run the following code in Connection 2 and notice you are blocked:

```
UPDATE Sales.OrderDetails
  SET discount = discount + 0.05
WHERE orderid = 10249;
```

2-3c

Run the following code in Connection 1 to read the data again and commit the transaction:

```
  SELECT orderid, productid, unitprice, qty, discount
  FROM Sales.OrderDetails
  WHERE orderid = 10249;

COMMIT TRAN;
```

You get the two rows with discount values 0.00 again, giving you repeatable reads. Note that if your code was running under a lower isolation level (READ UNCOMMITTED or READ COMMITTED), the UPDATE statement wouldn't have been blocked, and you would have gotten non-repeatable reads.

2-3d

Go to Connection 2 and notice that the update finished.

2-3e

Run the following code for cleanup:

```
UPDATE Sales.OrderDetails
  SET discount = 0.00
WHERE orderid = 10249;
```

2-4

2-4a

Run the following code in Connection 1 to set the isolation level to SERIALIZABLE and query Sales.OrderDetails:

```
SET TRANSACTION ISOLATION LEVEL SERIALIZABLE;

BEGIN TRAN;

  SELECT orderid, productid, unitprice, qty, discount
  FROM Sales.OrderDetails
  WHERE orderid = 10249;
```

2-4b

Run the following code in Connection 2 to attempt to insert a row to Sales.OrderDetails with the same order ID that is filtered by the previous query and notice that you are blocked:

```
INSERT INTO Sales.OrderDetails
    (orderid, productid, unitprice, qty, discount)
  VALUES(10249, 2, 19.00, 10, 0.00);
```

Note that in lower isolation levels (READ UNCOMMITTED, READ COMMITTED, REPEATABLE READ), this *INSERT* statement wouldn't have been blocked.

2-4c

Run the following code in Connection 1 to query Sales.OrderDetails again, and commit the transaction:

```
  SELECT orderid, productid, unitprice, qty, discount
  FROM Sales.OrderDetails
  WHERE orderid = 10249;

COMMIT TRAN;
```

You get the same result set that you got from the previous query in the same transaction, and because the *INSERT* statement was blocked, you get no phantom reads.

2-4d

Go back to Connection 2 and notice that the *INSERT* statement finished.

2-4e

Run the following code for cleanup:

```
DELETE FROM Sales.OrderDetails
WHERE orderid = 10249
  AND productid = 2;
```

2-4f

Run the following code in both Connection 1 and Connection 2 to set the isolation level to the default READ COMMITTED:

```
SET TRANSACTION ISOLATION LEVEL READ COMMITTED;
```

2-5

2-5a

Run the following code to allow SNAPSHOT isolation level in the TSQLFundamentals2008 database:

```
ALTER DATABASE TSQLFundamentals2008 SET ALLOW_SNAPSHOT_ISOLATION ON;
```

2-5b

Run the following code in Connection 1 to open a transaction, update rows in Sales. OrderDetails, and query it:

```
BEGIN TRAN;

  UPDATE Sales.OrderDetails
    SET discount = discount + 0.05
  WHERE orderid = 10249;

  SELECT orderid, productid, unitprice, qty, discount
  FROM Sales.OrderDetails
  WHERE orderid = 10249;
```

2-5c

Run the following code in Connection 2 to set the isolation level to SNAPSHOT and query Sales.OrderDetails. Notice that you're not blocked—instead you get an earlier, consistent version of the data that was available when the transaction started (discount values 0.00):

```
SET TRANSACTION ISOLATION LEVEL SNAPSHOT;

BEGIN TRAN;

  SELECT orderid, productid, unitprice, qty, discount
  FROM Sales.OrderDetails
  WHERE orderid = 10249;
```

2-5d

Go to Connection 1 and commit the transaction:

```
COMMIT TRAN;
```

2-5e

Go to Connection 2 and query the data again; notice that you still get discount values 0.00:

```
  SELECT orderid, productid, unitprice, qty, discount
  FROM Sales.OrderDetails
  WHERE orderid = 10249;
```

2-5f

In Connection 2 commit the transaction and query the data again; notice that now you get discount values 0.05:

```
COMMIT TRAN;

SELECT orderid, productid, unitprice, qty, discount
FROM Sales.OrderDetails
WHERE orderid = 10249;
```

2-5g

Run the following code for cleanup:

```
UPDATE Sales.OrderDetails
  SET discount = 0.00
WHERE orderid = 10249;
```

Close all connections.

2-6

2-6a

Turn on READ_COMMITTED_SNAPSHOT in the TSQLFundamentals2008 database:

```
ALTER DATABASE TSQLFundamentals2008 SET READ_COMMITTED_SNAPSHOT ON;
```

2-6b

Open two new connections (we will refer to them as Connection 1 and Connection 2).

2-6c

Run the following code in Connection 1 to open a transaction, update rows in Sales.OrderDetails, and query it:

```
BEGIN TRAN;

  UPDATE Sales.OrderDetails
    SET discount = discount + 0.05
  WHERE orderid = 10249;

  SELECT orderid, productid, unitprice, qty, discount
  FROM Sales.OrderDetails
  WHERE orderid = 10249;
```

2-6d

Run the following code in Connection 2 which is now running under the isolation level READ COMMITTED SNAPSHOT because the database flag READ_COMMITTED_SNAPSHOT is turned on. Notice that you're not blocked—instead, you get an earlier, consistent version of the data that was available when the statement started (discount values 0.00):

```
BEGIN TRAN;

  SELECT orderid, productid, unitprice, qty, discount
  FROM Sales.OrderDetails
  WHERE orderid = 10249;
```

2-6e

Go to Connection 1 and commit the transaction:

```
COMMIT TRAN;
```

2-6f

Go to Connection 2, query the data again, and commit the transaction; notice that you get the new discount values 0.05:

```
SELECT orderid, productid, unitprice, qty, discount
FROM Sales.OrderDetails
WHERE orderid = 10249;
```

```
COMMIT TRAN;
```

2-6g

Run the following code for cleanup:

```
UPDATE Sales.OrderDetails
  SET discount = 0.00
WHERE orderid = 10249;
```

Close all connections.

2-6h

Change the database flags back to the defaults, disabling snapshot isolation levels:

```
ALTER DATABASE TSQLFundamentals2008 SET ALLOW_SNAPSHOT_ISOLATION OFF;
ALTER DATABASE TSQLFundamentals2008 SET READ_COMMITTED_SNAPSHOT OFF;
```

Exercises 3-1 through 3-7 deal with deadlocks.

3-1

Open two new connections (we will refer to them as Connection 1 and Connection 2).

3-2

Run the following code in Connection 1 to open a transaction and update the row for product 2 in Production.Products:

```
BEGIN TRAN;

  UPDATE Production.Products
    SET unitprice = unitprice + 1.00
  WHERE productid = 2;
```

3-3

Run the following code in Connection 2 to open a transaction and update the row for product 3 in Production.Products:

```
BEGIN TRAN;

  UPDATE Production.Products
    SET unitprice = unitprice + 1.00
  WHERE productid = 3;
```

3-4

Run the following code in Connection 1 to query product 3. You will be blocked.

```
  SELECT productid, unitprice
  FROM Production.Products
  WHERE productid = 3;

COMMIT TRAN;
```

3-5

Run the following code in Connection 2 to query product 2. You will be blocked, and a deadlock error will be generated either in Connection 1 or Connection 2.

```
  SELECT productid, unitprice
  FROM Production.Products
  WHERE productid = 2;

COMMIT TRAN;
```

3-6

Can you suggest a way to prevent this deadlock?

Hint: Refer back to what you read in the "Deadlocks" section.

3-7

Run the following code for cleanup:

```
UPDATE Production.Products
  SET unitprice = 19.00
WHERE productid = 2;

UPDATE Production.Products
  SET unitprice = 10.00
WHERE productid = 3;
```

Chapter 10
Programmable Objects

This chapter provides a brief overview of programmable objects to familiarize you with the capabilities of Microsoft SQL Server in this area and with the concepts involved. The chapter covers variables; batches; flow elements; cursors; temporary tables; dynamic SQL; routines such as user-defined functions, stored procedures, and triggers; and dynamic SQL. The purpose of this chapter is to provide a high-level overview, not to delve into technical details. Try to focus on the logical aspects and capabilities of programmable objects rather than trying to understand all code elements and their technicalities. For details and more in-depth coverage of programmable objects, please refer to the book *Inside Microsoft SQL Server 2008: T-SQL Programming* (Microsoft Press, 2009).

Variables

Variables allow you to store data values temporarily for later use in the same batch where they were declared. I describe batches later in the chapter, but for now, suffice it to say that a batch is one T-SQL statement or more sent to SQL Server for execution as a single unit.

Use a *DECLARE* statement to declare one or more variables, and use a *SET* statement to assign a value to a single variable. For example, the following code declares a variable called *@i* of an *INT* data type and assigns it the value 10:

```
DECLARE @i AS INT;
SET @i = 10;
```

SQL Server 2008 introduces support for declaring and initializing variables in the same statement like so:

```
DECLARE @i AS INT = 10;
```

Throughout this chapter, I use separate *DECLARE* and *SET* statements so that you can also run the code in SQL Server 2005 and earlier versions.

When assigning a value to a scalar variable, the value must be the result of a scalar expression. The expression can be a scalar subquery. For example, the following code declares a variable called *@empname*, and assigns it the result of a scalar subquery returning the full name of the employee with ID 3:

```
USE TSQLFundamentals2008;

DECLARE @empname AS NVARCHAR(61);

SET @empname = (SELECT firstname + N' ' + lastname
                FROM HR.Employees
                WHERE empid = 3);

SELECT @empname AS empname;
```

This code returns the following output:

```
empname
----------
Judy Lew
```

The *SET* statement can operate only on one variable at a time, so if you need to assign values to multiple attributes, you need to use multiple *SET* statements. This can involve unnecessary overhead when you need to pull multiple attribute values from the same row. For example, the following code uses two separate *SET* statements to pull both the first and the last names of the employee with ID 3 to two separate variables:

```
DECLARE @firstname AS NVARCHAR(20), @lastname AS NVARCHAR(40);

SET @firstname = (SELECT firstname
                  FROM HR.Employees
                  WHERE empid = 3);
SET @lastname = (SELECT lastname
                 FROM HR.Employees
                 WHERE empid = 3);

SELECT @firstname AS firstname, @lastname AS lastname;
```

This code returns the following output:

```
firstname  lastname
---------- ---------
Judy       Lew
```

SQL Server also supports a nonstandard assignment *SELECT* statement, allowing you to query data and assign multiple values obtained from the same row to multiple variables using a single statement. Here's an example:

```
DECLARE @firstname AS NVARCHAR(20), @lastname AS NVARCHAR(40);

SELECT
  @firstname = firstname,
  @lastname  = lastname
FROM HR.Employees
WHERE empid = 3;

SELECT @firstname AS firstname, @lastname AS lastname;
```

The assignment *SELECT* has predictable behavior when exactly one row qualifies. However, note that if the query has more than one qualifying row, the code doesn't fail. The assignments take place per each qualifying row, and with each row accessed, the values from the current row overwrite the existing values in the variables. When the assignment *SELECT* finishes, the values in the variables are those from the last row that SQL Server happened to access. For example, the following assignment *SELECT* has two qualifying rows:

```
DECLARE @empname AS NVARCHAR(61);

SELECT @empname = firstname + N' ' + lastname
FROM HR.Employees
WHERE mgrid = 2;

SELECT @empname AS empname;
```

The employee information that ends up in the variable after the assignment *SELECT* finishes depends on the order in which SQL Server happens to access those rows. When I ran this code I got the following output:

```
empname
----------
Sven Buck
```

The *SET* statement is safer than the assignment *SELECT* because it requires you to use a scalar subquery to pull data from a table. Remember that a scalar subquery fails at run time if it returns more than one value. For example, the following code fails:

```
DECLARE @empname AS NVARCHAR(61);

SET @empname = (SELECT firstname + N' ' + lastname
                FROM HR.Employees
                WHERE mgrid = 2);

SELECT @empname AS empname;
```

Because the variable was not assigned with a value, it remains *NULL*, which is the default for variables that were not initialized. This code returns the following output:

```
Msg 512, Level 16, State 1, Line 3
Subquery returned more than 1 value. This is not permitted when the subquery follows =, !=,
<, <= , >, >= or when the subquery is used as an expression.
empname
--------
NULL
```

Batches

A batch is one or more T-SQL statements sent by a client application to SQL Server for execution as a single unit. The batch undergoes parsing (syntax checking), resolution (checking the existence of referenced objects and columns, permissions checking), and optimization as a unit.

Don't confuse transactions and batches. A transaction is an atomic unit of work. A batch can have multiple transactions, and a transaction can be submitted in parts as multiple batches. When a transaction is cancelled or rolled back in midstream, SQL Server undoes the partial activity that has taken place since the beginning of the transaction, regardless of where the batch began.

Client APIs such as ADO.NET provide you with methods for submitting a batch of code to SQL Server for execution. SQL Server utilities such as SQL Server Management Studio, SQLCMD, and OSQL provide a client command called *GO* that signals the end of a batch. Note that the *GO* command is a client command and not a T-SQL server command.

A Batch as a Unit of Parsing

A batch is a set of commands that are parsed and executed as a unit. If the parsing is successful, SQL Server will then attempt to execute the batch. In the event of a syntax error in the batch, the whole batch is not submitted to SQL Server for execution. For example, the following code has three batches, the second of which has a syntax error (FOM instead of FROM in the second query):

```
-- Valid batch
PRINT 'First batch';
USE TSQLFundamentals2008;
GO
-- Invalid batch
PRINT 'Second batch';
SELECT custid FROM Sales.Customers;
SELECT orderid FOM Sales.Orders;
GO
-- Valid batch
PRINT 'Third batch';
SELECT empid FROM HR.Employees;
```

Because the second batch has a syntax error, the whole batch is not submitted to SQL Server for execution. The first and third batches pass syntax validation and therefore are submitted for execution. This code produces the following output showing that the whole second batch was not executed:

```
First batch
Msg 102, Level 15, State 1, Line 4
Incorrect syntax near 'Sales'.
Third batch
empid
-----------
2
7
1
5
6
8
3
9
4

(9 row(s) affected)
```

Batches and Variables

Variables are local to the batch in which they are defined. If you try to refer to a variable that was defined in another batch, you get an error saying that the variable was not defined. For example, the following code declares a variable and prints its content in one batch, and then tries to print its content from another batch:

```
DECLARE @i AS INT;
SET @i = 10;
-- Succeeds
PRINT @i;
GO

-- Fails
PRINT @i;
```

The reference to the variable in the first *PRINT* statement is valid because it appears in the same batch where the variable was declared, but the second reference is invalid. Therefore the first *PRINT* statement returns the variable's value (10), while the second fails. Here's the output returned from this code:

```
10
Msg 137, Level 15, State 2, Line 3
Must declare the scalar variable "@i".
```

Statements That Cannot Be Combined in the Same Batch

The following statements cannot be combined with other statements in the same batch: *CREATE DEFAULT*, *CREATE FUNCTION*, *CREATE PROCEDURE*, *CREATE RULE*, *CREATE SCHEMA*, *CREATE TRIGGER*, and *CREATE VIEW*. For example, the following code has an *IF* statement followed by a *CREATE VIEW* statement in the same batch and therefore is invalid:

```
IF OBJECT_ID('Sales.MyView', 'V') IS NOT NULL DROP VIEW Sales.MyView;

CREATE VIEW Sales.MyView
AS

SELECT YEAR(orderdate) AS orderyear, COUNT(*) AS numorders
FROM Sales.Orders
GROUP BY YEAR(orderdate);
GO
```

An attempt to run this code generates the following error:

```
Msg 111, Level 15, State 1, Line 3
'CREATE VIEW' must be the first statement in a query batch.
```

To get around the problem, separate the *IF* and *CREATE VIEW* statements into different batches by adding a *GO* command after the *IF* statement.

A Batch as a Unit of Resolution

A batch is a unit of resolution. This means that checking the existence of objects and columns happens at the batch level. Keep this fact in mind when designing batch boundaries. When you apply schema changes to an object and try to manipulate the object data in the same batch, SQL Server may not be aware of the schema changes yet and fail the data manipulation statement with a resolution error. I'll demonstrate the problem through an example and then recommend best practices.

Run the following code to create a table called T1 in tempdb with one column called col1:

```
USE tempdb;
IF OBJECT_ID('dbo.T1', 'U') IS NOT NULL DROP TABLE dbo.T1;
CREATE TABLE dbo.T1(col1 INT);
```

Next, try to add a column called col2 to T1 and query the new column in the same batch:

```
ALTER TABLE dbo.T1 ADD col2 INT;
SELECT col1, col2 FROM dbo.T1;
```

Even though the code might seem to be perfectly valid, the batch fails during the resolution phase with the following error:

```
Msg 207, Level 16, State 1, Line 2
Invalid column name 'col2'.
```

At the time the *SELECT* statement was resolved, T1 had only one column, and the reference to the column col2 caused the error. One best practice you can follow to avoid such problems is to separate DDL and DML statements into different batches, as in the following example:

```
ALTER TABLE dbo.T1 ADD col2 INT;
GO
SELECT col1, col2 FROM dbo.T1;
```

The GO n Option

The *GO* command was enhanced in the client tools in SQL Server 2005 to support an argument indicating how many times you want to execute the batch. You use the new option when you want the batch repeated. To demonstrate the enhanced *GO* command, first create the table T1 in tempdb with an identity column:

```
IF OBJECT_ID('dbo.T1', 'U') IS NOT NULL DROP TABLE dbo.T1;
CREATE TABLE dbo.T1(col1 INT IDENTITY);
```

Next, run the following code to suppress the default output produced by DML statements indicating how many rows were affected:

```
SET NOCOUNT ON;
```

Finally, run the following code to define a batch with an *INSERT DEFAULT VALUES* statement and to execute the batch 100 times:

```
INSERT INTO dbo.T1 DEFAULT VALUES;
GO 100
```

Keep in mind that *GO* is a client command and not a server T-SQL command. This means that regardless of the version of the database engine you are connected to, the *GO n* command is supported as long as the client tool you are using is SQL Server 2005 or later.

Flow Elements

Flow elements allow you to control the flow of your code. T-SQL provides very basic forms of control of flow elements including the *IF ... ELSE* element and the *WHILE* element.

The IF ... ELSE Flow Element

The *IF ... ELSE* element allows you to control the flow of your code based on a predicate. You specify a statement or statement block that is executed if the predicate is TRUE, and optionally a statement or statement block that is executed if the predicate is FALSE or UNKNOWN.

For example, the following code checks whether today is the last day of the year (today's year is different than tomorrow's year). If true, the code prints a message saying that today is the last day of the year; if else, the code prints a message saying that today is not the last day of the year:

```
IF YEAR(CURRENT_TIMESTAMP) <> YEAR(DATEADD(day, 1, CURRENT_TIMESTAMP))
  PRINT 'Today is the last day of the year.'
ELSE
  PRINT 'Today is not the last day of the year.'
```

In this example I use *PRINT* statements to demonstrate which parts of the code were executed and which weren't, but of course you can specify other statements as well.

Keep in mind that T-SQL uses three-valued logic and that the ELSE block is activated when the predicate is either FALSE or UNKNOWN. In cases where both FALSE and UNKNOWN are possible outcomes of the predicate (for example, when NULLs are involved), and you need different treatment for each case, make sure you have an explicit test for NULLs with the IS NULL predicate.

If the flow you need to control involves more than two cases, you can nest *IF* … *ELSE* elements. For example, the code below handles the following three cases differently:

1. Today is the last day of the year.

2. Today is the last day of the month but not the last day of the year.

3. Today is not the last day of the month.

```
IF YEAR(CURRENT_TIMESTAMP) <> YEAR(DATEADD(day, 1, CURRENT_TIMESTAMP))
  PRINT 'Today is the last day of the year.'
ELSE
  IF MONTH(CURRENT_TIMESTAMP) <> MONTH(DATEADD(day, 1, CURRENT_TIMESTAMP))
    PRINT 'Today is the last day of the month but not the last day of the year.'
  ELSE
    PRINT 'Today is not the last day of the month.';
```

If you need to run more than one statement in the IF or ELSE sections, use a statement block. You mark the boundaries of a statement block with the *BEGIN* and *END* keywords. For example, the following code runs a full backup of the sample database TSQLFundamentals2008 if today is the first day of the month, and a differential backup (changes since last full backup) if today is not the last day of the month:

```
IF DAY(CURRENT_TIMESTAMP) = 1
BEGIN
  PRINT 'Today is the first day of the month.';
  PRINT 'Starting a full database backup.';
  BACKUP DATABASE TSQLFundamentals2008
    TO DISK = 'C:\Temp\TSQLFundamentals2008_Full.BAK' WITH INIT;
  PRINT 'Finished full database backup.';
END
```

```
ELSE
BEGIN
  PRINT 'Today is not the first day of the month.'
  PRINT 'Starting a differential database backup.';
  BACKUP DATABASE TSQLFundamentals2008
    TO DISK = 'C:\Temp\TSQLFundamentals2008_Diff.BAK' WITH INIT;
  PRINT 'Finished differential database backup.';
END
```

Note that the *BACKUP DATABASE* statements in the preceding code assume that the folder C:\Temp exists.

The WHILE Flow Element

T-SQL provides the *WHILE* element to enable you to execute code in a loop. The *WHILE* element executes a statement or statement block repeatedly while the predicate you specify after the *WHILE* keyword is *TRUE*. When the predicate is FALSE or UNKNOWN, the loop terminates.

T-SQL doesn't provide a built-in looping element that executes a predetermined number of times, but it's very easy to mimic such an element with a *WHILE* loop and a variable. For example, the following code demonstrates how to write a loop that iterates 10 times:

```
DECLARE @i AS INT;
SET @i = 1
WHILE @i <= 10
BEGIN
  PRINT @i;
  SET @i = @i + 1;
END;
```

The code declares an integer variable called *@i* that serves as the loop counter and initializes it with the value 1. The code then enters a loop that iterates while the variable is smaller than or equal to 10. In each iteration the code in the loop's body prints the current value of *@i* and then increments it by 1. This code returns the following output showing that the loop iterated 10 times:

```
1
2
3
4
5
6
7
8
9
10
```

If at some point in the loop's body you want to break out of the current loop and proceed to execute the statement that appears after the loop's body, use the *BREAK* command. For example, the following code breaks from the loop if the value of *@i* is equal to 6:

```
DECLARE @i AS INT;
SET @i = 1
WHILE @i <= 10
BEGIN
  IF @i = 6 BREAK;
  PRINT @i;
  SET @i = @i + 1;
END;
```

This code produces the following output showing that the loop iterated five times, and terminated at the beginning of the sixth iteration:

```
1
2
3
4
5
```

Of course, this code is not very sensible; if you want the loop to iterate only five times, you should simply specify the predicate @i <= 5. Here I just wanted to demonstrate the use of the *BREAK* command with a simple example.

If at some point in the loop's body you want to skip the rest of the activity in the current iteration and evaluate the loop's predicate again, use the *CONTINUE* command. For example, the following code demonstrates how to skip the activity of the sixth iteration of the loop from the point where the *IF* statement appears and until the end of the loop's body:

```
DECLARE @i AS INT;
SET @i = 0;
WHILE @i < 10
BEGIN
  SET @i = @i + 1;
  IF @i = 6 CONTINUE;
  PRINT @i;
END;
```

The output of this code shows that the value of *@i* was printed in all iterations but the sixth:

```
1
2
3
4
5
7
8
9
10
```

An Example of Using IF and WHILE

The following example combines the use of the *IF* and *WHILE* elements. The purpose of the code in this example is to create a table called dbo.Nums in the tempdb database and populate it with 1,000 rows with the values 1 through 1000 in the column n:

```
SET NOCOUNT ON;
USE tempdb;
IF OBJECT_ID('dbo.Nums', 'U') IS NOT NULL DROP TABLE dbo.Nums;
CREATE TABLE dbo.Nums(n INT NOT NULL PRIMARY KEY);
GO

DECLARE @i AS INT;
SET @i = 1;
WHILE @i <= 1000
BEGIN
  INSERT INTO dbo.Nums(n) VALUES(@i);
  SET @i = @i + 1;
END
```

The code uses the *IF* statement to check whether the table Nums already exists in tempdb, and if it does, the code drops it. The code then uses a *WHILE* loop to iterate 1,000 times and populate the Nums table with the values 1 through 1000.

Cursors

In Chapter 2, "Single-Table Queries," I explained that a query without an ORDER BY clause returns a set (or a multiset), while a query with an ORDER BY clause returns what ANSI calls a cursor—a nonrelational result with order guaranteed among rows. In the context of the discussion in Chapter 2, the use of the term cursor was conceptual. T-SQL also supports an object called *cursor* that allows you to process rows from a result set of a query one at a time and in requested order. This is in contrast to using set-based queries—normal queries without a cursor where you manipulate the set or multiset as a whole, and cannot rely on order.

I want to stress that your default choice should be to use set-based queries; only when you have a compelling reason to do otherwise should you consider using cursors. This recommendation is based on several factors:

- First and foremost, when you use cursors you pretty much go against the relational model that wants you to think in terms of sets.

- Second, the record-by-record manipulation done by the cursor has overhead. A certain extra cost is associated with each record manipulation by the cursor compared to set-based manipulation. Given a set-based query and cursor code that do similar physical processing behind the scenes, the cursor code is usually several dozens of time slower than the set-based code.

- Third, with cursors you spend a lot of code on the physical aspects of the solution, or in other words, on *how* to process the data (declaring the cursor, opening it, looping through the cursor records, closing the cursor, deallocating the cursor). With set-based solutions you mainly focus on the logical aspects of the solution—in other words, on *what* to get instead of on how to get it. Therefore, cursor solutions tend to be longer, less readable, and harder to maintain compared to set-based solutions.

For most people, it is not simple to think in terms of sets immediately when they start learning SQL. In contrast to how the relational model wants us to think, it is more intuitive for most people to think in terms of cursors—processing one record at a time in a certain order. As a result, cursors are widely used, and in most cases they are misused; that is, they are used where much better set-based solutions exist. Make a conscious effort to adopt the set-based state of mind and to truly think in terms of sets. It can take time—in some cases years—but as long as you're working with a language that is based on the relational model, that's the right way to think.

Working with cursors is like fishing with a rod and catching one fish at a time. Working with sets, on the other hand, is like fishing with a net and catching a whole group of fish at one time. As another analogy, consider two kinds of orange-packing factories—an old-fashioned one and a modern one. The factories are supposed to arrange oranges in three different kinds of packages based on size—small, medium, and large. The old-fashioned factory works in cursor mode, which means that conveyer belts loaded with oranges come in, and a person at the end of each conveyer belt examines each orange and places it in the right kind of box based on its size. This type of processing is, of course, very slow. Also, order can matter here: If the oranges arrive on the conveyer belt already sorted by size, processing them is easier, so the conveyer belt can be set to a higher speed. The modern factory works in a set-based mode: All oranges are placed in a big container with a grid at the bottom with small holes. The machine shakes the container and only the small oranges go through the holes. The machine then moves the oranges to a container with medium holes and shakes the container, allowing the medium oranges to go through. The big oranges are left in the container.

Assuming you are convinced that set-based solutions should be your default choice, it is important to understand the exceptions, when you should consider cursors. One example is when you need to apply a certain task per each row from some table or view. For example, you may need to execute some administrative task per each database in your instance, or per each table in your database. In such a case it makes sense to use a cursor to iterate through the database names or table names one at a time, and execute the relevant task per each of those. I'll provide examples of this in the section "Dynamic SQL" later in the chapter.

Another example of when you should consider cursors is when your set-based solution performs badly and you exhaust your tuning efforts using the set-based approach. As I mentioned, set-based solutions tend to be much faster, but in some cases the cursor solution is faster. Those cases tend to be calculations that, if done by processing one row at a time in certain order, involve much less data access compared to the way SQL Server currently (in SQL Server 2008 and previous versions) optimizes corresponding set-based solutions. One such example is running aggregates. I provided a set-based solution to running aggregates using subqueries in Chapter 4, "Subqueries," in the section "Running Aggregates." Optimization is outside the scope of this book, so I won't go into detail here regarding why the cursor solution to running aggregates is currently more efficient than the set-based solution. When you feel ready to deal with optimization aspects of T-SQL querying, you can find details in *Inside Microsoft SQL Server 2008: T-SQL Querying* (Microsoft Press, 2009). At this point I just want you to understand that in most cases set-based solutions tend to be much faster than cursor solutions, but in some cases cursors are still faster because of optimization.

In the chapter's introduction, I mentioned that I'll provide a high-level overview. Still, an example of cursor code is probably appropriate here.

Working with a cursor generally involves the following steps:

1. Declare the cursor based on a query.

2. Open the cursor.

3. Fetch attribute values from the first cursor record into variables.

4. While the end of the cursor is not reached (the value of a function called *@@FETCH_ STATUS* is 0), loop through the cursor records; in each iteration of the loop fetch attribute values from the current cursor record into variables, and perform the processing needed for the current row.

5. Close the cursor.

6. Deallocate the cursor.

The following example with cursor code calculates the running total quantity for each customer and month from the Sales.CustOrders view:

```
SET NOCOUNT ON;
USE TSQLFundamentals2008;

DECLARE @Result TABLE
(
  custid      INT,
  ordermonth DATETIME,
  qty         INT,
  runqty      INT,
  PRIMARY KEY(custid, ordermonth)
);

DECLARE
  @custid     AS INT,
  @prvcustid  AS INT,
  @ordermonth DATETIME,
  @qty        AS INT,
  @runqty     AS INT;
```

```
DECLARE C CURSOR FAST_FORWARD /* read only, forward only */ FOR
  SELECT custid, ordermonth, qty
  FROM Sales.CustOrders
  ORDER BY custid, ordermonth;

OPEN C

FETCH NEXT FROM C INTO @custid, @ordermonth, @qty;

SELECT @prvcustid = @custid, @runqty = 0;

WHILE @@FETCH_STATUS = 0
BEGIN
  IF @custid <> @prvcustid
    SELECT @prvcustid = @custid, @runqty = 0;

  SET @runqty = @runqty + @qty;

  INSERT INTO @Result VALUES(@custid, @ordermonth, @qty, @runqty);

  FETCH NEXT FROM C INTO @custid, @ordermonth, @qty;
END

CLOSE C;

DEALLOCATE C;

SELECT
  custid,
  CONVERT(VARCHAR(7), ordermonth, 121) AS ordermonth,
  qty,
  runqty
FROM @Result
ORDER BY custid, ordermonth;
```

The code declares a cursor based on a query that returns the rows from the CustOrders view ordered by customer ID and order month, and iterates through the records one at a time. The code keeps track of the current running total quantity in a variable called *@runqty* that is reset every time a new customer is found. Per each row, the code calculates the current running total by adding the current month's quantity (*@qty*) to *@runqty*, and inserts a row with the customer ID, order month, current month's quantity, and running quantity into a table variable called *@Result*. When the code is done processing all cursor records, it queries the table variable to present the running aggregates. Here's the output returned by this code, shown in abbreviated form:

```
custid      ordermonth qty         runqty
----------- ---------- ----------- -----------
1           2007-08    38          38
1           2007-10    41          79
1           2008-01    17          96
1           2008-03    18          114
```

```
1       2008-04     60      174
2       2006-09     6       6
2       2007-08     18      24
2       2007-11     10      34
2       2008-03     29      63
3       2006-11     24      24
3       2007-04     30      54
3       2007-05     80      134
3       2007-06     83      217
3       2007-09     102     319
3       2008-01     40      359
...
89      2006-07     80      80
89      2006-11     105     185
89      2007-03     142     327
89      2007-04     59      386
89      2007-07     59      445
89      2007-10     164     609
89      2007-11     94      703
89      2008-01     140     843
89      2008-02     50      893
89      2008-04     90      983
89      2008-05     80      1063
90      2007-07     5       5
90      2007-09     15      20
90      2007-10     34      54
90      2008-02     82      136
90      2008-04     12      148
91      2006-12     45      45
91      2007-07     31      76
91      2007-12     28      104
91      2008-02     20      124
91      2008-04     81      205

(636 row(s) affected)
```

Temporary Tables

When you need to store data temporarily in tables, in certain cases you may prefer not to work with permanent tables. For example, suppose you need the data to be visible only to the current session, or even only to the current batch. As another example, suppose that you do want to make data available to all users, allowing them full DDL and DML access, but you don't have permissions to create tables in any user database.

SQL Server supports three kinds of temporary tables that you may find more convenient to work with in such cases: local temporary tables, global temporary tables, and table variables. The following sections describe the three kinds and demonstrate their use with code samples.

Local Temporary Tables

You create a local temporary table by naming it with a single number sign as a prefix, such as #T1. All three kinds of temporary tables are created in the tempdb database.

A local temporary table is visible only to the session that created it, in the creating level and all inner levels in the call stack (inner procedures, functions, triggers, and dynamic batches). A local temporary table is destroyed automatically by SQL Server when the creating level in the call stack gets out of scope. For example, suppose that a stored procedure called Proc1 calls a procedure called Proc2, which in turn calls a procedure called Proc3, which in turn calls a procedure called Proc4. Proc2 creates a temporary table called #T1 before calling Proc3. The table #T1 is visible to Proc2, Proc3, and Proc4 but not to Proc1, and is destroyed automatically by SQL Server when Proc2 finishes. If the temporary table is created in an ad-hoc batch in the outermost nesting level of the session (the value of the @@*NESTLEVEL* function is 0), it is visible to all subsequent batches as well, and is destroyed by SQL Server automatically only when the creating session disconnects.

You might wonder how SQL Server prevents name conflicts when two sessions create local temporary tables with the same name. SQL Server internally adds a suffix to the table name that makes it unique in tempdb. As a developer, you shouldn't care—you refer to the table using the name you provided without the internal suffix, and only your session has access to your table.

One obvious scenario where local temporary tables are useful is when you have a process that needs to store intermediate results temporarily—such as during a loop—and later query the data.

Another scenario is when you need to access the result of some expensive processing multiple times. For example, suppose that you need to join the Sales.Orders and Sales.OrderDetails tables from the TSQLFundamentals2008 database, aggregate order quantities by order year, and join two instances of the aggregated data to compare each year's total quantity with the previous year. The Orders and OrderDetails tables in the sample database are very small, but think in more practical terms, where such tables can have millions of rows. One option is to use table expressions, but remember that table expressions are virtual. The expensive work involving scanning all the data, joining the Orders and OrderDetails tables, and aggregating the data happens twice. Instead, it makes sense to do all the expensive work only once— storing the result in a local temporary table—and then join two instances of the temporary table, especially because the result of the expensive work is a very tiny set with only one row per each order year.

The following code illustrates this scenario using a local temporary table:

```
USE TSQLFundamentals2008;

IF OBJECT_ID('tempdb.dbo.#MyOrderTotalsByYear') IS NOT NULL
  DROP TABLE dbo.#MyOrderTotalsByYear;
GO
```

```
SELECT
  YEAR(O.orderdate) AS orderyear,
  SUM(OD.qty) AS qty
INTO dbo.#MyOrderTotalsByYear
FROM Sales.Orders AS O
  JOIN Sales.OrderDetails AS OD
    ON OD.orderid = O.orderid
GROUP BY YEAR(orderdate);

SELECT Cur.orderyear, Cur.qty AS curyearqty, Prv.qty AS prvyearqty
FROM dbo.#MyOrderTotalsByYear AS Cur
  LEFT OUTER JOIN dbo.#MyOrderTotalsByYear AS Prv
    ON Cur.orderyear = Prv.orderyear + 1;
```

This code produces the following output:

```
orderyear    curyearqty   prvyearqty
-----------  -----------  -----------
2007         25489        9581
2008         16247        25489
2006         9581         NULL
```

To verify that the local temporary table is visible only to the creating session, try accessing it from another session:

```
SELECT orderyear, qty FROM dbo.#MyOrderTotalsByYear;
```

You get the following error:

```
Msg 208, Level 16, State 0, Line 1
Invalid object name '#MyOrderTotalsByYear'.
```

Global Temporary Tables

When you create a global temporary table, it is visible to all other sessions. They are destroyed automatically by SQL Server when the creating session disconnects, and there are no active references to the table. You create a global temporary table by naming it with two number signs as a prefix, such as ##T1.

Global temporary tables are useful when you want to share temporary data with everyone. No special permissions are required and everyone has full DDL and DML access. Of course, the fact that everyone has full access means that anyone can even drop the table, so consider the alternatives carefully.

For example, the following code creates a global temporary table called ##Globals with columns called id and val:

```
CREATE TABLE dbo.##Globals
(
  id  sysname     NOT NULL PRIMARY KEY,
  val SQL_VARIANT NOT NULL
);
```

This table is supposed to mimic global variables that are not supported by SQL Server. The id column is of a *sysname* data type—the type SQL Server uses internally to represent identifiers, and the val column is of a *SQL_VARIANT* data type—a generic type that can store within it a value of almost any base type.

Anyone can insert rows into the table. For example, run the following code to insert a row representing a variable called *i* and initialize it with the integer value 10:

```
INSERT INTO dbo.##Globals(id, val) VALUES(N'i', CAST(10 AS INT));
```

Anyone can modify and retrieve data from the table. For example, run the following code from any session to query the current value of the variable *i*:

```
SELECT val FROM dbo.##Globals WHERE id = N'i';
```

This code returns the following output:

```
val
-----------
10
```

> **Note** Keep in mind that as soon as the session that created the global temporary table disconnects and there are no active references to the table, SQL Server automatically destroys it.

If you want a global temporary table to be created every time SQL Server starts, and you don't want SQL Server to try to destroy it automatically, you need to create the table from a stored procedure that is marked as a startup procedure. (For details, see "Automatic Execution of Stored Procedures" in SQL Server Books Online.)

Run the following code from any session to destroy the global temporary table explicitly:

```
DROP TABLE dbo.##Globals;
```

Table Variables

Table variables are similar to local temporary tables in some ways and different in others. You declare table variables similarly to the way you declare other variables, by using the *DECLARE* statement.

As with local temporary tables, table variables have a physical presence as a table in the tempdb database, contrary to the common misconception that they exist only in memory. Like local temporary tables, table variables are visible only to the creating session, but have a more limited scope, which is only the current batch. Table variables are visible neither to inner batches in the call stack nor to subsequent batches in the session.

If an explicit transaction is rolled back, changes made to temporary tables in that transaction are rolled back as well; however, changes made to table variables by statements that completed in the transaction aren't rolled back. Only changes made by the active statement that failed or was terminated before completion are undone.

Temporary tables and table variables also have optimization differences, but those are outside the scope of this book. For now, I'll just say that in terms of performance, usually it makes more sense to use table variables with very small volumes of data (only a few rows) and to use local temporary tables otherwise.

For example, the following code uses a table variable instead of a local temporary table to compare total order quantities of each order year with the year before:

```
DECLARE @MyOrderTotalsByYear TABLE
(
  orderyear INT NOT NULL PRIMARY KEY,
  qty       INT NOT NULL
);

INSERT INTO @MyOrderTotalsByYear(orderyear, qty)
  SELECT
    YEAR(O.orderdate) AS orderyear,
    SUM(OD.qty) AS qty
  FROM Sales.Orders AS O
    JOIN Sales.OrderDetails AS OD
      ON OD.orderid = O.orderid
  GROUP BY YEAR(orderdate);

SELECT Cur.orderyear, Cur.qty AS curyearqty, Prv.qty AS prvyearqty
FROM @MyOrderTotalsByYear AS Cur
  LEFT OUTER JOIN @MyOrderTotalsByYear AS Prv
    ON Cur.orderyear = Prv.orderyear + 1;
```

This code returns the following output:

```
orderyear   curyearqty  prvyearqty
----------- ----------- -----------
2006        9581        NULL
2007        25489       9581
2008        16247       25489
```

Table Types

SQL Server 2008 introduces support for table types. By creating a table type you preserve a table definition in the database and can later reuse it as the table definition of table variables and input parameters of stored procedures and user-defined functions.

For example, the following code creates a table type called dbo.OrderTotalsByYear in the TSQLFundamentals2008 database:

```
USE TSQLFundamentals2008;

IF TYPE_ID('dbo.OrderTotalsByYear') IS NOT NULL
  DROP TYPE dbo.OrderTotalsByYear;
```

```
CREATE TYPE dbo.OrderTotalsByYear AS TABLE
(
  orderyear INT NOT NULL PRIMARY KEY,
  qty       INT NOT NULL
);
```

Once the table type is created, whenever you need to declare a table variable based on the table type's definition, you won't need to repeat the code—instead you can simply specify dbo.OrderTotalsByYear as the variable's type like so:

```
DECLARE @MyOrderTotalsByYear AS dbo.OrderTotalsByYear;
```

As a more complete example, the following code declares a variable called *@MyOrderTotalsByYear* of the new table type, queries the Orders and OrderDetails tables to calculate total order quantities by order year, stores the result of the query in the table variable, and queries the variable to present its contents:

```
DECLARE @MyOrderTotalsByYear AS dbo.OrderTotalsByYear;

INSERT INTO @MyOrderTotalsByYear(orderyear, qty)
  SELECT
    YEAR(O.orderdate) AS orderyear,
    SUM(OD.qty) AS qty
  FROM Sales.Orders AS O
    JOIN Sales.OrderDetails AS OD
      ON OD.orderid = O.orderid
  GROUP BY YEAR(orderdate);

SELECT orderyear, qty FROM @MyOrderTotalsByYear;
```

This code returns the following output:

```
orderyear   qty
----------- -----------
2006        9581
2007        25489
2008        16247
```

The table type of a table variable only helps you shorten your code, but doesn't really introduce a new capability conceptually. But as I mentioned, you can also use a table type as the type of input parameters of stored procedures and functions, which is an extremely useful capability that is conceptually new.

Dynamic SQL

SQL Server allows you to construct a batch of T-SQL code as a character string, and then execute that batch. This capability is called dynamic SQL. SQL Server provides two ways of executing dynamic SQL: using the *EXEC* (short for *EXECUTE*) command and using the sp_executesql stored procedure. I will explain the difference between the two and provide examples for using each.

Dynamic SQL is useful for several purposes, including:

- **Automating administrative tasks.** For example, querying metadata and constructing and executing a *BACKUP DATABASE* statement per each database in the instance

- **Improving performance of certain tasks.** For example, constructing parameterized ad-hoc queries that can reuse previously cached execution plans (more on this later)

- **Constructing elements of the code based on querying the actual data.** For example, constructing a PIVOT query dynamically when you don't know ahead of time which elements should appear in the IN clause of the PIVOT operator

> **Note** Be extremely careful when concatenating user input as part of your code. Hackers can attempt to inject code you did not intend to run. The best measure you can take against SQL injection is to avoid concatenating user input as part of your code (for example, by using parameters). But if you do concatenate user input as part of your code, make sure you thoroughly inspect the input and look for SQL injection attempts. You can find an excellent article on the subject in SQL Server Books Online under "SQL Injection."

The EXEC Command

The *EXEC* command is the original way provided in T-SQL for executing dynamic SQL. *EXEC* accepts a character string as input in parentheses and executes the batch of code within the character string. *EXEC* supports both regular and Unicode character strings as input.

I'll start with a very basic example of using *EXEC* to invoke dynamic SQL. The following example stores a character string with a *PRINT* statement in the variable *@sql* and then uses the *EXEC* command to invoke the batch of code stored within the variable:

```
DECLARE @sql AS VARCHAR(100);
SET @sql = 'PRINT ''This message was printed by a dynamic SQL batch.'';';
EXEC(@sql);
```

Notice the use of two single quotes to represent one single quote in a string within a string. This code returns the following output:

```
This message was printed by a dynamic SQL batch.
```

The following example uses a cursor to query the INFORMATION_SCHEMA.TABLES view to get the names of the tables in the TSQLFundamentals2008 database. Per each table, the code constructs and executes a batch of code that calls the sp_spaceused procedure against the current table to get space usage information:

```
USE TSQLFundamentals2008;

DECLARE
  @sql AS NVARCHAR(300),
  @schemaname AS sysname,
  @tablename  AS sysname;
```

```
DECLARE C CURSOR FAST_FORWARD FOR
  SELECT TABLE_SCHEMA, TABLE_NAME
  FROM INFORMATION_SCHEMA.TABLES
  WHERE TABLE_TYPE = 'BASE TABLE';

OPEN C

FETCH NEXT FROM C INTO @schemaname, @tablename;

WHILE @@fetch_status = 0
BEGIN
  SET @sql =
    N'EXEC sp_spaceused N'''
    + QUOTENAME(@schemaname) + N'.'
    + QUOTENAME(@tablename) + N''';';

  EXEC(@sql);

  FETCH NEXT FROM C INTO @schemaname, @tablename;
END

CLOSE C;

DEALLOCATE C;
```

In case you're curious about the use of the *QUOTENAME* function, it is used to delimit the input value. If a second argument with the quote character is not specified, the function uses square brackets by default. So if *@tablename* is *N'My Table'*, *QUOTENAME(@mytable)* returns *N'[My Table]'*, making it a valid identifier.

This code returns the following output with space usage information for all tables in the database:

```
name          rows  reserved  data    index_size   unused
------------- ----- --------- ------  -----------  -------
Suppliers     29    48 KB     8 KB    40 KB        0 KB

name          rows  reserved  data    index_size   unused
------------- ----- --------- ------  -----------  -------
Categories    8     32 KB     8 KB    24 KB        0 KB

name          rows  reserved  data    index_size   unused
------------- ----- --------- ------  -----------  -------
Products      77    64 KB     8 KB    56 KB        0 KB

name          rows  reserved  data    index_size   unused
------------- ----- --------- ------  -----------  -------
Customers     91    104 KB    24 KB   80 KB        0 KB

name          rows  reserved  data    index_size   unused
------------- ----- --------- ------  -----------  -------
Shippers      3     16 KB     8 KB    8 KB         0 KB

name          rows  reserved  data    index_size   unused
------------- ----- --------- ------  -----------  -------
Orders        830   416 KB    152 KB  232 KB       32 KB
```

```
name            rows   reserved  data   index_size  unused
------------    -----  --------- ------  ----------- -------
OrderDetails    2155   224 KB    72 KB   104 KB      48 KB

name            rows   reserved  data   index_size  unused
------------    -----  --------- ------  ----------- -------
Employees       9      48 KB     8 KB    40 KB       0 KB
```

The sp_executesql Stored Procedure

The sp_executesql stored procedure was introduced after the *EXEC* command. It is more secure and more flexible in the sense that it has an interface; that is, it supports input and output parameters. Note that unlike *EXEC*, sp_executesql supports only Unicode character strings as the input batch of code.

The fact that you can use input and output parameters in your dynamic SQL code can help you write more secure and more efficient code. In terms of security, parameters that appear in the code cannot be considered part of the code—they can only be considered operands in expressions. So by using parameters, you can remove exposure to SQL injection.

The sp_executesql stored procedure can perform better than *EXEC* because its parameterization aids in reusing cached execution plans. An execution plan is the physical processing plan that SQL Server produces for a query, with the set of instructions regarding which objects to access, in what order, which indexes to use, how to access them, which join algorithms to use, and so on. To simplify things, one of the requirements for reusing a previously cached plan is that the query string be the same as the one for which the plan exists in cache. The best way to efficiently reuse query execution plans is to use stored procedures with parameters. This way even when parameter values change, the query string remains the same. But if for your own reasons you decide to use ad-hoc code instead of stored procedures, at least you can still work with parameters if you use sp_executesql and therefore increase the chances for plan reuse.

The sp_executesql procedure has two input parameters and an assignments section. You specify the Unicode character string holding the batch of code you want to run in the first parameter called *@stmt*. You provide a Unicode character string holding the declarations of input and output parameters in the second input parameter called *@params*. Then you specify the assignments of input and output parameters separated by commas.

The following example constructs a batch of code with a query against the Sales.Orders table. The example uses an input parameter called *@orderid* in the query's filter:

```
DECLARE @sql AS NVARCHAR(100);

SET @sql = N'SELECT orderid, custid, empid, orderdate
FROM Sales.Orders
WHERE orderid = @orderid;';

EXEC sp_executesql
  @stmt = @sql,
  @params = N'@orderid AS INT',
  @orderid = 10248;
```

This code assigns the value *10248* to the input parameter, but even if you run it again with a different value, the code string remains the same. This way you increase the chances for reusing a previously cached plan.

To use an output parameter, simply specify the keyword *OUTPUT* both in the parameter declaration and in the parameter assignment. The following example demonstrates using output parameters. The code queries the INFORMATION_SCHEMA.TABLES view to get the list of table and view names in the database. The code uses a cursor to iterate through the object names. In each iteration, the code constructs a dynamic SQL batch that queries the count of rows in the current object and stores the result in an output parameter called *@n*. The value of the output parameter *@n* is passed to the local variable *@numrows* that is assigned to the output parameter. The code inserts a row into a table variable called *@Counts* with the name and the count of rows of the current object. When the code is done iterating through the cursor records, it queries the table variable to present the counts. Here's the complete example code:

```
DECLARE @Counts TABLE
(
  schemaname sysname NOT NULL,
  tablename sysname NOT NULL,
  numrows INT NOT NULL,
  PRIMARY KEY(schemaname, tablename)
);

DECLARE
  @sql AS NVARCHAR(350),
  @schemaname AS sysname,
  @tablename  AS sysname,
  @numrows    AS INT;

DECLARE C CURSOR FAST_FORWARD FOR
  SELECT TABLE_SCHEMA, TABLE_NAME
  FROM INFORMATION_SCHEMA.TABLES;

OPEN C

FETCH NEXT FROM C INTO @schemaname, @tablename;

WHILE @@fetch_status = 0
BEGIN
  SET @sql =
    N'SET @n = (SELECT COUNT(*) FROM '
    + QUOTENAME(@schemaname) + N'.'
    + QUOTENAME(@tablename) + N');';

  EXEC sp_executesql
    @stmt = @sql,
    @params = N'@n AS INT OUTPUT',
    @n = @numrows OUTPUT;

  INSERT INTO @Counts(schemaname, tablename, numrows)
    VALUES(@schemaname, @tablename, @numrows);
```

```
    FETCH NEXT FROM C INTO @schemaname, @tablename;
END

CLOSE C;

DEALLOCATE C;

SELECT schemaname, tablename, numrows
FROM @Counts;
```

This code returns the following output:

```
schemaname   tablename           numrows
-----------  ------------------  --------
HR           Employees           9
Production   Categories          8
Production   Products            77
Production   Suppliers           29
Sales        Customers           91
Sales        CustOrders          636
Sales        OrderDetails        2155
Sales        Orders              830
Sales        OrderTotalsByYear   3
Sales        OrderValues         830
Sales        Shippers            3

(11 row(s) affected)
```

Using PIVOT with Dynamic SQL

This section is advanced and optional in case you feel very comfortable with pivoting techniques and dynamic SQL. In Chapter 7, "Pivot, Unpivot, and Grouping Sets," I explained how to use the PIVOT operator to pivot data. I mentioned that in a static query, you have to know ahead of time which values to specify in the IN clause of the PIVOT operator. Following is an example of a static query with the PIVOT operator:

```
SELECT *
FROM (SELECT shipperid, YEAR(orderdate) AS orderyear, freight
      FROM Sales.Orders) AS D
  PIVOT(SUM(freight) FOR orderyear IN([2006],[2007],[2008])) AS P;
```

This example queries the Sales.Orders table, and pivots the data so that it returns shipper IDs on rows, order years on columns, and the total freight in the intersection of each shipper and order year. This code returns the following output:

```
shipperid   2006          2007           2008
-----------  ------------  -------------  -------------
3           4233.78       11413.35       4865.38
1           2297.42       8681.38        5206.53
2           3748.67       12374.04       12122.14
```

With the static query, you have to know ahead of time which values (order years in our case) to specify in the IN clause of the PIVOT operator. This means that you need to revise the code every year. Instead, you can query the distinct order years from the data, construct a batch of dynamic SQL code based on the years that you queried, and execute the dynamic SQL batch like so:

```
DECLARE
  @sql      AS NVARCHAR(1000),
  @orderyear AS INT,
  @first    AS INT;

DECLARE C CURSOR FAST_FORWARD FOR
  SELECT DISTINCT(YEAR(orderdate)) AS orderyear
  FROM Sales.Orders
  ORDER BY orderyear;

SET @first = 1;

SET @sql = N'SELECT *
FROM (SELECT shipperid, YEAR(orderdate) AS orderyear, freight
      FROM Sales.Orders) AS D
  PIVOT(SUM(freight) FOR orderyear IN(';

OPEN C

FETCH NEXT FROM C INTO @orderyear;

WHILE @@fetch_status = 0
BEGIN
  IF @first = 0
    SET @sql = @sql + N','
  ELSE
    SET @first = 0;

  SET @sql = @sql + QUOTENAME(@orderyear);

  FETCH NEXT FROM C INTO @orderyear;
END

CLOSE C;

DEALLOCATE C;

SET @sql = @sql + N')) AS P;';

EXEC sp_executesql @stmt = @sql;
```

Routines

Routines are programmable objects that encapsulate code to calculate a result or to execute activity. SQL Server Supports three types of routines: user-defined functions, stored procedures, and triggers.

As of SQL Server 2005 you can chose whether to develop a routine with T-SQL or with .NET code based on the Common Language Runtime (CLR) integration in the product. Because this book's focus is T-SQL, the examples here use T-SQL. Generally speaking, when the task at hand mainly involves data manipulation, T-SQL is usually a better choice. When the task is more about iterative logic, string manipulation, or computationally intensive operations, .NET is usually a better choice.

User-Defined Functions

The purpose of a user-defined function (UDF) is to encapsulate logic that calculates something, possibly based on input parameters, and return a result.

SQL Server supports scalar and table-valued UDFs. Scalar UDFs return a single value; table-valued UDFs return a table. One benefit of using UDFs is that you can incorporate them in queries. Scalar UDFs can appear anywhere in the query where an expression that returns a single value can appear (for example, in the SELECT list). Table UDFs can appear in the FROM clause of a query. Here I provide an example of a scalar UDF.

UDFs are not allowed to have any side effects. This obviously means that UDFs are not allowed to apply any schema or data changes in the database. But other ways of causing side effects are less obvious. For example, invoking the *RAND* function to return a random value or the *NEWID* function to return a globally unique identifier (GUID) has side effects. Whenever you invoke the *RAND* function without specifying a seed, SQL Server generates a random seed that is based on the previous invocation of *RAND*. For this reason, SQL Server needs to store information internally whenever you invoke the *RAND* function. Similarly, whenever you invoke the *NEWID* function the system needs to set some information aside to be taken into consideration in the next invocation of *NEWID*. Because *RAND* and *NEWID* have side effects, you're not allowed to use them in your UDFs.

For example, the following code creates a UDF called dbo.fn_age that returns the age of a person with a given birth date (*@birthdate argument*) at a given event date (*@eventdate argument*):

```
USE TSQLFundamentals2008;
IF OBJECT_ID('dbo.fn_age') IS NOT NULL DROP FUNCTION dbo.fn_age;
GO

CREATE FUNCTION dbo.fn_age
(
  @birthdate AS DATETIME,
  @eventdate AS DATETIME
)
RETURNS INT
AS
BEGIN
  RETURN
```

```
        DATEDIFF(year, @birthdate, @eventdate)
      - CASE WHEN 100 * MONTH(@eventdate) + DAY(@eventdate)
                < 100 * MONTH(@birthdate) + DAY(@birthdate)
            THEN 1 ELSE 0
        END
END
GO
```

The function calculates the age as the difference, in terms of years, between the birth year and the event year, minus 1 year in case within the year, the event month and day is smaller than the birth month and day. The expression *100 * month + day* is simply a trick to concatenate the month and day. For example, for month February and day 12 the expression yields the integer 0212.

Note that a function can have more than just a RETURN clause in its body. It can have code with flow elements, calculations, and so on. But the function must have a RETURN clause that returns a value.

To demonstrate using a UDF in a query, the following code queries the HR.Employees table and invokes the *fn_age* function in the SELECT list to calculate the age of each employee today:

```
SELECT
  empid, firstname, lastname, birthdate,
  dbo.fn_age(birthdate, CURRENT_TIMESTAMP) AS age
FROM HR.Employees;
```

For example, if you were to run this query on February 12, 2009, you would get the following output:

```
empid       firstname  lastname              birthdate                 age
----------- ---------- --------------------- ------------------------- ----
1           Sara       Davis                 1958-12-08 00:00:00.000   50
2           Don        Funk                  1962-02-19 00:00:00.000   46
3           Judy       Lew                   1973-08-30 00:00:00.000   35
4           Yael       Peled                 1947-09-19 00:00:00.000   61
5           Sven       Buck                  1965-03-04 00:00:00.000   43
6           Paul       Suurs                 1973-07-02 00:00:00.000   35
7           Russell    King                  1970-05-29 00:00:00.000   38
8           Maria      Cameron               1968-01-09 00:00:00.000   41
9           Zoya       Dolgopyatova          1976-01-27 00:00:00.000   33

(9 row(s) affected)
```

Note that if you run the query in your system, the values that you get in the age column depend on the date on which you run the query.

Stored Procedures

Stored procedures are server-side routines that encapsulate T-SQL code. Stored procedures can have input and output parameters, they can return result sets of queries, and they are allowed to invoke code that has side effects. Not only can you modify data through stored procedures, but you can also apply schema changes through them.

Compared to using ad-hoc code, the use of stored procedures gives you many benefits:

- Stored procedures encapsulate logic. If the implementation of a stored procedure needs to change, you apply the change only in one place in the database and all users of the procedure start using the altered procedure.

- Stored procedures give you better control of security. You can grant a user with permissions to execute the procedure without granting the user with direct permissions to perform the underlying activities. For example, suppose that you want to allow certain users to delete a customer from the database, but you don't want to grant them direct permissions to delete rows from the Customers table. You want to ensure that requests to delete a customer are validated—for example, checking whether the customer has open orders, open debts, and so on—and you may also want to audit the requests. By not granting direct permissions to delete rows from the Customers table directly but instead granting permissions to execute a procedure that handles the task, you ensure that all the required validations and auditing always take place. In addition, stored procedures can help prevent SQL injection, especially when they replace ad-hoc SQL from the client with parameters.

- You can incorporate all error handling code within a procedure, silently taking corrective action where relevant. I discuss error handling later in the chapter.

- Stored procedures give you performance benefits. Earlier I talked about reuse of previously cached execution plans. Stored procedures reuse execution plans by default, while SQL Server is more conservative with the reuse of ad-hoc plans. Also, the aging of procedure plans is less rapid than that of ad-hoc plans. Another performance benefit of using stored procedures is reduction of network traffic. The client application needs to submit only the procedure name and its arguments to SQL Server. The server processes all of the procedure's code and returns only the output back to the caller. No back and forth traffic is associated with intermediate steps of the procedure.

As a simple example, the following code creates a stored procedure called Sales.usp_GetCustomerOrders. The procedure accepts a customer ID (*@custid*) and a date range (*@fromdate* and *@todate*) as inputs. The procedure returns rows from the Sales.Orders table representing orders placed by the requested customer in the requested date range as a result set, and the number of affected rows as an output parameter (*@numrows*):

```
USE TSQLFundamentals2008;
IF OBJECT_ID('Sales.usp_GetCustomerOrders', 'P') IS NOT NULL
  DROP PROC Sales.usp_GetCustomerOrders;
GO
```

```
CREATE PROC Sales.usp_GetCustomerOrders
  @custid    AS INT,
  @fromdate AS DATETIME = '19000101',
  @todate    AS DATETIME = '99991231',
  @numrows   AS INT OUTPUT
AS
SET NOCOUNT ON;

SELECT orderid, custid, empid, orderdate
FROM Sales.Orders
WHERE custid = @custid
  AND orderdate >= @fromdate
  AND orderdate < @todate;

SET @numrows = @@rowcount;
GO
```

When executing the procedure, if you don't specify a value in the *@fromdate* parameter, the procedure will use the default *19000101*, and if you don't specify a value in the *@todate* parameter, the procedure will use the default *99991231*. Notice the use of the keyword *OUTPUT* to indicate that the parameter *@numrows* is an output parameter. The *SET NOCOUNT ON* command is used to suppress messages indicating how many rows were affected by DML statements, like the *SELECT* statement within the procedure.

Here's an example of executing the procedure, requesting information about orders placed by customer with ID 1 in the year 2007. The code absorbs the value of the output parameter *@numrows* in the local variable *@rc* and returns it to show how many rows were affected by the query:

```
DECLARE @rc AS INT;

EXEC Sales.usp_GetCustomerOrders
  @custid   = 1,
  @fromdate = '20070101',
  @todate   = '20080101',
  @numrows  = @rc OUTPUT;

SELECT @rc AS numrows;
```

The code returns the following output showing three qualifying orders:

```
orderid      custid       empid        orderdate
-----------  -----------  -----------  -----------------------
10643        1            6            2007-08-25 00:00:00.000
10692        1            4            2007-10-03 00:00:00.000
10702        1            4            2007-10-13 00:00:00.000

numrows
-----------
3
```

Run the code again providing a customer ID that doesn't exist in the Orders table (for example, customer ID 100), and you get the following output indicating that there are zero qualifying orders:

```
orderid      custid      empid       orderdate
-----------  ----------- ----------- -----------------------


numrows
-----------
0
```

Of course, this is just a basic example. You can do much more with stored procedures.

Triggers

A trigger is a special kind of stored procedure—one that cannot be executed explicitly. Instead, it is attached to an event. Whenever the event takes place, the trigger fires and the trigger's code runs. SQL Server supports associating triggers with two kinds of events—data manipulation events (DML triggers) such as *INSERT*, and data definition events (DDL triggers) such as *CREATE TABLE*.

You can use triggers for many purposes including auditing, enforcing integrity rules that cannot be enforced with constraints, enforcing policies, and so on.

A trigger is considered part of the transaction that includes the event that caused the trigger to fire. Issuing a *ROLLBACK TRAN* command within the trigger's code causes a rollback of all changes that took place in the trigger, and also of all changes that took place in the transaction associated with the trigger.

Triggers in SQL Server fire per statement and not per modified row.

DML Triggers

SQL Server supports two kinds of DML triggers—*after* and *instead of.* An *after* trigger fires after the event it is associated with finishes and can only be defined on permanent tables. An *instead of* trigger fires instead of the event it is associated with and can be defined on permanent tables and views.

In the trigger's code, you can access tables called *inserted* and *deleted* that contain the rows that were affected by the modification that caused the trigger to fire. The inserted table holds the new image of the affected rows in the case of *INSERT* and *UPDATE* statements. The deleted table holds the old image of the affected rows in the case of *DELETE* and *UPDATE* statements. In the case of *instead of* triggers, the inserted and deleted tables contain the rows that were supposed to be affected by the modification that caused the trigger to fire.

The following simple example of an *after* trigger audits inserts to a table. Run the following code to create a table called dbo.T1 in the tempdb database, and another table called dbo.T1_Audit that holds audit information for insertions to T1:

```
USE tempdb;

IF OBJECT_ID('dbo.T1_Audit', 'U') IS NOT NULL DROP TABLE dbo.T1_Audit;
IF OBJECT_ID('dbo.T1', 'U') IS NOT NULL DROP TABLE dbo.T1;

CREATE TABLE dbo.T1
(
  keycol  INT         NOT NULL PRIMARY KEY,
  datacol VARCHAR(10) NOT NULL
);

CREATE TABLE dbo.T1_Audit
(
  audit_lsn  INT         NOT NULL IDENTITY PRIMARY KEY,
  dt         DATETIME    NOT NULL DEFAULT(CURRENT_TIMESTAMP),
  login_name sysname     NOT NULL DEFAULT(SUSER_SNAME()),
  keycol     INT         NOT NULL,
  datacol    VARCHAR(10) NOT NULL
);
```

In the audit table the column audit_lsn has an identity property and it represents an audit log serial number. The column dt represents the date and time of the insertion using the default expression *CURRENT_TIMESTAMP*. The column login_name represents the name of the login that performed the insertion using the default expression *SUSER_SNAME()*.

Next, run the following code to create the *AFTER INSERT* trigger *trg_T1_insert_audit* on the table T1 to audit insertions:

```
CREATE TRIGGER trg_T1_insert_audit ON dbo.T1 AFTER INSERT
AS
SET NOCOUNT ON;

INSERT INTO dbo.T1_Audit(keycol, datacol)
  SELECT keycol, datacol FROM inserted;
GO
```

As you can see, the trigger simply inserts into the audit table the result of a query against the inserted table. The values of the columns in the audit table that are not listed explicitly in the *INSERT* statement are generated by the default expressions described earlier. To test the trigger run the following code:

```
INSERT INTO dbo.T1(keycol, datacol) VALUES(10, 'a');
INSERT INTO dbo.T1(keycol, datacol) VALUES(30, 'x');
INSERT INTO dbo.T1(keycol, datacol) VALUES(20, 'g');
```

The trigger fires after each statement. Next, query the audit table:

```
SELECT audit_lsn, dt, login_name, keycol, datacol
FROM dbo.T1_Audit;
```

You get the following output, only with *dt* and *login_name* values that reflect the date and time when you ran the inserts, and the login you used to connect to SQL Server:

```
audit_lsn   dt                      login_name         keycol      datacol
----------- ----------------------  -----------------  ----------- ----------
1           2009-02-24 09:04:27.713 QUANTUM\Gandalf    10          a
2           2009-02-24 09:04:27.733 QUANTUM\Gandalf    30          x
3           2009-02-24 09:04:27.733 QUANTUM\Gandalf    20          g
```

DDL Triggers

SQL Server 2005 introduced support for DDL triggers. Those can be used for purposes like auditing, enforcing policies, change management, and others.

SQL Server supports creating DDL triggers at two scopes, database and server scope, depending on the scope of the event. You create a *database* trigger for events with a database scope such as *CREATE TABLE*. You create an *all server* trigger for events with a server scope such as *CREATE DATABASE*. SQL Server supports only *after* DDL triggers; it doesn't support *before* or *instead of* DDL triggers.

Within the trigger you obtain information on the event that caused the trigger to fire by querying a function called *EVENTDATA* that returns the event info as an XML value. You can use XQuery expressions to extract event attributes such as post time, event type, login name, and others from the XML value.

This example of a DDL trigger audits all DDL activities in a database. First, run the following code to create a database called testdb and use it:

```
USE master;
IF DB_ID('testdb') IS NOT NULL DROP DATABASE testdb;
CREATE DATABASE testdb;
GO
USE testdb;
```

Next, run the following code to create the table dbo.AuditDDLEvents, which holds the audit information:

```
IF OBJECT_ID('dbo.AuditDDLEvents', 'U') IS NOT NULL
  DROP TABLE dbo.AuditDDLEvents;

CREATE TABLE dbo.AuditDDLEvents
(
  audit_lsn        INT      NOT NULL IDENTITY,
  posttime         DATETIME NOT NULL,
  eventtype        sysname  NOT NULL,
  loginname        sysname  NOT NULL,
  schemaname       sysname  NOT NULL,
  objectname       sysname  NOT NULL,
  targetobjectname sysname  NULL,
  eventdata        XML      NOT NULL,
  CONSTRAINT PK_AuditDDLEvents PRIMARY KEY(audit_lsn)
);
```

Notice that the table has a column called eventdata of an XML data type. Besides the individual attributes that the trigger extracts from the event information and stores in individual attributes, it also stores the full event information in the eventdata column.

Run the following code to create the audit trigger *trg_audit_ddl_events* on the database using the event group *DDL_DATABASE_LEVEL_EVENTS* representing all DDL events at the database level:

```
CREATE TRIGGER trg_audit_ddl_events
  ON DATABASE FOR DDL_DATABASE_LEVEL_EVENTS
AS
SET NOCOUNT ON;

DECLARE @eventdata AS XML;
SET @eventdata = eventdata();

INSERT INTO dbo.AuditDDLEvents(
  posttime, eventtype, loginname, schemaname,
  objectname, targetobjectname, eventdata)
  VALUES(
    @eventdata.value('(/EVENT_INSTANCE/PostTime)[1]',          'VARCHAR(23)'),
    @eventdata.value('(/EVENT_INSTANCE/EventType)[1]',         'sysname'),
    @eventdata.value('(/EVENT_INSTANCE/LoginName)[1]',         'sysname'),
    @eventdata.value('(/EVENT_INSTANCE/SchemaName)[1]',        'sysname'),
    @eventdata.value('(/EVENT_INSTANCE/ObjectName)[1]',        'sysname'),
    @eventdata.value('(/EVENT_INSTANCE/TargetObjectName)[1]', 'sysname'),
    @eventdata);
GO
```

The trigger's code first stores the event info obtained from the *EVENTDATA* function in the *@eventdata* variable. The code then inserts a row into the audit table with the attributes extracted using XQuery expressions by the *.value* method from the event info, plus the XML value with the full event information.

To test the trigger, run the following code that contains a few DDL statements:

```
CREATE TABLE dbo.T1(col1 INT NOT NULL PRIMARY KEY);
ALTER TABLE dbo.T1 ADD col2 INT NULL;
ALTER TABLE dbo.T1 ALTER COLUMN col2 INT NOT NULL;
CREATE NONCLUSTERED INDEX idx1 ON dbo.T1(col2);
```

Next, run the following code to query the audit table:

```
SELECT * FROM dbo.AuditDDLEvents;
```

You get the following output (split here into two sections for lack of room), but with values in the *posttime* and *loginname* attributes that reflect the post time and login name in your environment:

```
audit_lsn posttime                  eventtype       loginname
--------- ------------------------- --------------- ----------------
1         2009-02-12 09:06:18.293   CREATE_TABLE    QUANTUM\Gandalf
2         2009-02-12 09:06:18.413   ALTER_TABLE     QUANTUM\Gandalf
3         2009-02-12 09:06:18.423   ALTER_TABLE     QUANTUM\Gandalf
4         2009-02-12 09:06:18.423   CREATE_INDEX    QUANTUM\Gandalf
```

audit_lsn	schemaname	objectname	targetobjectname	eventdata
1	dbo	T1	NULL	<EVENT_INSTANCE>...
2	dbo	T1	NULL	<EVENT_INSTANCE>...
3	dbo	T1	NULL	<EVENT_INSTANCE>...
4	dbo	idx1	T1	<EVENT_INSTANCE>...

When you're done, run the following code for cleanup:

```
USE master;
IF DB_ID('testdb') IS NOT NULL DROP DATABASE testdb;
```

Error Handling

SQL Server provides you with tools to handle errors in your T-SQL code. The main tool you use for error handling is a construct called TRY...CATCH that was introduced in SQL Server 2005. SQL Server also provides a set of functions that you can invoke to get information about the error. I'll start with a basic example demonstrating the use of TRY...CATCH, followed by a more detailed example demonstrating the use of the error functions.

You work with the TRY...CATCH construct by placing the usual T-SQL code in a TRY block (between the *BEGIN TRY* and *END TRY* keywords), and all the error handling code in the adjacent CATCH block (between the *BEGIN CATCH* and *END CATCH* keywords). If the TRY block has no error, the CATCH block is simply skipped. If the TRY block has an error, control is passed to the corresponding CATCH block. Note that if a TRY...CATCH block captures and handles an error, as far as the caller is concerned, there was no error.

Run the following code to demonstrate a case with no error in the TRY block:

```
BEGIN TRY
  PRINT 10/2;
  PRINT 'No error';
END TRY
BEGIN CATCH
  PRINT 'Error';
END CATCH
```

All code in the TRY block completed successfully; therefore, the CATCH block was skipped. This code generates the following output:

```
5
No error
```

Next, run similar code, but this time divide by zero, and an error occurs:

```
BEGIN TRY
  PRINT 10/0;
  PRINT 'No error';
END TRY
BEGIN CATCH
  PRINT 'Error';
END CATCH
```

When the *divide by zero* error happened in the first *PRINT* statement in the TRY block, control was passed to the corresponding CATCH block. The second *PRINT* statement in the TRY block was not executed. Therefore, this code generates the following output:

```
Error
```

Typically, error handling involves some work in the CATCH block investigating the cause of the error and taking a course of action. SQL Server gives you information about the error via a set of functions. The *ERROR_NUMBER* function returns an integer with the number of the error and is probably the most important of the error functions. The CATCH block usually includes flow code that inspects the error number to determine what course of action to take. The *ERROR_MESSAGE* function returns error message text. To get the list of error numbers and messages, query the catalog view sys.messages. The *ERROR_SEVERITY* and *ERROR_STATE* functions return the error severity and state. The *ERROR_LINE* function returns the line number where the error happened. Finally, the *ERROR_PROCEDURE* returns the name of the procedure where the error happened, and returns NULL if the error did not happen within a procedure.

To demonstrate a more detailed error handling example with the use of the error functions, first run the following code that creates a table called dbo.Employees in the tempdb database:

```
USE tempdb;
IF OBJECT_ID('dbo.Employees') IS NOT NULL DROP TABLE dbo.Employees;
CREATE TABLE dbo.Employees
(
  empid   INT        NOT NULL,
  empname VARCHAR(25) NOT NULL,
  mgrid   INT        NULL,
  CONSTRAINT PK_Employees PRIMARY KEY(empid),
  CONSTRAINT CHK_Employees_empid CHECK(empid > 0),
  CONSTRAINT FK_Employees_Employees
    FOREIGN KEY(mgrid) REFERENCES dbo.Employees(empid)
);
```

The following code inserts a new row into the Employees table in a TRY block, and if an error occurs, shows how to identify the error by inspecting the *ERROR_NUMBER* function in the CATCH block. The code also prints the values of the other error functions simply to show what information is available to you upon error:

```
BEGIN TRY

  INSERT INTO dbo.Employees(empid, empname, mgrid)
    VALUES(1, 'Emp1', NULL);
  -- Also try with empid = 0, 'A', NULL

END TRY
BEGIN CATCH
```

```
IF ERROR_NUMBER() = 2627
BEGIN
  PRINT '    Handling PK violation...';
END
ELSE IF ERROR_NUMBER() = 547
BEGIN
  PRINT '    Handling CHECK/FK constraint violation...';
END
ELSE IF ERROR_NUMBER() = 515
BEGIN
  PRINT '    Handling NULL violation...';
END
ELSE IF ERROR_NUMBER() = 245
BEGIN
  PRINT '    Handling conversion error...';
END
ELSE
BEGIN
  PRINT '    Handling unknown error...';
END

PRINT '    Error Number  : ' + CAST(ERROR_NUMBER() AS VARCHAR(10));
PRINT '    Error Message : ' + ERROR_MESSAGE();
PRINT '    Error Severity: ' + CAST(ERROR_SEVERITY() AS VARCHAR(10));
PRINT '    Error State   : ' + CAST(ERROR_STATE() AS VARCHAR(10));
PRINT '    Error Line    : ' + CAST(ERROR_LINE() AS VARCHAR(10));
PRINT '    Error Proc    : ' + COALESCE(ERROR_PROCEDURE(), 'Not within proc');

END CATCH
```

When you run this code for the first time, the new row is inserted into the Employees table successfully, and therefore the CATCH block is skipped. You get the following output:

```
(1 row(s) affected)
```

When you run the same code a second time, the *INSERT* statement fails, control is passed to the CATCH block, and a primary key violation error is identified. You get the following output:

```
Handling PK violation...
Error Number  : 2627
Error Message : Violation of PRIMARY KEY constraint 'PK_Employees'. Cannot insert duplicate
key in object 'dbo.Employees'.
Error Severity: 14
Error State   : 1
Error Line    : 3
Error Proc    : Not within proc
```

To see other errors, run the code with the values *0*, *'A'*, and *NULL* as the employee ID.

Here, for demonstration purposes, I used *PRINT* statements as the actions when an error was identified. Of course, error handling usually involves more than just printing a message indicating that the error was identified.

Note that you can create a stored procedure that encapsulates reusable error handling code like so:

```
IF OBJECT_ID('dbo.usp_err_messages', 'P') IS NOT NULL
  DROP PROC dbo.usp_err_messages;
GO

CREATE PROC dbo.usp_err_messages
AS
SET NOCOUNT ON;

IF ERROR_NUMBER() = 2627
BEGIN
  PRINT 'Handling PK violation...';
END
ELSE IF ERROR_NUMBER() = 547
BEGIN
  PRINT 'Handling CHECK/FK constraint violation...';
END
ELSE IF ERROR_NUMBER() = 515
BEGIN
  PRINT 'Handling NULL violation...';
END
ELSE IF ERROR_NUMBER() = 245
BEGIN
  PRINT 'Handling conversion error...';
END
ELSE
BEGIN
  PRINT 'Handling unknown error...';
END

PRINT 'Error Number  : ' + CAST(ERROR_NUMBER() AS VARCHAR(10));
PRINT 'Error Message : ' + ERROR_MESSAGE();
PRINT 'Error Severity: ' + CAST(ERROR_SEVERITY() AS VARCHAR(10));
PRINT 'Error State   : ' + CAST(ERROR_STATE() AS VARCHAR(10));
PRINT 'Error Line    : ' + CAST(ERROR_LINE() AS VARCHAR(10));
PRINT 'Error Proc    : ' + COALESCE(ERROR_PROCEDURE(), 'Not within proc');
GO
```

In your CATCH block, you simply execute the stored procedure:

```
BEGIN TRY

  INSERT INTO dbo.Employees(empid, empname, mgrid)
    VALUES(1, 'Emp1', NULL);

END TRY
BEGIN CATCH

  EXEC dbo.usp_err_messages;

END CATCH
```

This way you can maintain the reusable error handling code in one place.

Conclusion

This chapter provided a high-level overview of programmable objects so that you can be aware of SQL Server's capabilities in this area and start building your vocabulary. This chapter covered variables, batches, flow elements, cursors, temporary tables, dynamic SQL, user-defined functions, stored procedures, triggers, and error handling—quite a few subjects. I hope that you focused on concepts and capabilities rather than getting sidetracked by every bit of code in the examples.

Because this is the last chapter in the book, I should add a few of words about the next recommended step. If reading this book was your first step in learning T-SQL, you should let all this information sink in by practicing a lot. If you skipped the parts of the book marked as advanced, you may want to try tackling those when you feel more comfortable with the material. When you feel very comfortable with the material and are ready for more advanced querying, query tuning, and programming, I suggest reading the books *Inside Microsoft SQL Server 2008: T-SQL Querying* and *Inside Microsoft SQL Server 2008: T-SQL Programming*.

Appendix A
Getting Started

The purpose of this appendix is to help you get started and set up your environment so that you have everything you need to get the most out of this book.

The first section, "Installing SQL Server," walks you through the installation process in case you don't already have an instance of Microsoft SQL Server 2008 to connect to for practicing the materials from the book. If you already have an instance of SQL Server to connect to, feel free to skip the first section.

The second section, "Downloading Source Code and Installing the Sample Database," explains where you can download the source code for the book and provides instructions for installing the book's sample database.

The third section, "Working with SQL Server Management Studio," explains how to develop and execute T-SQL code in SQL Server using SQL Server Management Studio (SSMS).

The last section, "Working with SQL Server Books Online," describes SQL Server Books Online and explains its importance in helping you get information about T-SQL.

Installing SQL Server

To practice all materials from the book and run all code samples you can use any edition of SQL Server 2008 except SQL Server Compact, which doesn't have full-fledged T-SQL support like the other editions. Assuming that you don't already have an instance of SQL Server to connect to, the following sections describe where you can obtain SQL Server and how to install it.

1. Obtain SQL Server

As I mentioned, you can use any edition of SQL Server 2008 except SQL Server Compact to practice the materials from the book. If you have a subscription to MSDN, you can use the SQL Server 2008 Developer for learning purposes. You can download it from *http://msdn.microsoft.com/en-us/sqlserver/default.aspx*. Otherwise, you can use SQL Server 2008 Enterprise 180-day evaluation, free trial software that you can download from *http://www.microsoft.com/sqlserver/2008/en/us/trial-software.aspx*. In this appendix, I demonstrate the installation of SQL Server 2008 Enterprise 180-day evaluation.

2. Create a User Account

Prior to installing SQL Server, you need to create a user account that you will later use as the service account for SQL Server services.

To create a user account:

1. Right-click My Computer (or Computer in some operating systems) and choose Manage to open the Computer Management snap-in.

2. Navigate to Computer Management (Local) | System Tools | Local Users and Groups | Users.

3. Right-click the Users folder and choose New User.

4. Fill in the details for the new user account in the New User dialog box as shown in Figure A-1.

FIGURE A-1 The New User dialog box

    4-1. Type a user name (for example, **SQL**), optionally a full name (for example, **SQL Server Services Account**), optionally a description (for example, **Account for SQL Server services**), and a secure password, and then confirm the password.

    4-2. Clear the User Must Change Password At Next Logon check box.

    4-3. Select the User Cannot Change Password and Password Never Expires check boxes.

    4-4. Click Create to create the new user account.

3. Install Prerequisites

At this point you can start the setup.exe program from the SQL Server installation CD or folder. Before installing SQL Server, the setup program checks whether all the prerequisites are already installed. The prerequisites include the Microsoft .NET Framework and updated Windows Installer. If the setup program doesn't find the prerequisites, it will install those first, and when they are installed, you may be required to restart the computer and rerun the setup program.

4. Install the Database Engine, Documentation, and Tools

Once all prerequisites are installed, you can move on to installing the actual product.

To install the database engine, documentation, and tools:

1. After all prerequisites are installed, run the setup.exe program. You should see the SQL Server Installation Center dialog box shown in Figure A-2.

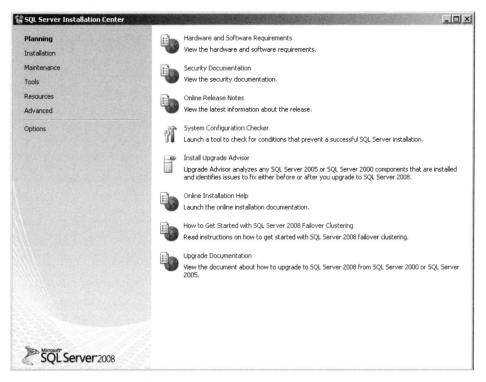

FIGURE A-2 SQL Server Installation Center

2. From the left pane, choose Installation. Note that the screen changes.

3. From the right pane, choose New SQL Server Stand-Alone Installation Or Add Features To An Existing Installation. The Setup Support Rules dialog box appears.

4. Click Show Details to view the status of the setup support rules as shown in Figure A-3, and ensure that no problems are indicated.

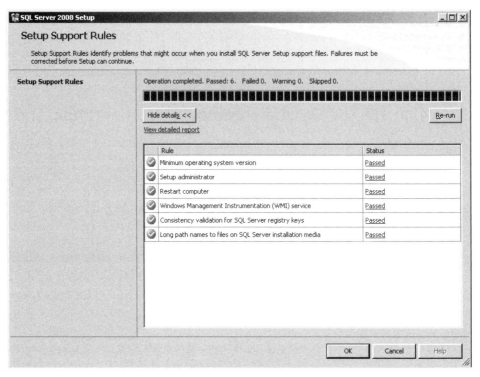

FIGURE A-3 The Setup Support Rules dialog box

5. When done, click OK to continue. The Product Key dialog box appears as shown in Figure A-4.

Note that in certain circumstances the dialog boxes Setup Support Files and Setup Support Rules described in steps 7-9 may appear before the Product Key dialog box. If they do, simply follow the instructions in steps 7-9 now instead of later.

6. Make sure that under the option Specify a Free Edition, Enterprise Evaluation is chosen and click Next to continue. The License Terms dialog box appears.

7. Confirm that you accept the license terms and click Next to continue. The Setup Support Files dialog box appears.

8. Click Install to continue. The Setup Support Rules dialog box appears again.

9. Click Show Details to view the status of the setup support rules and ensure that no problems are indicated. Click Next to continue. The Feature Selection dialog box appears. Select the features to install as shown in Figure A-5.

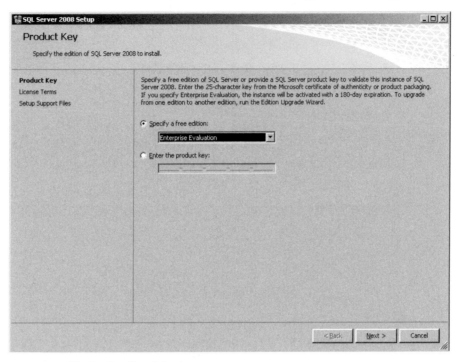

FIGURE A-4   The Product Key dialog box

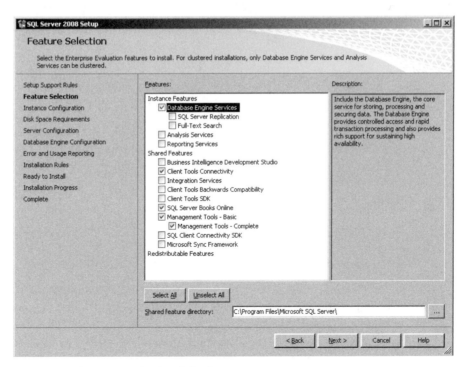

FIGURE A-5   The Feature Selection dialog box

Select the following features:

❏ Database Engine Services

❏ Client Tools Connectivity

❏ SQL Server Books Online

❏ Management Tools - Complete

For the purposes of this book you don't need any of the other features.

When done, click Next to continue. The Instance Configuration dialog box appears as shown in Figure A-6.

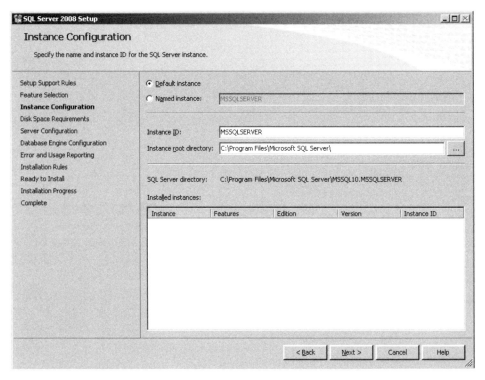

FIGURE A-6 The Instance Configuration dialog box

If you are not familiar with the concept of SQL Server instances, you can find details in Chapter 1, "Background to T-SQL Querying and Programming," in the section "SQL Server Architecture."

10. If a default instance of SQL Server is not installed in the computer and you would like to configure the new instance as the default, simply confirm that the option Default Instance is selected. If you want to configure the new instance as a named instance, make sure the option Named Instance is selected and specify a name for the new instance (for example, SQL08). When you later connect to SQL Server you will specify

only the computer name for a default instance (for example, QUANTUM), and the computer name\instance name for a named instance (for example, QUANTUM\SQL08).

11. When you're done, click Next to continue. The Disk Space Requirements dialog box appears. Make sure that you have enough disk space for the installation as required.

12. Click Next to continue. The Server Configuration dialog box appears.

13. As shown in Figure A-7, for the service account for the SQL Server Agent and SQL Server Database Engine services, specify the user name and password of the user account you created earlier.

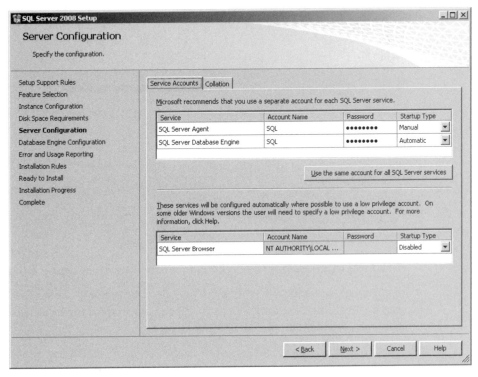

FIGURE A-7 The Server Configuration dialog box

Of course, if you named your user account something other than SQL, specify the name you assigned to the account.

For the purposes of the book, you do not need to change the default choices in the Collation dialog box, but if you want to know more about collation, you can find details in Chapter 2, "Single-Table Queries," in the section "Working with Character Data."

14. Click Next to continue. The Database Engine Configuration dialog box appears.

15. On the Account Provisioning tab, ensure that under Authentication Mode the option Windows Authentication Mode is selected. Under Specify SQL Server Administrators, click Add Current User to assign the current logged-on user with the System Administrator

(sysadmin) server role as shown in Figure A-8. SQL Server administrators have unrestricted access to the SQL Server database engine.

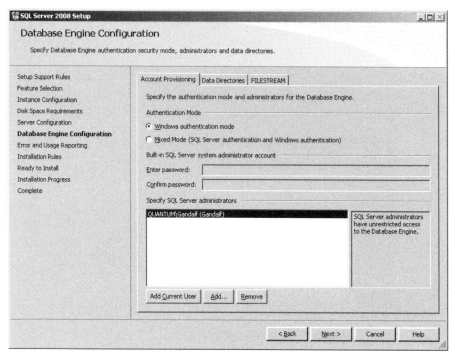

FIGURE A-8 The Database Engine Configuration dialog box

Of course, in your case your current user name will appear instead of QUANTUM\Gandalf.

If you want to change the setup program's defaults in terms of data directories you can do so on the Data Directories tab. For the purposes of the book, you don't need to configure anything on the FILESTREAM tab.

16. Click Next to continue. The Error And Usage Reporting dialog box appears. Make your choices based on your preferences and click Next to continue. The Installation Rules dialog box appears.

17. Click Show Details to view the status of the installation rules and ensure that no problems are indicated. Click Next to continue. The Ready To Install dialog box appears with a summary of the installation choices.

18. Ensure that the summary indicates your choices correctly and click Install to start the actual installation process. The Installation Progress dialog box appears and remains open throughout the remainder of the installation process. This dialog box provides a general progress bar as well as indicating the status of each feature that is being installed. When the installation is complete, a message saying Setup Process Complete appears above the general progress bar as shown in Figure A-9.

19. Click Next to continue. The Complete dialog box appears as shown in Figure A-10.

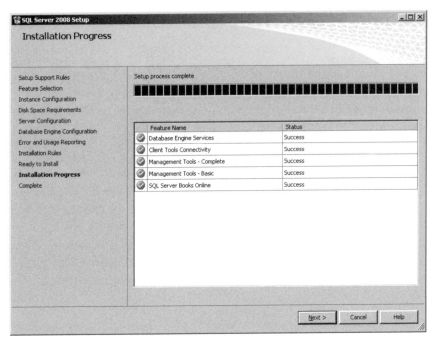

FIGURE A-9 The Installation Progress dialog box

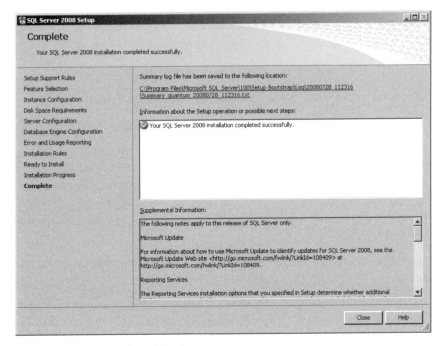

FIGURE A-10 The Complete dialog box

This dialog box should indicate the successful completion of the installation.

20. Click Close to finish.

Downloading Source Code and Installing the Sample Database

You can download the source code for the book from *http://www.insidetsql.com*. The entire book's source code script files plus the script file to create the book's sample database reside in a single compressed file. Uncompress the files to a local folder (for example, C:\TSQLFundamentals).

You will find up to three .sql script files associated with each chapter of the book. One file contains the source code for the corresponding chapter and is provided for your convenience, in case you don't want to type the code that appears in the book; this filename matches that of the corresponding chapter. A second file contains the exercises for the chapter; this filename matches that of the corresponding chapter but includes the suffix "Exercises." A third file contains the solutions to the chapter's exercises; this filename matches that of the corresponding chapter but includes the suffix "Solutions." You use SQL Server Management Studio (SSMS) to open the files and run their code. The next section explains how to work with SSMS.

You will also find a text file called orders.txt, for use when practicing the materials from Chapter 8, "Data Modification."

You will also find a script file called TSQLFundamentals2008.sql that creates the book's sample database, TSQLFundamentals2008. Run this if you're already familiar with running script files in SQL Server. If you aren't familiar with running script files in SQL Server, perform the following steps:

To run the script that creates the sample database:

1. Double-click the filename in Windows Explorer to open the file in SSMS. A Connect To Database Engine dialog box appears.

2. In the Server name box, ensure that the name of the instance you want to connect to appears. For example, type the name QUANTUM if your instance was installed as the default instance in a computer called QUANTUM, and type QUANTUM\SQL08 if your instance was installed as a named instance called SQL08 in a computer called QUANTUM.

3. In the Authentication box, make sure Windows Authentication is chosen. Click Connect.

4. When you are connected to SQL Server press F5 to run the script. When done, the message "Command(s) completed successfully" should appear in the Messages pane. You should see the TSQLFundamentals2008 database in the Available Databases combo box.

5. When done, you can close SSMS.

The data model of the TSQLFundamentals2008 database is provided in Figure A-11 for your convenience.

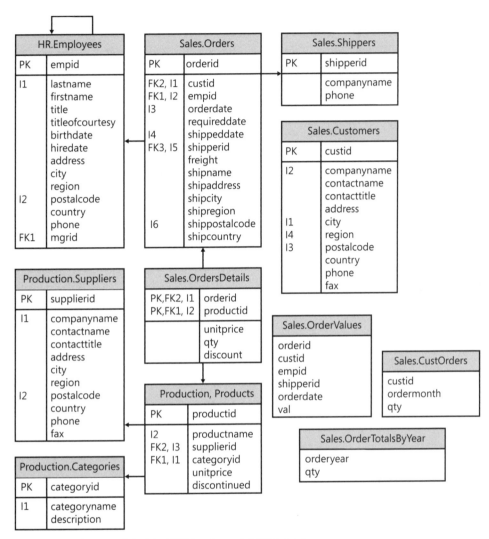

FIGURE A-11 Data model of the TSQLFundamentals2008 database

Working with SQL Server Management Studio

SQL Server Management Studio (SSMS) is the client tool you use to both develop T-SQL code and manage SQL Server. The purpose of this section is not to provide a complete guide to working with SSMS, but rather just to help you get started writing and executing T-SQL code against SQL Server.

To start working with SSMS:

1. Start SSMS from the Microsoft SQL Server program group.

If this is the first time you have run SSMS, I recommend setting up the startup options so that the environment is set up the way you want it.

If a Connect To Server dialog box appears, click Cancel for now.

2. Choose the menu item Tools | Options to open the Options dialog box. Under Environment | General, set the At Startup option to Open Object Explorer and New Query. This choice tells SSMS that whenever it starts it should open the Object Explorer and a new query window.

Object Explorer is the tool you use to manage SQL Server and graphically inspect object definitions, and a query window is where you develop and execute T-SQL code against SQL Server. Feel free to navigate the tree to explore the options that you can set, but few of them are likely to mean much at this point. After you gain some experience with SSMS, you will find many of the options more meaningful and will likely want to change some of them.

3. When you're done exploring the Options dialog box click OK to confirm your choices.

4. Close SSMS and start it again to verify that it actually opens the Object Explorer and a new query window. You should see the Connect To Server dialog box as shown in Figure A-12.

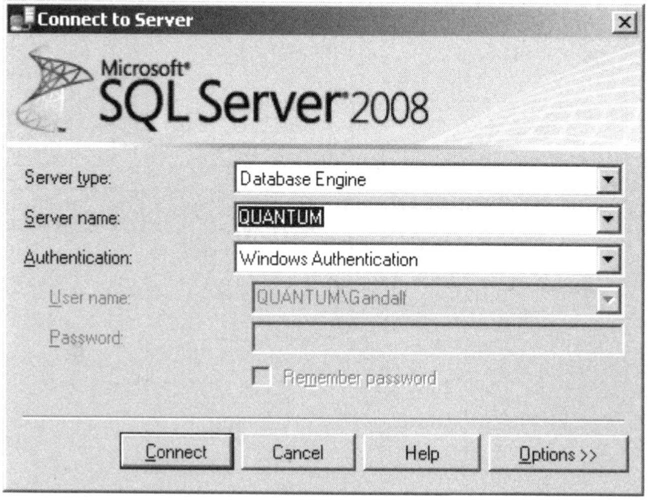

FIGURE A-12 The Connect To Server dialog box

5. In this dialog box, you specify the details of the SQL Server instance you want to connect to:

5-1. Type the name of the instance you want to connect to in the Server Name box.

5-2. Make sure Windows Authentication is chosen in the Authentication box.

5-3. Click Connect. SSMS should start as shown in Figure A-13.

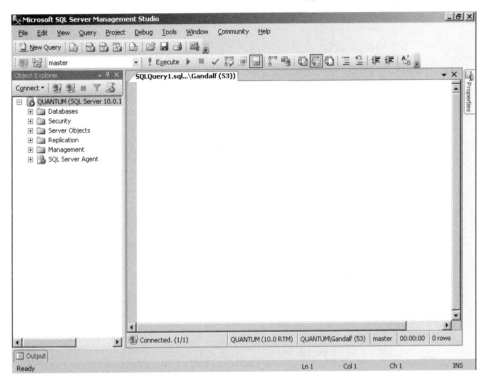

FIGURE A-13   SSMS started

The Object Explorer window appears on the left, and the query window appears to the right of Object Explorer. Although the focus of this book is developing T-SQL code and not SQL Server management, I urge you to explore the Object Explorer by navigating the tree and by right-clicking the various nodes. You will find Object Explorer a very convenient tool to graphically inspect your databases and database objects as shown in Figure A-14.

Note that you can drag items from the Object Explorer to the query window.

> **Tip** If you drag the Columns folder of a table from the Object Explorer to the query window, SQL Server will list all table columns separated by commas.

In the query window you develop and execute T-SQL code. The code you run is executed against the database you are connected to. You can choose the database you want to connect to from the Available Databases combo box as shown in Figure A-15.

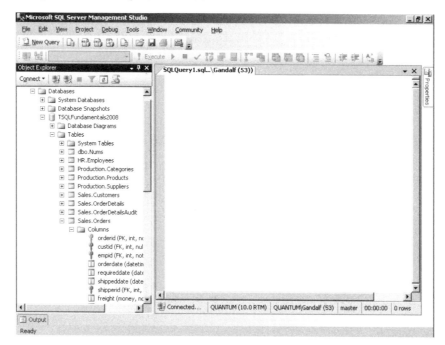

FIGURE A-14   Object Explorer

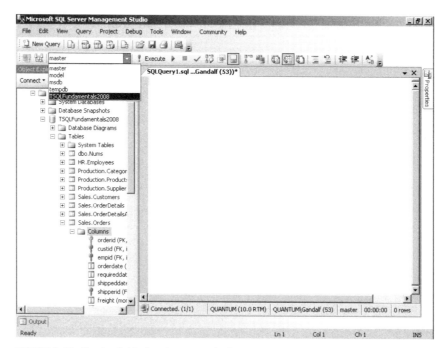

FIGURE A-15   The Available Databases combo box

6. Make sure you are currently connected to the TSQLFundamentals2008 sample database.

   Note that at any point you can change the instance you are connected to by right-clicking an empty area in the query window and then choosing Connection | Change Connection.

7. You are now ready to start developing T-SQL code. Type the following code in the query window:

```
SELECT orderid, orderdate FROM Sales.Orders;
```

8. Press F5 to execute the code. Alternatively, you can click Execute (the icon with the red exclamation point; not the green arrow, which starts the debugger). You will get the output of the code in the Results pane as shown in Figure A-16.

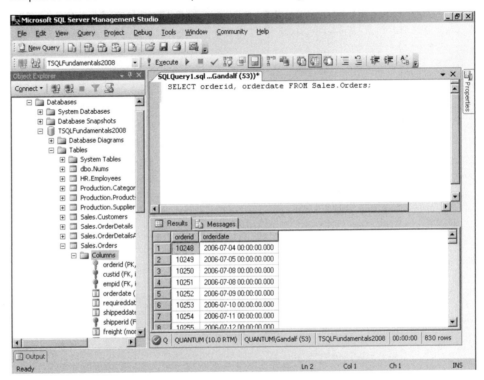

FIGURE A-16 Executing your first query

You can control the target of the results from the Query | Results To menu item or by clicking the corresponding icons in the SQL Editor toolbar. You have the following options: Results To Grid (default), Results To Text, and Results To File.

Note that if some of the code is highlighted, as shown in Figure A-17, when you execute the code, SQL Server executes only the selected part. SQL Server executes all code in the script only if no code is highlighted.

> **Tip** If you press and hold the Alt button before you start highlighting code, you can highlight a rectangle block that doesn't necessarily start at the beginning of the lines of code for purposes of copying or executing, as shown in Figure A-18.

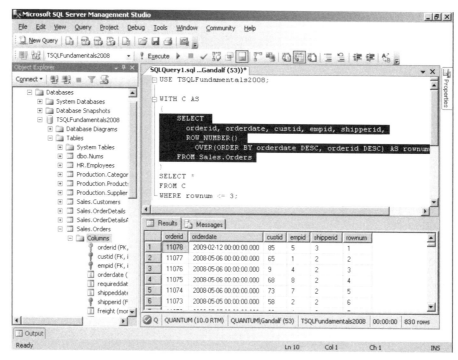

FIGURE A-17 Executing only selected code

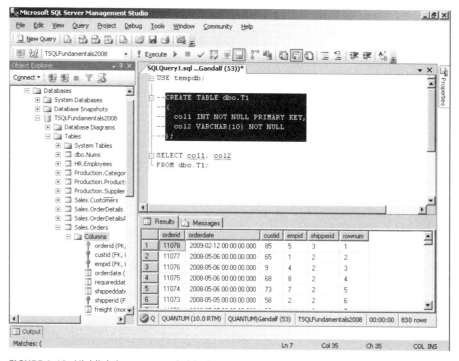

FIGURE A-18 Highlighting a rectangle block

Finally, before I leave you to your own explorations, I'd like to remind you that all of the source code of the book is available for download from the book's Web site. The previous section in this appendix, "Downloading Source Code and Installing the Sample Database," provides the details. Assuming you downloaded the source code and extracted the compressed files to a local folder, you can open the script file you want to work with from the menu item File | Open | File or the Open File icon on the Standard toolbar. Alternatively, you can double-click the script file's name in Windows Explorer to open the script file within SSMS.

Working with SQL Server Books Online

Microsoft SQL Server Books Online is the online documentation that Microsoft provides for SQL Server. It contains a huge amount of useful information. When developing T-SQL code, think of Books Online as your best friend—besides the T-SQL Fundamentals book, of course.

If you installed Books Online on your computer you will find a shortcut to it in the Microsoft SQL Server program group, Documentation and Tutorials folder. Books Online is also available on the Internet. For SQL Server 2005 Books Online, go to *http://msdn.microsoft.com/en-us/library/ms130214.aspx*. For SQL Server 2008 Books Online, go to *http://msdn.microsoft.com/en-us/library/bb543165(sql.100).aspx*. The examples that I demonstrate here assume a local installation of Books Online.

Learning to use Books Online is not rocket science, and I don't want to insult anyone's intelligence by explaining the obvious. Dedicating a section to Books Online in the "Getting Started" appendix is more about making you aware of its existence and emphasizing its importance rather than explaining how to use it. Too often people ask others for help about a SQL Server–related topic when they can easily find the answer if they only put a little effort into searching for it in Books Online.

I'll explain a few of the ways available in Books Online to get information. One of the windows that I use most in Books Online to search for information is the Help Index window shown in Figure A-19.

Type what you are looking for in the Look For box. As you type the letters of the subject you are looking for (for example, **OVER**), Books Online positions the cursor on the first qualifying item in the sorted list of subjects below. You can type T-SQL keywords for which you need syntax information, for example, or any other subject of interest.

Notice in Figure A-19 that when you choose a topic, the topic's URL in Books Online appears in the URL box. You can add the URL to the Help Favorites, and even send it to people if you want them to visit the same subject instead of explaining how to navigate to the subject.

When you are looking for a general item rather than a specific item, such as What's New In SQL Server 2008 or the T-SQL Programming Reference, you will probably find the Help Contents window useful (Figure A-20).

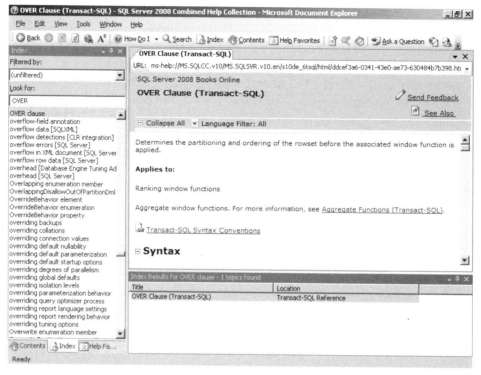

FIGURE A-19   The Books Online Help Index window

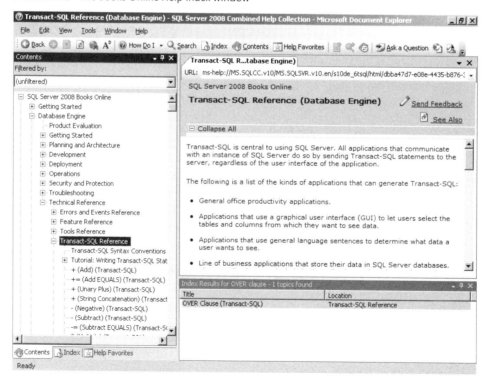

FIGURE A-20   The Books Online Help Contents window

Here you need to navigate the tree to get to the topic of interest. Note that in the Filtered By box you can filter on SQL Server 2008 Database Engine to refine both searches and lookups.

Another very useful window is the Help Search window shown in Figure A-21.

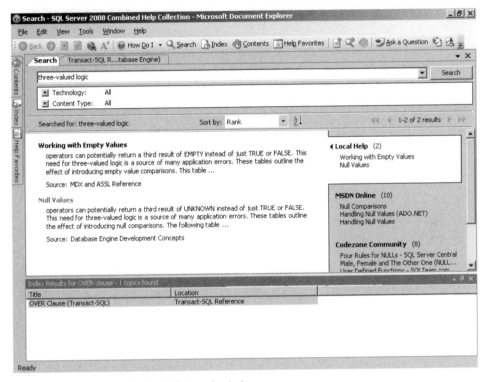

FIGURE A-21   The Books Online Help Search window

You use the Search window when looking for articles that contain words you are looking for. This is a more abstract search than a search in the Help Index window—somewhat similar to an Internet search engine. Books Online can look for information in the Local Help, MSDN Online, and the Codezone Community. Note that if you want to find a certain word in an open article, press **Ctrl+F** to open the Find dialog box.

> **Tip**   Finally, before I leave you to your own explorations, let me add a last tip. If you need help on a syntax element while writing code in SQL Server Management Studio, make sure your cursor is positioned somewhere in that code element and then press **Shift+F1**. This will load Books Online and open the syntax page for that element, assuming such a Help item exists.

Index

Symbols and Numbers

A

Itzik Ben-Gan

Itzik is a mentor and cofounder of Solid Quality Mentors. A SQL Server Microsoft MVP (Most Valuable Professional) since 1999, Itzik has delivered numerous training events around the world focused on T-SQL querying, query tuning, and programming. Itzik is the author of several books about T-SQL. He has written many articles for *SQL Server Magazine* as well as articles and white papers for MSDN. Itzik's speaking engagements include Tech Ed, DevWeek, PASS, SQL Server Magazine Connections, presentations to various user groups around the world, and Solid Quality Mentors events.

Resources for SQL Server 2008

**Microsoft® SQL Server® 2008
Administrator's
Pocket Consultant**
William R. Stanek
ISBN 9780735625891

**Programming Microsoft
SQL Server 2008**
Leonard Lobel, Andrew J. Brust,
Stephen Forte
ISBN 9780735625990

**Microsoft SQL Server 2008
Step by Step**
Mike Hotek
ISBN 9780735626041

**Microsoft SQL Server 2008
T-SQL Fundamentals**
Itzik Ben-Gan
ISBN 9780735626010

**MCTS Self-Paced
Training Kit (Exam 70-432)
Microsoft SQL Server 2008
Implementation and
Maintenance**
Mike Hotek
ISBN 9780735626058

**Smart Business Intelligence
Solutions with Microsoft
SQL Server 2008**
Lynn Langit, Kevin S. Goff,
Davide Mauri, Sahil Malik
ISBN 9780735625808

COMING SOON

Microsoft SQL Server 2008 Internals
Kalen Delaney *et al.*
ISBN 9780735626249

Inside Microsoft SQL Server 2008: T-SQL Querying
Itzik Ben-Gan, Lubor Kollar, Dejan Sarka
ISBN 9780735626034

Microsoft SQL Server 2008 Best Practices
Saleem Hakani and Ward Pond
with the Microsoft SQL Server Team
ISBN 9780735626225

**Microsoft SQL Server 2008 MDX
Step by Step**
Bryan C. Smith, C. Ryan Clay, Hitachi Consulting
ISBN 9780735626188

**Microsoft SQL Server 2008 Reporting Services
Step by Step**
Stacia Misner
ISBN 9780735626478

**Microsoft SQL Server 2008 Analysis Services
Step by Step**
Scott Cameron, Hitachi Consulting
ISBN 9780735626201

microsoft.com/mspress